Your Rights

Your Rights

The Liberty Guide

Edited by John Wadham,
Philip Leach and Penny Sergeant

Sixth Edition

National Council for Civil Liberties

with

LONDON · CHICAGO, ILLINOIS

Sixth edition published 1998 by
Pluto Press
345 Archway Road, London N6 5AA
and
1436 West Randolph, Chicago, Illinois 60607, USA

Previous editions published 1972, 1973, 1978, 1989 by Penguin; and
1994 by Pluto Press

British Library Cataloguing in Publication Data
A catalogue record for this book is available from the British Library

ISBN 0 7453 1163 6 hbk

Library of Congress Cataloging in Publication Data

Designed and produced for Pluto Press by
Chase Production Services, Chadlington, OX7 3LN
Typeset by Stanford DTP Services, Northampton
Printed in the EC by WSOY, Finland

Contents

List of contributors

Ruth Bundy is a solicitor practising in Leeds; she specialises in criminal and immigration work and prisoners' rights and is also involved in the conduct of inquests.

Simon Creighton is a solicitor who has been employed by the Prisoners' Advice Service since 1993. He is the co-author (with Vicky King) of *Prisoners and the Law* (Butterworths, 1996) and has contributed a chapter to *The Prisons Handbook* (ed. Mark Leech, Pluto Press 1997).

Jo Cooper is a solicitor advocate with a Higher Courts Qualification who specialises in public order law, particularly cases concerning demonstrations. He writes a regular column, 'Public Order Review' for *Legal Action*.

Fiona Fairweather is a solicitor and principal lecturer in law at the University of East London. She has written and lectured widely on police powers and is the author (with Howard Levenson and Ed Cape) of the Legal Action Group's *Police Powers: A Practitioners' Guide*, now in its third edition.

Bill Forrester has been Gypsy Liaison Manager for Kent County Council since 1989, and held a similar position within Essex County Council from 1980. He has been involved with traveller issues from 1973, first with NCCL (now Liberty) and later for the Minority Rights Group. He is chair of the Advisory Council for the Education of Roman and other Travellers and author of *The Travellers' Handbook*, published in 1985.

Maurice Frankel is director of the Campaign for Freedom of Information and has worked with the Campaign since it was set up in 1984. He previously worked with the corporate responsibility pressure group Social Audit.

Tess Gill is a barrister specialising in employment and industrial law, health and safety and the environment. She was previously a solicitor with trade union and private practice experience. She was appointed a part-time industrial tribunal chairman in 1995 and is co-author and editor of *Health and Safety Liability and Litigation* published in 1995 by FT Law & Tax.

Malcolm Hurwitt is a solicitor and a former president of mental health review tribunals. He was a member of the Executive Committee of NCCL (now Liberty) for thirty years and has twice been chair of NCCL. He was formerly a part-time adjudicator under the Immigration Act, and is now a Trustee of the Civil Liberties Trust.

Philip Leach worked for a firm of City solicitors before becoming Liberty's Legal Officer in 1993. He is the Assistant Cases Editor of the *European Human Rights Law Review* and he writes a regular column about human rights cases for *Legal Action*.

Ijeoma Omambala is a barrister in private practice specialising in discrimination law.

Robin Oppenheim is a barrister practising at Doughty Street Chambers, London. He has a particular interest and expertise in media and public law and civil liberty-related cases.

Penny Sergeant is Caseworker at Liberty and runs the Criminal Justice Network. She is on the Management Committee of the Prisoners' Advice Service.

Jay Sharma has worked in law centres since 1987 and is now at Central London Law Centre. His areas of work and interest are migration, asylum and related public law. He is on the Executive Committee of the Law Centres' Federation.

Rabinder Singh is a practising barrister, specialising in public law, employment law and human rights. He is also a Visiting Fellow at Queen Mary and Westfield College, London.

John Wadham is a solicitor and Director of Liberty. He has acted on behalf of applicants in a substantial number of cases before the European Commission and Court of Human Rights. He is the editor of the civil liberties section of the *Penguin Guide to the Law* and the case reports for the *European Human Rights Law Review*. He has also contributed to many other publications and written many articles on human rights and civil liberties.

Nicola Wyld is a solicitor who has worked in private practice, the Children's Legal Centre and the Family Rights Group.

Liberty is one of the UK's leading civil liberties and human rights organisations. Through a combination of test case litigation, lobbying, campaigning and research, Liberty has been working to promote civil rights and protect civil liberties for over sixty years. Liberty is the largest organisation of its kind in Europe and we pride ourselves on being democratically run.

Producing this book is part of our commitment to promote and protect the rights of everyone in the UK. If you would like to help Liberty's work please make a donation or become a member, or find out about our Lawyers for Liberty Network.

Please photocopy this form, fill it out and return it to Liberty, Freepost, 21 Tabard Street, London SE1 6BP.

Surname/s ....

Forenames ....

Title .... (Mr/Mrs/Miss/Other)

Address ....

....

Town ....

County .... Postcode...............................

(BLOCK CAPITALS PLEASE)

☐ I wish to make a donation of £10 ☐ £25 ☐ £50 ☐ £100 ☐ Other ☐
☐ I wish to become a member of Liberty

£20 Individual membership ☐ £25 Two people at same address ☐

£6 Full-time student, Social Security claimant ☐

£6 Pensioner ☐

£6 Couple, both unwaged, at the same address ☐

£3 Prisoner ☐

☐ I am a lawyer, please send me details about *Lawyers for Liberty*

Please tick the method of payment:

Cheque/PO made payable to Liberty ☐

Visa/Access Card No.: ☐☐☐☐ ☐☐☐☐ ☐☐☐☐ ☐☐☐☐

Expiry date: ..../..........

Amount enclosed £ ....

Signature of cardholder ....Date ....

Introduction

Since the 1930s, Liberty (the National Council for Civil Liberties) has been working to defend and extend human rights and civil liberties in this country. We have taken up important test cases, campaigned on a very wide range of issues and lobbied Parliament on proposed new laws. An important element of this work has been the free advice and information service which we offer to members of the public. Now in its sixth edition, *Your Rights* complements this service by providing a guide to your rights, liberties and responsibilities.

Your Rights has again been written by experts in their fields. It is intended primarily for people who have no specialist legal knowledge, although we hope it will also serve as a useful resource for lawyers and other advisers. It is written in an accessible way, avoiding unnecessary jargon, but seeks at the same time to explain the basics of what are often very complex procedures. The scope of the book is very wide and so where it is not possible to be comprehensive we have suggested relevant organisations which can offer specific help and advice.

The last edition of *Your Rights* was published in 1994 and since then there have been numerous changes to the law which are now included in this new edition. The effects on travellers and on peaceful protest of the Criminal Justice and Public Order Act 1994 are explained, as are the changes to a suspect's 'right of silence' and new police powers to stop and search without needing reasonable suspicion of any offence contained in the 1994 Act and the Prevention of Terrorism (Additional Powers) Act 1996. It was this latter Act which passed through the House of Commons in just twelve hours.

The procedures of the new Criminal Cases Review Commission (which was set up in 1997) in considering miscarriage of justice cases are explained and we summarise the new provisions of the Asylum and Immigration Act 1996 which denies nationals from certain countries the right to claim asylum and further restricts the appeals procedure for asylum seekers. The effects on the rights of workers of the Employment Rights Act 1996 and the EC Working Time Directive (which came into force in November 1996) are analysed and the important, but limited, rights established by the Disability Discrimination Act 1996 are explained.

Your Rights also explains how to use the Code of Practice on Access to Government Information (which came into force in April 1994), when to complain to the new Broadcasting Standards Commission (which was set up in April 1997) and how to complain to the European Ombudsman (who has been operating since September 1995). Each chapter considers relevant decisions of the European Court of Human Rights and the effects of European Union law.

The law is stated as at 1 April 1997. The most significant change is of course the proposal by the new government to incorporate the European Convention on Human Rights into domestic law. The rights in the Convention are set out in Chapter 5 and cover virtually every issue dealt with in this book. A Bill to incorporate the Convention is due to be published in the autumn of 1997 and this is likely to become an Act by July 1998 and to come into force not before January 1999. It is not clear at the time of writing exactly what effect this will have on our laws. It is likely that the Convention will be able to be used to challenge some of the existing procedures and judge-made law although whether the Convention will be given a higher status than statute is not so clear. Nevertheless the rights set out in this book may be enhanced by the Convention and in future the rights in the Convention will have to be considered much more seriously than they have been in the past.

We have also explained the effect of a number of Bills which have become law, such as the Police Act 1997, the Crime (Sentences) Act 1997, the Protection from Harassment Act 1997, the Sex Offenders Act 1997, the Social Security (Administration) Fraud Act 1997 and the Knives Act 1997. We do not consider the position in Scotland or Northern Ireland because the law there is different to the law in England and Wales and further information on those jurisdictions can be obtained from Liberty's sister organisations, the Scottish Council for Civil Liberties and the Committee for the Administration of Justice (in Northern Ireland).

We would like to thank all of our contributors for their generosity. Their services have again been given free of charge so that the income from this book will go to support Liberty's work. Our thanks also to all the staff and volunteers at Liberty and, finally, to everyone at Pluto.

John Wadham
Philip Leach
Penny Sergeant

Liberty
April 1997

Table of Statutes

Regulations

1

The right of peaceful protest

This chapter deals with:

- The historic right of peaceful protest.
- The regime for regulating public protest.
- In practice – organising a protest action.
- Public order offences.

1.1 The historic right of peaceful protest

The historic right to demonstrate is as deeply rooted in our political culture as the right to govern. It is one of the basic building blocks of our constitution. And like most of our 'constitutional rights' it is difficult to trace to a single source because our constitution has never been written down in a single place, like the American constitution, for example. There is no specific law which confers a legal right to demonstrate.

However, senior judges have often referred to the right of peaceful protest. One of the most famous judges of the last forty years, Lord Denning, said:

> The right to demonstrate and the right to protest on matters of public concern are rights which it is in the public interest that individuals should possess; and indeed, that they should exercise without impediment so long as no wrongful act is done. *Hubbard* v. *Pitt* (1976)

These very important rights are not 'given' to us by Parliament, but are ones which, as individuals, we already possess. They are rights which, in principle, we can exercise how we want and when we want, subject only to the restrictions that our elected governments or the courts impose.

There have been many times in the past – even in the recent past – when the public demonstration of support for a cause, or opposition to a policy or government, have changed the course of history. 'People power' remains a very potent political force, whether at a national or

1

local level; whether to do with political causes or single issues; whether in support of striking workers or bereaved families or in opposition to road-building, live animal exports, or the Poll Tax. Even when people have nothing else to fight with, it is often their solidarity with each other – to stand together and be counted – which proves their most powerful weapon.

However, for as long as there have been governments there have been rules to restrict forms of dissent. Over the centuries the law in this area has developed piecemeal, adapting to the prevailing attitudes and concerns of the governments and courts of the day. This dynamic process reflects the struggle which is at the heart of public order law – the natural tension between the amount of freedom we demand as demonstrators and the amount of restriction we as electors want our Parliament to impose.

Not all public protest takes the form of organised marches through town centres by people carrying placards and chanting slogans. Although the Public Order Act 1986 introduced extensive controls on such traditional forms of political expression, there has been a movement away from formal protest in favour of a proliferation of imaginative and diverse actions, many on private land, which have enabled political messages to be sent, and damaging practices to be frustrated, away from the restrictive controls of the police.

Inevitably, one of the stated reasons given in 1994 for extending the provisions of the Public Order Act 1986 was that police needed additional powers to regulate these new and varied methods of mass action, including raves, festivals, roads protests and hunt sabotage. The result is a statutory regime that is broader than ever before, with extensive powers that can be used not just against these and other 'targeted' groups, but against all manifestations of political protest, formal and informal.

These extensive powers put responsibilities on the shoulders of the police. Choosing which powers to exercise, which protests to control, and how, will often involve very careful policy considerations. In practice, sensitive to criticism on political and human rights grounds, police use their considerable powers against *protest* less often than the frequent use of criminal charges against *protesters* themselves.

In this chapter we set out

- the regime for regulating public protest;
- the practical consequences for organisers;
- the principal public order offences directed at demonstrators.

Where to find the law
The most important statutory provision is the Public Order Act 1986, as extended by the Criminal Justice and Public Order Act 1994. These

statutes together set out the powers of the police to impose conditions on marches, and on static demonstrations such as rallies, pickets and vigils. The Public Order Act 1986 also sets out the main public order offences such as riot, affray, and threatening behaviour, which are directed at people on demonstrations. Another significant statute is the Police and Criminal Evidence Act 1984 which gives the police powers to arrest and detain people suspected of committing criminal offences (see Chapter 6). The full text of these statutes is set out in legal reference books such as Blackstone's *Criminal Practice* or Stone's *Justices Manual* (see 'Further information' at the end of this chapter).

Even after these major pieces of legislation, public order law is far from unified. This is because, as well as their powers under these recent statutes, the police retain some historic 'common law' powers, such as the power to take action to prevent a breach of the peace. There are also numerous bye-laws, passed by local authorities which are specific to a particular area and often restrict our rights or impose obligations on us. Other legislation sometimes refers to rights to demonstrate. Picketing during industrial disputes, for example, is regulated by employment laws.

STOP PRESS

The new government proposes to incorporate the European Convention on Human Rights into domestic law. The rights in the Convention are set out in Chapter 5. A Bill to incorporate the convention is due to be published in the autumn of 1997 and this is likely to become an Act by July 1998 and to come into force not before January 1999. It is not clear at the time of writing exactly what effect this will have on our laws. It is likely that the Convention will be able to be used to challenge some of the existing procedures and judge-made law although whether the Convention will be given a higher status than statute is not so clear. Nevertheless the rights set out in this book may be enhanced by the convention and in future the rights in the Convention will have to be considered much more seriously than they have been in the past.

Another important source for today's law are reported cases, showing how the courts have approached particular situations in the past. All laws have to be interpreted – what exactly counts as a 'public place', for example – and the precedents from previous court decisions are a useful indication of how they might react if the same situation were to occur again. Many of these cases are reported regularly in publications such as *Legal Action* (see 'Further information').

Finally, the European Convention on Human Rights contains provisions (see Chapter 5) which are relevant to fundamental rights and freedoms such as the right to liberty (Art. 5), fair trial (Art. 6), respect for private and family life (Art. 8), freedom of thought, conscience and religion (Art. 9), freedom of expression (Art. 10) and of peaceful assembly (Art. 11). In addition, the Convention outlaws discrimination over the exercise of those rights on the basis of race, sex, religion, colour and political or other opinion (Art. 14). The Convention has provided a useful international yardstick against which Britain's public order regime can be judged and once incorporated it is expected that it could be used as a defence to criminal charges. Liberty is willing to look carefully at potential breaches of the Convention and supports test cases which raise points of principle.

1.2 The regime for regulating public protest

Marches
The Public Order Act 1986 refers to marches as 'processions' and to all other static demonstrations as 'assemblies'. A 'procession' is simply defined as people moving together along a route; the law does not provide a minimum number to constitute a procession, so even a handful of people going to a Town Hall to hand in a petition will constitute a procession. The Act gives police extensive controls over processions. Organisers of most processions must give advance notice to the police. The police may impose conditions on processions and, in limited circumstances, have them banned. Failure to comply with these provisions is a criminal offence.

Who is the organiser?
There is no legal definition. For a big procession an official organiser will probably have been selected well in advance of the date. For a spontaneous event the organiser could be anyone who takes the lead.

Advance notice
The rules are designed to ensure that the police are told, in advance, about the vast majority of political marches. Specifically, they say that notice should be given of any procession if it is intended to:

- Demonstrate support for or opposition to the views or actions of any group.
- Publicise a cause or campaign.
- Mark or commemorate an event.

Notice need not be given if it is not reasonably practicable to do so in advance. This is intended to allow for a completely spontaneous procession, for example, when a meeting turns itself into a march or, as Christian CND put it, when it is necessary 'to call acts of witness or protest at short notice'. If a prosecution is brought it will be for the magistrates' court to decide whether notice of any kind could have been given. A last-minute telephone call to the police is advisable to show you are prepared to follow the spirit of the law – a record should be kept of the call.

Notice is also not required if it is a funeral procession or a procession commonly or customarily held. This will include the Lord Mayor's Show in the City of London, the Notting Hill Carnival, and other annual local parades including those organised by religious groups. If a protest march occurs regularly (weekly, annually) at the same time along the same route then no notice should be required.

Where notice is required it must be in writing and must include:

- The date of the procession.
- The time it will start.
- The proposed route.
- The name and the address of the organiser.

The written notice must be delivered to a police station in the area where the procession is planned to start (or the first police area in England on the route if it starts in Scotland) either by hand or by recorded delivery six clear days in advance. 'Six clear days' means, effectively, a full week in advance, for example on Saturday for a procession the following Saturday.

If a procession is planned at short notice (less than one week) then the organiser is required to deliver written notice by hand as soon as reasonably practicable.

Offences connected with notice
The organiser commits an offence (maximum penalty fine up to £1,000) if either:

- Notice was not given as required.
- The date, starting time or route differs from that given on the notice.

There is no power of arrest, but the police could rely on their general power of arrest (see – s25 PACE Power of Arrest – p. 168). In practice it has proved very difficult for the police, in the handful of prosecutions brought under this section of the Act since 1987, to prove that a particular person was the organiser of a march. Unless the police can do so, their powers to prosecute are greatly curtailed. Even if they can, it is a defence if you can prove either:

- You were not aware that notice had not been given or not given in time.
- The different date, starting time or route was due to circumstances beyond your control or was changed with the agreement of the police or by direction of the police.

Police conditions on marches

There is no guarantee that the police will allow your proposed procession to take place as you want it. In advance, the Chief Constable (or the Commissioner in London) can impose conditions relating to the route, number of marchers, types of banners, duration, or restrict entry to a public place. These conditions must be in writing. After the procession has begun the most senior officer on the spot can impose similar conditions which do not have to be in writing. The Public Order Act 1986 says that conditions can only be imposed if the senior officer reasonably believes that the procession may result in:

- serious public disorder; or
- serious damage to property; or
- serious disruption to the life of the community.

The senior officer may also impose conditions if he or she reasonably believes that the purpose of the organisers is to intimidate others 'with a view to compelling them not to do an act they have a right to do, or to do an act they have a right not to do'. The conditions must be ones which the officer believes are necessary to prevent disorder, damage, disruption or intimidation. Where organisers have sufficient notice of proposed conditions, they can be challenged in the courts – see section 1.3 below. Failure to comply with a valid condition is a criminal offence with different penalties for organisers and other participants (see below).

Banning marches

The Public Order Act 1986 gives police power to ban all or a 'class' of processions in a local area for up to three months, by way of a banning order. If a Chief Constable (or the Commissioner in London) is satisfied that the powers to impose conditions will not be sufficient to prevent serious public disorder if the procession takes place, then he must apply for a banning order.

Outside London, the Chief Constable applies to the district council for a banning order. The district council is not obliged to make the order, and it must have the Home Secretary's consent to any banning order it makes. In London, the Commissioner makes the order with the Home Secretary's consent.

A banning order can cover all or part of a district (or all or part of the Metropolitan Police area or the City of London) and can ban all processions or just those within a certain class (for example, processions marking the death of a political terrorist). A blanket ban of all processions is often imposed, even though it is designed to prevent one march only. The standard formula is to ban 'all public processions other than those of a traditional or ceremonial character'. Failure to comply with a banning order is a criminal offence (see below).

Static demonstrations, rallies and other assemblies

In addition to the powers that the police have used effectively for many years (breach of the peace, obstruction of the highway, local bye-laws, etc., see p. 27) to move or disperse a crowd which has assembled for a common purpose, the Public Order Act 1986 gives the police specific powers to control public assemblies. These are similar to the powers which the police have to impose conditions on processions (see above). A 'public assembly' is twenty or more people gathered together in a public place which is at least partly in the open air. A public place is any highway (including the pavement) and any other place to which the public or a section of the public can have access and therefore includes parks and gardens, shopping precincts, shops and offices, restaurants and pubs, cinemas, football stadia, rights of way, etc. A public assembly could be twenty people spaced across a wide entrance, but probably not four sets of five pickets at different factory gates. Any static group of *less than twenty people* will not constitute a public assembly and therefore cannot be regulated under the Public Order Act 1986.

Police conditions on public assemblies

Conditions may be imposed on a public assembly which restrict:

* The place – for example, by forcing pickets to move from the embassy gates.
* The duration – for example, by reducing a twenty-four hour vigil to four hours.
* The numbers – for example, by reducing a mass picket from thousands to twenty.

Similar to the powers concerning processions, the Chief Constable (Commissioner in London) can impose conditions in advance (in writing) or the most senior officer on the spot can impose conditions as soon as twenty people have assembled. The grounds for doing so –

such as the fear of serious public disorder – are also the same as for processions. Note, however, that there is no power to ban a public assembly altogether, and no advance notice need be given of any public assembly.

Police powers to ban 'trespassory assemblies'

The situation is rather different for trespassory assemblies. A 'trespassory assembly' is twenty or more people on land in the open air without the permission, or in excess of the permission, of the occupier. A group of thirty celebrators at Stonehenge without permission would constitute a trespassory assembly.

The police have been given a new power to ban any trespassory assembly where there is a risk of serious disruption to the life of the local community, or where there is a risk to an important site or building. The police can impose a ban over an area up to five miles around the site, prevent people travelling to the assembly, and can arrest those who organise or take part in the assembly itself.

Offences

If you know that a condition has been imposed on either a procession or a public assembly, it is an offence if you do not comply, either as an organiser or as an ordinary participant. It is also an offence to incite others not to comply. If you know that a procession or trespassory assembly has been banned, it is an offence for you to organise, to take part or to incite others to take part in it.

In principle the police can arrest organisers or demonstrators, which in a large gathering gives them extremely wide discretionary powers as to whom they choose to remove from the scene. The maximum penalty for organisers or inciters is three months' imprisonment or a fine at level 4 (currently £2,500) and for participants a fine at level 3 (currently £1,000). It is a defence to prove that any failure to comply with a condition was beyond your control.

Additional powers in London and other towns

There are several nineteenth-century statutes (Metropolitan Police Act 1839, City of London Police Act 1839, Town Police Clauses Act 1847) which enable the Commissioners of Police in London and the City or local councils outside London to make regulations and give directions to prevent obstruction and to keep order. Directions are given to constables and are not required to be made public. There are no conditions that must be satisfied before directions can be given, and, therefore, little scope to challenge them as excessive or unjustified. When lawful directions have been issued (for example, not to continue down a particular street), and you have been 'acquainted' with them, you commit an offence if you do not comply. You could also be charged with obstructing the police (see p. 31).

Police directions are often used to restrict protest events, but over the last decade police forces in different parts of the country seem to have been more ready to turn to these discretionary powers to regulate not just political demonstrations but also raves and festivals, and the movement around the country of groups of people such as pickets, football supporters, new age travellers or roads protesters. When directions are made, police can be given very wide powers indeed, as the following examples – all from the last few years – show. When a 'Stop the City' demonstration was planned, the City of London Commissioner issued directions under which the police arrested people who distributed leaflets or gathered in groups of three or more. During the News International dispute at Wapping the Metropolitan Commissioner's directions, which were renewed monthly during the dispute, gave the police authority to close streets – even to residents – and stop any person walking or driving in any street in Tower Hamlets. In Salisbury the district council made an order banning 'hippies' from the town centre for two days and restricted them to a designated route.

In the City of London, the 'Ring of Steel' anti-terrorist roadblocks were originally set up in 1992 under police powers to stop and search suspected offenders (see p. 157 – Stop and Search). But after protests the police conceded in practice that they had no special grounds to think that the people caught up in the roadblocks were terrorist suspects. The roadblocks continued, but were then justified by reference to directions issued by the City of London Police Commissioner. In due course, the Government brought in specific statutory powers, but the episode highlighted the use of 'Commissioner's Directions' in anticipation of powers not yet granted under statute.

Liberty is prepared to challenge the use of these powers, believing that fundamental decisions about our civil rights should be taken by Parliament and not left to the discretion of Chief Officers.

Demonstrations near the Houses of Parliament

At the beginning of each Parliamentary session, the Metropolitan Police Commissioner is instructed by Parliament to give directions under the Metropolitan Police Act 1839 to police officers 'to disperse all assemblies or processions of persons causing or likely to cause an obstruction, disorder or annoyance' within a specified area around Westminster whenever Parliament is sitting (see map overleaf).

The police must rely on their general powers of arrest or powers to prevent a breach of the peace (see p. 34). You commit an offence (maximum sentence, a fine of £400) if you fail to disperse after you

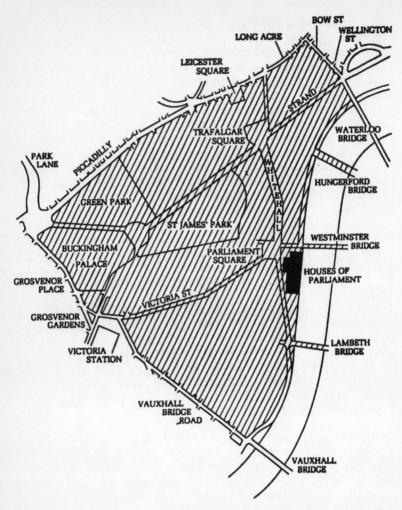

are made aware of the Commissioner's Directions, which normally means that the police must read them to you, or at least summarise their effect, before they can arrest you. It is a defence to show that the free passage of MPs would not have been obstructed. The directions do not affect processions or meetings on a day when Parliament is not sitting.

Picketing
For more than a century, trade unions and organised groups of workers have used picketing as a powerful means of protecting their

employment rights and improving the conditions in which they are expected to work. In recent years, picketing has been used by campaigning and protest groups as an effective way of bringing their views to public attention, for example, by picketing premises where politicians are due to attend, demonstrating outside head offices of organisations, and 'blockading' ports and airports supporting live animal exports. The law gives special status to picketing when it is related to an industrial dispute but no special exemption under the criminal law. However, most picketing is lawful unless it causes an obstruction of the highway or is designed to intimidate (see p. 32).

You are protected under the civil law if you picket in connection with an industrial dispute at or near your workplace for the purpose of peacefully obtaining or communicating information or peacefully persuading any person to work or abstain from working (Trade Union and Labour Relations Act 1992). Employers have increasingly used the civil courts to get injunctions in order to limit the effectiveness of picketing. Injunctions have been granted on the basis that it was not the workplace of some or all of the pickets or that the picketing was not peaceful. Unions who continue to picket in breach of an injunction are in contempt of court and liable to pay very heavy fines. By injunction the court can limit the location and number of pickets and impose conditions on their conduct.

No legal case has been decided which specifies that a particular number of pickets at the location of an industrial dispute will always be lawful. But a government Code of Practice, which the courts can refer to, suggests that the number of pickets at any entrance to a workplace should not generally exceed six. In applications for injunctions, the civil courts have tended to set the upper limit of the number of pickets that must be allowed at six. Other cases have given the police very wide discretion to limit the number of pickets if they believe it to be necessary to prevent a breach of the peace or an obstruction of the highway.

Secondary picketing – picketing at a workplace or premises where you do not work – does not have the same civil law protection, but is not a criminal offence. It is worth remembering that the police do not have any enhanced powers over secondary picketers and it is not their job to enforce the civil law on picketing, even if an injunction is in force. Their general powers in this area are dealt with below.

Police powers and picketing

Giving the police greater power to control and restrict picketing was a primary purpose of the Public Order Act 1986. Any picket of twenty or more people is a 'public assembly' and therefore subject to police conditions under the Act (see above). In addition to the power to impose conditions, the police possess a wide range of public order powers to restrict and control picketing and to arrest pickets for various offences, including:

- Obstruction of the highway (see p. 32) – on the basis of too many pickets, even if they are moving, or a single picket trying to compel a driver to stop and listen.
- Obstruction of the police (see p. 31) – for example, refusing to comply with lawful directions when the police are acting to prevent a breach of the peace.
- Using threatening, abusive or insulting words or behaviour (section 4 Public Order Act 1986, see p. 29).
- Disorderly conduct likely to cause harassment, alarm or distress (Section 5 Public Order Act 1986, see p. 29).
- Aggravated trespass (Section 68 CJPOA 1994, see p. 30).

Meetings

Public meetings

A public meeting is one which is open to the public to attend, with or without payment, and is held in a public place (a place to which the public have access on payment or otherwise). Many private premises, including town halls and council buildings, church halls, football stadia, pubs, etc., become 'public places' when public meetings are held there. A meeting could be any number of people and there is no duty to advertise it or to offer tickets widely. Local council meetings are public (except for confidential parts of the agenda).

If you are the organiser of a public meeting on private premises you must ensure that you comply with the terms and conditions for the use of the hall, etc., including all fire and safety regulations, and that the meeting is conducted in an orderly manner. Stewards should be easily identifiable but they should not wear a uniform to promote a political objective or signify membership of a political organisation. They must not try to take over the functions of the police or use force to promote a political objective (these acts would be illegal). They can assist in the admission and seating of members of the public and in the control of disorder or to remove members of the public who go too far in their heckling.

It is an offence under the Public Meeting Act 1908 to try to break up a lawful public meeting by acting in a disorderly manner or to incite others to do so. The maximum penalty is six months' imprisonment and/or a fine on level 5. If a police officer is present and reasonably suspects you of trying to disrupt the meeting then, at the chairperson's request, he or she can ask you for your name and address and it is an offence if you fail to give these details or give a false name or address (maximum penalty a fine on level 1). These offences do not carry a power of arrest, although the police could rely on their general powers of arrest (see p. 168).

If there is serious disruption or aggressiveness, and if the police believe that you are involved, then, relying on their common law powers to prevent a breach of the peace, the police could ask you to leave the meeting, threatening you with arrest if you refused, or they could arrest you for an offence under section 4 or section 5 of the Public Order Act 1986 (see p. 29).

Any meeting of twenty or more people which is wholly or partly in the open air is a 'public assembly' and subject to conditions being imposed by the police under the Public Order Act 1986 (see p. 7). Such a meeting held on land without the owner's permission may be a trespassory assembly and could be subject to a banning order (see above). Organisers should be aware that plain-clothes police officers may attend political meetings without authority for the purpose of collecting information.

Election meetings
The Representation of the People Act 1983 makes special provision for public meetings held at the time of local or national elections. All candidates are entitled to use rooms in local schools and other publicly owned meeting halls, free of charge, for election meetings provided that the meetings are open to the public and are intended to further the candidate's prospects by discussion of election issues.

Some local authorities have refused permission to the National Front to use their premises for election meetings on the grounds that they did not intend their meetings to be genuinely open to the public or because damage was likely to be caused to the premises. In 1986, the Court of Appeal upheld the right of a British National Party candidate to be allowed to use a schoolroom for an election meeting and ruled that a candidate who was refused such access could sue the local authority to enforce his rights under the election law.

The Representation of the People Act makes it an offence, punishable with a fine up to £1,000, to disrupt, or to incite others to disrupt, an election meeting. If a police officer reasonably suspects you of trying to disrupt the meeting, then, at the chairperson's request, he or she can ask you for your name and address and it is an offence if you fail to give these details or falsify them. Police powers for public meetings also apply to election meetings.

Private meetings
A meeting is private if members of the public are not free to attend, in payment or otherwise (for example, the meeting of a trade union

branch or a political party). A private meeting remains private even though it is held in a public building like a town hall. Organisers can refuse entry or require someone to leave. Private meetings are governed by the rules of the organisation involved, or by conditions specified by the organisers together with any requirements, for example, as to maximum numbers which apply to the premises where the meeting takes place. Unless the police are invited by the organisers they have no right to enter a private meeting and can be asked to leave unless they are present to prevent crime or an imminent breach of the peace.

Using the highway

The law provides a specific right to use a public highway: the right to pass and repass along the highway (including the pavement), and the right to make ordinary and reasonable use of the highway, which includes processions. The leading cases on the offence of highway obstruction show that the right to meet together, to go in a procession, to demonstrate and to protest on matters of public concern are undoubted in the law of England and Wales. However, the use of the highway must be reasonable; any unreasonable obstruction of the highway is a criminal offence (see p. 32 below). There may also be bye-laws – laws relating to a particular area – that restrict activities which are incidental to the right to use the highway (see the following two sections).

Street collections, leafleting, petitions, posters and newspapers

Generally speaking, the law allows a wider latitude for collecting money for charitable operations than for commercial or political ones, both of which are more closely regulated by licensing. 'Charitable purposes' means any charitable, benevolent or philanthropic purpose. It includes the relief of poverty and the advancement of religion or education at home or abroad, but it does not include collections to raise funds for a political party or for a political campaign, like CND or animal liberation. However, the law relating to these subjects is confused and inconsistently applied by the police. If in doubt, check bye-laws with the local authority and the police beforehand.

There is no need to obtain a licence or certificate for handing out leaflets or collecting signatures for a petition. A leaflet must have on it the name and address of the printer. Some bye-laws contain restrictions on the places where leafleting may take place; check the bye-laws at the town hall. The police may also move leafleters if they appear to be causing an obstruction. It is an offence to hand out leaflets which are threatening, abusive or insulting or which are intended to stir up racial hatred.

A petition to Parliament is governed by special rules and must conform to special wording. Copies of the rules can be obtained from:

House of Commons,
Westminster
London SW1A OAA
Tel: 0171 219 3000

Sticking up posters in public places is quite legal, so long as:

* You have the consent of the owner of the hoarding, fence or wall in question.
* The poster is no more than six feet square.
* It advertises a non-commercial event, including political, educational, or social meetings.
* There is no bye-law to prevent it.

Persons over eighteen may sell newspapers in the street or from door to door, as long as the sale is for campaigning purposes. If the sale is for profit it becomes street trading or peddling (if door to door), both of which are illegal without a licence. Sometimes difficulty is caused because the police believe that the newspaper or magazine is less of a campaigning document and more a device to raise money for a political organisation. Also, the sale of newspapers may obstruct the highway, which is a criminal offence (see p. 32).

Bye-laws

Many activities on the highway and in other public places such as parks and gardens and on common land are restricted by local bye-laws. Bye-laws for parks may, for example, prohibit public meetings, bill-posting, the erection of notices, stalls and booths, and the sale or distribution of pamphlets and leaflets. They will usually give the police and local authority officials the power to remove anybody who breaches the bye-laws.

Ministry of Defence bye-laws are used, for example, to keep trespassers out of United States Air Force bases. The RAF Greenham Common bye-laws listed twelve prohibited activities, beginning with entering the protected area except by way of an authorised entrance, and including affixing posters to perimeter fences.

A copy of local bye-laws should be on sale at the local town hall and also available for inspection. Bye-laws for land owned by an authority such as British Rail or British Coal, or by a government department, will be available directly from that authority. Often bye-laws have to be prominently displayed near entrances to private land, and they should show the address to obtain copies from.

It is an offence to breach a bye-law. The penalty is set out in the particular bye-law or, if not, is a fine up to £100. Recent cases supported by Liberty have shown that when a charge is brought, bye-laws can be challenged on the basis that they are *ultra vires*, that is, beyond the scope of the Act of Parliament which creates them, or that they are obviously unreasonable or inconsistent with or repugnant to the general law.

For the right to use the highway for industrial and consumer picketing, see p. 32.

1.3 In practice – organising a protest action

It is easy to be intimidated by all the laws that exist to regulate the expression of public protest. But the most successful protest groups see the restrictive legal framework as one of the necessary challenges that their own good organisation can overcome, or at least accommodate. Although the police have been given very wide powers under the Public Order Act 1986, the actual exercise of these powers has been remarkably rare since the Act came into force. Conditions are not routinely imposed on demonstrations, and banning orders have not been used as extensively as opponents of the legislation first feared. In fact, only a handful of the hundreds of thousands of prosecutions brought under the Act since 1987 have been for offences connected with organising marches or assemblies, defying banning orders or even breaching conditions imposed by police. The vast majority have been for the public order offences ranging from riot to disorderly conduct (see p. 27), each of which involved allegations of specific offensive conduct by the person concerned, usually at the demonstration itself.

The following sections show how complying with the law and negotiating with the police might be accommodated in the arrangements that organisers will be making, in any event, in preparation for a protest of significant size; and how structures developed to support the action itself can be adapted to support protesters who get arrested. Obviously, organisers will choose which of the following are appropriate or desirable for the particular sort of protest they are planning.

Organising the protest action

Stewards and legal observers
An efficient stewarding operation avoids many of the interactions between protesters and police that have the potential for conflict. Protesters are usually quite happy to follow sensible instructions so long

as they know that they are part of the organisers' plan rather than some arbitrary decision made on the spot by an officious police officer. Stewarding therefore gives confidence to your protesters, whilst also enabling information about particular difficulties to reach the organisation room, or chief stewards at the protest, very quickly.

It is important to appreciate, however, that police and organisers may have very different views of what 'efficient stewarding' means. From the organisers' point of view the real job of the stewards is to make sure that the event takes the course that the organisers want, not necessarily to solve problems for the police or to smooth things over where real conflicts exist. What the stewards are told to do might differ quite substantially from what the police want them to do. Police sometimes put conditions on demonstrations and assemblies which need to be challenged in practice as unreasonable. Stewards can then play a very important role in that challenge (see below, 'Challenging police decisions').

Stewards should be briefed prior to the protest on what exactly they should be doing, and who they should report to in the event of difficulty. They are part of the organisation of the event and should be identifiable as such both to police and protesters by bibs, armbands, special T shirts or badges (but obviously not a quasi-military uniform, see p. 12). At the event itself they should have a map of the proposed route, and the telephone number of the organisation room (see below).

Some organisations have ad hoc groups of legal observers who are prepared to attend demonstrations and make an independent note of numbers and movements of police and protesters. In the event of arrests, they will make immediate notes of witnesses' names and addresses. Observers can be a great help if events turn sour, but in any case their presence at a demonstration can be reassuring to protesters and police alike. It is important that they perceive themselves to be independent of the protest itself and its organisation. They may therefore wish to be identified in a way that distinguishes them from other people on the march, including stewards, for example by special badges, armbands or bibs. Often law students or lecturers from local colleges are prepared to provide this service if given enough notice. Inexperienced legal observers should be briefed by a solicitor, perhaps the standby solicitor (see legal cover section on p. 18), preferably in good time before the protest.

Stewards and legal observers should know where to meet immediately after the event for a debriefing where any feedback or information they have , for example, notes from legal observers, can be retrieved. They should also be available to come to a defendants' meeting (see below), which should be pencilled in for two or three days after the event, in case anyone at the demonstration is arrested. Arranging such a meeting provides a safety net which will enable you to begin to draw all your resources together should there ever be a defendants' group that needs to rely on them.

Advance publicity and press liaison

Prior to the event itself, advance publicity should include a clear statement of the venue for assembly, the time of departure (for a march) and the time and place of the eventual rally. Any venues you advertise ought – as a matter of good practice – to have been agreed with the owners/local authority/police in advance (see below). Otherwise, if you are forced to change any of these arrangements your supporters may never get to the protest.

Protest actions are designed to be widely seen and their intended message understood. You might prepare a brief press statement to be sent out to the media in advance setting out the message you want them to grasp – and, hopefully, to broadcast on your behalf – about why the event is taking place. Ideally, this should include contact telephone numbers of one or two people who are prepared to be quoted speaking on your behalf and a reference point at the protest itself so that journalists know where to go if they want to get an official statement or reaction to something that has happened. Journalists might be given the telephone number of the organisation room, but telephone interviews during the protest itself should be kept short.

The advantage of preparing a press release in advance is that local journalists will put the event in their news diary, which may ensure fuller coverage. Also, they may be more interested in difficulties you have with the police in the run-up to the event, especially if you decide to tell the press that you are preparing to challenge proposed conditions.

Organisation room

On the day of the event itself there ought to be a reference point away from the demonstration – a union office, for example – with at least two separate phone lines. One of these numbers should be circulated widely on a leaflet which arrested people will be likely to have with them when in the police station. This will also be the number used by stewards or legal observers if they want to contact the organisation room where necessary during the event itself. The other phone line can be used for outgoing calls – to the police station, to the standby lawyer (see below), or perhaps to the press.

Legal cover

Ideally you will have arranged a standby lawyer well in advance of the action who is prepared to be contacted during the demonstration itself and to follow through with representation for arrested demonstrators if they require it. The standby lawyer should be a criminal solicitor with particular experience of dealing with demonstrations. If you do not know of such a lawyer, organisations like those listed below will help you find one in your area. If you experience difficulties negotiating with the police in advance, the standby lawyer may be prepared to help you.

Debriefing

Taking time to listen to feedback from those who have helped you organise the event is more than just good practice – where there have been arrests such an exercise is essential. It is also an opportunity to recognise the job done by stewards and legal observers, to thank them and to make sure you have their contact numbers for the next time you need them.

Defendants' meeting

At the briefing for stewards and legal observers you will probably have arranged a defendants' meeting at a given venue and time two or three days after the event. Although you hope it will not be needed, such a meeting may make a very significant difference to those who may attend (see p. 23).

Dealing with police

Deciding whether to make contact

Whenever it is anticipated there may be police interest in a proposed action it will be worth weighing the benefits and costs of speaking to the police well in advance as part of your preparations. Sometimes it will be a legal obligation to do so (see p. 4).

The benefits of establishing contact with the police are likely to include, if not always good will, at least some cooperation. With some or all of the above measures in place you will be in a strong position to satisfy the police that you will be able to regulate your own event without needing outside help. Confident organisers who impress with their thoroughness and practicality are more likely to be able to convince sceptical police that a proposed event should proceed exactly as planned. Where they are able to do so, the worry that the event might be hijacked by police interference will be eased, and organisers will then be able to concentrate on getting their political message across to the public.

The costs of contacting the police might include the fact that they may use your information to trigger the use of their powers to restrict a protest or, exceptionally, to ban it altogether. It is worth remembering that communications to police – especially those in writing – could be used in court if the police wanted to show that a particular person was an organiser of an illegal demonstration.

Despite their substantial human resources and weaponry, the police are very often intimidated by the idea of large numbers of people taking to the streets to make their protest heard. Where police react in a hostile way, it is often through fear of the unknown. In practice, many police forces respond positively to constructive engagement – they like to know that someone who is organising a demonstration has anticipated the likely numbers and thought about the route, stewarding and safety. They also like to know that there will be someone at the protest to whom they can talk sensibly in an emergency. In a protest that continues over days or weeks, maintaining clear channels of communication with a senior officer, even where you consider police tactics to be unhelpful, can have positive benefits for protesters.

Meeting the police in advance
When you tell the police you are holding a demonstration they often ask you to a meeting with them. There is no requirement that you attend but it is probably sensible that you do. You will have to prepare for the meeting quite carefully with details of arrangements for stewarding and crowd control, first aid and access by emergency vehicles, maps and plans, a detailed timetable and an estimate of numbers. Relying on your own knowledge of the community and any other events likely to take place on the same date, try to anticipate police objections.

For the police this meeting can be an information-gathering session. The Metropolitan Police, for instance, have an official-looking form which asks you for the information you must give in advance by law, but also a lot of other information – such as names of speakers, for example. It is important to be aware of the information you must provide, and to decide in advance how much you wish to say to the police beyond that. If in doubt at the meeting on how to respond, you can always say that you want to consult your committee or co-organisers, etc. You don't have to agree to everything the police propose. You can tell the police directly that you do not agree to a certain condition, or that you will consider whether to or not.

If the demonstration is likely to be big in size or impact, especially if it is in the centre of a big city, there may be a large number of police present at this meeting – traffic police, public order police, local area police and note-takers, etc. It is always worth taking another person with you (or maybe one or two more) – a fellow committee member, a friend or even a friendly solicitor. It is best to agree in advance on how you will handle this, so that everyone is clear who is there to speak to police, to make decisions, or to take notes. Since police forces probably differ quite a lot, it may be worth talking to other groups who have organised demonstrations in your area before going to a meeting with the police.

Who to put forward

Choose as your own representative(s) for such a meeting the person on your team who is likely, for whatever reason, to get the most constructive and sympathetic response from the police side. This person need not be a 'spokesperson' in a formal sense, or have any position of responsibility for your organisation or even for the direction of the protest itself. Indeed it is often better that the person's only role is to facilitate communication between the parties rather than to be a decision maker in her/his own right. This ensures the person has a good reason to report back to others to consider police proposals, and it may lessen the personal pressure that can be brought to bear on the negotiator by police.

Challenging police decisions

Even when the police threaten to impose conditions, organisers have a great deal of discretion about whether and when to challenge the police decision. Sometimes organisers are prepared to agree to police alterations to their original proposals – a minor alteration to the proposed route, perhaps – knowing that this means in practice that the police are unlikely to interfere further with a route they have themselves adopted. Organisers may even prefer to adapt their protest to what they consider to be unreasonable police requests simply to ensure the event goes ahead without its political message being blunted by unnecessary conflict with the police. But where organisers decide to challenge unacceptable police conditions it is perfectly possible for them to do so with dignity. This section suggests some starting points.

Mobilising political support

Although the police regard their own decisions as 'operational', in practice they involve setting priorities between the interests of different groups in society. Ultimately, where the right balance lies is really a political matter and the police are sensitive to criticism from MPs and councillors, local interest groups or trades councils. Members of the police committee may be concerned by 'operational' policing decisions they consider to be oppressive.

Mounting a legal challenge

With the help of legal advisers, organisers could test the legality of police conditions through a court case in advance of the action itself. In order to seek a judicial review of a police decision you would need to argue that either:

- The decision was improperly reached (for example, because the proper procedure was not followed or improper considerations were taken into account).
- The decision was so unreasonable or arbitrary that no reasonable chief officer could have reached that conclusion.

It would be relevant to show that negotiations were still open. Cases brought to challenge banning orders show that courts are very unwilling to interfere with police decisions, especially if to do so would involve substituting their own assessment of the facts, and the possible prospects of disorder, damage, disruption or intimidation, for the assessment made by senior police officers.

Applications for judicial review must be made to the High Court in London. Urgent applications can be heard quickly. In many instances, however, you will be informed of conditions to restrict processions or assemblies too late to apply to the court. There is no one with immediate power to overrule the senior officer on the spot if he decides to impose conditions.

Where protesters themselves defy police conditions it will be for the police to decide whether to make arrests and seek prosecutions. If in a subsequent trial it turns out that the conditions were indeed invalid, the prosecutions would fail and arrested persons may be entitled to damages.

Help from Liberty

Liberty has been able to advise many of its supporters, including unions and political groups, about the best way to challenge police operations which threaten to defeat civil liberties. In the past the organisation has supported lawyers and lay people who have challenged such decisions and has itself been prepared to take test cases where important issues of principle have been at stake. In the first instance, you or your solicitor may want to contact Liberty's Legal Officer at the address below. Liberty will either be able to help you or will refer you to a specialist solicitor or campaigning group who have dealt with similar problems in the past.

Liberty
21 Tabard Street
London SE1 4LA
Tel: 0171 403 3888

Supporting defendants

Where people have been arrested at a protest event and charged with offences, they become defendants in the criminal process, facing the possibility of a criminal record and sometimes a substantial fine or even prison. It is often very frightening for protesters to be torn from a demonstration to find themselves facing the music all on their own. An important part of what organisers can do for defendants, as their cases progress over the months that may elapse before a trial, is to provide support. Defendants may be helped by support and reassurance in many different ways – it will often be a question of adapting your resources to the calls that are made on them – but one of the most straightforward and practical measures is to ensure that there is always someone from your organisation at court with defendants for each appearance.

In the immediate aftermath of the event, however, there are some standard procedures to be performed, starting with the defendants' meeting. This will have been pencilled in for two or three days after the event just in case it may be needed. Too soon, and defendants may still be in custody. Too late, and a lot of your resources, especially witnesses, will have dispersed, perhaps forever.

Defendants' meeting

A defendants' meeting puts people who have been charged with offences in touch with the people who organised the event, sometimes for the first time. Defendants may need immediate help to get lawyers or legal aid, for example, or even just floors to sleep on if they have to remain away from home for a court hearing. The meeting is an opportunity to give defendants reassurance if they need it, and to tell them what support they can expect from your organisation. There may be questions about bail conditions, legal aid or bind-overs, for example, or how their cases are likely to develop. The standby lawyer may be prepared to attend such a meeting, but will not give specific legal advice to defendants about their individual cases.

The defendants' meeting is a very important practical opportunity to match defendants to the witnesses who saw them being arrested. It is useful to do this quickly while memories are fresh. Often witnesses will not have met the defendants before and will not know them by name. Unless they come to a meeting and see the defendant, the only method of matching them to the right arrest is by their description of the arrested person, or by the time and location of the arrest. Where there have been many arrests, particularly at a mobile protest like a march, there is often great confusion about location, order and times of arrests. Often the only way to sort out which witnesses saw which arrests is to have everyone in the same room at the same time.

Defendants might want to provide passport photos of themselves or, if you have a camera at the meeting, might want you to take photos of them, to help with identification. This is often an enormous help for you, for witnesses and for lawyers where there are more than a handful of arrests. Make sure defendants are happy for you to circulate their photos and other information about themselves they want to give you.

Legal aid and self help (see Chapter 7)

Defendants charged with 'less serious' criminal offences may find it difficult – in some cases impossible – to get legal aid. The first priority will be to complete the legal aid application as fully as possible, pointing out, for example, that a particular defendant may have a special need for representation because of the complexity of the case, or the consequences of conviction, which might include the loss of a job, or the loss of previous good character. Completing the application is a skilled job – lawyers will help defendants to apply for legal aid if necessary. If legal aid is refused, lawyers will usually offer to represent the client at their normal hourly charging rate which is often out of the reach of all but well-off defendants. Occasionally lawyers will represent defendants for a lower fee, or even for free. It is always worth asking, especially if a particular lawyer is already representing other defendants from the same demonstration.

Defendants who are unable to obtain, or afford, legal representation will have to rely on self-help – and your help – to conduct their defence. Some organisations have proved that they can be very effective in supporting defendants who defend themselves, often by establishing a legal team within the organisation that pools knowledge and experience, and which provides a clear reference point for defendants. It is worth remembering that even if a defendant is denied legal aid for *representation*, s/he may still qualify for a number of hours of *advice and assistance* from a solicitor under the Green Form Scheme. Following a test-case taken by Liberty during opposition to the Poll Tax, it is now clear law that defendants are entitled to the assistance of a 'Mackenzie friend' to advise them in court if they are otherwise unrepresented. A friend in court can be a great source of practical, as well as moral, support (see 'Representation and legal aid' in Chapter 7, 'The rights of defendants').

An excellent reference book on self-representation is available from the Civil Liberties Trust. Michael Randle represented himself (successfully) at the Old Bailey in 1991 when he stood trial for assisting the escape from prison of George Blake. Randle's book, *How to defend yourself in court* draws on his experiences and is a very useful resource and inspiration for defendants and their supporters, whether legally represented or not.

Supporting the legal team

Once a lawyer is instructed by a person arrested for a criminal offence, the relationship is a personal one between the client and the lawyer and is therefore subject to professional confidentiality. Although the lawyer will not be prepared to speak about the details of the client's case to anyone else, most sympathetic lawyers will wish to retain a close contact with any organisation that has their clients' best interests at heart. Moreover they may wish to rely on you to get things done that they do not have the knowledge or resources to do themselves.

Sometimes several different solicitors will be acting for different defendants. Unless you are able to help them with an overview of what happened when and where during the course of the whole event, individual solicitors may never get the full picture. It is very important, for example, for them to know which arrests may be linked with each other. Accurate information about the time and location of arrests will be very helpful when defence lawyers seek film or photographs of the event from journalists who covered it. It is best to get this overview completed when events are fresh in everyone's mind and you have willing supporters to help.

Preparing material for defendants and their solicitors

At the earliest opportunity – within a few days of the defendants' meeting – organisers should marshal all the material they have at their disposal and make it available to defendants and their lawyers. This will include brief accounts of the following matters. Where more is needed later, defendants will know exactly who to ask:

- Facts about the event itself – who you are, how you prepared for the event. Negotiations with the police before and at the event. Who spoke for the organisation, who represented the police. What conditions were imposed/agreed. What steps were taken by police/organisers to publicise conditions. Whether any conditions were broken. Include a map of the route showing, if possible, location and time of arrests. Also reports – in the form of brief statements – where stewards and legal observers have made observations about the event that might be relevant. Include telephone numbers to enable lawyers to contact individuals directly if their evidence may be helpful.
- Full list of defendants' names, addresses and telephone numbers, including, if possible, time and location of arrest, police station taken to, offence they are charged with, date and venue of first court appearance. If defendants are happy to supply passport-sized

photos of themselves (or wanted you to take photographs at the defendants' meeting), you can include a photocopied sheet with them all on.

- Full list of witnesses' names, addresses and telephone numbers, marked (if known) with the names of the defendants whose arrest they saw.
- List of media representatives – especially photographers and television news teams – who you think were at the event. A useful source are the bylines on media coverage – this can be followed up in the local library without having to buy all the newspapers. Wherever a news story might be helpful it should be circulated. You might also include the list of organisations you sent your press release to. Lawyers may then be able to follow up whether they had anyone at the event.
- List of defence solicitors, so you know who to circulate information to. It will also help solicitors to communicate with each other if they know who else is being represented by whom.

Dealing with the press

In the run-up to the trials of defendants who plead not guilty – sometimes a delay of many months – you may want to look closely at the media coverage of the event and respond constructively by telephone to journalists, by 'letters to the editor' or by press release to anything that is said that you know is not true.

The police are adept at public relations and will normally have their own publicists, who are experienced journalists, handling press enquiries about the event and its aftermath. It is a sad fact that the media often takes this version as gospel, presuming the guilt of anyone unfortunate enough to have been arrested. Whilst there are no doubt other factors at play, this may sometimes be due to their perception that there is no other reliable source to challenge what the police say.

As well as supplying information from your organisation, you may be able to put the media in touch with ordinary protesters who had a very different impression of the way the event took place. If you know that celebrities at the event, such as local politicians, are likely to be supportive, you can ask them if they, too, are prepared to be interviewed.

It will give confidence to defendants to see that you are active about putting media coverage right. It also advertises the work that you are doing just in case defendants or potential witnesses did not know how to get in touch.

Practical help

It is often useful to talk to people who are experienced at organising protest events to get ideas on ways to get the most impact from the available resources and, in the event of unexpected arrests, on ways of supporting defendants and their legal teams. Liberty can help put you in touch with many groups nationwide, and up-to-date information can be obtained via the Internet if you search for links to 'politics', 'protest', and 'action'.

1.4 Public order offences

The right of protest may only be exercised peacefully. Otherwise, a wide variety of offences may be committed. The Public Order Act 1986 contains many of the more common public order offences such as riot, affray and threatening behaviour. But there are many offences elsewhere in the law which may be used against activities in public, such as assault, criminal damage and having an offensive weapon. Some specific offences connected with marches, assemblies and meetings were set out earlier in this chapter.

Serious offences of violence
The three main offences in the Public Order Act 1986 for group violence are riot, violent disorder and affray.

Riot
It is an offence of riot if you use violence where at least twelve people are together using or threatening violence for a common purpose and in such a way that 'a person of reasonable firmness' witnessing the events would fear for his or her safety.

This is the most serious of public order offences. Prosecutions are becoming less common because of the difficulty of proving a 'common purpose'. The offence can only be tried in the Crown Court and the Director of Public Prosecutions must consent to the case being brought. The maximum penalty is ten years' imprisonment.

Violent disorder
You are guilty of violent disorder if you use or threaten violence where at least three people are together using or threatening violence and in such a way that a person 'of reasonable firmness' would fear for his or her personal safety.

This offence is used especially for group violence, such as disturbances commonly associated with football hooliganism, or where weapons are used. It can be tried in either the Crown Court or the magistrates' court. The maximum penalty is five years' imprisonment.

Affray
It is an affray if you use or threaten violence to somebody else in such a way that a person 'of reasonable firmness' would fear for his or her personal safety (*effrayer* is the French word meaning 'to frighten').

Street fighting, with or without weapons or missiles, is an affray. It can be tried in either the Crown Court or the magistrates' court. The maximum penalty is three years' imprisonment.

Grievous bodily harm and actual bodily harm

Serious assaults on individuals include the offences of inflicting grievous bodily harm and assault occasioning actual bodily harm. These offences are set out in the Offences Against the Person Act 1861.

If you cause or inflict grievous bodily harm on somebody or wound them (that is, cut the skin), the maximum penalty is life imprisonment. If the person dies, the charge may be murder or manslaughter. If the injury is less serious, such as bruising or grazes, the charge may be assault occasioning actual bodily harm, with a maximum penalty of five years' imprisonment.

Less serious offences

Assault

You are guilty of common assault (under the common law) if you engage in an act which intentionally or recklessly causes another person to expect immediate personal violence, anything from a punch or a kick to throwing something at somebody. If injury is caused, a more serious charge of assault may be brought (see above). Common assault can only be tried in the magistrates' court. The maximum penalty is six months' imprisonment.

You are guilty of a separate offence with a similar penalty if you assault a police officer in the execution of his or her duty. At a trial the prosecution would have to show that the police officer was acting lawfully. In practice, especially in a confused demonstration situation, proving beyond doubt that police action was lawful is often difficult. This offence is the highest level summary only offence (see trial by jury or trial by magistrates?' in Chapter 7, below) and a custodial sentence, even for a first offender is a real possibility.

Threatening, abusive or insulting words or behaviour

It is an offence under Section 4 of the Public Order Act 1986 if you use threatening, abusive or insulting words or actions towards somebody else, and:

* You intend the other person to fear that violence is going to be used; or
* The other person is likely to expect violence; or
* Violence may well be provoked.

This offence is normally used where threats, abuse or insults are likely to cause a breach of the peace: rival football supporters hurling abuse, threats at the picket line, abusive language by rival demonstrators. The charge is often used against protesters who, in the view of the police, go beyond the bounds of ordinary protest, but in all cases the behaviour must be directed towards another person. It is also an offence if threatening words are on a banner or placard or even a T shirt or badge.

This offence can only be tried in the magistrates' court; there is no right to trial by jury. The maximum penalty is six months' imprisonment and/or a fine of £5,000.

Harassment

It is an offence under Section 4A of the same Act if you use threatening behaviour with intent to cause a person harassment, alarm and distress. Introduced to deal with cases of racial harassment, the section has been used more frequently, but with little success, to prosecute 'stalkers'. The penalties are as for Section 4 (above).

In addition, as a result of concern about the ability of the courts to deal with stalkers, in March 1997 the Protection from Harassment Act 1997 received Royal Assent. Section 1 of the Act makes it an offence for a person to pursue a course of conduct which the person knows or ought to know amounts to harassment of another person. The offence is punishable by imprisonment of up to six months and/or a fine of £5,000. The Act also introduces an offence of aggravated harassment where a complainant is also put in fear of violence (with a sentence of up to five years' imprisonment and an unlimited fine). The Act creates a statutory tort of harassment and makes it a criminal offence to breach a civil injunction restraining any conduct of harassment, and criminal courts will be able to make restraining orders on convicted defendants.

Disorderly conduct

It is an offence under Section 5 of the Public Order Act 1986 if you use threatening, abusive or insulting words or behaviour or disorderly behaviour within the hearing or sight of a person likely to be caused harassment, alarm or distress. There must be a victim present at the scene of the crime. That person must be identified but need not be brought to court. Police officers are unlikely to be victims of this offence.

This is the lowest-level public order offence. It is intended to cover minor acts of hooliganism, especially behaviour directed at the elderly and other vulnerable groups. It was much criticised when it was introduced in the Public Order Act because it covered behaviour which was generally not considered to be criminal. In particular, it covers behaviour which falls short of violence or the threat or fear of violence.

The offence carries a unique two-stage power of arrest, allowing police to arrest only if the demonstrator has been warned to stop the disorderly conduct and has then gone on to repeat it. The offence can only be tried in the magistrates' court. The maximum penalty is a fine up to £1,000; there is no power to send a person convicted of this offence to prison.

Aggravated Trespass

The offence of aggravated trespass is committed when a person

- trespasses on land
- when a lawful activity is taking place on that land or land nearby
- and he or she does anything intending to intimidate, obstruct or disrupt that activity.

The offence, under Section 68 of the Criminal Justice and Public Order Act 1994, goes hand-in-hand with new powers to prevent protesters joining an aggravated trespass. The powers are similar to the exclusion zone powers for trespassory assemblies (see above, p. 8). Once protesters are within a five-mile radius exclusion zone they can be turned back, and can be arrested and charged with an offence if they refuse to comply. The offences carry imprisonment of up to three months or a fine up to £2,500.

Criminal damage

You are guilty under the Criminal Damage Act 1971 if you damage or destroy property or threaten to do so intentionally or recklessly and without lawful excuse. There is a full range of offences from arson with intent to endanger life (maximum penalty life imprisonment) to damage of property under £5,000 in value (magistrates' court only with a maximum penalty of three months' imprisonment and/or a fine up to £2,500). The damage need not be permanent. Even graffiti designed to wash away with rain may be criminal damage.

Offensive weapons

You are guilty under the Prevention of Crime Act 1953 if you have an offensive weapon in a public place without lawful authority or reasonable excuse. There are three types of weapon: one designed for causing injury such as a knuckle-duster, dagger or flick-knife; one adapted for causing injury like a broken bottle; and one intended for use to cause injury, such as an ordinary knife or a spanner. The offence can be tried in the Crown Court (maximum penalty two years' imprisonment) or in the magistrates' court (maximum penalty six months' imprisonment and/or a fine up to £5,000).

Under the Criminal Justice Act 1988 it is an offence to have a knife in a public place without reasonable excuse. The section does not apply to a folding pocket-knife with a blade not more than three inches long. Mere possession of any other kind of knife or other article with a blade is an offence (maximum penalty a fine of £1,000 in the magistrates' court) unless you can prove you had a good reason for carrying it, for example, for use at work, for a hobby, for religious reasons or as part of a national costume (for stop and search powers, see p. 157). The courts have said that the 'good reason' has to relate to the time the knife is found. A good reason for having it five days before was not good enough, and nor was just forgetting you had it with you.

The Knives Act 1997 created a new power for the police to stop and search for knives or offensive weapons without needing reasonable suspicion of a particular offence. The power can be exercised where a senior police officer gives authorisation on the basis of a reasonable belief that there are people in the locality carrying such weapons without good reason.

Police obstruction

It is an offence if you wilfully obstruct a police officer in the execution of his or her duty. This is widely used by the police at demonstrations and in other public order contexts. Wilful obstruction of a police officer means simply doing any act which makes it more difficult for police to carry out their lawful duty (magistrates' court only, maximum penalty one months' imprisonment and/or a fine up to £1,000). It is used against those who refuse to move on or to keep back, or against those who interfere with police work, for example, by objecting to a lawful arrest or search. In practice, proving officers were acting 'in the execution of their duty' can be very difficult for the prosecution, especially in complicated situations involving multiple arrests. There is no specific power of arrest for this offence and so the police have to rely on their 'general arrest powers' where the circumstances permit (see Chapter 6). Where an arrest can be justified, no warning need be given in advance.

'Watching and besetting'

It is an offence under the Trade Union and Labour Relations (Consolidation) Act 1992 (maximum penalty six months' imprisonment and/or a fine up to £5,000) to intimidate others, if, for example, you:

- Use violence to intimidate someone or their family or damage property.
- Persistently follow someone.

- Hide someone's tools or clothes.
- 'Watch and beset' or picket someone's home or place of work (NB: it is not unlawful to picket peacefully at your own place of work).
- Follow someone in the street, with two others, in a disorderly manner.

But this applies only if you do any of these acts with the intention of compelling the person not to do something he or she has a legal right to do (for example, the right to use the highway to go to work) or to do something he or she has a legal right not to do (for example, the right not to join the picket). Persuasion, even vigorous persuasion, will not amount to an offence unless it crosses into the realm of compulsion.

Highway obstruction

You commit an offence if, without lawful authority or excuse, you wilfully obstruct the free passage of the highway.

This is a widely drawn offence. It is often seen in practice as a police licensing power over public gatherings. The police use it to remove sit-down demonstrators, to keep marchers from leaving the agreed police route, to control pickets, and in every conceivable public order context on the highway. The offence does not require violence or the threat of violence.

When cases reach court, prosecutors commonly agree to offer no evidence if the defendant agrees to be bound over (see below). Often the police will give a warning to move before making an arrest, although there is no legal requirement to do so. Nevertheless, a failure to give a warning may be relevant to the reasonableness or otherwise of the use of the highway.

The offence is obstructing the *highway*, not other highway *users*. So it is not necessary to prove that any other person was actually obstructed – the 'obstruction' can be made out if you simply occupy a section of highway. In practice the offence usually turns on whether a particular obstruction was *reasonable* rather than whether there was, in fact, an obstruction. The test of reasonableness is always objective. Was there an actual obstruction? If there was, how long did it last? Where was it? What was its purpose? The police often decide to make an arrest on the basis that other people are prevented from passing along the highway or going into shops or business premises. But it is a question of fact in each case and the test of reasonableness can very often be argued successfully in demonstration cases, particularly where the police have taken no action in the past, or where the place of protest is a regular post or where the obstruction was trivial. It is often helpful to have photographs to show just how extensive – or limited – a particular obstruction was.

The offence can only be tried in the magistrates' court. The maximum penalty is a fine of £1,000. There is no power to send a person convicted of highway obstruction to prison.

Offences connected with processions, assemblies and meetings

It is an offence to breach a condition imposed by the police on a procession or an assembly or to breach an order banning processions in your locality (see p. 8). You may commit an offence if you wear a uniform in public signifying association with any political organisation or with the promotion of any political objective (trial in the magistrates' court, maximum penalty three months' imprisonment and/or a fine up to £500).

For offences connected with picketing see p. 11.

For offences connected with meetings see p. 12.

For offences of stirring up racial hatred see p. 238.

Sentences

In deciding an appropriate sentence, courts will always consider the gravity of the offence, the circumstances of its commission, and the previous character of the defendant. Defendants who plead guilty are entitled to credit because a guilty plea indicates remorse for their behaviour.

There are powers to sentence to imprisonment in all serious cases. Prison has to be considered a real possibility in offences such as threatening behaviour and assault, especially where police are involved. However the majority of public order cases dealt with in the magistrates' courts are disposed of by way of community penalty (such as community service) or a fine. Wherever there is a real risk of imprisonment, defendants are entitled to legal aid, subject to their means.

Two of the most frequent offences, highway obstruction and disorderly conduct are not imprisonable under any circumstances, and a third offence, obstructing police is technically imprisonable but this power is used very rarely indeed.

Fine levels

In fixing the amount of a fine the court must take into account the means of the offender. The court may give the offender time to pay, for example, within three months, or at so much a week. If the court imposes a sentence of imprisonment in default and the fine is not paid, the court may send the offender to prison, but only after a careful means enquiry.

Breach of the peace

There is no offence of breach of the peace. But if a police officer sees a breach of the peace or reasonably believes that a breach of the peace is about to be committed or that a renewal of a breach of the peace is threatened, he or she may arrest, disperse or detain those involved and, if necessary, take them before a magistrates' court to be bound over.

There is a breach of the peace whenever harm is actually done or is likely to be done to a person, or in his or her presence to his or her property, or a person is in fear of being so harmed. The law allows a person to be arrested for an anticipated breach of the peace even where violence is anticipated from a third party, rather than from the person being arrested.

If a breach of the peace occurs, one or more of the public order offences of threatening behaviour, disorderly conduct, assault or criminal damage (see above for these offences) is likely to have been committed. In such a case, the police can choose whether to charge an offence or go before the magistrates for a bind-over order.

Bind-overs

The magistrates' court may bind you over to keep the peace and or be of good behaviour for a specified period in a number of different circumstances:

*   You may be brought before the court for committing a breach of the peace (under the Justices of the Peace Act 1361).
*   You may be brought before the court on a complaint made by any person at the court.
*   In proceedings for a criminal offence, a witness or a defendant (even if acquitted) may be bound over.

A bind-over order is not a conviction or a penalty. It is an undertaking as to future conduct. Its purpose is to prevent offences being committed in the future. The order will bind you over to keep the peace for a period of time for a specified sum, say £200 for twelve months. If you breach the order and are brought back to court, you will have to pay up to the whole amount. Sometimes sureties are taken, in which case the person who has put up the surety would have to forfeit some or all of the amount of their surety too. If you refuse to be bound over in the first place, you can be sent to prison for up to six months. You should always be given the opportunity to say in court why you should not be bound over, if you wish to, or why you are not in breach of an order.

Bind-over orders are often used against demonstrators and protesters. Sometimes a charge, such as obstruction of the highway, is dropped by the prosecution if the defendant agrees to be bound over and the court also agrees. In some cases, unions will advise their members who have been picketing not to accept bind-overs if they wish to return to the picket line. A bind-over cannot of itself prevent someone returning to the picket line (see the right to bail, p. 202) but it is an inhibiting factor.

Liberty believes that the bind-over order is an outdated form of justice and that it is wrong to give the courts the power to send somebody to prison for refusing to be bound over, particularly when no offence has been committed. Liberty has supported challenges to the use of the power to bind over, and hope that a test case before the European Court of Human Rights will limit the arbitrary way the power can be exercised.

1.5 Further information

Bibliography

Archbold's Criminal Pleading Evidence and Practice, Sweet and Maxwell, 1997.

Blackstone's Criminal Practice, Blackstone Press, 1997.

R. Card and R. Ward, *The Criminal Justice and Public Order Act 1994*, Jordans, 1995.

J. Cooper, *Public Order Review*, Legal Action (regular round-up of recent public order decisions each February and August).

M. Randle, *How to Defend yourself in Court*, Civil Liberties Trust, 1995.

Stone's Justices' Manual, Butterworths 1997.

P. Thornton, *Public Order Law*, Blackstone Press, 1987.

2

The right of free expression

This chapter deals with:

- The right to freedom of expression.
- Defamation – libel and slander.
- Other remedies.
- Copyright and allied property rights.
- Criminal law restrictions on freedom of expression.
- Contempt of court and restrictions on court reporting.
- Controls on broadcasting, films, video and cable.
- The balance of conflicting rights and interests.
- Further information.

2.1 The right to freedom of expression

It may seem strange that English law confers no positive right to freedom of speech on the individual. We are not all free to pitch our soapbox on the street corner and tell the world whatever we want or more relevantly today to sit in front of our computer screen and send across the Internet any material we wish. The law provides a battery of restrictions on our right to say, publish or print what we want.

Our right to freedom of expression is a negative one. We are all free to express ourselves except where the law forbids it. The only members of society who have a positive right to freedom of speech are Members of Parliament. They gave themselves that right under the Bill of Rights of 1688. However, it is not a right which the rest of us enjoy. We do not have the constitutional rights of freedom of expression and of the press available to all American citizens under the First Amendment of the US Constitution.

The nearest individuals get to a right to freedom of expression is under Article 10 of the European Convention on Human Rights which binds the state in international law but is not enforceable in domestic courts, except as an aid to intepretation of ambiguous statutes. Article 10 of the Convention provides:

1. Everyone has the right of free expression. This right shall include
    freedom to hold opinions and to receive and impart information
    and ideas without interference by public authority and regardless
    of frontiers. This Article shall not prevent states from requiring the
    licensing of broadcasting, television or cinema enterprises.
2. The exercise of these freedoms, since it carries with it duties and
    responsibilities, may be subject to such formalities, conditions,
    restrictions or penalties as are prescribed by law and necessary in
    a democratic society, in the interests of national security, territorial
    integrity or public safety, for the prevention of disorder or crime,
    for the protection of health and morals, for the protection of the
    reputation or rights of others, for preventing the disclosure of
    information received in confidence, or for maintaining the
    authority and impartiality of the judiciary.

Article 10 therefore provides a right and then sets out exceptions to
that right. Further, Article 10 has to be seen in the context of the
competing right to privacy and family life under Article 8 which is
foreshadowed in Article 10. Article 8 provides:

1. Everyone has the right to respect for his private and family life,
    his home and his correspondence.
2. There shall be no interference by a public authority with the
    exercise of this right except such as is in accordance with the law
    and is necessary in a democratic society in the interests of national
    security, public safety or the economic well-being of the country,
    for the prevention of disorder or crime, for the protection of
    health or morals, or for the protection of the rights and freedoms
    of others.

The European Court of Human Rights has in its case law strictly
limited the scope of the exceptions to these conflicting rights. In order
to take advantage of the right to freedom of expression under Article
10 of the Convention, the individual must first exhaust all his or her
remedies in the English courts and then wearily tread the lengthy path
to the European Court of Human Rights. As we will see, Article 10 has
struck at the heart of much of English law on freedom of expression.

If incorporation of the Convention into domestic law takes place it
is to be hoped a coherence and liberal spirit can be brought to the
domestic law relating to freedom of expression. Then perhaps truly we
can lay claim to popular notions of free speech.

Without Article 10 of the Convention as part of English law, 'the
right of free expression' has only the limited legal meaning that a
person is free to say anything which is not prohibited. This chapter
examines the scope of those restrictions on our freedom to say, print

---

STOP PRESS

The new government proposes to incorporate the European Convention on Human Rights into domestic law. The rights in the Convention are set out in Chapter 5. A Bill to incorporate the Convention is due to be published in the autumn of 1997 and this is likely to become an Act by July 1998 and to come into force not before January 1999. It is not clear at the time of writing exactly what effect this will have on our laws. It is likely that the Convention will be able to be used to challenge some of the existing procedures and judge-made law although whether the Convention will be given a higher status than statute is not so clear. Nevertheless the rights set out in this book may be enhanced by the Convention and in future the rights in the Convention will have to be considered much more seriously than they have been in the past.

---

and publish what we want. We will see that there is a perpetual and unresolved tension between the right to freedom of expression and the right to protection of property in all its varied forms, privacy, reputation, confidential ideas and from criminal or perceived anti-social behaviour. As the means of communication becomes ever more varied and complex, so this tension becomes more acute and is expressed more frequently.

The following sections give an outline of the principal restrictions that limit the right of free expression.

2.2 Defamation – libel and slander

The distinction between libel and slander

Libel and slander are intended to protect reputations and provide compensation for injury to them. Libel is used if a damaging statement takes a permanent form (books, magazines, films, electronic publications, etc., and broadcasts which have been included in this category by Parliament); slander is used if it does not take a permanent form. The obvious type of statements are words. However, the Defamation Act 1996 provides that not only words, but pictures, visual images, gestures or any other method of signifying meaning are actionable if defamatory (see below).

The distinction between slander and libel is an arcane one. It is still relevant in that normally a litigant in an action for spoken words (slander) must prove financial loss, where if the words had been written down, he or she would not because the law presumes damage from the written and not the spoken word. However, this distinction is one without point if the spoken words are accusations of an imprisonable crime; that he or she is a carrier of a contagious disease; that the victim is unfit for his or her office, business or profession; if the communication is an attack on the credit of tradespeople; or an accusation of unchastity or adultery to a woman or girl. Here, as with all libels, damage is presumed and need not be proved.

Meaning and defamation

Defamation law provides that a statement is only defamatory if it damages the reputation of the victim in the eyes of 'right-thinking' members of society. This quaint nineteenth-century idea does not really accord with most people's idea of what damages reputation. Luckily, by and large, it is juries and not judges who interpret what the standard of the right-thinking person is.

The motive of an author is not relevant. Statements that on their face appear harmless can be defamatory if there is a secondary or innuendo meaning to the reasonable reader in possession of extra information that was likely to come to the attention of readers of the statement.

A statement may be untrue or hurtful, but this does not make it defamatory unless it has an effect on the person's reputation in the eyes of the 'right-thinking' member of society. A good example of the strange way in which this works is a case in the 1920s when a striking fisherman sued his fellow striker for saying that he had gone to the owners to ask for a ship to work. It was found that whilst untrue, it would only injure the litigant's reputation in the eyes of his striking colleagues, who plainly were not regarded as right-thinking members of society. How times change (or do not change).

A statement that is understood as mere vulgar abuse is not defamatory if in the form of a slander because no one would think the worse of its object. For historical reasons, the defence of vulgar abuse is not available if the statement is a libel.

Publication

The statement must have been 'published' by the person sued. This expression has a much wider meaning than its colloquial meaning. It covers any means of communication even if only to one other person. Due to the breadth of the term 'publication', many individuals can find themselves ensnared in defamation proceedings who have only a slight connection with the work. The Defamation Act 1996 provides a defence to persons who are not authors, editors or commercial publishers of the statement if they took reasonable care in relation to its publication and they did not know and had no reason to believe that what they did caused or contributed to the publication of a defamatory statement. This is supposed to cover printers, distributors, on-line service providers and live broadcasters.

Whether the 1996 Act will put an end to actions against all and sundry connected to a particular work to which a litigant objects, with the purpose of stifling dissemination of the defendant's views, is yet to be seen. It will also be interesting to see how this defence affects the growth area of Internet libel actions where there are a multiplicity of people potentially responsible for disseminating material around the world. It will still remain prudent for carriers of risky material to obtain pre-publication advice from a lawyer that there is nothing defamatory included in the publication.

Identification

The litigant must show that the defamatory statement refers to him or her. This is straightforward where the litigant is named. Otherwise it is a matter of inference. The anonymous victim of an attack can sue if there are sufficient clues in the piece pointing to his or her identity. Sometimes the reference to the victim is unintentional, for instance, the character in a novel who, unwittingly, is given the name of a real person. In such circumstances under the Defamation Act 1996, a publisher can make an offer to publish a suitable correction and a sufficient apology and to pay the costs of the victim which if not accepted will provide a defence to proceedings, unless the victim can prove that the publisher knew or had reason to believe that the statement did refer or was likely to be understood to refer to him or her and that it was both false and defamatory of him or her.

Entitlement to sue

Not only can individuals sue, but any trading corporation can sue where the statement has a tendency to damage it in respect of its business. Non-trading corporations can sue in respect of defamatory statements damaging their property or financial interests. Trade unions can sue in respect of defamatory statements touching their union activities.

Groups without a legal identity cannot complain of libel. Therefore, victims of racism cannot get redress under defamation law where there is no pointer in the statement to an individual. Similarly, an unincorporated club cannot sue for libel, whatever the damage to its reputation. Whilst there is no remedy generally for group libels, there are some cases where the words can be read as libelling every member of the group; all the crime reporters who covered the Old Bailey once obtained damages for a story which implied they were all drunk.

In 1993 the House of Lords ruled that government bodies cannot sue for defamation. They considered it was of the 'highest public importance that a democratically elected body or any governmental body, should be open to uninhibited public criticism'. Unfortunately, domestic law does not apply this rule or any restriction to the politicians who people such bodies. Increasingly, politicians have recourse to the libel courts to protect not only their political but their personal reputations. Indeed, Parliament in the Defamation Act 1996 has breached the principle of parliamentary privilege in a selective manner so as to retain an MP's immunity from action for any defamatory statement made in Parliament, whilst giving the individual MP the right to sue where an issue arises as to parliamentary conduct which would otherwise be cloaked in parliamentary privilege. This amendment to the law was allowed principally to allow Neil Hamilton MP to restart libel proceedings against the *Guardian* over the 'cash for questions' row. Ironically, he subsequently withdrew his action at the last moment before trial.

This is an unnecessary infringement of freedom of expression in political matters, which could have been balanced by Parliament adapting the American doctrine that a public figure can only succeed in a defamation action where the statement complained of was made maliciously.

Only the living can sue for defamation. Thus, historians have considerably greater freedom of expression than current commentators, but even they must be careful that the things they write about the dead do not in some way damage the reputation of the living.

Time limits
The right to sue for defamation is now lost after one year rather than three years, subject to certain statutory exceptions.

The defences of truth, fair comment and privilege
The main defences available to a defendant in defamation proceedings are: truth, fair comment and privilege. Article 10 of the Convention does not provide a general 'free-speech' defence in domestic law, although increasingly judge-made defamation law is made by reference to, if not in conformity, with Article 10 case law.

Truth (or justification) is simple to state. If a publisher can show that the words were true, the litigant's claim fails. The only exception to this principle concerns defendants whose convictions have become 'spent' under the Rehabilitation of Offenders Act 1974. Publication of the details of these old convictions can lead to damages for libel, but only if the plaintiff can show that the publisher acted 'maliciously'.

The position is less clear-cut when a criminal prosecution for libel is brought. These cases are rare: the libel (slanders are not criminal) must be serious and, in the case of a newspaper or periodical, permission to bring the action must first be obtained from a High Court judge, who must be persuaded that the evidence is strong and that criminal charges are in the public interest. Historically, criminal libel was intended to prevent breaches of the peace (for example, caused by speakers at public meetings) and it was in this context that truth was recognised as being an aggravating feature of the publication. Truth is a defence provided publication of the true statement was in the public interest. Criminal libel is an anachronism. The Law Commission has recommended that it be abolished.

In civil actions for damages, there is no additional requirement of public interest. Truth on its own is a complete defence. The difficulty with the defence is not a legal one but a practical one. It can be very difficult to put together sufficient admissible evidence to persuade a jury that the statement is true. 'Reliable sources' may not be prepared to testify in court. The evidential burden can be an impossible one for the financially straightened defendant without libel insurance. Further, a failed defence of truth can boost the damages to be paid. Therefore, the defence has to be deployed with great care.

If a defendant can prove that the defamatory statement is an expression of opinion and not fact, the less stringent defence of fair comment may be available. Typically, this will be of use to the critic and reviewer, but the defence is often deployed where the burden of proving truth is too great or risky. Therefore, the boundary between a statement of fact and comment is crucial and subject to much pre-trial skirmishing between the parties. The defence covers any comment on a matter of public importance and based on true facts which are either contained in the publication or sufficiently referred to. The comment can be trenchantly expressed or misused, as long as it is honestly held. The plaintiff can undermine the defence only by showing that the comment was written with 'malice'. This is not the same as spite or ill-will, but rather it means abusing the commentator's position, such as publishing with the intention to injure or with reckless indifference to truth. Expressions of honestly held opinions are safe.

A defence of privilege arises from the law's recognition that, in particular situations, it is important for there to be open communication, even if that openness causes damage to reputation. No distinction is made between fact and comment. At common law, 'absolute privilege' provides a complete defence, however vindictive, vicious or untrue it is. 'Qualified privilege' provides a conditional defence at common law. If a statement which would attract qualified privilege is published maliciously, then the defence is lost.

Absolute privilege is confined to proceedings in Parliament or courts in this country. The Defamation Act 1996 has provided a statutory absolute privilege for contemporary or court-postponed fair and accurate reports of court proceedings in this country, of the European Court of Justice, the European Court of Human Rights and any international criminal tribunal established by the United Nations Security Council.

Qualified privilege is more common. The importance of common law qualified privilege has been largely superseded by the Defamation Act 1996. It is still important where the statutory privilege does not arise. At common law, where the person who publishes the words has a duty or interest in communicating them and his or her audience has a duty or interest in receiving them, a defence of qualified privilege arises. For instance, if a defendant is subjected to media attack by the litigant, he or she is entitled to reply in the media to that attack without being sued for that reply unless the original attack was true, or he or she has gone beyond reply and on to an unconnected attack on the litigant. Similarly, complaints or information passed under a public or private legal, social or moral duty to the relevant authorities are protected by common law qualified privilege.

The Defamation Act 1996 provides a statutory qualified privilege for material which is of public concern and for the public benefit in the form of fair and accurate reports of public proceedings of parliaments, courts, official inquiries, international organisations/conferences anywhere in the world, and certain materials published by governments and other specified public bodies. A more limited qualified privilege, subject to suitable and reasonable explanation or contradiction required by the litigant, extends to publication of other material specified in the 1996 Act: fair and accurate reports of public proceedings before local authorities, justices of the peace acting in a non-judicial capacity, official inquiries or other statutory bodies, public meetings in European Union states and general meetings of UK public companies. Also covered by this more limited form of qualified privilege are fair and accurate reports of the findings and decisions of all EU associations which promote the interests of and adjudicate upon matters concerned with trade, business, industry, the professions, education, culture, leisure or charity and fair and accurate copies of materials issued to the public by EU parliaments and governmental bodies, international organisations/conferences and of materials relating to the employment of UK public company directors which are circulated to the members of the company.

Remedies

Injunctions to prevent defamatory statements being made where the exact words to be published are not known with reasonable certainty cannot be obtained. Similarly a pre-trial injunction will not be granted where the publisher (or broadcaster) swears an affidavit that it is true.

Judges regard it as a matter for the jury at the trial to decide the dispute and will not prevent publication (or transmission) in advance. Unfortunately, this judicial self-restraint does not apply outside defamation, and injunctions are all too readily granted against the media to prevent disclosure of material which is said to be in breach of confidence (see below).

The principal restraint on freedom of expression is through the fear of being subjected to hitherto 'casino-style' justice by juries awarding substantial damages. The European Court of Human Rights in July 1995 found an award of £1.5 million in 1989 to be in breach of Article 10 of the Convention. Since then the Appeal Court has tried to rein in jury awards. In December 1995, it said that it is

> in our view offensive to public opinion, and rightly so, that a defamation plaintiff should recover damages for injury to reputation greater, by a significant factor, than if that same plaintiff had been a helpless cripple or an insensate vegetable.

Juries will now be reminded what an appropriate range of awards is and of the range of awards for personal injury. Hopefully, this will produce awards which no longer bring the law into disrepute and deter legitimate debate. However, the costs burden to the unsuccessful defamation defendant remain a significant deterrent to defending gagging writs issued by the rich and powerful.

Juries still retain the anomalous power to award additional punitive damages to punish defendants who recklessly publish without any genuine belief in the truth of the statement in order to make a profit. It remains the case that legal aid is unavailable either to bring or defend defamation proceedings.

2.3 Other remedies

There are other remedies which may be used by a litigant angered by a false publication. 'False attribution of authorship' may be relied on when a publisher fabricates quotations under the law of copyright.

Occasionally it is possible for individuals who qualify for legal aid but who could not afford to bring a defamation action to bring an action in malicious falsehood against the media. It requires proof that the words were untrue, published maliciously and that they were likely to cause financial loss. In 1992 an ex-royal maid successfully used this civil wrong against a newspaper which accused her of stealing love letters between Princess Anne and Commander Lawrence. It has also been used to stop the press from publishing photographs of a famous television actor whilst he lay semi-conscious in hospital. Normally, the preferable course to remedy such gross invasions of privacy will be to bring an action for breach of confidence.

An alternative which has recently opened up is to restrain behaviour which amounts to harassment. It is now possible to sue for the persistent telephone harasser even if there is no threat of violence, providing it is likely to cause psychiatric injury. Criminal sanctions may also apply (see p. 50 below) and the Protection from Harassment Bill may provide new remedies.

Additionally, an ex-employee can now sue with the benefit of legal aid in negligence where his or her ex-employer provides an inaccurate and otherwise defamatory reference to a prospective employer. However, for negligence to limit freedom of speech, there must be an assumed responsibility to ensure accuracy to the recipient of the information which the courts are prepared to recognise. The situations are limited primarily to business or analogous relationships.

Complaints about the unethical behaviour of newspapers and magazines can be made to the Press Complaints Commission (PCC). The behaviour need not have resulted in a libel or any of the other legal wrongs considered above; the PCC is not a court but a voluntary body set up by the newspaper industry. It cannot award damages or any other redress other than a decision vindicating (or rejecting) the complaint. Its decisions are usually well publicised.

2.4 Copyright and allied property rights

A multiplicity of rights

Copyright law both provides rights in works to writers, musicians, artists, photographers and the like and correspondingly grants a multiplicity of rights over the same material. The creative process, and thereby freedom of expression, is restricted and shaped by giving other copyright owners a power of veto over the incorporation of their work in some new work. For instance, the practice of sampling is fraught with copyright difficulty for the musician and the recording company. The use of sampled material from another musician without his or her permission in combination with other material may create copyright in the musical end product, but it can never be exploited without the risk of proceedings for infringement of copyright by the owner of the musical copyright in the sampled work. It does not matter that the infringing track is only a few bars on a 20-track album – the court will still grant a final injunction preventing exploitation of the album.

The collage artist, the scratch video-maker, the popular songwriter, the cartoonist, and the journalist in possession of a leaked memorandum can all encounter copyright obstacles in creating their work, yet none of them would want others to be free to plagiarise their final product. However, there are limits to the reach of copyright law to restrain freedom of expression. In 1993 broadcasters who proposed to broadcast an interview with the serial killer Denis Neilsen could not be prevented from broadcasting the interview by the Home Office on the basis that it owned copyright to the film since to do so would stifle freedom of speech in circumstances where there was no pressing need to ban the broadcast.

Meaning of copyright

Copyright is a statutory right to stop others copying or exploiting in various other ways authors' works without permission typically for the duration of the author's life plus fifty years thereafter. The Copyright, Designs and Patents Act 1988 is one of the most bewildering statutes. It creates several different categories of 'work' in which copyright can exist and different owners or authors of works. The principal categories of protected work are: literary, dramatic, musical and artistic works (including photographs); sound recordings (such as records, tapes and CDs); films, television and sound broadcasts, and cable programmes.

Copyright does not exist in a work until it is recorded in some written or other form. For example, a musical work is not protected until recorded on a digital audio tape or the like. It is generally the reproduction of that form which is restricted. This means, for instance, that newspapers do not have a monopoly even in their 'exclusive' news stories. They can stop others using their photographs, their text (or a substantial part of it) or an imitation of their work, but the information conveyed is not theirs to control. Ideas themselves are not protected and recourse in such cases is made to the developing law of confidence.

No copyright exists in a literary, dramatic, musical or artistic work unless it is 'original'. This simply means that some limited work or effort must have gone into the work. For instance, even street directories or television programme schedules can attract copyright as literary works. Therefore, great care has to be taken in using apparently mundane material which may result in copyright infringement proceedings, stifling distribution of the end product.

The owner or author of the copyright is normally the creator or creators of it in the case of a literary, dramatic, musical or artistic work. Special rules apply in relation to copyright of other works and all works created in the course of employment. The ownership of copyright is distinct from the ownership of the physical record of the work. For instance, a photographer may own the copyright of the artistic work he or she creates, but not the film on which it is recorded. Separate ownership of the physical property can restrict the use of the work.

Defences to infringement of copyright

Copyright is not infringed if the owner consents to the copying or other exploitation of the work. The first difficulty is identifying who is the owner or owners of the various copyrights. In some works (a television play, for instance) it is possible for different people to own the copyright in the script, the photographs, the sound track, the dramatic screenplay, the film recording, the play and the broadcast. Even if the owners can be identified there is generally no obligation on them to sell reproduction rights.

In the absence of the owner's licence, there are two important defences to a claim for infringement of copyright. The first is fair dealing. This includes the fair use of another's work for the purpose of criticism or review, or the reporting of current events. The originator of the work must be acknowledged in a criticism or review and in the print media's news reporting (but not in the broadcast media). In an important case concerning a critical book about Scientology, which made use of unpublished internal Scientology documents, the courts confirmed that the defence of fair dealing could apply, even though the work had not previously been published and even though the criticism was directed at the contents of the work rather than its style.

The second important defence is public interest. This does not appear in the statute, but the courts have said that (just as they will not stop publication of confidential information which is in the public interest) so, too, they would not prohibit the infringement of another's copyright where the public interest in publication outweighed the private right of property. The defence is based on the idea that the public 'need to know' should sometimes override the copyright's owner's right to restrict or prevent publication.

Criminal sanctions

It should be noted that there are criminal sanctions for infringement of copyright in certain circumstances. As a result of the growth in national and international piracy of copyright material (bootleg videos and the like), the criminal provisions and penalties for commercial copyright piracy have been made more severe. There are a range of offences committed by those who infringe copyright, generally for commercial purposes, when they know or have reason to believe, that they are infringing. Penalties range from imprisonment, heavy fines and forfeiture of infringing material and equipment for making infringing material.

The civil courts in response to growing copyright piracy have also been prepared enthusiastically to grant to copyright owners what in practice are private search warrants to track down the sources for bootleg operations.

'Moral rights'

The 1988 Act introduced new 'moral rights' for the authors of copyright works. Subject to complex limitations and qualifications, authors of copyright works have the right to be identified as such and the right not to have their works subjected to derogatory treatment. A new right of privacy was also introduced to limit the use of photographs commissioned for private and domestic purpose, for example, wedding photographs, etc.

Passing off

In addition to copyright protection, the law will prevent one trader passing off its goods as those of another. These commercial disputes often have little to do with free speech, but their over-zealous application (or the minimal investigation of a litigant's claim on an application for a pre-trial injunction) can lead to the suppression of parody, spoof and satire.

The civil law of confidence

The law of confidence in recent years has been used by private citizen and state alike to attempt to stifle freedom of expression. From ex-spies and traitors selling their secrets of yesteryear to paparazzi with photographs of royalty seeking the highest price in Fleet Street – all have been caught up in the web of confidence. A civil duty of confidence is said to be owed by someone in receipt of confidential information from another. This has application not only in the commercial field (for instance, when sensitive commercial information is leaked to the press) but also to people's private lives.

Domestic law does not recognise an enforceable right to privacy, as set out in Article 8 of the Convention. However, the law of confidence is being stretched to fill this gap. In 1988, a court held that confidences given to a friend about a secret lesbian relationship could be protected. In 1995, it was suggested by a judge that if a photographer took a photograph with a telephoto lens of a person engaged in a private act, then the photographer and the press could be restrained from using the photograph. Again in 1995, the Appeal Court refused to vary an order preventing disclosure of any matter relating to a child's education on the grounds it was confidential. This was even though the mother wanted to do so in order that a film company could make a film about the treatment the child was receiving in a specialist institution for her special educational needs. The court said that it had a supervisory jurisdiction over children to preserve their confidences.

The forces of free speech in this context do not always give way to the protection of privacy. In 1994 the Court of Appeal refused an application of the ex-wife of a man convicted of indecency offences who wanted to ensure that the identity of her ex-husband was obscured in a television programme to protect her anonymity and that of her child. The Court placed great emphasis on not whittling away freedom of the press by extending judge-made law protecting a child's right to privacy in matters of education and upbringing.

If the judicial trend towards recognising a right to privacy continues, then real force would be given in domestic law to the right under Article 8 of the European Convention. The fear would be that without firm limits placed on such a right, it may be used by the rich and famous to suppress embarrassing and inconvenient material adversely affecting their public role. The government continues to vacillate as to whether it will legislate to provide a civil right to privacy.

The law of confidence has also been used by the State in an attempt to suppress the disclosure of state secrets, rather than the criminal law. Unlike the criminal law, the civil law of confidence will generally only protect material which is still confidential. It was the widespread publication of *Spycatcher* by ex-spy Peter Wright which powerfully influenced the House of Lords to refuse a final injunction to the government. Further, Article 10 of the Convention has been used by the courts in 1996 to allow George Blake to profit from his book revealing his activities as a spy for this country, notwithstanding the government's attempt to use the law of confidence to prevent him. George Blake was said by the courts to be entitled not to have his right to free speech curtailed, notwithstanding his life-long duty of confidence to the government. These two decisions provide some hope that Article 10 rights to freedom of expression will obtain greater recognition and prevail over government obsession with needless secrecy.

Any recipient of confidential information always retains the defence that the disclosure of such material is in the public interest. It used to be said that only crime or serious wrongdoing would justify the breach of a confidence, but now the test is more open and the court must strike a balance between the interest in preserving confidence and the public interest in publication. However, there remains a judicial bias in giving priority to the protection of confidence at the expense of free speech.

If a litigant can find out in advance that publication of a leak or other alleged breach of confidence is planned, and is willing to go to court, then the inevitable first step will be an application for an injunction to stop publication until trial. The test which the courts apply in deciding whether to grant such injunctions is extremely favourable to the litigant. Usually the judges will grant an injunction, unless there is clear evidence of public interest, and in the case of the *Spycatcher* pre-trial injunction even that was not sufficient. The argument for this 'balance of convenience test' is that at the pre-trial stage, the evidence is incomplete and the court is often required to make a hasty decision because publication is imminent. The objection is that the time between injunction and trial is usually so great that the story will have gone cold by the time that full argument on the merits is heard. This in turn means that the defence is not pursued and there never is a full hearing of the case.

2.5 Criminal law restrictions on freedom of expression

Blasphemy

Blasphemy is an anachronistic relic of the common law of libel. It protects the Anglican faith against exposure to 'vilification, ridicule or indecency'. It applies to outrageous comment or immoderate or offensive treatment of the Anglican faith. Consequently, opponents of Salman Rushdie's *Satanic Verses* were unable to start a blasphemy prosecution – the book was about Mohammed and Islam, not Christ or Christianity. The intentions of the publisher are irrelevant. Moderate or reasoned criticism of Anglican doctrine is not a crime and the court must consider the likely audience in order to decide whether the publication would produce the necessary outrage. However, there is no defence of public good, namely that the material was published in the interests of science, literature or art.

For newspapers and periodicals, the prosecutor must first get permission to bring the case from a High Court judge who must be persuaded that the evidence is clear 'beyond argument' – that the offence is a serious one and that the public interest would justify a prosecution before proceeding.

There has only been one successful prosecution for blasphemy since 1922, and that a private one (brought by Mrs Mary Whitehouse) of the magazine *Gay News* for a poem on the homoerotic musings of the centurion guarding the body of Christ. It has been argued that the crime can no longer be justified in our pluralistic society. In 1985 the Law Commission recommended its abolition. The alternative of extending the offence to all religions (taken by Lord Scarman in the *Gay News* case) would seriously curtail freedom to criticise and ridicule some of the more bizarre cults which style themselves as religions.

In 1996 the European Court of Human Rights upheld the ban by the British Board of Film Classification that Nigel Wingrove's video film *Visions of Ecstasy* would infringe the criminal law of blasphemy. The Court considered that the blasphemy laws did not infringe the Article 10 right to freedom of expression which must be a matter for individual country. Wingrove's video concerned the erotic fantasies of a sixteenth-century Carmelite nun who experienced powerful ecstatic visions of Jesus Christ. As such, ironically, it would probably have escaped censorship in most European countries. It seems therefore that in matters of religion, freedom of expression is to be given little credence.

Obscenity

The law governing obscene publications is to be found principally in the Obscene Publications Act 1959. Commercial dealings in obscene items, or possession of them for these purposes, is an offence. With or without a prosecution, the items can be seized under a magistrate's warrant and, after a hearing to determine whether they contravene the statute, can be forfeited.

The test of obscenity – 'deprave or corrupt'

The 1959 Act adopted as the core of its test of obscenity the famous phrase of Lord Chief Justice Cockburn in 1868: does the article have a tendency to deprave or corrupt the persons who are likely to read, see or hear it? Courts have since interpreted 'deprave or corrupt' as implying a powerful and corrosive effect. There must be more than an immoral suggestion or persuasion or depiction; it must constitute a serious menace. Despite this, the 'deprave and corrupt' test is essentially nebulous. It is difficult to predict in advance whether juries or magistrates will be persuaded that it has been satisfied. This in turn can lead to incompatible decisions in different parts of the country.

However, the 1959 Act did not simply mimic the previous law. There had been a tendency for earlier prosecutors to focus on purple passages and to invite juries to consider them in isolation. The 1959 Act now requires courts to have regard to the effect of the item taken as a whole (where the article, for instance in a magazine, consists of two or more distinct items, they can be viewed separately). Again, what matters is the likely audience, and a publisher is entitled to rely on circumstances of distribution which will restrict those into whose hands the article might fall. The prosecution's case is not made by showing that the odd stray copy might be read by a more impressionable person; it is necessary to show that it would have the tendency to deprave or corrupt a significant proportion of the likely audience.

Defence of merit

The most important change introduced by the 1959 Act was a new defence that publication (in the case of magazines and books) is in the interests of science, literature, art or learning, or of other matters of general concern. A similar but rather narrower defence (the interests of drama, opera, ballet or any other art, or of literature or learning) applies to plays and films. The use of this defence was demonstrated in the first major case under the 1959 Act when the publishers of

D. H. Lawrence's *Lady Chatterley's Lover* were acquitted at the Old Bailey in 1960.

Obscenity – drugs and violence
Obscenity cases do not necessarily involve sex. There have been occasional prosecutions and forfeitures of books which advocated the taking of prohibited drugs. In 1968, while allowing the appeal of the publishers of *Last Exit to Brooklyn*, the Court of Appeal said that the encouragement of brutal violence could come within the test of obscenity. In recent years, video 'nasties' have also been dealt with under the Act.

Children
There are special and much more rigorous offences to try to stop the taking or distribution of indecent photographs of children.

Indecency offences
Obscenity is concerned with the harmful effect of the article on its reader or audience; another group of offences regulates indecency where the complaint is more that the material is offensive to public susceptibilities – a nuisance rather than a danger. No easy definition of indecency exists. The courts have said that this is something that 'offends against the modesty of the average man, offending against recognised standards of propriety at the lower end of the scale'. It depends on the circumstances and current (and in some cases, local) standards. This vagueness is dangerous. Posters for causes such as animal rights which are deliberately intended to shock their audience have sometimes had to contend with indecency prosecutions. Indecency is easier to prove than obscenity because there is no defence of public good, there is no need to consider the article as a whole and there is no need to satisfy the 'deprave and corrupt' test.

There is no general crime of trading in indecent articles (as there is with obscene ones) but a number of specific offences incorporate the indecency test. Thus, it is a crime to send indecent matter through the post, or to put it on public display unless entry is restricted to persons over eighteen and payment is required, or the display is in a special part of a shop with an appropriate warning notice. The indecency offences do not apply to television broadcasts (although, as we shall see, both the BBC and private TV companies operate under internal prohibitions on indecent matter (see p. 60 below)), to exhibitions inside art galleries or museums, to exhibitions arranged by or in premises occupied by the Crown or local authorities, or to performances of a play or films in licensed cinemas.

Telephone calls of an obscene nature can also be caught by the indecency laws as a public nuisance. In fact, the Court of Appeal ruled in 1996 a telephone call or calls which cause psychiatric injury can amount to an assault/grievous bodily harm. The potential scope of this extension of the criminal law to catch 'stalkers' which restricts free speech across all media is worrying.

In addition to these offences, local councils can now adopt powers to regulate sex shops and sex cinemas in their areas. Council licences always prohibit the public display of indecent material and licences can be revoked if breaches of these conditions occur. Similarly, the music and entertainment licences granted by local authorities will often be conditional on the licensee ensuring that no indecent display takes place. Breach of this condition is both an offence and a ground for withdrawing the licence.

Customs regulations also prohibit the importation of indecent articles. The bookshop Gay's the Word was prosecuted under these provisions for importing books concerned with homosexuality. However, these restrictions have been substantially undermined by an unlikely source – the EU provisions on free trade. A cardinal principle of the EU is that one member state should not set up trade barriers to goods from another member state if there is a legitimate internal market in the same goods. In the case of the UK there is a legitimate market in indecent (but not obscene) articles as long as the traders observe the restrictions noted above. Consequently, Britain cannot discriminate against the importation of the same indecent books from other EU countries. European law prevails over the British customs regulations. For these reasons the prosecution of Gay's the Word was dropped.

Racial hatred

The offences of inciting or stirring up racial hatred have been progressively expanded since they were first introduced in 1965. They are currently contained in the Public Order Act 1986. In brief, they prohibit the use of threatening, abusive or insulting words, behaviour or displays with the intention of stirring up racial hatred or where racial hatred is likely to be stirred up.

The acts do not have to be done in public, but they are not crimes if done in a private dwelling and cannot be seen or heard from the outside. The inadvertent use of words which are threatening, abusive or insulting is not an offence. Only since the Public Order Act 1986 have the police had a limited power of arrest without a warrant for the offence. There are other offences of publishing or distributing material; presenting or directing a play; distributing, showing or playing visual images or sounds; broadcasting a television programme (except programmes transmitted by the BBC or IBA); or distributing a cable programme with the same characteristics (i.e. threatening, abusive or insulting) and which is either intended to stir up racial hatred or likely to have this effect. In addition, it is an offence to possess racially inflammatory material unless ignorant of its contents. The police can obtain a search warrant for such material and magistrates can order its forfeiture.

Very few prosecutions have been brought for racial hatred offences. In fact, in the past four years only fifteen people have been prosecuted under the 1986 Act. Yet the Commission for Racial Equality received 494 complaints about written material alone and recommended prosecution in fifty-five cases. One of the reasons for this is that no prosecution can be brought without the consent of the Attorney General and successive Attorneys General have expressed their reluctance to authorise prosecutions giving the reason that unsuccessful prosecutions do more harm than good to racial equality.

The Official Secrets Acts

The Official Secrets Act 1911, whilst it does provide punishment for spies, has become notorious for its Section 2 which was intended to curb civil service leaks and their publication in the press. On one occasion in 1978 the government did try to use Section 1 (the spying charge, carrying a maximum of fourteen years' imprisonment) on journalists investigating signals intelligence and its disturbing implications. This trial, known as the 'ABC case' after the initials of the defendants, was notable for the judge's round denunciation of the Section 1 charges as 'oppressive'. The defendants were convicted under Section 2 but the journalists were given conditional discharges. While the government has on rare occasions (such as Tisdale and Ponting) prosecuted their sources, it has not, since the ABC case, tried again to prosecute the media itself under this Act.

Official Secrets Act 1989

Section 2 was replaced in 1989 by another Official Secrets Act. Instead of a broad catch-all provision of the 1911 vintage there is now a series of offences prohibiting disclosure of information relating to intelligence, security, defence and crime. Members or ex-members of the security and intelligence service can be prosecuted for the unauthorised revelation of any information whether truly secret or not, relating to security or intelligence. It is not necessary to prove that the State has been harmed. Other Crown servants, contractors and employees of various private companies and regulatory bodies may be prosecuted for the unauthorised disclosure of information concerning security or intelligence, defence or international relations, providing that the disclosure damages the work of the security and intelligence services or is likely to do so. There is a further offence of disclosing information which would be likely to result in the commission of a criminal offence or information obtained from a telephone tap without proof of damage.

None of these offences provide for a defence of public interest or moral duty. There is only a weak defence that the defendant did not know or have reason to believe that the information concerned security, defence, international relations or crime. Journalists, the media and others outside government will commit offences if they publish information which they know has been leaked in breach of the Act and whose publication would be damaging.

The right to jury trial
The fact that anyone charged with most official secrets offences can elect for a jury trial has a real effect in curbing the impact of the Act. Whatever the law may say, if the information leaked was already public knowledge or if its disclosure is in the public interest (as in the case of Clive Ponting's memorandum on the government's policy on the sinking of the *Belgrano* in the Falklands War), convictions are far from certain. Even if a conviction is achieved, it will be at the price of attracting considerable press attention to the prosecution and the 'secret' at its centre will attract substantial press coverage. Hence, the official secrets legislation has fallen by and large into disuse and recourse is made to the civil law of confidence.

Other secrecy offences
Apart from the Official Secrets Acts, there are dozens of specific statutory offences of disclosing information in the hands of the government. Frequently, they are imposed where a government department has powers to acquire information under compulsion. These 'mini' Official Secrets Acts also lack a public interest defence.

2.6 Contempt of court and restrictions on court reporting

The scope of contempt law
Contempt of court covers a variety of situations, where the courts regard the exercise of free speech as a sufficient threat to the administration of justice, to require action to be taken. The most obvious example is disobedience to a court's order or the failure to observe an undertaking given to the court.

Publication of a secret document in defiance of an injunction prohibiting its disclosure would thus be punishable as contempt. Until

1987, it was thought that orders of this kind only affected the immediate person to whom they were directed (and their servants or agents). Third parties, it was thought, would only be in contempt if they aided the defendant to break the court's order. However, one of the most serious encroachments on press freedom in the *Spycatcher* litigation was the decision of the Court of Appeal that other publishers, acting on their own behalf, could be in contempt of court by publishing the same material where this would frustrate the court's intention to keep the material secret. This was the ultimate extension of the web of the law of confidence to ensnare those who know of an injunction against another party to prevent them betraying the confidential information covered by the injunction.

Judge-made law

The *Spycatcher* litigation further illustrates a general problem of the law of contempt: it has been developed almost exclusively by the judges who have not given equal weight to the right to free speech. By using contempt law, the courts have invented offences of disclosing the identity of blackmail victims who had remained anonymous in court, day-by-day re-enactments on television of court hearings, and (in certain circumstances) of disclosing details of a jury's deliberations. These were matters more properly left to Parliament. Parliament did subsequently enact restriction to jury disclosures, ironically much more severe than the judge-made law. It is now an offence to disclose any details of a jury's deliberations or votes taken, other than to give their verdict at the end of the trial.

Another type of contempt is the deliberate interference with current proceedings. Understandably, there is no freedom to intimidate or threaten reprisals against witnesses. A more controversial question is whether it is permissible to put pressure on a party to abandon a law suit. A publication may constitute a contempt because it puts public pressure on a litigant to pursue a particular course of action in relation to legal proceedings in which it is involved. *Private Eye*, in its own special way, castigated Sir James Goldsmith for his various suits against the magazine. The magazine was held not to be guilty of contempt because nothing of what they published was likely to have any effect on the outcome of the proceedings. In the early 1970s, the *Sunday Times* campaigned for compensation on behalf of the victims of the drug thalidomide and urged Distiller's, its UK distributor, to reach a generous settlement with the plaintiffs. The Attorney General successfully obtained an injunction to stop further stories on the grounds that they would be in contempt of court. The principal basis for the decision has now been reversed by legislation, but two of the Law Lords suggested that it was contempt to pressurise a party into settling. The current position is probably that fair and temperate criticisms of a litigant is not contempt, but that abusive or misrepresentative articles would run the risk of contempt proceedings.

It is still said that it is contempt to do any act or publish anything which is calculated to bring a court or judge into contempt or lower his or her authority. The origins of this type of contempt are both dubious and controversial. Historically, it was used as a weapon to suppress radical ideas, but was last used successfully in this country in 1931. The present attitude appears to be that judges should tolerate even misplaced criticism. It is probable that only serious allegations of corruption or other impropriety could possibly prompt a prosecution.

Strict liability – the *sub judice* rule

Strict liability contempt is the form of contempt that most frequently restricts what the media can say. For specified periods before and during the time that a case is going through the courts, the media are liable if they publish anything that would cause a substantial risk of serious prejudice to the proceedings. During these periods, the case is 'active' although the older phrase *sub judice* is still used. Criminal proceedings are active from the time an arrest takes place or a warrant or summons is issued. Civil proceedings do not become active until a date is fixed for the hearing.

The degree of restriction that this imposes depends on the court or tribunal which will hear the case. If it is to be tried by a jury, nothing should be written or broadcast which might prejudice the jury against the defendant; in particular, no past misdeeds should be referred to and care should be taken that reports do not assume the defendant's guilt. Even irreverent comment about defendants in a forthcoming criminal trial may be caught. In 1996 the Court of Appeal found that the makers of the television programme *Have I Got News For You* were in contempt of court when jokes were made that the Maxwell brothers (who were to be tried for the Mirror Group pension fraud) were obviously guilty of fraudulent conduct, even though the programme was broadcast six months before the trial.

At the other end of the spectrum are cases on appeal and civil cases heard by judges alone. These will be heard by professional judges who are trained to exclude extraneous considerations such as press reports. Consequently, it will be very rare for a publication to be in contempt of such proceedings. However, the Court of Appeal banned Channel 4 from broadcasting a dramatic re-enactment of the appeal of the Birmingham Six until after the case was over for fear that it might prejudice a retrial.

Defences to strict liability contempt

There are two important special defences to charges of strict liability contempt. The first is that a discussion in good faith of public affairs or other matters of general public importance will not be contempt if the risk of prejudice is merely incidental to the discussion and there was no bad faith. Thus Malcolm Muggeridge was free to write about the issues of terminating medical support to deformed babies even though a doctor was on trial at the same time for the killing of a Down's Syndrome child. Muggeridge focused on a by-election in which the issues of principle had been raised and did not mention the trial. The House of Lords held that the newspaper could rely on the public interest defence.

A second important defence is that it is not generally contempt to publish a fair, accurate and contemporaneous report of legal proceedings held in public in good faith. This is important because things are sometimes said in trials which might reflect adversely either on participants in those proceedings or in other active cases.

However, the media's freedom to report is subject to the power of the court to make a postponement order. These can delay full reporting until the end of either the proceedings in question or the others which are at risk of prejudice. Postponement orders can effectively prevent anything being published about a case for many months, as in the case of a long fraud trial. There is considerable variation in the propensity of Crown Court judges to make postponement orders. Recent cases suggest that when the media appeal such orders, the higher courts tend to favour the principle of open justice. It is now accepted that the media should be permitted to make arguments against gagging orders. These can be made to the judge before the order (if the media learn of the application in time), after the order in an effort to persuade the judge to set it aside, or to the Court of Appeal.

Other restrictions on court reporting

These powers are in addition to restrictions on reporting which apply without the need for a specific order. Only very brief reports can be carried, for instance, of proceedings in a magistrates' court of a case which might eventually be sent to trial by a judge and jury at a Crown Court. Newspapers can name the parties, their lawyers and whether bail was granted, but very little else until the trial is over. A defendant has the right to have these restrictions lifted, but if the co-accused differ in their attitude to publicity, the bench decides.

In sex offence cases the victim must remain anonymous unless the court orders otherwise. Until 1988, the defendant was given the same protection (unless convicted). The press (unlike the rest of the public) have a right to attend juvenile court hearings, but are prohibited from identifying defendants or witnesses, or from publishing their photographs. Young people do not have automatic anonymity in other courts, but the courts can make orders in specific cases.

In civil cases the problem is not so much that reporting is prohibited (though this is so in certain cases involving children and others to do with trade secrets), but that journalists (and other members of the public) frequently do not have the right to be present and so cannot learn what has transpired unless one of the parties involved is willing to talk. This restriction may be acceptable in disputes over custody or access to children. It is not justifiable in a large and important category of cases heard in the judge's private chambers.

Anonymity in some cases can be waived. In the Jaymee Bowen case in 1995, her father was successful in persuading the Court of Appeal to lift a ban on disclosure of her identity in order that he could sell her story to the press so that he could raise money for what was hoped would be life-saving cancer treatment which the local health authority had refused to fund.

Before a civil dispute comes to trial it is common for there to be pre-trial applications. Classic examples are injunctions against the press to prevent disclosure of an allegedly secret document, or orders prohibiting industrial action. If the plaintiff has chosen to bring the case in the Chancery Division of the High Court, these applications are heard by a judge in public (subject to any special orders to preserve legitimate confidences). However, if the case is brought in the Queen's Bench Division of the High Court, the applications are heard in chambers and the press are excluded. Plaintiffs are generally free to choose in which division to bring their case and can thus effectively select the degree of publicity they prefer.

These cases apart, it is very unusual for courts to depart from the principle of open justice. There is a statutory power to do so in particular cases (for example, official secrets prosecutions) and a general power where the public's presence would defeat the ends of justice. The courts have repeatedly stressed that it is only exceptional circumstances which will justify excluding the public or restricting reporting. The public may be present in court, but sketching and photography are prohibited.

In 1981, Parliament permitted the limited use of tape recorders in court with the judge's leave. There are administrative directions that applications should be treated sympathetically. Taping can be used only as an aid in compiling an accurate record of what was said: public reproduction is banned.

Reporting the proceedings of tribunals

In addition to the regular criminal and civil courts, there is a bewildering array of 'courts', tribunals and enquiries. It is impossible to generalise about when the public have a right of access. If they do, there will usually be a qualified privilege to protect the publisher of a fair and accurate report from libel actions (see above at p. 42). The 'strict liability contempt' provisions will only apply if the body is 'exercising the judicial power of the state'. By way of example, licensing authorities act administratively and therefore their proceedings are never 'active'. Industrial tribunals and mental health review tribunals, on the other hand, do exercise a statutory judicial jurisdiction – their proceedings will be active from the time a hearing date is set, but of course there will be no contempt unless the publication poses a serious threat to the integrity of the proceedings.

Enforcement

Prosecutions under the strict liability rule can be brought only with the Attorney General's consent. This was intended to ensure that some consideration was given to the public interest before prosecutions were brought. If the Attorney General refuses to prosecute, there is no right to challenge such a decision. In 1995 the Taylor sisters, whose convictions for murder were quashed by the Court of Appeal after a trial by media, failed in their attempt to get the Courts to review the refusal of the Attorney General to prosecute the press for contempt. In recent years, Crown Court judges have been more prepared to discharge defendants in criminal trials who have been the subject of media coverage commenting on their guilt or innocence.

While private parties cannot prosecute for contempt, they can, if they would suffer particularly from a publication which offended against the rule, seek an injunction to stop publication.

2.7 Controls on broadcasting, films, videos and cable

The BBC, by its charter, is intended and expected to 'censor' the programmes it transmits. The Independent Broadcasting Authority (the IBA) had similar duties in relation to commercial broadcasting. The IBA's successors, the Independent Television Commission (ITC) and the Radio Authority, are intended to regulate with a lighter touch, but their powers to penalise their licensees and ultimately to revoke licences mean that they wield considerable influence.

The ITC regulates through its code of practice. This requires that commercial television programmes do not offend against good taste or decency and are not likely to encourage crime or lead to disorder; that news is presented with due accuracy and impartiality, and that due impartiality is preserved in regard to matters of political or industrial controversy or relating to current public policy.

Unlicensed broadcasters are prohibited. It is a criminal offence which requires no proof of intent. Therefore, pirate radio stations have to keep one step ahead of the Department of Trade Inspectors, who can forfeit equipment as well as prosecute for infringements.

The government has a power to direct that certain matters should not be broadcast both on commercial television and on the BBC. It used this power in 1988 to ban spoken comment by or in support of Sinn Fein, the UDA or any of the organisations proscribed under the anti-terrorism laws, now revoked. A challenge to the gagging order by the National Union of Journalists (NUJ), on the basis that it infringed the guarantee of freedom of expression in Article 10 of the European Convention on Human Rights, failed in the House of Lords and the application was rejected by the European Court of Human Rights.

In 1993 the government exercised its power to control what is broadcast by proscribing the Red Hot satellite channel, a carrier of pornographic material. This was upheld after an initial legal challenge, although there may have been an infringement of EU broadcasting law. The government even retains the power to send in troops to take control of the BBC in the name of the Crown in extreme circumstances.

Unlike newspapers which can openly propagate their own views, the television companies cannot editorialise on matters (other than broadcasting issues) which are politically or industrially controversial or relate to current public policy. Subliminal messages are prohibited and religious broadcasting is specifically controlled.

Political advertising is controlled by the ITC and the Radio Authority. In effect, advertising on behalf of an organisation whose objects are mainly or wholly political or advertising which is directed towards a political end is banned. Notwithstanding a court challenge, this covers radio advertising about atrocities in Rwanda and Burundi by Amnesty International. The magazine *Index on Censorship* has suffered a similar ban. Article 10 of the Convention was held not to be contravened.

There are limits to these duties. Thus the Court of Appeal has accepted that in judging whether all the constituent parts of a programme satisfy the 'good taste' canon, the ITC can take account of the purpose and character of the programme as a whole. The duties set out above have also to be reconciled with the Commission's other duties, for instance to secure a wide showing of programmes of merit. Channel 4 was deliberately created to provide programmes 'calculated to appeal to tastes and interests not generally catered for by ITV', and 'to encourage innovation and experimentation in the form and content of programmes'. Inevitably, this can only be done in some cases at the risk of causing offence to those with mainline tastes. The requirement of impartiality in non-news programmes can be satisfied over a series of programmes and a tradition has developed of allowing more latitude to 'personal view' programmes that are 'balanced' by others.

The courts have discouraged legal challenges to the ITC and its predecessor, the IBA, for vetting programmes, and their decisions on individual programmes can (generally) only be quashed if they are so perverse as to be unreasonable. The BBC has accepted similar restraints to those imposed on commercial television, but the legal position of the restraints remains uncertain.

The Obscene Publications Act now applies to television and radio broadcasts, although no prosecutions have yet been brought (since 1990).

The Broadcasting Standards Commission

The 1996 Broadcasting Act set up a new quango to deal with broadcasting regulation. The new body has taken over the functions of the old Broadcasting Standards Council (BSC) which was set up by the government to monitor sex and violence on radio and television and the Broadcasting Complaints Commission which dealt with complaints in relation to unjust or unfair treatment and unwarranted infringements of privacy. The two regimes now operate under the one roof.

Radio or television programmes put out by the independent broadcasters or the BBC can be reviewed by the BSC. Complaints of unjust or unfair treatment or unwarranted infringements of privacy in, or in connection with, the obtaining of material included in sound or television broadcasts, may be made by a person affected (fairness complaints). Complaints cannot be made in connection with someone who has died more than five years previously, but within this period a member of the family, a personal representative or someone closely connected can make a fairness complaint to the BSC. Written complaints can be made by anyone about the portayal of violence or sexual conduct or about alleged failures of programmes to attain standards of taste and decency (standards complaints) within two months of a television programme and three weeks of a radio programme.

The Commission cannot order the payment of any money to the complainant, but they can insist on the responsible body publishing the Commission's findings and, more significantly, can insist on an approved summary being broadcast within a stipulated time.

The British Board of Film Classification

The British Board of Film Classification (BBFC) is a hybrid system. There is no general requirement that a film must have a BBFC certificate before being shown, but this position is achieved indirectly by the power of local councils to licence cinemas. Most licences have a condition attached that only films with a BBFC certificate will be shown. Like television and radio programmes, films can be prosecuted under the Obscene Publications Act although feature films (not less than 16 mm) can only be prosecuted or forfeited with the approval of the Director of Public Prosecutions.

The BBFC has been given an enlarged role in relation to video cassettes. Here it is a censor in law as well as in practice and it is an offence to supply an unclassified video or to breach any restrictions which have been imposed by the BBFC (as to minimum age, type of supplier, etc.). Videos concerned with sport, religion, music and education are exempt, but not if they show or are designed to encourage human sexual activity (or force or restraint associated with it), or mutilation, torture or other gross acts of violence towards humans or animals. Videos are not exempt either if they show human genitalia or human urinary or excretory functions. The BBFC has to consider whether videos are suitable for viewing in the home. There is an appeal structure for those who submit videos to the BBFC, but the sizeable fees charged by the Board and the delays that the process necessarily entails can cause grave difficulties for producers.

Cable

Cable programming is still in its infancy but the regulatory framework has been established on a similar model to that for broadcasting. Thus, the ITC has the power to license operators. It must do all that it can to see that its licensees do not include in their programmes material which offends against good taste or decency or is likely to encourage or incite crime or lead to public disorder or to be offensive to public feeling. Subliminal images are, again, banned. News must be presented with due accuracy and impartiality, but only if it originates in the UK. Non-news programmes are considerably less inhibited than broadcasts; instead of a requirement of 'balance' there is only the duty to see that undue prominence is not given to the views and opinions of particular persons or bodies on religious matters, matters of public controversy or issues relating to current public policy. Editorialising on religious, political, industrial controversy or current public policy is, as with broadcasting, prohibited. The ITC has the ultimate sanction of withdrawing an operator's licence if these or the other conditions are broken.

2.8 The balance of conflicting rights and interests

We have seen that the law relating to freedom of expression is contradictory and fragmented. There is no entrenched right of freedom to say, read and publish what we want. Intrusions on that right are recognised both in criminal and civil law and pre-eminence is given to the right to privacy of information, person and property. These legal restrictions affect not only the press and broadcast media, but also the individual artist, writer, publisher and broadcaster. Organisations such as a radical bookshop, a community radio station or a local video project are as much affected by the restrictions on free expression discussed here as the multinational media organisation. These restrictions are equally important to those who receive rather than broadcast information and ideas. The law relating to freedom of expression controls and censors what we are allowed to read, see and listen to. From this perspective, it can be seen that the absence of a positive right to that flow of information, our right as citizens to freedom of expression is easily curtailed and in some cases lost completely to the conflicting interests of the state and private citizen jealously guarding their interests.

2.9 Further information

Useful organisations

Campaign for Freedom of Information
Suite 102
16 Baldwin Gardens
London EC1N 7KJ
Tel: 0171 831 7477

Campaign for Press and Broadcasting Freedom
8 Cynthia Street
London N1 9JF
Tel: 0171 278 4430

National Union of Journalists
314 Gray's Inn Road
London WC1X 8PD
Tel: 0171 278 7916

Newspaper Society
Bloomsbury House
Bloomsbury Square
74–77 Great Russell Street
London WC1 3DA
Tel: 0171 636 7014

Bibliography

F. Klug and others, *The Three Pillars Of Liberty*, Routledge, 1996.

G. Robertson, *Obscenity*, Weidenfeld and Nicolson, 1976.

G. Robertson and A. Nicol, *Media Law: The Rights of Journalists and Broadcasters*, Penguin, 1992.

3

The right of privacy

This chapter deals with

- Confidential information.
- Spent convictions and the rehabilitation of offenders.
- Tapping, bugging and recording of telephone conversations.
- Interception of post.
- Other types of bugging and surveillance.
- Unwanted letters and telephone calls.
- Intrusion or harassment by neighbours and others.
- Power of officials to enter your home.
- Searches by Customs and Excise officials.
- Privacy and the media.

There is no right of privacy as such in English law. The English courts have to date refused to follow the pioneering course of their American counterparts, which have spelt out from the common law and the US Constitution general principles which protect an individual's right to be left alone. Recent statements from some senior judges indicate that the English courts may come to recognise a right of privacy in the common law but it is too early to tell whether this will happen or whether legislation will be necessary to create such a right.

Article 8 of the European Convention on Human Rights follows a similar model to Article 10 (freedom of expression), that is, it begins with a ringing declaration, in this case of the right of a person to respect from the State for his or her private and family life, home and correspondence. This is then qualified with an acknowledgement that intrusions are permitted if they are prescribed by law and are necessary in a democratic society in the interests of national security, public safety and the economic well-being of the country; for the prevention of disorder or crime; for the protection of health or morals; or for the protection of the rights and freedom of others. The European Convention is not part of English law, but applications can be made directly to the European Commission of Human Rights (see Chapter 5).

STOP PRESS

The new government proposes to incorporate the European Convention on Human Rights into domestic law. The rights in the Convention are set out in Chapter 5. A Bill to incorporate the Convention is due to be published in the autumn of 1997 and this is likely to become an Act by July 1998 and to come into force not before January 1999. It is not clear at the time of writing exactly what effect this will have on our laws. It is likely that the Convention will be able to be used to challenge some of the existing procedures and judge-made law although whether the Convention will be given a higher status than statute is not so clear. Nevertheless the rights set out in this book may be enhanced by the Convention and in future the rights in the Convention will have to be considered much more seriously than they have been in the past.

Although there is no general right of privacy in English law, there is what one senior judge has called 'piecemeal protection' of privacy, which is considered in the rest of this chapter.

3.1 Confidential information

The law of confidence has its origins in the commercial world of trade secrets and confidential lists of business contacts. However, it has grown far beyond this. Three main elements have to be proved before the courts will grant an injunction to preserve a secret:

- The information must be confidential in nature (such as health records).
- The person with the information must be under a duty to keep it confidential.
- The proposed use must be incompatible with that duty.

The duty can be created by a contract. Members of the Royal households, for instance, have to promise never to reveal what they learn in the course of their employment. But many secrets are shared by people who never think in terms of contracts. There are many relationships which are by their nature confidential: for example, between a lawyer and a client and between a doctor and a patient. The courts have been willing to recognise that duties of confidence can be owed between spouses and even friends. As importantly, third parties who acquire information and who know or learn of its confidential character can also be required to respect the confidence. This means that a newspaper to whom a secret is sold or given can be ordered not to publish it. Secret documents which are accidentally sent to third parties must be returned. The language of 'duty of confidence' is even applied to a thief who steals private papers.

The requirement that the information must be confidential is loosely applied. The court will not refuse an injunction because the information has leaked out to a limited extent. However, there will come a point (as in the *Spycatcher* saga) when it is plainly silly to pretend that there is any secret left to be preserved.

There is obvious potential for a clash of interests here: between the original confider who wants the secret kept and the press who appeal to the principle of freedom of expression. Although there is a public interest defence to breach of confidence, the balance between these two interests is still unsatisfactory (see Chapter 2 on freedom of expression).

Most breach of confidence cases take the form of applications for injunctions but, if a person wishes to stop publication pending a full trial of the case, he or she is usually expected to give an undertaking to pay the defendant compensation if the action eventually fails: since most people are unlikely to have the income to be able to give this kind of undertaking, such injunctions tend to be available only to the rich. If publication takes place before the plaintiff can act, the courts can still award damages or order the defendant to account for any profits made as a result of the disclosure.

3.2 Spent convictions and the rehabilitation of offenders

One particular kind of information that a person may understandably want to keep confidential is that relating to a past criminal conviction. On the other hand, other people may have a legitimate need to know about previous convictions so as to protect vulnerable people, for example. The Rehabilitation of Offenders Act 1974 allows people to start with a clean slate after they have paid their debt to society, but provides for exceptions to this general principle.

How a sentence becomes spent
The Act applies to all types of sentence, whether it is prison, a fine, probation, absolute or conditional discharge, findings in a juvenile court that an offence has been committed, and convictions of certain offences in service disciplinary proceedings.

The rehabilitation period depends on the sentence and runs from the date of conviction. When the period has expired, the conviction becomes 'spent' and need not be revealed in the future, for example, when you are applying for a job, completing an insurance proposal form, or applying for credit facilities or a tenancy of property. Table 3.1 sets out the rehabilitation periods according to sentence.

Table 3.1 Spent convictions and the rehabilitation of offenders

Sentence	Rehabilitation period
Prison for more than two and a half years	never*
Prison for more than six months but less than two and a half years	10 years*
Prison for six months or less	7 years*
Fine	5 years*
Dismissal with disgrace from Her Majesty's service	10 years*
Dismissal from Her Majesty's service	7 years*
Detention in respect of conviction in service disciplinary proceedings	5 years*
Borstal	7 years
Detention for over six months but less than two and a half years	5 years
Detention for six months or less	3 years
Hospital order under Mental Health Act 1983	5 years or 2 years after order ceases to have effect, whichever is the longer
Absolute discharge	6 months
Conditional discharge, probation order, binding over, care order, supervision order	1 year after conviction of the order or 1 year after the order ends, whichever is the longer
Disqualification	The period of disqualification

* Note: These periods are reduced by half if the offender was under seventeen at the date of conviction.

The following sentences can never become spent:

- A sentence of imprisonment of more than two and a half years.
- A life sentence.
- Detention during Her Majesty's pleasure.

If you are convicted during the rehabilitation period of an offence which can only be tried in a magistrates' court, the new sentence will carry its own rehabilitation period and will not affect the earlier one. If the second offence is more serious and you receive a sentence covered by the Act, the earlier conviction will become spent only when the later one becomes spent. If a person is given a sentence which can never become spent, this also prevents an earlier unspent conviction from becoming spent.

It should be noted that it is the *length of the sentence imposed by the court* which is relevant and not, for example, the length of time actually served in prison. A sentence counts in the same way whether you are actually sent to prison or the sentence is 'suspended'. In each case, the periods of rehabilitation are as set out in Table 3.1.

Where a person receives two or more prison sentences in the course of the same court case, the rehabilitation period depends on whether the sentences are ordered to take effect 'concurrently' (i.e. at the same time) or 'consecutively' (i.e. one after another). For example, if two six-month sentences are concurrent, the offences are treated separately, giving each conviction a rehabilitation period of seven years. However, if the sentences are consecutive, they are treated as a single term of twelve months, with a rehabilitation period of ten years.

The effect of rehabilitation
Once the rehabilitation period has expired, not only do you not have to reveal it, but also it cannot be revealed by anyone else without your permission.

Evidence in legal proceedings
A spent conviction cannot be used in evidence in a civil court, tribunal, arbitration or disciplinary or similar hearing. You should not be asked questions about spent convictions and, if you are, you need not answer them unless you wish to do so.

This does not apply in:

- Service disciplinary proceedings.
- Applications for adoption, custody, wardship or guardianship or in care proceedings.

- Where the court or tribunal is satisfied that justice cannot be done except by hearing evidence about the spent conviction.
- Criminal proceedings, but the Lord Chief Justice has ruled that no one should refer in open court to a spent conviction without the authority of the judge, whose authority should not be given unless the interests of justice so require.

Employment

Questions are often asked by potential employers about a person's previous convictions. The general rule under the Act is that you can treat such questions as *not* relating to spent convictions. Therefore if you decide not to disclose a spent conviction you cannot be denied employment or subsequently dismissed on the ground that you failed to disclose it: however, in exceptional circumstances, you may be prosecuted for the criminal offence of 'obtaining a pecuniary advantage by deception'. Likewise, failing to disclose a spent conviction is not a lawful ground for excluding you from any office or profession. Nor can a spent conviction be a lawful ground for prejudicing you in the way you are treated in an occupation or employment.

If, therefore, you are excluded or dismissed from employment on the ground of a spent conviction, you may be able to take the matter to a court or to an industrial tribunal. However, you should first seek legal advice. Many occupations and offices are specifically excluded from the general rule and are dealt with below. You should read these carefully.

Some employers are adopting the practice of asking prospective or existing employees to obtain a copy of their criminal record under the provisions of the Data Protection Act 1984, which allows people to see computer records about themselves (see Chapter 4). This record will list all convictions, including spent ones. Although this practice is not unlawful, it is a misuse of the data protection laws and has been criticised by the Data Protection Registrar. If you are concerned about agreeing to such a request, you should seek help from a union official or the Data Protection Registrar's Office at:

Wycliffe House
Water Lane
Wilmslow
Cheshire SK9 5AF
Tel: 01625 545745.

Provision of services

Some contracts, such as insurance policies, are governed by the legal principle that all relevant information must be disclosed by the person seeking insurance, whether or not it is asked for – otherwise the contract could be treated as invalid. Clearly, the existence of a driving offence or an offence of dishonesty could be relevant to an insurance company's assessment of the risk and the appropriate level of the premium. However, the Act clearly states that your duty to disclose all relevant information does *not* extend to disclosing convictions which are spent.

Going abroad

It should be remembered that the Act applies only to the United Kingdom and has no effect so far as the laws of other countries are concerned. This means, for example, that applicants for immigration and work permits or for visas to countries such as the USA will be under a duty to disclose spent convictions (unless the law of the relevant country has an Act similar to ours, in which case the extent of your duty will often be made clear on the application form). If in doubt about the law of the country concerned, ask their embassy or high commission in this country.

Defamation proceedings

A reference to a spent conviction in a newspaper article, for example, can give rise to a claim for defamation. However, in order to protect free speech, the Act states that a person who is sued for disclosing a spent conviction may rely on the defences of 'justification' (i.e. the statement is true) and/or 'fair comment' (i.e. the statement was a fair comment on a matter of public interest). In order to succeed when such a defence is raised, you would have to prove that the statement was made with 'malice', that is with some irrelevant, spiteful or improper motive.

In addition, the reporting of certain events and the making of statements in certain circumstances can give rise to the defences of 'absolute' or 'qualified privilege'. For example, fair and accurate reports of judicial proceedings are 'absolutely privileged' (i.e. immune) from defamation actions (see Chapter 2).

As the law relating to defamation is complicated, you should seek specialist legal advice but remember that legal aid is not available for defamation actions.

Exceptions to the Act

The Act is often criticised for the many and wide exceptions made to its general principles. If you fall within any of the exceptions, you will be treated as if the Act had never been passed and you will not be entitled to rehabilitation for an otherwise spent conviction. These exceptions are listed in the Orders made by a relevant government minister and relate mainly to matters of national security, the care of those who are considered to be vulnerable and to the administration of justice.

Excepted professions, occupations and offices

A number of professions, occupations and offices have been excepted from the Act's general rule that a person does not have to disclose a spent conviction: see Table 3.2. If you apply to join one of the professions, occupations or offices listed in Table 3.2, you will normally be asked to disclose all previous convictions including spent ones (and you must be told why). Furthermore, a spent conviction, or the failure to disclose it, may be a good ground to exclude or dismiss you from one of the professions, occupations or offices listed in Table 3.2.

Table 3.2 Excepted professions, occupations and offices

Accountants	Nurses and midwives
Dealer in securities	Opticians
Dentists	Pharmaceutical chemists
Director, controller, etc.	Police constables
of insurance company or	Prison board of visitors
building society	Prison officers
Firearms dealers	Probation officers
Judicial appointments	Teachers
Lawyers	Traffic wardens
Manager or trustee of unit trust	Veterinary surgeons
Medical practitioners	

Other excepted occupations include:

- Any office or employment where the question about spent convictions is asked for the purpose of safeguarding national security – for example, if you wish to be employed by the UK Atomic Energy Authority, the Civil Aviation Authority or as an officer of the Crown.
- Certain types of work in health and social services where the work involves access to people over sixty-five, people suffering from serious illness or mental disorder, alcoholics or drug addicts, blind, deaf or dumb people, or where the work is concerned with the provision of care, recreation or leisure facilities to people under eighteen (see below for further details).
- Applications for certain certificates or licences (for example, those for firearms, explosives or gaming) require that your spent convictions must be disclosed and allow the licensing authority

to take them into account. Failure to disclose a spent conviction could lead to the refusal or loss of the certificate or licence and even to prosecution.

Disclosure of criminal background of those with access to children

Since 1986 procedures have been adopted to check any possible criminal background with local police forces of those applying for work (including voluntary work) with substantial access to children in the statutory sector (i.e. local authorities and health authorities), for example, in day nurseries, playgroups, children's homes, social work, teaching, and community and youth work. Since 1989 this has been extended to the voluntary sector as well. The check also applies to prospective foster parents, adoptive parents and childminders, and extends to other adults in their households.

Where a police check is required in relation to such a job with a local authority or a health authority, you will be requested to list any convictions, including spent convictions, binding-over orders or cautions, and will be asked to consent in writing to a police check being carried out. It should also be pointed out to you that, because of an exception in the Act, the police will disclose spent convictions and that they may be taken into account in deciding whether to employ you.

Where the information provided by the police differs from that provided by you, this must be discussed with you before a decision is taken. If you think that the police information is incorrect, you are entitled to make representations to the police through a nominated person. The police must also disclose 'other relevant information' concerning you. This must be restricted to factual information which the police would be prepared to present as evidence in court, or details of acquittals or decisions not to prosecute where the circumstances of the case would give cause for concern.

It is for the prospective employers to decide your suitability, taking into account only those offences which may be relevant to the particular job in question – for example, they will consider the nature of the offence, when it occurred and its frequency. The fact that you have a criminal record does not automatically mean that you are unfit to work with children. On the other hand, it is not only sexual offences which may render a person unsuitable for such work.

If you are concerned that a prospective employer may take into account a conviction that you consider to be irrelevant to the job applied for, you should attach a note to the original disclosure form explaining the circumstances of the offence and why you consider it to be irrelevant. If you are denied employment on the basis of that conviction, you should seek legal advice: in limited circumstances, it may be possible to challenge the decision.

Prospective employers may also use the Department of Health's Consultancy Service and the Department for Education and Employment's 'List 99' as further check on a person's suitability. These departments hold lists of people who, because of a previous conviction or incident, are considered to be unfit to work with children or young people. You should have been informed at the time by the relevant Department that your name had come to its attention and why. You should also have been given the opportunity to make representations about the incident in question.

For further information see Home Office Circular No. 47/93 *Protection of Children: Disclosure of Criminal Background of those with Access to Children* (in respect of the statutory sector) and Home Office Circular No. 42/94 (in respect of the voluntary sector). Copies of these circulars are available free from:

Police, Science & Technology Unit
Room 535
Home Office
Horseferry House
Dean Ryle Street
London SW1P 2AW
Tel: 0171 217 8609

Police reporting of convictions

The general rule is that police information (including information on convictions) should not be disclosed unless there are important considerations of public interest to justify departure from the general rule of confidentiality. Exceptions to this rule are made where there is a need:

- To protect vulnerable members of society.
- To ensure good and honest administration of the law.
- To protect national security.

The effect of this means that under Home Office Circular No. 45/86 *Police Reports of Convictions and Related Information*, the police may disclose, when it is requested, information on a person's past convictions, cases pending and other such background information as would be admissible in court in the circumstances listed in respect of:

- Persons to be appointed to posts with substantial access to children (see above).
- Members of or visitors to the same household as a child subject to a case conference on non-accidental injury to children.

- Parents (and any co-habitees) to whom a local authority propose to return a child in care.
- Applicants for compensation for criminal injury.
- Applicants to join the police.
- Applicants for certain licences: for example, gaming, lottery, sex establishment and entertainment licences.
- Applicants for and holders of licences as operators of heavy goods vehicles and passenger service vehicles.
- Applicants for licences as dealers in securities.
- Applicants for consumer credit licences.
- Applicants for casual Post Office work.
- Potential jurors in cases involving national security or terrorism.
- Social enquiry reports and other reports by probation officers.
- Welfare reports for courts determining the care and custody of children.
- People subject to national security vetting.

Under the same Circular, the police are asked to report convictions as they occur to the supervising authorities or professional bodies of those groups listed in Table 3.3, particularly where the offences involve violence, dishonesty, drink or drugs, as they may affect a person's suitability to continue in a profession or occupation.

Table 3.3 Reporting convictions of those in certain professions and occupations.

British Telecom staff	Post Office staff
Civil Aviation Authority staff	Probation officers
Civil servants	Social workers
Dentists	Teachers (including student
Lawyers	teachers) and ancillary staff
Magistrates	UK Atomic Energy Authority
Medical practitioners	and British Nuclear Fuels staff
(and various professions	Youth workers
supplementary to medicine)	
Nurses and midwives	
Pharmaceutical chemists' staff	

Unauthorised disclosure of convictions
The Act makes it an offence if:

- An official unlawfully discloses someone else's spent conviction, in the course of their official duties. The penalty is a maximum fine of £2,500 (level 4 on the standard scale).

- Any person who obtains details of a spent conviction from any official record by means of fraud, dishonesty or a bribe. The penalty is up to six months' imprisonment and/or a maximum fine of £5,000 (level 5 on the standard scale).

If someone wrongfully reveals that you have a spent conviction, you can:

- Report the matter to the police and ask that the incident be investigated with a view to prosecution of the person responsible.
- Sue the person concerned for defamation (see above).
- Make a formal police complaint.

If, for example, the police reveal to a person who is not responsible for people listed in Table 3.3, you may be able to bring a claim for breach of confidence (see section 3.1 above). You should seek legal advice about this, since it is a developing area of the law. Its advantage over defamation proceedings is that legal aid is (at least in principle) available.

The Sex Offenders Act 1997 imposes a requirement on people who have been convicted (or found not guilty by reason of insanity) *or cautioned* for sex offences to notify the police of their name and address (Sections 1 and 2). Although the Act is often regarded as creating a 'paedophiles' register', the definition of sex offences in Schedule 1 to the Act is very wide and is not confined to offences against children or to non-consensual offences. In the case of those who have been cautioned, the requirement will apply if they have admitted the offence in question (Section 1(1)(c)). It will be an offence to fail to comply with the notification requirement, punishably by either a fine not exceeding scale 3 or a maximum of one month's imprisonment or both (Section 3). The requirement will remain in place indefinitely if a person has been imprisoned for a period of thirty months or more or has been admitted to a hospital subject to a restriction order. The requirement will remain in place for a period of ten years if a person has been imprisoned for a term of more than six months but less than thirty months and for a period of seven years if a person has been imprisoned for six months or less or has been admitted to a hospital without a restriction order. The notification requirement will remain in place for five years for other people (Section 1(4)). The relevant periods are halved if the person concerned is under eighteen on the relevant date as defined in Section 1(8) and Section 4(2)).

At the time of writing the details of how the police will use this system were not clear. It is likely that information from the register will only be disclosed very selectively.

3.3 Tapping, bugging and the recording of telephone conversations

Telephone tapping

The Interception of Communications Act 1985 makes private telephone tapping an offence. We add the qualification 'private' because the Act perpetuates the system for the interception of telephone calls on the warrant of the Home Secretary. Warrants ought to be confined to cases involving national security, serious crime or the economic well-being of the UK, but the scope for investigating the propriety of an official tap or intercept is extremely limited. The Interception of Communications Tribunal can investigate whether there was a warrant and, if so, whether it was properly issued. However, the complainant will not be told the government's story or have a proper chance to test it.

Where it is found that a warrant has been improperly issued, the tribunal has power to order compensation and the destruction of the recorded material. If the interception took place without a warrant the only sanction is a criminal prosecution (to which the Director of Public Prosecutions must consent). There is no offence under the 1985 Act if the interception has the consent of either party to the telephone call. The 1985 Act does not apply to calls made from cordless telephones – it is therefore not unlawful to intercept such calls without a warrant. Application forms for the Tribunal can be obtained from: Interception of Communications Tribunal, P. O. Box 44, London SE1 OTX.

Bugging

No offence is committed under the 1985 Act if a third party does not interfere with the telephone line itself but instead listens in by placing a bug on or near the telephone. The person who places the device may commit some other offence (such as criminal damage) or a civil wrong (such as trespass to land) in installing the bug but it is difficult to trace such people, especially if they are officers of the state and/or act undercover. Bugging by the police has for many years been subject only to Home Office guidelines published in 1984 ('Guidelines on the Use of Equipment in Police Surveillance Operations'). However, the Police Act 1997, puts police bugging on a statutory footing for the first time. This means that the use of bugs by the police in relation to homes, offices and hotel bedrooms will have to have prior authorisation by a Commissioner (a serving or retired High Court Judge) unless the need for surveillance is 'urgent' in which case a Commissioner must be informed as soon as practicable. The police still do not need prior authority of a judge if the surveillance can be carried out without the need to go onto, or interfere with, private property.

Recording

It is not an offence for one party to a telephone call to make a recording of it, even if the other party is unaware of what is being done. Indeed, this can often be a useful way of proving that someone has been making malicious or nuisance calls. However, the evolving doctrine of breach of confidence may be available to stop a person revealing what was said and recorded in such a situation if it was apparent that the conversation was confidential and there is no public interest in such disclosure.

3.4 Interception of post

The official system for interception of post is as old as the Post Office itself. Private interception is an offence (under the Post Office Act 1953). The Interception of Communications Act 1985 provides a system for interception of post with the warrant of the Home Secretary which is similar to the system for telephone tapping.

3.5 Other types of bugging and surveillance

Your private conversations may be listened to and recorded through use of a bug even if you are not using the telephone. Often the bug is installed in or attached to the outside of a building. The person who owns or rents the property will have a claim for trespass. There may also be other offences such as criminal damage committed. This will be of limited use if the person who planted the bug cannot be traced, but the apparatus can at least be disabled.

The Security Service (MI5) was given legal recognition in 1989. Burglary and other interferences with property can only be authorised by the Home Secretary personally. The intrusion must be necessary to obtain information for one of MI5's functions. These are broadly defined as the protection of national security and safeguarding the economic well-being of the UK against threats posed by persons outside the country. As with telephone tapping there is a complaints procedure (to a senior judge who is appointed to act as Security Service Commissioner in the case of intrusions into property, and another tribunal in the case of other MI5 activities). However, if the intrusion is skilfully done, the victim will be ignorant of it. The Commissioner's and tribunal's powers are limited, and again the process denies the complainant a proper opportunity to hear the case against him or her.

Complaints about MI5 should be sent to: Security Service Tribunal, P.O. Box 18, London SE1 0TZ.

The Intelligence Services Act 1994 set up a similar complaints procedure for the Security Intelligence Service (MI6 – responsible for the foreign secret services) and the Government Communications Head Quarters (GCHQ – the government's listening centre). The Act also set up a parliamentary committee to supervise the work of all three security services. Unfortunately, this is unlikely to provide any significant level of accountability. Complaints about MI6 should be sent to: Intelligence Services Tribunal, P. O. Box 4823, London SW1A 9XD. If the surveillance (whether by the government, the press or by others) does not involve physical intrusion to property, there are even fewer restrictions. Snooping which employs radio transmitters is an offence under the Wireless Telegraphy Act 1949 which prohibits the use of unlicensed transmitters (or receivers).

Other listening devices such as long-range microphones and the use of long-range telephoto lenses are not barred under the current state of the law, although there have been increasingly loud demands for their use as a means of intruding on personal privacy to be prohibited. Surveillance in public places (whether overhearing conversations or taking photographs) is often treated only as a public order issue. If no breach of the peace is threatened there will usually be no offence. However, the developing doctrine of breach of confidence may be available to stop distribution of recordings of conversations in a public place if it was apparent that the conversation was confidential but the law is not clear at the moment. There have also been suggestions in the courts that the publication of photographs of private acts, obtained for example by a telephoto lens, may be restrained under the breach of confidence doctrine. Closed circuit television (CCTV) systems have been set up in many towns and cities, usually by local authorities and often in partnership with the police. CCTV is still completely unregulated by statute. If you are concerned about an aspect of a local CCTV system you should take the matter up with the local authority or the police. Many organisations have agreed to bide by codes of practice relating to CCTV, but these codes are entirely voluntary. A particularly comprehensive code of practice has been drawn up by the Local Government Information Unit (1–5 Bath Street, London EC1V 9QQ).

3.6 Unwanted letters and telephone calls

It is a criminal offence to telephone grossly offensive messages or make indecent or obscene or menacing telephone calls or calls which cause annoyance, inconvenience or needless anxiety (Telecommunications Act 1984). If the perpetrator is known and is persistent in making calls the courts are increasingly willing to grant injunctions to prevent this type of harassment. They have even made these orders at the request of a relative of the property owner. 'Nuisance', the legal category into which these claims fall, may thus be moving away from being exclusively an aspect of property ownership and more openly a means of protecting domestic privacy. The criminal courts may in certain circumstances treat such harassment as 'grievous bodily harm'. The Protection from Harassment Act introduces a new offence of pursuing a course of conduct which amounts to harassment of a person. This also enables a person to obtain a civil court injunction to stop harassment occurring.

Hate mail is usually anonymous, but if it can be traced the sender can be prosecuted under the Malicious Communications Act 1988. This makes it an offence to send a letter or other article which conveys an indecent or grossly offensive message or a threat or which contains information known to be false and the purpose of the letter is to cause distress or anxiety.

Inertia selling used to be common before the Unsolicited Goods and Services Act 1971. The technique was to send goods to customers who were then charged for them if they did not go to the trouble to return them. The 1971 Act allows recipients of unsolicited goods to keep them as free gifts after six months (thirty days if the recipient writes to the sender asking for them to be collected). The 1971 Act also makes it an offence to send obscene or indecent books, magazines, leaflets or advertising material describing or illustrating human sexual techniques (see Chapter 2 for more on obscenity).

3.7 Intrusion or harassment by neighbours and others

Property is a concept which English law can understand. The right to keep others out is one of the defining characteristics of property ownership. Those who are fortunate enough to own or rent their home are entitled to injunctions to prevent intrusion and damages to compensate for trespass. Harassment of tenants by their landlords for the purpose of encouraging the tenants to leave can be particularly expensive for landlords. The tenants can claim the additional value which the house or flat has for the landlord with vacant possession (Housing Act 1988). Harassment of this kind can also be a criminal offence (Protection from Eviction Act 1977).

Neighbours who do not physically intrude may none the less make life intolerable in a variety of ways. Their unreasonable use of their land can be the tort of private nuisance. Again such behaviour can be restrained by injunction or lead to a claim in damages.

People who come to your door to sell goods, ask you to give to a charity, persuade you to support a particular religion or political party or ask questions for a market research survey have no right to enter your home. You can refuse to talk to them and they must leave when you ask them to.

3.8 Power of officials to enter your home

A house on fire, or infested with rats, or with a gas leak, or where building works have been carried out in a dangerous manner, is something which concerns the whole community. To cope with problems such as these, many officials are given the right to enter your home whether you like it or not.

There are, in fact, tens of thousands of officials in the UK who have the power, in certain circumstances, to enter private premises, but most of them only have the power to enter business premises and are not dealt with here. This section describes the most important powers of entry which may involve officials entering your home. (The powers of the police to enter and search private premises are dealt with in Chapter 6.)

Each type of official is subject to different rules of procedure because each is governed by a different Act of Parliament and there is no general code which covers their conduct. Quite commonly, however, the procedure is that the official must produce evidence of identity and authority before entering and may not insist on entering without first giving you at least twenty-four hours' notice. If, after such notice, you refuse to let him or her in, the magistrates' court may give authority to enter without your consent, by force if necessary. In general, if someone asks to come into your home, claiming to be an official, you should:

- Ask to see the caller's identity card.
- Ask the caller what authority he or she has to enter your home.
- If in doubt, refuse entry and contact the office from which the official claims to come in order to check his or her credentials.

If you have a complaint to make about the way an official behaves, you should approach the appropriate authority. For example, in the case of a local authority official, you should complain to your local councillor; in the case of a gas or electricity official, the gas or electricity company; in the case of a VAT inspector, the collector in charge of VAT at the local office; or, in the case of a tax inspector, the Commissioners for the Inland Revenue. There may also be the possibility of a complaint to an official regulator or an ombudsman (see Chapter 5 on the right to complain).

Fire brigade

A member of a local authority fire brigade who is on duty (or a police officer) may enter any premises where a fire has broken out, or where there is reason to believe a fire has broken out. Other premises, such as neighbouring houses, may also be entered if this is necessary for fire-fighting purposes. The fire officer can force entry, if necessary. The permission of the owner or occupier does not have to be obtained. It is an offence to obstruct or interfere with any member of a fire brigade who is involved in fighting a fire; the maximum penalty is a fine of level 3 (currently £1,000) (Fire Services Act 1947).

Gas and electricity boards

An official of a gas or electricity company may enter your home if:

- You agree to let the official enter.
- A magistrate has given the official a warrant authorising the official to enter.
- There is an emergency and the official has reason to believe that there is danger to life or property.

A gas or electricity board official is entitled to ask to enter your home, or to apply to a magistrate for a warrant, in order to:

- Inspect the meter or any other fittings.
- Disconnect the supply in certain circumstances.

In order to obtain a warrant, the official must show that:

- You have been given at least twenty-four hours' notice; and
- He or she has asked to be admitted and you have refused; or
- The premises are unoccupied.

Entry must be at a 'reasonable' time and the official must leave the house as secure against trespassers as it was when he or she arrived, and make good any damage caused.

It is a criminal offence to obstruct a person who has a warrant or who asks to be admitted in an emergency; the maximum penalty is a fine of level 3 (currenty £1,000). It is not an offence to refuse to let the official enter if there is no emergency and the official does not have a warrant (Rights of Entry (Gas and Electricity Boards) Act 1954; Electricity Act 1989 and Gas Act 1995).

Water companies

An authorised official of a water company may enter any premises at a 'reasonable' hour in order to:

- Inspect water meters.
- Ascertain whether there has been any contravention of the law relating to water supplies.
- Detect waste or misuse of water.

In the first two cases (but not the last), twenty-four hours' notice must be given. Entry can be obtained in an emergency or under a warrant.

Housing

An official authorised by the local authority may enter any house in the area at any 'reasonable' time in order to:

- Make a valuation or survey, where a compulsory purchase order is being considered or has been issued.
- Examine the premises and make a survey where a notice requiring repairs, a demolition order, a closing order or a clearance order has been issued.
- Measure the rooms, etc., to determine whether there is or has been overcrowding.
- Ascertain whether there is or has been a contravention of the Housing Act regulations.

The official must have a written document of authority and must give at least twenty-four hours' notice. It is an offence to obstruct the official, providing the official is authorised and has given notice; the maximum penalty is a fine of level 2 – currently £500 (Housing Act 1985).

Planning

An authorised local authority official may enter premises at any 'reasonable' time for various planning purposes, including:

- Preparing or approving development plans.
- Dealing with applications for planning permission.
- Making a valuation in connection with compensation.
- Making a survey in connection with a compulsory purchase order.

• Investigating whether development has occurred without planning permission.

The official must give twenty-four hours' notice. The local authority must also pay compensation for any damage caused. It is an offence to obstruct the official, provided that proper notice has been given; the maximum penalty is a fine of level 2 – currently £500 (Town and Country Planning Act 1990).

Rating

A local assessor may enter any property in the area in order to carry out a survey or make a valuation for the purposes of drawing up rating valuation lists. The official must give three days' notice. It is an offence to obstruct the official provided that proper notice has been given; the maximum penalty is a fine of level 2 – currently £500 (Local Government Finance Act 1992).

Social security

An inspector may enter business premises at any 'reasonable' time in order to interview employers, employees and self-employed people about their contributions record. It is an offence not to produce National Insurance Certificates or other relevant documents. It is also an offence to refuse to answer the inspector's questions, except that you are not obliged to give information which will incriminate yourself or your spouse – this does not include a common law husband or wife (Social Security Administration Act 1992). The maximum penalty for either offence is a fine of level 3 (currently £1,000) and a fine of £40 for each day that the offence continues.

An investigator (such as an official trying to find out if a person is cohabiting) does not have a right to enter your home. If the official forces entry, or refuses to leave after you ask him or her to do so, he or she is committing a trespass and you may be able to take legal action.

Tax

A tax inspector can obtain a warrant from a circuit judge if he or she reasonably suspects that an offence involving serious fraud in relation to tax has been committed. The warrant authorises the inspector to enter and search private premises and remove documents. Any application for a warrant must be made with the approval of a Commissioner for the Inland Revenue (Taxes Management Act 1970).

VAT

A VAT official may enter any premises at a 'reasonable' time for any purposes connected with administering value added tax. The official may enter without a warrant, and may also inspect goods which are liable to tax. If the official has reasonable grounds for suspecting you of an offence related to VAT, he or she may apply to a magistrate for a warrant authorising him or her to:

- Enter, by force if necessary, at any 'reasonable' time within fourteen days of the warrant being issued.
- Seize any documents relating to the investigation.
- Search any people on the premises (but a woman can only be searched by another woman).

Obstructing a VAT official could amount to an assault for which you could be prosecuted (Value Added Tax Act 1984).

Mental health

An approved social worker may at all 'reasonable' times, after producing identity if requested, enter and inspect any premises in which a mentally disordered person is living if there is reasonable cause to believe that he or she is not being properly cared for.

Magistrates have the power to issue a warrant authorising a police officer to enter premises (by force, if necessary) if they have reasonable cause to suppose that a mentally disordered person is being ill-treated there, or is unable to look after him- or herself. The police officer must be accompanied by a social worker and a doctor (Mental Health Act 1983).

Infectious diseases and illness

In the case of 'notifiable diseases' (for example, plague and cholera) a magistrate may make an order for the compulsory medical examination of suspected sufferers and carriers and for the removal to and detention in hospital of anyone suffering from such a disease where it appears that proper precautions are not being taken to prevent the spread of the disease (Public Health (Control of Diseases) Act 1984). AIDS is dealt with similarly to notifiable diseases, but slightly less stringently; there is no provision for compulsory examination provided the suspected sufferer or carrier is already receiving treatment from a doctor (Public Health (Infectious Diseases) Regulations 1985).

On a certificate from the appointed local authority officer, the local authority may serve notice on an occupier to disinfect or destroy articles likely to retain infection within a fixed period, if doing so would tend to prevent the spread of any infectious disease. The occupier has twenty-four hours to inform the local authority that he or she will comply, failing which the local authority has the right to enter and to do the necessary work. The occupier can be forced to reimburse the local authority and the provision for compensation for articles destroyed is not very satisfactory. Where an infectious disease occurs in a house, the local authority may also, at their own cost, remove persons from the premises, acting with a magistrates' warrant if there is no consent. This is not limited to the notifiable diseases mentioned above.

Magistrates also have the power to issue a warrant authorising an officer of a local authority to enter premises to remove to hospital persons who are so chronically ill or old as to be unable to look after themselves, and who are not being properly looked after by others. Seven days' notice to the person of such an application must be given (National Assistance Act 1948).

Pests and vermin

The occupier of land is under an obligation to notify the local authority if rats or mice in substantial numbers live on or resort to the land. The local authority may serve notice on the owner or occupier (or both) of land (including buildings), requiring them to take specified steps within a specified time to keep the land free of mice or rats.

Where premises are so filthy or unwholesome as to be prejudicial to health, or are verminous, the local authority may require corrective measures, including, for example, disinfection or the removal of wallpaper. If necessary, the notice may require the occupiers of infested premises (and neighbouring premises which might be affected) to vacate the premises while gas is employed to destroy vermin. In such a case, the local authority must provide temporary alternative accommodation at its own expense.

It is an offence to disobey the notice (maximum penalty level 1 (£200), or level 3 (£1,000) in the case of a mice or rat notice). In the event of disobedience, the local authority also has the power to enter the land to do the work itself (Public Health Act 1936, Prevention of Damage by Pests Act 1949).

Foster homes

A local authority can authorise someone (for example, a social worker) to inspect any home where a child is being fostered. The inspector must produce an official document, showing that he or she has the right to enter. It is an offence to refuse to allow the inspector to enter; the maximum penalty is a fine of level 3 – currently £1,000 (Children Act 1989).

The Anton Piller order

Over the past ten to fifteen years, the courts have developed a form of civil search warrant called an 'Anton Piller' order (named after a case of the same name). This is usually issued in cases involving 'pirate' goods, such as unauthorised video copies of popular films, but it can be issued in any case where the court is persuaded that the defendant is the sort of person who might destroy relevant evidence in his or her possession if the order is not made. Strictly speaking, an Anton Piller order is not a search warrant because it does not directly empower the holder to enter or search premises. What the order does is to instruct the person in charge of the premises to let the holder in. But since it is a contempt of court to refuse to let him or her in, the order has much the same effect as a search warrant. The order must be served by a 'supervising solicitor', but it will usually allow him or her to be accompanied by others. The solicitor should be experienced and should not be a member or employee of the firm acting for the person who obtains the Anton Piller order. If you are served with an Anton Piller order, ask the supervising solicitor for an explanation of what is going on: he or she has a duty to offer to explain the effect of the order to you fairly and in everyday language. Take a good look at the terms and conditions attached to the order, many of which explain your rights in the situation. For example, you are entitled to refuse entry before 9.30 a.m. or after 5.30 p.m. or at all on Saturday and Sunday. The supervising solicitor must give you an opportunity to take legal advice. In view of the seriousness of the matter, it would be sensible to do so. It would, however, be a very rare case in which your lawyer would advise you not to comply with the order. Nearly all Anton Piller orders contain a provision forbidding you to tip off others (apart from your lawyer) about their existence. In fact, the plaintiff often has means of telling whether others have been tipped off; he or she may have persons watching for such activity and, if you were caught arranging for others to dispose of inconvenient evidence, you would risk prison for contempt of court.

The supervising solicitor is under a strict duty to behave responsibly. In one case where it was held that the solicitor acted oppressively, he was ordered to pay substantial compensation.

Bailiffs

Bailiffs are officers of the court, although they may be employed by private companies, and their job is to seize property. Courts can make a variety of orders which are enforced by bailiffs. Their rights to enter your home are complex and will depend on the order made by the court. In virtually all cases they are entitled to enter your home but only in a few cases, such as eviction orders, are they entitled to force their way in. They can, however, climb through unlocked windows and break down internal doors and may put pressure on you to invite them in.

If they are employed by the court following a judgment debt they can seize any goods or possessions belonging to the debtor but cannot seize anything needed personally for his or her job (for instance, tools, books and vehicles) or used for basic needs (clothing, bedding, furniture, household equipment and food). Thus they can take stereo equipment, televisions, video recorders, etc. Bailiffs cannot seize property belonging to people other than the debtor.

The goods are then usually impounded for a short period (five days) before being sold by auction. Often the goods are left on the premises until sold. This is known as taking 'walking possession'.

3.9 Searches by Customs and Excise officials

Approximately 40,000 travellers each year are stopped and bodily searched at customs points throughout the country under powers conferred by the Customs and Excise Management Act 1979. The nature of the search may take a number of forms, from a 'pocket search' to a full strip or intimate body search. Most people find such searches distressing and humiliating, and frequently ask the question 'Why me?'

When you may be searched
A customs officer may ask to search you or anything you have with you if he or she reasonably suspects that you are carrying:

* Any item which is liable to excise duty or tax which has not been paid; for example, perfume, alcohol, cigarettes, in excess of the duty-free allowance.
* Any item which is prohibited or restricted from being imported or exported; for example, illegal drugs.

A request to search you does not mean that you are under arrest; it means that you are to be detained whilst a search is carried out. If you are placed under arrest, you must be told.

Length of detention
How long you may be detained for will depend on the circumstances, but in all circumstances the length of detention must be reasonable and not exceed the time taken for the actual search, which is usually completed in under ten minutes. If you decide to leave before being searched, the customs officer may let you go or you may be arrested (see below). You may also (exceptionally) be charged with the offence of obstructing or impeding a customs officer.

What amounts to reasonable suspicion?

A customs officer does not have to be certain that you are carrying an unlawful item in order to justify a search. But there must be some concrete basis for the officer's suspicion which relates to you. The mere fact that you have arrived from a particular destination, that you are dressed in a certain way or that you are carrying particular items such as condoms, cigarette papers or petroleum jelly, which could be associated with drug use or drug trafficking, is not in itself sufficient justification. However, a combination of these or other factors, such as suspicious behaviour, an unusual quantity of luggage, unexplained journeys abroad, etc., may give rise to enough reasonable suspicion to justify your being searched.

What you must be told

The customs officer must tell you what you are suspected of: for example, 'I have reasonable grounds to suspect that you are carrying illegal drugs.' Although you should ask why you are suspected of a particular offence, the customs officer does not, in fact, have to tell you.

If you are asked to submit to a 'rub-down' search (see below), you must be told that you have the right to go before a senior customs officer if you do not agree with the search. In the case of a strip or intimate search (see below), you must be told that you have the right to be taken before either a senior customs officer or a magistrate who will then decide whether or not the search should take place.

Going before a senior customs officer or magistrate

If you decide to exercise your right to go before a senior customs officer or a magistrate, you are entitled to be present to hear the reasons why you should submit to a body search and have the opportunity to say why you disagree. If you wish someone to speak on your behalf, you should say so.

If you decide that you wish to go before a magistrate there may be some delay, but arrangements should be made to ensure that a magistrate is available at all times. It would not be reasonable to expect you to wait more than a couple of hours. If you are told or if it appears that the delay will be any longer than this, you should ask to see the most senior officer in attendance at the airport or port so that you may make an official complaint. If you decide to leave because of the unreasonable delay, you should ensure that the customs officer knows that this is the reason. As mentioned above, you do run the risk of being arrested if you decide to leave prior to the search taking place.

After hearing the evidence from both the customs officer requesting the search and yourself, the senior officer or magistrate (depending on whom you request to be taken before) will then direct whether or not the search is to take place and the form that the search may take.

What form may the search take?
The nature and extent of the search depends on what you are suspected of carrying and where. It may take any of the following forms:

- A 'pocket search' (i.e. removal of all items from pockets).
- A 'rub-down' (i.e. the body is frisked).
- A search of outer clothing (i.e. removal of outer coat, jacket, hat or gloves).
- A strip search (see below).
- An intimate search (see below).

Customs officers are instructed to ensure that any person searched is treated courteously and considerately. All 'rub-down' and strip searches can be carried out only by a person of the same sex as the person being searched. (For those who may carry out an intimate search see below.)

Strip search
A strip search is essentially a visual search of your body. You will be accompanied by two customs officers of the same sex as yourself to a private room and asked to remove your clothing. Customs officers are under a duty to make every reasonable effort to reduce to the minimum the embarrassment that you may experience. For example:

- You need not be completely naked at any time. It will usually be possible for the top and bottom halves of the body to be unclothed and reclothed separately. If this is not suggested to you, you should ask that you be allowed to undress in this way.
- If you are required to be naked, a blanket or other suitable covering should be provided. Again, if this is not offered to you, you should request it.

An intimate search
An intimate search consists of the physical examination of one or more of your body orifices (i.e. mouth, nose, ears, anus and genitalia) and may only be done if an officer of at least the rank of senior executive officer authorises it. The reason why it is thought necessary must be explained to you. The examination may only be carried out by a doctor or a nurse. No person of the opposite sex to yourself who is not a doctor or nurse should be present, nor should anyone whose presence is unnecessary. An intimate search of a juvenile (i.e. under the age of seventeen) or of a person who is mentally ill or mentally handicapped

may only take place in the presence of an appropriate adult (for example, a relative or social worker) who is of the same sex as the person being searched – unless the juvenile requests otherwise and the adult agrees.

If you do not consent to an intimate search, it is most unlikely that the doctor or nurse will agree to carry it out. However, you must remember that you run the risk of being arrested if you do not consent, particularly if the search has been authorised by a magistrate.

If you are arrested

A customs officer may arrest you if he or she has reasonable grounds to suspect that you are committing, or have committed, an offence as described above. You must be informed of why you are being arrested. The customs officer has the same powers to search you as described above if you are not under arrest and you have the same rights to be taken before a senior officer or a magistrate (see above). In addition, if you are under arrest, customs officers have the power to request that you submit to an intimate search if they believe you have an article on you that may cause a physical injury to yourself or others whilst in detention.

A customs officer of the same sex as yourself may carry out this search but only where a senior officer has authorised that it is not practicable for a doctor or nurse to do so. If you are under arrest, you may be detained for longer: up to twenty-four hours, or if it is alleged that you have committed a 'serious arrestable offence', up to thirty-six hours and to a maximum of ninety-six hours if a magistrate authorises further detention.

During detention you have the right:

- To inform someone of your arrest.
- To consult a solicitor in private.

However, exercising these rights may be delayed by thirty-six hours if you have been arrested for a 'serious arrestable offence'. You are entitled to a copy of your custody record (see Chapter 6). An intimate body sample such as urine or blood can only be taken with your consent in writing.

If you wish to make a complaint

If you feel that you have been unreasonably subjected to a body search or have any objections to the way in which it was carried out, you may complain in writing to the Collector (the person in overall charge of the airport or port) at the address of the airport or port at which the search took place. You may also take up the matter with your MP and request that your complaint be referred to the Paymaster General at the Treasury (the minister responsible for Customs and Excise).

3.10 Privacy and the media

The laws about breach of confidence, trespass, nuisance, surveillance, etc., apply equally to the media. Libel may restrict some intrusions on private life but only if the words are defamatory (see p. 39), and in reality it only helps the wealthy because legal aid is not available for libel actions.

'Malicious falsehood' is a growing cause of legal action. It was used against a newspaper which photographed a famous actor who was recovering in hospital from brain surgery. The court said that the remarks which the patient had made were wrongly portrayed as a voluntary and exclusive interview. Malicious falsehood can also be pursued even though the published material is at the same time a libel. The ban on legal aid does not apply to malicious falsehood. However, the ingredients are more difficult to establish: the victim must show that the words are false, that they were published maliciously (i.e. for some improper purpose), and that they have either caused financial loss or, in some cases, were likely to cause such loss.

Copyright can also be used as a way of preventing publication of private papers or pictures, but working out who owns copyright (and who is therefore the right person to bring an action) can be a complicated matter. Additional protection is given to a person who commissions photographs for private or domestic purposes. Even if copyright is owned by the photographer, that person can prevent their publication.

If the makers of television and radio programmes intrude on a person's privacy, a complaint can be made to the Broadcasting Standards Commission, a new body set up in April 1997 under the Broadcasting Act 1996. This new body took over the powers of the Broadcasting Complaints Commission and the Broadcasting Standards Council. The Commission can also consider complaints of unjust or unfair treatment which may overlap with intrusions of privacy but goes far wider. The complaint must relate to a programme which has been broadcast, but the Commission can insist on reviewing material which was filmed or recorded but not used. The Commission has no power to ban a programme in advance and cannot award compensation. However, it can insist that its findings are published and/or broadcast. See Chapter 5 for the address of the Commission.

The Broadcasting Standards Commission is a statutory body. There is no equivalent legislation for the press, but there is a Press Complaints

Commission which has been set up by the industry itself. The PCC has drawn up a code of conduct which prohibits intrusions into an individual's private life unless this is justified in the public interest. The PCC publishes its own findings. There is no obligation on a newspaper which is found to have breached the code to report the findings or to give it any particular prominence, although rival titles may be quick to report PCC criticism. See Chapter 5 for the address of the PCC. The PCC replaced the previous Press Council in 1991 after a report by the Calcutt Committee in 1990 condemned the inadequate protection for individual privacy. Three years later, Sir David Calcutt QC again reviewed the performance of the press and considered that it was still lamentable in its disrespect for privacy. He proposed a range of new measures including a statutory tribunal with the power to order compensation and publication of its adjudications on privacy matters. He also recommended that there should be new criminal offences of trespass on private property or the use of surveillance devices for the purposes of obtaining personal information. Calcutt considered that there should be public interest defences, but only in tightly defined situations. His proposals caused concern not only in the press itself, but amongst others who feared that the new rights would be used to spike stories of real public interest which did not fit neatly into the proposed defences. There was also concern that his suggestions might lead to new grounds for granting injunctions before trial and that the usual cautious approach of the courts to injunctions at that stage (where priority is given to preserving the status quo) would mean that even stories within his categories of public interest would not see the light of day.

In a consultation paper in 1993 the government suggested that there should be a statutory right to privacy which would allow individuals to sue for compensation in specific circumstances. In response, the newspaper industry in January 1994 appointed an ombudsman to deal with complaints. In 1995 the government decided not to introduce a statutory system for the regulation of the press.

3.11 Further information

Useful organisations
Consult your telephone directory for local addresses and telephone numbers of the following organisations:

- Law centres
- Citizens' Advice Bureaux

Bibliography

'Report of the Committee on Privacy and Related Matters', HMSO Cm 1102, 1990.

Sir David Calcutt, 'Review of Press Self-Regulation', HMSO Cm 2135, 1993.

'Privacy and Media Intrusion: The Government's Response', HMSO Cm 2918, 1995.

4

The right to know

Many organisations, both public and private, hold files on the people they deal with. Important decisions about you may be taken on the basis of your file, often by people who have never met or spoken to you. All they know about you is what the file says. If the information is incomplete, inaccurate or unfair, your rights may be at risk or you could be denied a benefit or service that you need. The best safeguard is a right to see the file for yourself, so you can challenge unjustified statements, correct factual inaccuracies and make your views known before – not after – decisions are taken.

Several laws allow people to see certain files held on them, and some information can also be obtained under the non-statutory 'open government' code of practice.

This chapter describes the rights you *do* have, to see:

- computer records
- government records
- health records
- housing records
- social work records
- school records.
- credit reference agency records
- other rights of access

STOP PRESS

The government has promised to create a new right to freedom of information. It is proposed that a consultation paper (a White Paper) will be published in 1997 and that a Bill to create this right will be published in 1998. This is a very important development but it is unlikely to be in force until 1999.

4.1 Computer records

The Data Protection Act 1984 gives you the right to see personal data about yourself held on computer. The Act applies to computerised information held by anyone, including government departments, public bodies, the NHS, the police, private sector and commercial organisations, employers and even individuals such as a GP or college lecturer.

But even the most highly computerised organisation usually has at least some information on paper too. There is no right to see these 'manual' files unless they are covered by one of the specific rights described later. However, new legislation providing access to many manual files will have to be introduced by October 1998 to comply with a European Directive. A White Paper concerning the Directive was published in July 1997.

The exemptions
The Data Protection Act allows certain information to be withheld. The main exemptions apply to:

National security
The Act does not apply to data which a cabinet minister has certified needs to be exempted to safeguard national security. Neither the courts nor the Data Protection Registrar, who enforces the Act, can challenge a ministerial certificate.

Law enforcement
Personal data held for the purpose of preventing or detecting crime, apprehending or prosecuting offenders, or assessing and collecting any tax or duty are exempt from access, but only if disclosure would prejudice one of those purposes.

The exemption is not restricted to bodies like the police or Inland Revenue. For example, information about suspected fraud held by a bank or a social security office would also be covered.

Not all law enforcement information is necessarily exempt. For example, if you are the victim of a crime you should be able to see what is held about you without much risk of prejudicing the purpose for which the record is held. But if you are the suspect, the chance of it being withheld will be much greater.

Personal information about someone else
This information will not be released to you without that person's consent. However, if the information can be disclosed to you in a way that does not identify the individual – for example, by deleting the name – then it must be.

The 'data user' (the person using the computer) is not required to ask someone who is referred to in your file for consent to let you see the information. But if you think you know who may be mentioned – for example, a family member – you can ask if they will sign a letter of consent which you can include with your application.

Details that would identify someone who has supplied information about you
These are exempt – though the information they have provided is not. Only identifiable individuals, not organisations, are protected.

Intentions
The intentions of the data user towards you are exempt. A note in your employment file saying your employer intended to promote or make you redundant could be withheld. However, opinions about you must be disclosed.

Word processing
The text of a document which is being written or stored on a computer does not have to be disclosed. A journalist writing an article on a computer does not have to let someone mentioned in it see it. But if the computer is used to process or analyse the data in any way – for example, to identify people with particular characteristics – then it is accessible.

Other exemptions
Other exemptions apply to data used purely to calculate pay or pensions or for business accounting purposes or for managing an individual's personal or family affairs; to some kinds of club membership records; to information kept solely for statistical or research purposes and published anonymously; and to lawyer–client communications. Additional exemptions, described later in this chapter, apply to medical and social work records.

Incomplete disclosure
One of the weaknesses of the Data Protection Act is that you need not be told if exempt information has been withheld – whether you have been given the full file, or only an edited version. You may even get a deliberately ambiguous reply to your request, such as 'We hold no data on you which we are required to disclose to you.' This either means there is no file on you – or that there is a file, but it is regarded as totally exempt.

Nevertheless, it is worth asking if anything has been held back: it may be difficult for the person involved to evade a direct question. If you suspect you have been refused access to information which is not genuinely exempt you can ask the Data Protection Registrar to investigate.

Applying

To apply, write to the organisation which holds the data, saying that you are applying under Section 21 of the Data Protection Act for access to any personal information about yourself held on computer. Sending your request by recorded delivery will help avoid any later dispute about whether or not it was received. If the data user has different offices or branches and you're not sure which to write to, telephone first and ask. Alternatively, contact the Data Protection Registrar's office or look at the organisation's Register entry, which can be found on the Internet (see below). Organisations must register under the Act and provide an address for 'subject access' requests in their register entry.

The data user is entitled to ask you for proof of your identity and for information needed to locate any file on you. It may help if you say what your relationship to the organisation is (e.g. customer, employee, student, patient), give any relevant dates or reference numbers and say which of its offices or branches you have dealt with – but don't volunteer any information which you regard as sensitive. You do not need to say why you want the information. The data user cannot refuse access because you might use the data to criticise it, complain or take legal action.

Fees

You may have to pay a fee. At the time of writing, the maximum is £10, though some organisations charge less or nothing.

Unfortunately, the charge can sometimes exceed this. If the data user has more than one register entry, for example, if data is held for different purposes, a separate application fee can be charged for each entry applied for. An application to the Metropolitan Police for information about you held on computer files about vehicle owners, disqualified drivers and stolen cars is covered by a single £10 application fee. But you would have to pay a second fee if you also wanted a search of records on parking tickets or traffic offences. Checking the files on pedal cycles and licensed taxi cabs would involve another £10 apiece. If the data user has an application form, this may explain the different register entries – and help you narrow your request down.

The data user must give access within forty days of receiving your request and any supplementary details needed. It can supply either a print-out or a typed copy of the information. Any unintelligible terms, such as computer codes, must be explained.

Parents and children

The Act has no minimum age limit for applicants. Except in Scotland, children can apply for their own records provided they are capable of understanding the nature of the request. A parent or guardian can only apply on the child's behalf if (a) the child has given consent or (b) the child is too young to understand the nature of the request *and* access is in the child's interests. A parent concerned about a small child's health probably would be able to see the medical record. But a parent wishing to defend him- or herself against allegations of child abuse, or looking for evidence to support a custody claim, probably would not.

In Scotland, a child must be sixteen to apply on his or her own behalf. A child's guardian, normally the parent, would exercise the right on behalf of a child under sixteen.

Inaccurate information

If you find that computerised data about yourself is factually incorrect or misleading, you are entitled to have it corrected or erased. Opinions cannot be challenged unless they are based on wrong facts. If you have been damaged by inaccurate data, you are entitled to ask a court to award you compensation.

Disclosures to others

The Data Protection Act gives you little control over what is done with your details. It does say that information must be obtained 'fairly', and the Registrar interprets this to mean that when you are asked for information you must be told to whom it might be disclosed – unless it is obvious, or the disclosure is required by law or for law enforcement purposes. Once you have been told that the information may be used for, say, mailing list purposes, you have no specific right to know which organisations have bought a list which includes your details.

The data user's register entry must state in general terms the kinds of organisations to whom it may want to disclose data, but need not give the names of the specific organisations. For example, it may tell you that disclosures will be made to local authorities, but not which ones.

Enforcing the Act

If a data user fails to comply with any of the Act's requirements – for example, if it withholds information which is not exempt, fails to respond to your request within forty days, or refuses to correct demonstrably inaccurate information – you can complain either to a court or to the Data Protection Registrar. The Registrar is usually preferable, as this costs you nothing.

You can also complain to the Registrar if a data user has failed to comply with the Data Protection Principles laid down in the Act. Briefly, these require organisations to obtain and process personal data fairly and lawfully; to hold, use and disclose it only for specified purposes which they have identified in their register entries; to ensure that the data is accurate, up to date, relevant to and not excessive for the purpose for which it is held and not kept longer than necessary, and is protected against improper disclosure.

You can contact the Registrar at:

Office of the Data Protection Registrar
Wycliffe House
Water Lane
Wilmslow
Cheshire
SK9 5AF
Tel: 01625 535 711

4.2 Government records

You can see information held on you by government bodies under the Code of Practice on Access to Government Information (also known as the 'Open Government' Code of Practice), which came into force in April 1994. The Code, which is not legally binding, is supervised by the Parliamentary Ombudsman and applies to government departments and agencies plus a small number of other central government bodies within the Ombudsman's jurisdiction.

The Ombudsman cannot investigate complaints against the police, the security and intelligence services, publicly owned companies and many individual quangos, so these bodies are not covered by the Code. However, the Government has said that central government quangos should introduce disclosure policies of their own, similar to the Code. These may help you – but you will not be able to complain to the Ombudsman if information is refused.

What the Code of Practice covers
The Code:

* commits departments and agencies to releasing information on request. It applies to official information generally, as well as to personal information. It covers information that may have been recorded before the Code came into force as well as afterwards;

- promises that departments and agencies will publish the internal guidance they use in dealing with the public. This means you should be able to see the procedures meant to be followed by officials who deal with say, your benefit application and check that you have been fairly treated;
- commits departments to giving you reasons for administrative decisions which affect you.

One of the Code's limitations is that it only offers access to 'information' and not to copies of actual documents. Departments may not be prepared to let you see copies of the files held on you and instead ask you to specify what particular information you want. You may be sent this information in a letter, rather than be given photocopies of documents, correspondence or reports from your file. However, if you need to see the actual documents you should ask for them and if necessary complain to the Ombudsman if you don't get them. The Ombudsman has said that if a document is requested, he may recommend that a photocopy of it be disclosed, provided that it does not contain any exempt information and can be disclosed in full.

Exemptions

The Code exempts various classes of information from disclosure. Two of these apply to entire classes of personal files. Employment records are exempt, so civil servants cannot see their own personnel files. Information relating to particular nationality, consular and entry clearance cases is also exempt.

Disclosures which would be 'an unwarranted invasion of privacy' are exempt. This protects personal information about yourself: it also means you will not be able to see private information about someone else which might form part of your file.

There is a long list of other exemptions. These include information harmful to national security, defence and foreign relations; disclosures which would 'harm the frankness and candour of internal discussion' such as civil servants' advice, policy analysis and communications between different departments; information which would prejudice law enforcement, legal or other formal proceedings; public safety, public order, the management of the economy, the collection of taxes, a public authority's competitive position, its negotiations, its commercial or contractual activities or 'the proper and efficient conduct' of its operations. Incomplete statistics or research whose disclosure 'could be misleading' is exempt. So is information whose disclosure could harm the competitive position of a third party, information which was supplied to the government in confidence by a third party or information whose disclosure is prohibited by any of the statutory restrictions on access. Departments can also refuse requests which are 'vexatious or manifestly unreasonable or are formulated in too general a manner or which ... would require unreasonable diversion of resources'. There are other exemptions as well.

However, the Code does say that most classes of exempt information can be disclosed if any harm that might result from disclosure is outweighed by the public interest in making the information available. It may be difficult to argue that a request that you are making for your own personal files is a matter of public interest. But if the information you are seeking has wider implications (for example, if it shows that a department is routinely ignoring its own rules, or that people are not receiving a benefit they are entitled to) you may want to argue that there is a public interest in disclosure, even if the information is exempt.

Fees

Straightforward requests are generally handled free of charge. However, if your request is time-consuming, you may be asked to pay a fee which depends on the number of hours of staff time spent on the request. A certain number of free hours is normally allowed (usually between one and five, depending on the department) followed by an hourly charge of £15 or £20. You will be told the likely charges in advance, and asked if you agree to pay.

Applying for information

You should make your application in writing to the body which holds the information you want. If you are not sure who to address it to, a list of 'open government contacts' in each department and agency to whom requests can be sent can be obtained from the Office of Public Service or from the Internet (see below).

Your letter should say that you are asking for the information under the Open Government Code of Practice, and ask for a reply to be sent to you within twenty days – the Code's target response time. Make your request as specific as possible: this will reduce your chances of being charged a fee, or having your request turned down altogether. (Requests can be refused if they are 'too general' or would cause 'unreasonable diversion of resources'.)

Appeals

If you are refused information, you should be told which exemption has been relied on. If you think information is not in fact exempt, you should ask the body concerned to review its decision. The review will normally be carried out at a more senior level within the department or agency. If, after this, you are still dissatisfied you can complain to the Parliamentary Ombudsman. But you must normally have asked the body concerned to reconsider its own decision first.

Unfortunately, you cannot write to the Ombudsman directly, you must ask an MP to refer your complaint to him. This can be done by any MP, not just your own constituency MP. Send the Ombudsman all the relevant correspondence and set out any reasons you have for thinking that the information should have been disclosed to you. You can also complain to the Ombudsman about unreasonable delay, charges or replies which you suspect are misleading.

The Code of Practice is not legally binding – it is not a Freedom of Information Act. So although the Ombudsman can recommend that a department disclose information, he cannot compel it to do so. However, the Ombudsman's recommendations carry weight in Whitehall and are usually accepted.

New legal rights to see manual records are likely to come into force by October 1998, when legislation to implement a European Data Protection Directive is required to be introduced. The legislation should give people a right to see information held about them in many kinds of manual files, perhaps including police and employment records. Information recorded before the new law comes into force is likely to be accessible. A White Paper concerning the Directive was published in July 1997.

4.3 Non-computerised records: some common features

A series of individual laws provide rights of access to manually held health, social work, housing and school records. The laws generally have a number of common features, which are given here to avoid repeating them in each of the following sections:

- Applications must be in writing.
- Only information recorded after the law came into force is accessible. In general, earlier information can only be seen on a voluntary basis, if the record holder agrees.
- There is a very limited exception to the above: some earlier information is accessible if, in the record holder's opinion, it is necessary to understand information to which the right of access does apply. This is most likely to apply if recent information explicitly refers back to something recorded before the right came into force.
- You can be charged a £10 fee for applying for your records. Unfortunately the government has refused to rule out 'double' payments. This means you can be charged one fee for asking for

your computerised, say, social work records and another £10 for access to the manual record. Fortunately, some record holders reduce or waive these fees.

- You are entitled to inspect the records and get photocopies, on payment of copying and postage costs.
- You have the right to have factually inaccurate information corrected. If the record holder does not accept that it is inaccurate you can either appeal against the decision and/or insist that a statement setting out your views about the disputed information is added to the record.
- Information about another identifiable individual, and any details which will identify someone who has supplied information about you is exempt.
- Information which is likely to cause 'serious harm' to your or someone else's health is exempt.
- Information held for law enforcement purposes can be withheld if disclosure would prejudice those purposes.
- The record holder can withhold information about its intentions towards you.
- For certain records (housing records and medical reports to insurers and employers) you have to be told if exempt information has been withheld from you. But you have no right to know when information has been withheld from health, social work or school records.

If you think you have been injured, for example, as a result of an accident or a medical mistake, and could be entitled to compensation, your solicitor will be able to obtain your medical records in full in the course of litigation. You may be entitled to a wider range of information than you would otherwise get under the Access to Health Records Act or the Code of Practice, since 'exempt' information cannot be withheld. Obtaining your records in this way does not commit you to carrying on with an action for compensation. But unless you are eligible for legal aid, you may have to pay some legal expenses.

4.4 Health records

- If your health records are held on computer, you are entitled to see them under the Data Protection Act (see above).
- If your records are held manually (i.e. on paper), the Access to Health Records Act entitles you to see any information recorded after November 1991.
- You can see information recorded about you before November 1991 under the Code of Practice on Openness in the NHS.

- You have the right to see a report which your doctor sends to an employer or an insurance company.
- All the above rights apply to both NHS and private health records, except for the Code of Practice which only applies to the NHS.

Access to records compiled after November 1991

The Access to Health Records Act 1990 allows people to see information about their physical or mental health which has been recorded manually by or on behalf of a 'health professional' who has treated them. It applies both to NHS and private medical records. The Act only applies to information recorded after November 1991.

The health professionals whose records can be seen are doctors, dentists, opticians, pharmacists, nurses, midwives, health visitors, chiropodists, dieticians, occupational therapists, orthoptists, physiotherapists, clinical psychologists, child psychotherapists, osteopaths, speech therapists, art or music therapists employed by a health service body and scientists who head health service departments. Other kinds of health records, for example, those held by various kinds of psychotherapists or alternative practitioners, are not accessible.

Applications must be made to the holder of the record, usually the GP, health authority or board or NHS trust. In private practice, applications should go directly to the health professional. You must be given access within forty days. If all you want is information added to your file in the last forty days, you must be given it within twenty-one days. This reduces delays for someone who only wants to see a recent entry about a current health problem.

You can inspect your record in person or authorise someone to look at it for you. Unintelligible terms must be explained.

Access must be given without charge if information has been added to your file in the last forty days, though you can be charged for any photocopies you ask for. This should allow free access to the whole file, back as far as November 1991, to anyone who has recently been seen by a health professional. NHS bodies sometimes try and charge in cases where access should be free. Be prepared to insist on free access if information has recently been put on your file. However, if nothing has been added to your file in the last forty days you can be charged a £10 access fee, plus the cost of any copies.

Children can apply for their own records. Parents normally require their child's consent before they can see the child's records. If the child is incapable of understanding the nature of the request, the parent can have access only if the record holder is satisfied that access is in the child's best interests. Even then, parents will not be allowed to see information which the child has provided in confidence, for example, about contraception, or problems in the home.

The relatives of someone who has died, have no right to the deceased's records. The only exception is if the death may have been caused by negligence. The Access to Health Records Act allows someone who might be entitled to compensation – usually a dependent – to get records relating to the cause of death.

Exemptions
There are two main exemptions.

'Serious harm'
Information likely to cause serious harm to the patient's or someone else's physical or mental health is exempt. Doctors argue that this is necessary, but it inevitably provokes suspicion in patients. Its purpose is to allow information to be withheld from, for example, someone with a mental illness whose condition could be seriously aggravated by seeing the record. It is not, however, a blanket exemption for psychiatric, or any other class of, patients. Studies have shown that most psychiatric patients benefit from seeing their medical records, provided they have been written in the knowledge that they might be seen and someone is available to help explain them.

Note that the exemption refers to 'serious' harm – not, for example, to distress. It is not intended to allow doctors to withhold possibly upsetting news from a patient, particularly one who could be helped to come to terms with it by suitable support and counselling.

This decision must be based on the advice of a health professional, normally the doctor treating the patient. A similar exemption applies to requests for computerised health records under the Data Protection Act.

Information about, or given by, another individual
Information about, or provided by, another identifiable individual other than a health professional is exempt. Your GP does not need a consultant's permission before showing you a report on you written by the consultant.

Enforcement
If a record holder does not comply with the Act you can enforce your rights in the courts. Where NHS records are involved you can also complain under NHS complaints procedures.

Access to records compiled before November 1991
The Access to Health Records Act does not apply to information recorded before November 1991, except where access to such earlier information is necessary in order 'to make intelligible' any information

to which the right of access does apply. If something in your records cannot be understood without seeing a pre-November 1991 part of the record, you should be able to see it.

In other cases, you are entitled to information from your pre-1991 NHS health records under the Code of Practice on Openness in the NHS. This non-statutory Code came into force in June 1995 and commits health authorities and trusts and doctors, dentists, opticians and community pharmacists to release information on request. It applies to any information held by these bodies, including personal information held about you, and extends to information recorded before it came into effect.

The Code is broadly similar to the Open Government Code of Practice described above and contains similar exemptions. The NHS Code also offers access to 'information' rather than copies of actual documents, and this means that while NHS bodies are required to let you have details of what is recorded about you they do not have to show you the copies of the file itself. However, the Ombudsman's view is that provided that none of the information you have asked for is exempt, he or she may recommend that a photocopy of the original should be disclosed.

NHS bodies can set their own charges for information, but the Code recommends that these 'should be exceptional'. It says that where they are made they should not apply to the first hour of staff time; thereafter fees of up to £20 an hour may be charged.

Information should normally be provided to you within twenty days of your request. If you are dissatisfied with a decision to refuse information or with delays or charges you should complain to the Chief Executive of the body responsible. If that fails you can complain to the Health Service Ombudsman, who can be contacted at:

Church House
Great Smith Street
London
SW1P 3BW
Tel: 0171 276 3000.

Insurance and employment medical reports

If your doctor writes a report on your health for an insurance company or an employer you have the right to see it before it is sent under the Access to Medical Reports Act 1988.

Any doctor who is or has been involved in your medical care is covered. But a report by an independent doctor, who has never treated you, and acts solely for the insurer or employer will not be accessible.

An employer or insurer cannot contact your doctor unless it has your written consent and has informed you of your rights under the Act. You must be given the chance to say whether you want to see the report before it is sent. If you say yes, the doctor is supposed to wait twenty-one days before sending the report, to allow you to arrange to see it. Get in touch with your doctor straight away and ask to be contacted as soon as the report is ready.

No charge can be made if you just inspect the report; if you want a copy you can be charged a 'reasonable fee'.

If information has been withheld under an exemption (e.g. for 'serious harm') you are entitled to be told.

If you see the report and are unhappy with it – for example, if you feel it involves an unacceptable breach of your privacy, or misrepresents the true picture – you have the right to stop it being sent. But if you do, the employer or insurer may not be willing to offer you the job or insurance policy – so do not take this step lightly.

The doctor is required to keep a copy of the report for six months after sending it, and you have the right to see it during this period. You may want to do this if you are unexpectedly refused insurance or employment.

Enforcement

If you believe that a doctor, employer or insurance company has breached the Act you can apply to a court for an order requiring compliance. If a doctor has sent a report without your consent, this may be a breach of medical confidentiality. You may have grounds for a complaint to the General Medical Council.

4.5 Housing records

If you are or have been a local authority tenant, have applied to be one, or have bought your council home, you have the right to see the council's housing records on you. Regulations under the Access to Personal Files Act 1987 entitle you to information recorded after April 1989 – in Scotland, after August 1992.

Access must be given within forty days. Information likely to cause you or someone serious harm, and information about or provided by someone else can be withheld – but not if the person is a member of your family living with you or a housing officer or a health professional. If information about someone else is on your file, the authority is obliged to contact the person and ask if they will let you see it, a requirement which does not apply to other types of records. For further details see the Access to Personal Files (Housing)

Regulations 1989 and the Access to Personal Files (Housing)(Scotland) Regulations 1992.

There is no right of appeal to the courts. The regulations say that complaints must be considered either by a group of councillors who were not involved in the original decision or by the full council. You may also be able to complain to the Local Government Ombudsman, who investigates complaints about councils' 'maladministration'.

4.6 Social work records

Other regulations under the Access to Personal Files Act 1987 give you the right to see information about yourself recorded after April 1989 on a local authority's social work records.

The exemptions are generally the same as for housing records (see above). The main differences are:

- You can only see information about yourself – not other members of your family.
- Information about identifiable social workers or people paid by the social services department for doing related work (e.g. a foster parent or child minder) cannot be withheld.
- Information which would be likely to cause serious harm to your or someone else's physical or mental health or emotional condition can be withheld. The Department of Health's guidance says that only in the 'most exceptional' circumstances should information be withheld on these grounds.
- You have no legal right to be told if exempt information has been withheld.
- Appeals must be heard by a committee of three councillors, no more than one of whom may be a member of the social services committee.

Children
Children are entitled to apply for access to their own records and parents cannot normally see information about them unless (a) the child consents or (b) the child is too young to understand the nature of the application *and* access is in the child's best interests.

There is no exemption for information relating to child abuse as such. Disclosures likely to identify an informant who has reported suspected abuse can be withheld, but not where the person is a social worker or health professional. Information likely to expose the child or anyone else to serious risk is exempt. Parents will probably not be able to see information which the child has provided to social workers in confidence, or anything likely to expose the child to pressure to withdraw allegations, or risk of reprisals or continued abuse. But parents should normally be able to see information about themselves – as opposed to the child – such as a social worker's notes of an interview with the parent.

For further details see the Access to Personal Files (Social Services) Regulations 1989, the Access to Personal Files (Social Work) (Scotland) Regulations 1989 and the guidance contained in Department of Health Circular LAC(89)2.

4.7 School records

Parents, and older pupils, have the right to see information recorded in school records after September 1989 or, in Scotland, after October 1990. Local education authority (LEA) maintained schools, grant maintained schools and all special schools are covered – but records of independent schools are not.

The parents of a pupil under eighteen can see the records, as can a pupil who is sixteen or above. Access must be given within fifteen school days of a request and – unlike most other kinds of records – is free, though the costs of any copies supplied can be charged.

Any material in a pupil's educational record produced by a teacher, an education welfare officer or an employee of the LEA is accessible – but information supplied by others is not. A teacher's private notes, kept purely for his or her personal use are exempt – but not if they are available to other teachers. Other exemptions apply to information likely to cause serious harm to the pupil or anyone else, information relating to potential child abuse and references about a pupil sent to employers, colleges or universities. There is no right to be told when exempt information has been withheld. Appeals are dealt with by the school governors.

For further details see the Education (School Records) Regulations 1989 and the School Pupil Records (Scotland) Regulations 1990 and Department of Education and Science Circular No 17/89.

4.8 Credit reference records

When you apply for a loan, credit card, bank account or mortgage, the chances are that the company involved will run a check on you with a credit reference agency. These agencies check the electoral register to confirm that people live where they say they do, and report on bad debts, bankruptcies and perhaps on how well people keep up repayments of existing loans. If any of the information about you is wrong, it could be extremely damaging.

When they supply information about you, credit reference agencies may also include information about other people who live or used to live at your address. Following a legal ruling by the Data Protection Tribunal, agencies now can only supply information about other people if they are family members, living in the same household. But this still means you could be refused credit because someone else in your family is a bad credit risk.

Under the Consumer Credit Act 1974 you have the right to know whether a lender has consulted a credit reference agency, and if so which one. If you are refused credit, ask the lender to give you these details. Whether or not you have been refused credit, you are entitled to see what a credit reference agency holds about you.

To apply, write to the agency enclosing a £1 application fee. Give your full name and address and any other addresses you have lived at during the past six years. The information must be sent to you within seven days.

If the file contains mistakes, the agency must correct them and tell you what it has done within twenty-eight days. If it refuses, or you aren't satisfied with the amendment you can send it a note of correction of up to 200 words which it must add to your file and send out whenever information about you is supplied in future.

There are two main credit reference agencies:

CCN Group Ltd
Consumer Help Service
PO Box 40
Nottingham
NG7 2SS
Tel: 0115 986 8172

Equifax Europe Ltd
Dept 1E
PO Box 3001
Glasgow
G81 2DR
Tel: 01990 143 700

Enforcement

If you have a complaint about a credit reference agency, write to:

Director General of Fair Trading
Field House
Bream's Building
London
EC4A 1PR
Tel: 0171 242 2858.

4.9 Employment and other records

There are no rights of access at all to certain kinds of manual records, although the equivalent computerised records are available under the

Data Protection Act. Police records and those held in manual form by banks, building societies and other commercial organisations are not accessible. There is no right to see employment records, although some employers have introduced their own access policies. Even in the absence of a policy you may occasionally get access, if the person holding the record feels you have a good case and the request is made in a non-confrontational manner.

If you are dismissed and bring a tribunal complaint, you may be able to get your employment records during the case. But these are not available otherwise. Nor are job references. There is little you can do if you think your job prospects are being harmed by an unfair reference, unless you manage to get hold of the reference and can demonstrate that it is inaccurate. You may then have grounds for a negligence or defamation action or, if the information was derived from a computer file, be able to seek compensation under the Data Protection Act. But as there is no right to see references these are not usually options.

It may be worth trying to discuss the matter with the organisation giving the reference. If you think you know why you are getting the bad reference it may also be worth raising the matter directly with a prospective employer, so you can put your side of the story.

4.10 Other rights of access

This chapter has only dealt with access to personal files. There are also other rights to other information. For example, the Local Government (Access to Information) Act 1985 allows the public to attend meetings of local authorities and their committees and sub-committees and to see agendas, reports, minutes and background papers – subject to a series of exemptions. A meeting will usually be closed to the public if personal information about someone is being discussed and even if the information is about you, you will have no right to attend or see the papers. However, the local authority associations have published a Good Practice Note on Access to Information which encourages councils to introduce their own access policies and voluntarily allow people to see their own personal information and details about council policies.

At the time of the local authority's annual audit, a local authority must make available to 'any persons interested', all 'books, deeds, contracts, bills, vouchers and receipts' relating to the audit. These must be available for inspection for fifteen days, and the public notice given by advertising in local newspapers. This is one of the most powerful access rights on the UK statute books. There is no exemption for commercial confidentiality: indeed, the only information that can be withheld are details about identifiable members of the council's staff. An authority which fails to allow such inspection commits an offence under the Accounts and Audit Regulations 1983.

The Environmental Information Regulations 1992, which implement a European directive, provide a general right of access to information about the environment held by public bodies, again subject to broad exemptions. Government departments, local authorities and and other bodies with 'public responsibilities for the environment' must make available information about the state of the air, water, land, and animal and plant life; about activities which adversely affect any of these, and about measures designed to protect them from damage.

There are also many laws which forbid the disclosure of information. The best known of these is the Official Secrets Act 1989, which makes it an offence to disclose official information potentially harmful to defence, foreign relations, law enforcement, the work of the security and intelligence services, or any information about action taken under a warrant to intercept communications or enter premises. The government has rejected calls for a 'public interest defence' to this Act, so a defendant cannot argue that he or she was justified in releasing information which revealed serious wrongdoing. There are statutory restrictions on disclosure in some 250 other laws. Some protect personal information, but others prevent the disclosure of safety information and other matters of public interest.

Many countries now have freedom of information laws, giving the public an enforceable right of access to government records. These include the USA, Canada, Australia, New Zealand, France, Denmark, Holland, Norway, Greece, Hungary and Sweden – which has had a freedom of information act since 1766. Until Britain follows suit secrecy will too often still be the norm.

4.11 Further information

Useful organisations

Campaign for Freedom of Information
Suite 102
16 Baldwins Gardens
London EC1N 7RJ
Tel: 0171 831 7477

You can find the addresses and telephone numbers of the following in your telephone directory:

* Law Centres
* Citizens' Advice Bureaux

Bibliography

Patrick Birkinshaw, *Freedom of Information, the Law, the Practice and the Ideal*, Butterworths, 2nd edition, 1996

Testing the Open Government Code of Practice, a guide to the two Codes, and with a copy of the Open Government Code itself, from the Campaign for Freedom of Information (address above) price £1.50

Code of Practice on Access to Government Information, and a leaflet 'Explaining the Code of Practice' which contains a list of departmental open government contacts, from Room 417b, Office of Public Service, 70 Whitehall, London SW1A 2AS or by telephoning 0345 223242, or on the Internet at: http://www.open.gov.uk/m-of-g/code.htm

Code of Practice on Openness in the NHS, from Room 5/E/59, NHS Executive, Quarry House, Quarry Hill, Leeds LS2 7UE and on the Internet at: http://www.open.gov.uk/doh/codemain.htm

Open Government. Select Committee on the Parliamentary Commissioner for Administration, 2nd report, session 1995–96, HMSO, HC 84.

Annual Report on the Code of Practice on Access to Government Information, available from the Office of Public Service, address above.

Annual Report of the Data Protection Registrar, available from HMSO.

The Data Protection Register can be found on the Internet at http://www.open.gov.uk/dpr/dprhome.htm

5

The right of redress (complaints and legal action)

This chapter contains information on:

- Civil action and judicial review.
- Government departments.
- Local government.
- Health services and care services.
- The police.
- Courts and legal services.
- Financial professions.
- The media.
- Public utilities.
- Miscellaneous complaints.
- Compensation for the victims of crime.
- Complaints and European law.
- Other international treaties.
- The Citizen's Charter.
- Further information.

5.1 Civil action and judicial review

Civil action
If another person, or an organisation, has breached the terms of a contract made with you, or if in some other way they have infringed your rights (for example, by acting negligently in their treatment of you or assaulting you) you have the right to take civil legal proceedings against them. Unlike criminal proceedings (where the State almost always has the role of prosecuting individuals who are alleged to have broken the criminal law), in a civil action one party takes proceedings against another party. Many civil cases will concern a claim that one side has broken their contract with the other, but a civil action can also relate to the duties which are imposed by the common law without the need for there to be a contract. For example, a civil action can be brought if a person defames you or trespasses on your land.

Most civil cases will be brought in the County Court (although cases concerning very large sums of compensation will begin in the High Court). The usual remedy is financial (damages) and sometimes a court order instructing a party either to carry out a particular course of action or to stop doing so (an injunction). You can obtain the appropriate forms to start a civil action from your local County Court, but it is advisable to seek advice from a solicitor and you could be eligible for financial support to do so, under the Green Form legal aid scheme.

Judicial review

If you wish to challenge a decision of a public body, in addition to the complaints mechanisms explained below, you may be able to do so by taking judicial review proceedings in the High Court. Judicial review can be applied for in relation to any public body, including government departments, local authorities, the police and other organisations exercising a public function. The grounds for such cases will usually be that the body acted 'illegally' or 'irrationally' or that the decision was reached unfairly because of a defect in the procedure which led to the decision. The usual remedy if a case succeeds is that the public body will be ordered by the court to reconsider or change its decision. Damages may also be available in certain circumstances. Judicial review applications must usually be initiated very quickly (within three months of the decision being challenged). It is a complicated procedure and legal advice should be sought. Legal aid is available for judicial review cases.

STOP PRESS

The new government proposes to incorporate the European Convention on Human Rights into domestic law. The rights in the Convention are set out in Chapter 5. A Bill to incorporate the Convention is due to be published in the autumn of 1997 and this is likely to become an Act by July 1998 and to come into force not before January 1999. It is not clear at the time of writing exactly what effect this will have on our laws. It is likely that the Convention will be able to be used to challenge some of the existing procedures and judge-made law although whether the Convention will be given a higher status than statute is not so clear. Nevertheless the rights set out in this book may be enhanced by the Convention and in future the rights in the Convention will have to be considered much more seriously than they have been in the past.

5.2 Government departments

If you wish to complain about the way that your case has been handled by a department of central government, or by some non-departmental bodies (a list of which can be obtained from the address below) the Parliamentary Commissioner for Administration (or Parliamentary Ombudsman) exists for this purpose. The Ombudsman has the power to investigate complaints of injustice or loss arising from maladministration, a term which includes such faults as delay, bias and arbitrary decision making. These powers include making government departments show investigators all relevant documents. Regular reports are also made to Parliament and the Ombudsman has a committee of MPs who can follow up reports. The Ombudsman cannot award you damages, but in the past recommendations that money be paid back or compensation be given have been accepted by the departments concerned. The Ombudsman cannot go to court on your behalf, and the decision whether to take up a complaint and make an investigation is entirely up to the Ombudsman.

If you feel that you have a good complaint in that you have lost out in some way because of maladministration, you cannot complain directly to the Ombudsman but must do so via an MP (any MP). You should first have complained to the department and used up all internal tribunals and appeals. There is no charge for the Ombudsman's services and any expenses you incur during the investigation can be reimbursed. You can contact your own MP locally or write to him or her or any other MP at the House of Commons. The Ombudsman's address is:

The Parliamentary Commissioner for Administration
Church House
Great Smith Street
London SW1P 3BW
Tel: 0171 273 6450.

There are some areas in which the PCA cannot act: national security, civil service employment and government contracts being among them. The decision reached is not legally binding on the department involved but is usually followed. Northern Ireland has its own Commissioner, whose address is:

Office of the Northern Ireland Parliamentary Commissioner
33 Wellington Place
Belfast BT1 6HN
Tel: 01232 233821.

5.3 Local government

There are different ombudsmen for local government, but they exist to carry out the same sort of investigation. You can complain directly to the relevant ombudsman's office about maladministration by any local body such as the local authority or police authority, but only once you have exhausted all the procedures used by the body you are complaining about. The Commissioner for Local Administration can look into a local education authority but cannot examine matters relating to the direct provision of teaching. Nor can the Commissioner look into matters which should have been taken to a court or tribunal. There are several specific areas which do not come within the jurisdiction of the Commissioner, i.e. issues affecting all or most of the inhabitants of a council's area; personnel matters; the internal affairs of schools and colleges, and contracts for supply of goods and services to the Council. There is a twelve-month time limit for complaints to the Commissioner for Local Administration, but this can be extended in exceptional circumstances. Investigations into local health authorities may also be undertaken, but in some areas specialist bodies exist. England has three Commissioners for different regions and Wales and Scotland have one each. Their addresses are:

For London and the South
21 Queen Anne's Gate
London SW1H 9BU
Tel: 0171 915 3210

For the Midlands
The Oaks
Westwood Way
Westwood Business Park
Coventry CV4 8JB
Tel: 01203 695999

For the North
Beverly House
17 Shipton Road
York YO3 6FZ
Tel: 01904 663 200

For Scotland
23 Walker Street
Edinburgh EH3 7HX
Tel: 0131 225 5300

For Wales
Derwen House
Court Road
Bridgend
Mid Glamorgan CF31 1BL
Tel: 01656 661325

5.4 Health services and care services

The way to complain about matters connected to the provision of state
healthcare depends on the profession of the person about whom you
wish to complain and which aspect of their work you wish to complain
about. You should consider all the options below before taking any
action. Advice and assistance in all Health Service complaints is
available from your local Community Health Council (see your
telephone book) who can help write letters and present cases.

Complaints against general practitioners

These fall into two categories; those about breach of the GP's
conditions of employment and those relating to behaviour.

Complaints about a GP not meeting his or her contractual
obligations to the NHS as his or her employer, as well as complaints
about dentists, chemists and opticians go to the Family Health Services
Authority. The address of your local FHSA will be in your phone book
and it is also on your medical card. Complaints should be made in
writing to the General Manager. The FHSA can formally investigate
such matters as failure to come to a call-out outside surgery hours.
There is a time limit on complaints of thirteen weeks from the event
causing the complaint (thirteen weeks from finding the cause or six
months from the treatment in the case of dentists). You can make a
complaint for someone else who is unable to do so.

Informal complaints can cover any aspect of the service provided
by a surgery but only breaches of the GP's contract with the NHS can
be formally investigated by a committee of medical and lay members.
At this hearing, you can put your own case or have a friend's help. You
will receive a copy of the findings and if your complaint is proved, the
GP may be disciplined. You cannot receive compensation from the
committee – you would have to go to court for this – but you can claim
back expenses. The decision can be appealed to the Secretary of State
for Health and the Health Service Commissioner can investigate how
the FHSA handled your case (see below).

Complaints about hospitals

Initially, if you are dissatisfied with your treatment in hospital, you
should speak to the ward sister. Under the Patient's Charter, you are

allocated a named nurse whose name you should be told and who is responsible for your care. If this does not solve the problem, go to the Unit General Manager (hospital manager) or District General Manager or the Chair of the District Health Authority. If the hospital is a NHS trust, complain to the Chief Executive.

If you are still unhappy, you can go to the Health Service Commissioner (ombudsman) at:

Church House
Great Smith Street
London SW1P 3BW
Tel: 0171 276 3000

The ombudsman cannot investigate matters of clinical judgement. You should complain in writing within a year and you must have complained to the health authority first. The Commissioner has powers similar to the PCA and covers all hospital services such as ambulances, but not GPs. Ombudsmen exist also for Scotland and Wales. They can be contacted at:

First Floor, 28 Thistle Street
Edinburgh EH2 1EN
Tel: 0131 225 7465

Fourth Floor, Pearl Assurance House
Greyfriars Road
Cardiff CF1 3AG
Tel: 01222 394621

Complaints about nurses and midwives

These professions are covered by a national council which may take action on a complaint of conduct which brings the profession into disrepute. Its address is:

UK Central Council for Nursing, Midwifery and Health Visiting
23 Portland Place
London W1N 3AF
Tel: 0171 637 7181.

Complaints about doctors

If your complaint is about improper behaviour by a doctor (such as sexual harassment or fraud) address it to:

The General Medical Council
178 Great Portland Street
London W1N 6JE
Tel: 0171 580 7642.

The GMC is the governing body for doctors and may discipline its listed doctors, including disqualifying them from practice. It does not investigate complaints of medical negligence or incompetence. Leaflets exist to help you make a complaint – see your Community Health Council.

Complaints of negligence

In this case you should first go to the appropriate consultant. If this does not work, complain to the Regional Medical Officer at the Regional Health Authority, who may organise an investigation by specialists.

If this does not work, or you seek monetary damages, you could consider going to court in a private action for negligence. Be careful, as the law tends towards the doctor, although it is better than it used to be. Advice on this matter can be sought from a solicitor, from your Community Health Council or from:

Action for the Victims of Medical Accidents
Bank Chambers
1 London Road
Forest Hill
London SE23 8TP
Tel: 0181 291 2793.

Complaints about community care

Write first to the Director of Social Services. This may lead to informal problem solving, registering a complaint or a formal review by a panel which reports to the local authority. Leaflets telling you who to complain to in social services and the DSS are available from Citizens' Advice Bureaux and other advice centres. If the complaint is of mal-administration, it could go to the Commissioner for Local Administration.

If your complaint is about social security payments, you should go to your local office of the Benefits Agency, the address of which will be in the phone book. They have procedures for dealing with complaints and appeals, which include a system of tribunals.

5.5 The police

If you are dissatisfied with your treatment by the police, the first thing to do is to get as many details as possible about the officer(s) who dealt with you: their names, numbers, car number and so on, as well as details of any witnesses. Such information will be important. Write down what happened as soon as you can, this again will help later. Anyone can make a police complaint. You need not be a 'victim' as such of police misconduct. You might, for example, have been a witness to an incident which you feel should be the subject of a complaint.

Before making a complaint you should consider the following points:

- Complaints must be made within one year of the incident. If you are worried or uncertain, always take advice first. Do not allow yourself to be pressurised by the police or anyone else into making your complaint on the spot.
- Your complaint must be about a particular officer or officers, not about general police practice or policy. This is why it is important to try to identify the officer(s) involved. If you have a general complaint concerning policing practice, you should raise the matter with your MP and the Home Office. Complaints about local policing policy can be taken up through your Police Consultative Committee or Police Authority (or Home Secretary for the police in London).

Before making your complaint against the police, it is a good idea to get advice from a solicitor, law centre or Citizens' Advice Bureau (CAB), particularly if you are also considering a civil action against the police (see below). If you do not have much money, you should consult any solicitor who does legal aid work and ask for Green Form advice. This advice will be free, or virtually free, depending on your income and savings. For more information, see p. 131.

How should a complaint be made?

A complaint can be made verbally at a police station but your views will be more accurately recorded if you submit your complaint in writing and retain a copy for yourself. You should write to the appropriate Chief Constable or, if in London, to the Metropolitan Police Commissioner. Give as many details as you can and be honest and accurate, because the police could take legal action if they are falsely accused of wrongful conduct. The complaint must be registered by the police.

If you do not want to contact the police yourself, you may ask someone else to put your complaint forward for you, for instance, a Citizens' Advice Bureau, law centre, solicitor, your employer, trade union representative or a friend. You will need to give them written consent to do so.

In some cases the police may need to take action as soon as a complaint is received to get evidence which might not be available later. For example, if you complain about an assault while you are in custody, the police would normally ask a police doctor to examine you then and there but only if you are willing. Nobody can compel you to be examined.

The police may wish to try to settle the matter informally, with an officer of at least the rank of chief inspector mediating. This can only happen if you agree to it. Informal resolution is quicker and simpler than formal investigation. If you do not agree to informal resolution, if attempts at informal resolution do not work or if your complaint turns out to be more serious than originally thought, it can be formally investigated instead.

How does informal resolution work?

An officer of the rank of chief inspector, or at least of the rank of the officer(s) concerned, will be appointed to oversee the procedure. He or she must ask you and the officer(s) concerned for your views of the incident under investigation. Although the procedure is meant to be informal, you may still want to give your views in writing or have someone else with you when you are interviewed about your complaint. If there were witnesses to the incident who would support your complaint, you should ask the officer in charge to interview them. The officer should take any other appropriate steps, but no specific procedure is laid down. The appointed officer can apologise to you on behalf of the officer(s) concerned if that officer(s) admits the misconduct; even without the officer's admission, it is possible that an apology on behalf of the Chief Constable, or the force generally, will be made, but there is no power to require the police officer(s) to take part. If you are asked to attend a meeting to discuss your complaint, you can insist that it take place away from police premises and that you have someone to accompany you.

If you are not satisfied by the informal resolution, you can request that your complaint be formally investigated instead (minor complaints are rarely upheld using the formal procedure, however).

If a complaint is informally resolved, there will be no formal entry in the personnel record of the officer(s) concerned. A record will be kept, however, and you are entitled to a copy if you request it within three months of the complaint having been resolved.

What is the Police Complaints Authority and how does it work?

Investigation of all complaints is conducted by the police themselves. In certain cases, however, their investigation will be supervised by the

Police Complaints Authority (PCA). The PCA is a civilian body whose members are not, and never have been, members of the police. The chair is appointed by Her Majesty, and no fewer than eight other members are appointed by the Home Secretary. Members are appointed for a maximum of three years at a time. The Home Secretary appoints two of the members to the position of deputy chair.

The PCA must supervise any complaint alleging that the conduct of a police officer:

- resulted in death or serious injury to another person; or
- constituted assault causing actual bodily harm, or constitutes a 'serious arrestable offence'.

In addition, the Chief Constable or Commissioner may ask the PCA to supervise the investigation of any other complaint.

What happens when a complaint is formally investigated?

If the investigation is to be formal, the Chief Constable or Commissioner must appoint an investigating officer of at least the rank of chief inspector and not lower in rank than the officer(s) concerned. The investigating officer must be from a different sub-division or branch and can be appointed from a different police force.

The officer(s) you have complained about will be informed of your complaint and cautioned that any statement he or she (or they) makes may be used in disciplinary proceedings. The officer(s) and any police witnesses will be interviewed and statements taken. Then you and your witnesses will be asked to meet the investigating officer to give full statements.

The investigating officer will then report to the Chief Constable or Commissioner who may:

- Refer to the Director of Public Prosecutions (DPP) if the officer has committed a criminal offence.
- Not refer but notify the Police Complaints Authority of the possibility that there was a criminal offence and of any disciplinary action taken.
- Notify the Authority of any disciplinary charges made against the officer(s).
- Notify the Authority that he or she will take no action.

The Authority can order the Chief Constable or Commissioner to refer a case to the DPP or to bring disciplinary charges, even if he or she has said he or she does not intend to. Serious investigations may (and if very serious must) be supervised by the Authority who will consider the report itself.

When does a complaint involve prosecution by the DPP?

If the investigation report indicates that a criminal offence may have been committed, the Chief Constable or Commissioner will probably refer the complaint to the DPP. It remains for the DPP to decide whether the officer(s) should be prosecuted. But in fact very few officers are ever prosecuted.

What are the disciplinary charges and when can they be brought?

The Chief Constable or Commissioner must also consider whether disciplinary charges should be brought and must inform the PCA whether or not they intend to bring disciplinary proceedings. The PCA may recommend that the officer(s) be charged, and if the Chief Constable or Commissioner refuses to comply with this recommendation, the PCA can direct him or her to do so.

The possible disciplinary offences are set out in the Police Discipline Code. These include, for example, abuse of authority, improper disclosure of information, failing without good cause to follow the Codes of Practice established under the Police and Criminal Evidence Act 1984 and racially discriminatory behaviour.

An officer(s) against whom disciplinary charges are brought must face a disciplinary hearing; if the charge is upheld, a punishment will be awarded. Disciplinary hearings are conducted by the Chief Constable or Commissioner of the officer's own force, or by the Deputy Chief Constable or Commissioner to whom responsibility may be delegated. In some cases a Chief Constable from another force might take their place. If the officer(s) involved has already been prosecuted by the DPP, no disciplinary charge may be brought for an offence which is 'in substance' the same as the criminal offence, whether or not the officer(s) was acquitted or convicted.

What is the complainant's role at the disciplinary hearing?

If the officer(s) denies the charge, you will be expected to attend the disciplinary hearing to give evidence although it is likely that this is the only part of the hearing you will be allowed to attend. You may be accompanied by a friend but you cannot be legally represented by a lawyer. The police officer(s), however, is entitled to be legally represented at the disciplinary hearing in all serious cases and in other cases only at the discretion of the Deputy Chief Constable.

You will normally be called as the first witness. You should be told what the officer(s) has been charged with and whether he or she admits or denies it. You will be allowed to question the officer(s) but you will not be allowed to ask questions which are considered to be irrelevant, including any questions concerning previous disputes between yourself and the same officer(s).

If found guilty of a disciplinary offence, the police officer(s) can be punished in a variety of ways, including a reprimand or caution, a fine, a reduction in rate of pay or rank, a requirement to resign, or dismissal.

The officer(s) can appeal to the Home Secretary against both the finding of guilt and the punishment. The Home Secretary can appoint a three-member panel to enquire into the matter before deciding the appeal, and must do so if the officer(s) has been punished with the loss of either job or rank. In this case the complainant may have to give evidence again.

Bringing a complaint against senior officers

If your complaint concerns the conduct of an officer above the rank of superintendent, your complaint will be directed to the police authority for the officer's area (except in London where the Commissioner also deals with complaints about senior officers – other than those against him- or herself or the Deputy Assistant Commissioner or Commander, in which case the Home Secretary takes over). The police authority is an organisation made up of magistrates and local councillors and is responsible for the efficiency of the police.

The decision to deal with minor complaints against senior officers by informal resolution is at the police authority's discretion, and your consent to your complaint being dealt with in this way is not a legal requirement for this procedure to be pursued. If your complaint is to be investigated by the police authority, the officer appointed on behalf of the authority must be of at least the same rank as the officer about whom you have complained. The role of the PCA in supervising the investigation applies equally to complaints against senior officers (see 'The Police Complaints Authority' above).

Disciplinary charges against senior officers are drawn up by an independent solicitor and are heard by a single person appointed by the police authority or commissioner from a list provided by the Lord Chancellor.

Note: a senior officer cannot be suspended by a police authority whilst a complaint is being investigated unless the PCA approves the suspension.

The Police Act 1996 will make some changes to the complaints and discipline systems, when the relevant provisions of the Act are brought into force.

Conclusion

The police complaints system is criticised because it still involves the police investigating the police thus lacks the necessary independence. The Police Complaints Authority has itself advocated that in special cases an *ad hoc*, non-police investigating team should be appointed. Another problem faced by complainants is that proving complaints is difficult because the criminal standard of proof applies, so disciplinary proceedings must be proved beyond reasonable doubt. As the Police Complaints Authority has said, if a complainant's statement conflicts with statements made by the police it will be impossible to reconcile the different accounts and so the complaint will usually not be upheld.

If you wish to contact the Police Complaints Authority direct you may do so at:

10 Great George Street
London SW1P 3AE
Tel: 0171 273 6450.

Taking legal action yourself

Suing the police – civil action

You may bring a civil action against the police and seek damages to compensate you for your injuries and loss. The categories under which the police can be sued include the following:

* Assault and battery or the use of excessive force in arrest or detention.
* False imprisonment or restricting your liberty unlawfully (for example, detaining you without justification or for too long without charge).
* Trespass or searching property without proper authority.
* Malicious prosecution or bringing a prosecution without any good reason – which then fails.
* Negligence or failure to meet the standard of care which the police should show for the safety of people forseeably affected by their actions.

Many civil cases succeed where formal complaints fail. Under such circumstances, you should ask a lawyer as soon as possible to advise you on your chances of success and the possible amount of damages you might receive. In February 1997 the Court of Appeal laid down guidelines on the level of damages in civil actions against the police in the case of *The Commissioner of Police for the Metropolis* v. *Thompson and Hsu*. The Court proposed a figure of £500 for the first hour of false imprisonment and then a downward sliding scale, with £3,000 to be awarded for 24 hours' detention. The Court also proposed damages for malicious prosecution of between £2,000 and £10,000, and that exemplary damages (i.e. more akin to punitive rather than compensatory damages) awarded against the police should be between £5,000 and £50,000. Legal aid is available for actions against the police (subject to the merits of your case and your income and capital).

It is usual to sue the Chief Constable (who is generally responsible for the actions of police officers) of the relevant police force and so, unlike the position with police complaints, it is not essential to know the identities of the police officers involved.

If you are considering a civil action as well as making a formal complaint you should get legal advice from a solicitor or other adviser. You may be advised not to make a very detailed statement in support of your complaint because this might put you at some disadvantage in the civil action as the police will know at a very early stage the case you are going to make against them. If you have already made a complaint, refer the investigating officer to your solicitor. Be prepared for a considerable wait as civil cases can take several years to be concluded.

Prosecuting the police – criminal action

If you believe that there is good evidence to show that the police officer(s) has committed a criminal offence, for example, by assaulting you, you can bring a private prosecution. Normally you should wait to see if the DPP will prosecute since the outcome would be the same (see 'When does a complaint involve prosecution by the DPP?' on p. 126). If the officer(s) is convicted he or she would be sentenced and could be ordered to pay some compensation to you.

You must get legal advice before bringing a private prosecution since you will need strong evidence if you are to have any chance of success. Under these circumstances there is no legal aid available and a private prosecution can be very expensive, especially if the officer(s) elects for trial by jury. It is important to realise that the odds are against your winning and that you could be made liable for the police legal costs.

How are major incidents involving the police dealt with?

The Home Secretary can set up an independent enquiry into any matter concerning the police in England and Wales – not only misconduct by individuals or groups of officers but also as a result of police instructions and policing policies which result in serious conflict with members of the public. Such enquiries, however, are rarely held.

Police authorities can require chief police officers to report on any matter concerning the policing of their area; this is another way in which major incidents can be investigated.

Because the scope of public enquiries and reporting to police authorities is much wider than individual complaints, a campaign of public pressure is often needed before action is taken. If there has been an incident which needs to be examined in a public way, you should consider taking up the matter with Liberty, with relevant local organisations, your MP and elected members of the police authority and with the press.

Complaints about local policing practice

If you are not happy with the way the police are carrying out their responsibilities in your area – for example, if you think that their priorities are wrong, or that they are unfairly treating certain sections of the community – this can be addressed by a Police Consultative Committee. Almost all police authorities have set up Police Consultative Committees in their areas. Each committee covers quite a small area (in London they are based on boroughs). Their members are appointed by the police authority. They tend to meet quarterly, although in some areas it is more frequent, and at least part of each meeting is usually open to the public so that issues of concern may be raised. Details of meetings may be obtained from your town hall.

However, the committees are merely consultative in function and have no power actually to change police practice. They are just a forum for the police to meet the public, not a mechanism for investigating or rectifying complaints.

Useful organisations

Police Complaints Authority
10 Great George Street
London SW1 3AE
Tel: 0171 273 6450

Law Centres' Federation
18–19 Warren Street
London W1P 5DB
Tel: 0171 387 8570

5.5 Courts and legal services

This subject area includes the courts and the legal professions, and each has its own system for dealing with complaints.

Going to court

Before taking any complaint as far as court, you should always seek legal advice. This may be available free through a law centre or by going to a solicitor, many of whom now offer a free initial interview. Beyond this, if you are eligible, the Legal Aid Green Form Scheme covers pre-hearing advice given to you and the writing of letters and preparation of a written case. Advice is valuable because in some cases you could stand to pay both sides' costs if you lose.

For people on a low income, legal aid may be available to cover the costs of going to court, although obtaining full assistance has become more difficult after recent changes in the system, and the current limit for full aid is around £50 per week disposable income (allowances are also given for dependents). If your disposable income is over this amount, you will have to pay some of the costs of the case, worked out on a sliding scale. Legal aid is payable for the majority of criminal and civil cases, but not if you are bringing a defamation action or if your case will be decided in a tribunal. There are exceptions to the rule and you can check your situation by getting detailed advice.

If your case relates to a money claim of under £3,000 you can use the small claims procedure in the County Court. You can make such a claim without needing a solicitor and your local court has leaflets on how to submit a claim. There is an initial fee, but this is recoverable if you win. The case is heard by the judge in chambers – that is, not in a court room – and the procedure is designed to be quicker and easier than a full trial. You can apply to have judgment entered for you in fourteen days if no defence is put up. Sums of over £3,000 can be dealt with at the judge's discretion by referral to arbitration. If in doubt, ring your local court and ask; the number is under 'courts' in the Yellow Pages.

In cases where you are claiming compensation for negligence causing injury or loss, for breach of contract or for a civil offence such as assault, you must go to the County Court or, in some cases, the High Court. This will require a lawyer.

The magistrates' court usually deals with criminal matters where the police have summonsed or charged someone. They also deal with cases involving the poll tax (community charge) and the council tax.

The above is only an outline of the court system and before getting involved in your case you should get advice, which may often be free. Many complaints are not heard by courts as such but at tribunals like industrial tribunals which can deal with the matter in a less formal way. The rules on tribunals are varied and uneven, and you should seek advice on whether or not you can be represented and on how the tribunal in your case will work.

Complaints about the courts

If you are dissatisfied with the way the court system works (although not with the result of your case, which is a legal matter), for example, if you have been kept waiting excessively or you have not been given information by the court which you should have received, your rights as a complainant are now in the Courts' Charter which is available from the Court Service Secretariat at:

> The Lord Chancellor's Department
> Selborne House
> 54 Victoria Street
> London SW1E 6QW
> Tel: 0171 210 8500.

At a local level, the name of the Chief Clerk, to whom all complaints should be addressed, and the complaints procedure must now be on display in all court buildings.

Complaints against solicitors

There are three sorts of complaints you might have against a solicitor: a complaint about charges being too high, a general complaint about the way you have been dealt with by your solicitor, or a complaint involving negligence by your solicitor. In all cases you should complain in the first instance to the firm itself so that if possible, your grievance can be settled without taking the matter further. If the solicitor who has acted for you will not address your complaint, you should refer the matter to the senior partner in the firm, or the partner who has specific responsibility for dealing with complaints. If your complaint is not resolved in this way, the action you take next will depend on the nature of your complaint.

Complaints about overcharging

Once you have tried to resolve this informally, for matters which have not involved court proceedings, you can ask your solicitor to apply to the Law Society for a Remuneration Certificate. For further information about this you can call the Remuneration Certificate enquiry line on 01926 822022. Alternatively, if court proceedings were issued, you will need to apply to the court for taxation of your solicitors' bill. You should note that this may involve you in further costs, particularly if the bill is reduced by less than twenty per cent of its original total.

Complaints about professional conduct

If your complaint is about the way your lawyer has handled your case or how he or she has acted towards you, you can write or telephone the Office for the Supervision of Solicitors (see address below) who will investigate complaints of poor service and/or misconduct made against any solicitor in England or Wales. The OSS can order compensation up to £1,000, require a solicitor to correct a mistake, or discipline a solicitor for misconduct. If you are dissatisfied with a decision of the OSS, or the way your complaint was handled by them, you have three months from the date of their decision to refer the matter to the Legal Services Ombudsman who is appointed by the Lord Chancellor to ensure that complaints handling by the legal profession is well regulated.

Complaints about negligence

Complaints of this sort should also go in the first instance to the OSS. The OSS will review the complaint and if appropriate will refer the matter to one of the solicitors on their Negligence Panel. These are independent solicitors who have volunteered to give one hour's free advice on whether a solicitor was negligent and, if so, what to do next. Ultimately it may be necessary for you to take action in the courts to obtain compensation for the negligence of a solicitor. Enquiries should be directed to:

The Director
The Office for the Supervision of Solicitors
Victoria Court
8 Dormer Place
Leamington Spa
Warwickshire CV32 5AE
Tel: 01926 820082/3

The Office of the Legal Services Ombudsman
22 Oxford Court
Manchester
M2 3WQ
Tel: 0161 236 9532.

Complaints against barristers

You cannot sue a barrister for negligence in the way he or she presents your case in court although you may be able to sue for negligent advice. If you are dissatisfied with your barrister's professional conduct, for example, if your instructions have been ignored, you should complain to the profession's governing body at:

The General Council of the Bar
3 Bedford Row
London WC1R 4DB
Tel: 0171 242 0082.

This body may impose disciplinary sanctions on barristers.

5.7 Financial professions

The professions which deal with your financial affairs have regulatory bodies set up and run by these professions. You should complain to the company involved first and then to the appropriate regulator.

The Banking Ombudsman
70 Gray's Inn Road
5–11 Fetter Lane
London EC4A 1BR
Tel: 0171 583 1395

The Building Societies' Ombudsman
Millbank Tower
Millbank
London SW1P 4XS
Tel: 0171 931 0044

Corporate Estate Agents' Ombudsman
PO Box 1114
Salisbury SP1 1YO
Tel: 01722 333306

The Insurance Ombudsman Bureau
City Gate One
135 Park Street
London SE1 9EA
Tel: 0171 928 7600

Investment Managers' Regulatory Organisation (IMRO)
Lloyds Chambers
1 Port Soken Street
London E1 8BT
Tel: 0171 628 6022

The Investment Ombudsman
6 Fredrick's Place
London EC2R 8BT
Tel: 0171 796 3065

Pensions Ombudsman
11 Belgrave Road
London SW1V 1RB
Tel: 0171 834 9144.

5.8 The media

If you are upset by something shown on television or in the press or covered on radio, or feel that you personally have been misquoted or wrongly represented, you can complain directly to the organisation involved and/or to the regulatory bodies. For the press, the Press Complaints Commission is the current official watchdog. Initially, they operate a telephone helpline which can give you the name and address of the relevant editor so you can complain directly. You can call this on 0171 353 3732. Beyond this, the PCC upholds a code of practice which penalises inaccuracy and intrusiveness. Complaints should be in writing to:

> The Press Complaints Commission
> 1 Salisbury Square
> London EC4Y 3AE
> Fax: 0171 353 1248.

For radio and television, you should first complain to the programme's producer. You may address complaints about the BBC to the appropriate senior manager or directly to:

> The Director-General
> BBC Broadcasting House
> London W1A 1AA
> Tel: 0171 580 4468.

Complaints should be sent to the Programme Controller in the case of a commercial station.

If your complaint is not satisfactorily dealt with by the broadcaster, you should write to the Broadcasting Standards Commission at the address below:

> The Broadcasting Standards Commission
> 5–8 The Sanctuary
> London SW1P 3JS
> Tel: 0171 233 0544.

In April 1997 a new regulatory body, the Broadcasting Standards Commission, was set up under the Broadcasting Act 1996 to consider complaints of unjust or unfair treatment and unwarranted infringements of privacy, as well as the portrayal of violence and sex and standards of taste and decency. The new Commission took over the powers of both the Broadcasting Complaints Commission and the

Broadcasting Standards Council. Complaints to the Commission should be made within a reasonable time after the relevant broadcast (usually three months). The Commission has the power to require the broadcaster to publish a summary of a complaint and of the Commission's findings.

For independent television the umbrella body is:

The Independent Television Commission
33 Foley Street
London W1P 7LB
Tel: 0171 255 3000.

The Independent Television Commission (ITC) deals with matters of complaint against the commercial television companies: Channel 3 and 4, cable, satellite and Teletext (but not the BBC or S4C). The ITC Programme Code covers matters such as taste and decency, the portrayal of violence, privacy, impartiality, charitable appeals and religious programmes. Complaints about breaches of the Code should be made in writing to the ITC at the above address. The ITC can impose heavy fines or revoke licences in serious cases or ensure that an apology is broadcast. Complaints about S4C should either be made to the BSC or directly to S4C at Parc Ty Glas, Llanisien, Cardiff CF4 5DU (tel: 01222 747444 or 741414).

For independent radio the regulatory body is the Radio Authority:

Radio Authority
Holbrook House
14 Great Queen Street
Holborn
London WC2 5DG
Tel: 0171 430 2724

The Radio Authority monitors compliance with its three codes: the Advertising and Sponsorship Code, the Programme Code (covering, for example, taste and decency) and the News and Current Affairs Code (covering, for example, impartiality and election broadcasts). Complaints should be made to the Authority within forty-two days of the relevant broadcast. The Authority has similar powers to the ITC and can, for example, require an apology to be broadcast.

If your complaint is directed at the content or tone of an advertisement in any medium, you should complain to:

The Advertising Standards Authority
2 Torrington Place
London WC1E 7HN
Tel: 0171 580 5555.

If you feel that you have been personally defamed by the media, you may wish to bring a civil action for defamation. You should again seek legal advice before acting, although legal aid is only available for advice and not for representation. Starting such an action cannot occur simultaneously with the complaints procedures described above.

5.9 Public utilities

Since the privatisation of the gas, electricity, water and telephone companies, the government has created watchdog bodies for each industry. If a complaint to the company itself at a local or regional level (addresses will be in the phone book) does not lead to a solution, you should complain to the regulator. Such complaints may be about standards of service or matters relating to billing. Below are the relevant general addresses. If a local office exists, it will be listed in the phone book.

Telecommunications

OFTEL
50 Ludgate Hill
London EC4M 7JJ
Tel: 0171 634 8700
Consumer helpline: 0345 145000

The Secretary
Welsh Advisory Committee on Telecommunications
First Floor Caradog House
St Andrew's Place
Cardiff CF1 3BE
Tel: 01222 374028

The Secretary
Scottish Advisory Committee on Telecommunications
2 Greenside Lane
Edinburgh EH1 3AH
Tel: 0131 244 5576

The Secretary
Northern Ireland ACT
Chamber of Commerce and Industry
22 Great Victoria Street
Belfast BT2 7PU
Tel: 0232 244113

The Secretariat
Independent Committee for the Supervision of Standards of
Telephone Information Services (ICSTIS)
Third Floor Alton House
177 High Holborn
London WC1V 7AA
Tel: 0171 240 5511.

Electricity
OFFER – the regional office will be listed in the phone book or available
on request from the electricity company.

Water

OFWAT
Centre City Tower
7 Hill Street
Birmingham B5 4UA
Tel: 0121 625 1300

River and canal complaints to The National Rivers' Authority (see
phone book for local office) or:

Rio House
Waterside Drive
Aztec West
Almondsley
Bristol BS12 4UD
Tel: 01454 624400.

Gas
You should complain to your local office of the Gas Consumers'
Council, the address of which will be in the phone book or available
from the local gas company office. The national office of the council
is at:

Abford House
15 Wilton Road
London SW1V 1LT
Tel: 0171 931 9151.

You can also complain to the regulator whose national office is at:

OFGAS
Sixth Floor Stockley House
130 Wilton Road
London SW1V 1LQ
Tel: 0171 828 0898.

Complaints about the Post Office

For complaints about counter service, look under Post Office Counters Ltd in your phone book. For complaints about the letters service, look under Royal Mail in your phone book. This will include a freepost address. For complaints about the parcels service, look under Parcelforce in your phone book.

5.10 Miscellaneous complaints

Complaints about many consumer issues should be taken to the appropriate section of your local authority, or county council such as environmental health and trading standards. They may also be able to advise on housing complaints against private landlords, but specialist advisers in this field exist at Citizens' Advice Bureaux, law centres and similar organisations.

5.11 Compensation for the victims of crime

If you are the victim of a criminal act, there are three ways in which you could obtain compensation from the offender:

- A compensation order made by the court as part of a guilty verdict. This is not an award you can apply for, and it is important that the prosecution at the trial knows as much information as possible which might persuade the judge to make such an order.
- A civil action suing for damages. Seek advice from a solicitor or a Citizens' Advice Bureau before attempting this.
- An application to the Criminal Injuries Compensation Scheme which exists by law to award compensation to those injured by crimes of violence. You may apply for an award even if the offender has not been arrested, as long as you have not been awarded any compensation by either of the first two methods above.

Information on the latter scheme is available from:

The Criminal Injuries Compensation Board
Tay House
300 Bath Street
Glasgow G2 4JR
Tel: 0141 331 2726.

The scheme will not pay compensation assessed at under a certain amount (about £1,000) and will not accept claims made if the offence has not previously been promptly reported to the police or if any information is held back from them. Claims made later than three years after the event are also inadmissible. The Board can take other factors into account in deciding whether to award and how much to award, including whether or not they consider the injuries to be your fault. Unfortunately, they can also refuse or reduce the compensation if you have a criminal record or if you 'associate with criminals'. Different rules also apply to situations where the victim making the claim is in the same family as the offender. If your claim arises from a road traffic offence, unless it was a deliberate attempt to run you over, you should claim from the offender's insurance company. If the offender is uninsured, payments can be made by the Motor Insurers' Bureau, an organisation funded by the insurance companies. Their address is:

Motor Insurers' Bureau
152 Silbury Boulevard
Milton Keynes MK9 1NB
Tel: 01908 240000.

Victims may also receive advice and counselling from Victim Support, a national charity which is in contact with the police and will contact those it feels it can offer assistance to. You can contact the organisation through the local police's community involvement unit or phone Victim Support directly at their local address which will be in the phone book.

Other organisations exist to assist victims of crimes such as rape and they can be found in the phone book or by asking the police.

5.12 Complaints and European law

European law is having an increasingly important impact upon UK law. There are two major European Courts, each of which is based on a different organisation. The first is the European Court of Justice which is part of the European Union (formerly the 'EEC' currently comprising fifteen countries). It exists to rule on questions of European Community law put to it by national courts, and also to hear cases between member states and against Community institutions. If you feel that you have such a case, you should seek expert legal advice as the law is often complex. In respect of human rights, EC law has had most impact in relation to discrimination law and freedom of movement within the European Union (see Chapters 9 and 10).

The European Ombudsman
In September 1995 the new office of the European Ombudsman was created to adjudicate on complaints brought by European Union citizens about maladministration in the activities of EC institutions or bodies, such as the European Commission (but not the European Court of Justice or the Court of First Instance acting in their judicial capacities). Complaints can be made directly to the Ombudsman or through your MEP. The address is as follows:

The European Ombudsman
1, Avenue du President Schuman
F-67001 Strasbourg Cedex B.P. 403
France
Tel: 00 333 88 17 40 01.

The European Commission and Court of Human Rights
The second system is based on the Council of Europe (now composed of more than thirty countries). The United Kingdom is bound by many international treaties which oblige it to respect human rights. One of the most important of these is the European Convention for the Protection of Human Rights and Fundamental Freedoms (ECHR). This treaty offers the possibility of redress where a person's civil liberties have been infringed and no remedy can be obtained from the British courts or government.

The Convention was drawn up under the auspices of the Council of Europe, an organisation of West European countries which is based in Strasbourg, France, and is quite separate from the European Community. The Convention was adopted on 4 November 1950 and came into force on 3 September 1953. Its provisions guarantee most, but not all, civil liberties, including the right to life, freedom from torture, freedom from arbitrary arrest, the right to a fair trial, the right to privacy, freedom of religion, freedom of expression, and freedom of assembly and association. The rights guaranteed by the Convention have been expanded on several occasions by the adoption of 'protocols' (i.e. additions) but the UK has only accepted the first protocol (see p. 153). The Convention's principal shortcoming remains, however, the absence of any general prohibition of discrimination; at present it only prohibits discrimination affecting the enjoyment of the rights

STOP PRESS

The new government proposes to incorporate the European Convention on Human Rights into domestic law. The rights in the Convention are set out in Chapter 5. A Bill to incorporate the Convention is due to be published in the autumn of 1997 and this is likely to become an Act by July 1998 and to come into force not before January 1999. It is not clear at the time of writing exactly what effect this will have on our laws. It is likely that the Convention will be able to be used to challenge some of the existing procedures and judge-made law although whether the Convention will be given a higher status than statute is not so clear. Nevertheless the rights set out in this book may be enhanced by the Convention and in future the rights in the Convention will have to be considered much more seriously than they have been in the past.

and freedoms set out in the Convention and protocols. The text of those rights and freedom is set out on p. 148.

The enforcement of the Convention is entrusted to the European Commission and Court of Human Rights, together with the Committee of Ministers of the Council of Europe. The Commission and Court each consists of one person nominated by each of the countries belonging to the Council of Europe. These persons act in their individual capacity and cannot be government officials. The Committee of Ministers consists of the foreign ministers (or their deputies) of the member states of the Council of Europe.

There are two ways in which alleged breaches of the Convention's provisions by the UK can be brought to the attention of these bodies. The first is through a complaint made by one of the other countries which are also bound by the Convention. For example, it was as a result of a complaint by the Republic of Ireland against the UK that certain interrogation practices used in Northern Ireland were held to amount to inhuman and degrading treatment. Countries are, however, reluctant to bring cases against each other and will only do so in the most extreme cases or where their own interests are affected.

The second method of complaint – by the person whose rights have been infringed – is used much more frequently and with greater effect. Any person, non-governmental organisation or group of individuals (whatever their nationality) can complain about a country bound by the Convention where it has declared that it is prepared to accept such complaints. The UK has allowed complaints by individuals since 1966.

The complaints can be about the law, acts of governmental bodies or the decisions of courts. They will be dealt with first by the European Commission of Human Rights and may go later to either the European Court of Human Rights or the Committee of Ministers.

During 'war or other public emergency threatening life of the nation', governments can derogate from their obligations under the Convention. This enables them to restrict the exercise of some of the rights and freedoms, but only in so far as is necessary to deal with the emergency. The UK has, in the past, used this provision in Northern Ireland and one is in force now which allows the police to detain people under the terrorism laws for up to seven days. No derogation is ever possible in respect of the right to life (other than in respect of deaths resulting from lawful acts of war), freedom from torture and slavery and the prohibition of retrospective penalties.

Using the Convention

The procedure for making a complaint where you believe that any of your rights under the Convention have been violated is relatively straightforward. It is not, however, a speedy process (a case can take five years to be resolved) and the delays are undoubtedly exacerbated by the many complaints that do not fall within the ambit of the Convention or do not comply with its requirements which are rejected at the early stages. It is important, therefore, to check whether the subject matter of your complaint has previously been considered and to ensure that you have complied with the admissibility requirements set out below. It is not essential to be represented by a lawyer but it is better to get advice from a solicitor experienced in this type of case or from Liberty. Although the UK's legal aid scheme does not cover complaints under the Convention, limited legal aid may be provided by the Commission (but only towards the end of the examination of a complaint's admissibility and not before it is lodged) and legal costs are recoverable where a complaint is successful. There are no fees payable to the Commission and Court and there is no liability to meet the costs of the government even if your case is unsuccessful.

Making a complaint

A complaint does not have to be started on a special application form although you will eventually be asked to complete one. Complaints should be directed to:

Secretary of the Commission of Human Rights
Council of Europe
F-67075 Strasbourg Cedex
France
Tel: 00 333 88 41 2000 (for urgent cases only – see p. 145)
Fax: 00 333 88 41 27 30.

The following information will be required and should, therefore, be provided in your letter to the Commission:

- Your name, age, address and occupation.
- The name, address and occupation of anyone acting as your representative (for example, your lawyer).
- The country against whom you are complaining (for example, the UK).
- A clear and concise statement of the facts you are complaining about – it is important to describe the events in the order in which they occurred, the way in which the legislation or decision complained about has affected you and to give exact dates.
- The provisions of the Convention on which you are relying and an explanation as to why you consider that the facts involve a violation of them.
- The object of your application (for example, the repeal or amendment of certain legislation or the reversal of a decision and compensation).
- The details of all the remedies (including any appeal) which you have pursued within the country concerned and, where appropriate, an explanation as to why you have not pursued any available remedies.
- The judgments, decisions and any other documents relating to your complaint.

You can ask the Commission to keep your identity confidential. Liberty may also be able to assist with cases taken under the Convention.

Admissibility
The Commission then has to decide whether your application is admissible (i.e. falls within its terms of reference). The application will be referred to one of the Commission's members – the rapporteur – who may ask for further information from you or the government before reporting on the case to the Commission. The Commission itself may then decide to ask for further information or invite the government to make observations on whether or not the application should be admitted. You will be sent a copy of the government's observations and can in turn make observations yourself. The Commission may hold an oral hearing in Strasbourg at this stage.

All the proceedings before the Commission are confidential and you should be careful not to divulge information about them to the press or anyone else. Although divulging information will very rarely lead to the application being dismissed, it can happen and you should take expert advice. The following factors will lead to a ruling that your complaint is inadmissible:

- It was anonymous.
- It was not made within six months of the final decision relating to the alleged violation of the Convention.
- It concerned a matter already dealt with by the Commission or some other international process.
- It was incompatible with the Convention, i.e. it concerned a country, period in time or territory to which the Convention does not apply, or a right not guaranteed by it.
- The domestic remedies were not exhausted (i.e. any judicial or administrative procedure within the country concerned which could have resolved your complaint – it has to be a procedure that can lead to a binding decision and so would not include any discretionary or political remedies, such as a complaint to the ombudsman).
- It was 'manifestly ill-founded' (i.e. the facts did not disclose any prima facie violation of the Convention).
- It was an abuse of the right of petition (for example, the primary aim was political, the Commission was misled, the confidentiality of the proceedings was disregarded, insulting or threatening language was used before the Commission or the government).

The six-month time limit referred to above is very strict. You must lodge your case within six months of the last decision in the domestic courts or tribunals. If, however, there is no effective remedy at all in the UK courts you should write to the Commission within six months of the incident which you are complaining about.

The overwhelming majority (95 per cent) of applications are found to be inadmissible by the Commission. This underlines the importance of a thorough evaluation of your case before you write to the Commission. There is no appeal against its decision. Moreover, a case that has been admitted can, on further examination by the Commission (or even the Court), be rejected as inadmissible. It is likely to take at least a year before the Commission decides on the admissibility of a case but it will give priority to urgent cases (i.e. those where a person's life or well-being is immediately threatened by the action being complained about). In such cases, the Commission should be contacted by telephone, telex or fax. The Commission may then ask the government to refrain from acting until the application has been considered. Although not bound to do so, the government is likely to accede to such a request.

The later stages
If the Commission decides that your application is admissible, it will then examine the substance of your case. The Commission may hold a hearing in Strasbourg (or may have considered the merits at the same

time as it considered the issue of admissibility). When it has reached a provisional opinion on the merits of the case – which will not be published – the Commission will try to reach a 'friendly settlement' (i.e. a negotiated agreement) between you and the government.

The settlement may simply involve the payment of compensation or the making of a decision (for example, the revocation of a deportation order) but it may also require a change in the law or administrative practice which gave rise to the complaint. The Commission has to be satisfied that any settlement takes account of the general interest (for example, where a complaint arose from the application of the rules restricting access by prisoners to legal advice, the settlement would require the reform of those rules as well as the payment of compensation). If a friendly settlement is agreed and approved, the Commission will prepare a brief statement of the facts and the solution reached. This is all that will be published about the case.

Where no friendly settlement is achieved, the Commission draws up a report on the case which will state whether in its opinion there has been a breach of the Convention. The report will include any dissenting views from individual members of the Commission. There is then a period of three months during which the decision whether to refer the case to the Court of Human Rights must be made. Such a decision can only be taken where the respondent state has accepted the jurisdiction of the Court (the UK has) and can only be made by the Commission or any government of a Council of Europe country involved (or whose citizen is involved) in the case; the individual applicant has no part to play in this decision (although a newly designed procedure that does give a right will be brought in as soon as it has been agreed by the governments). Cases tend to be referred to the Court where they involve problems of interpretation or where the commission is divided. A referral is unlikely where the Court has already resolved the issue in an earlier case brought against the same government.

The proceedings before the Court amount to a fresh examination of your complaint. It is likely to involve written and oral submissions by the Commission, the government and yourself. You may be represented by a lawyer for this purpose. It is also possible for the Court to allow any person, organisation or government to make submissions relevant to the case (Liberty has put in submissions in the past – for example, on issues connected with long detention periods in terrorist cases and right-to-silence cases). The case will be heard either by a chamber of seven judges or (where it raises serious questions affecting the interpretation of the Convention) the full Court. The Court will issue a judgment stating whether or not the Convention has been violated. Where it considers that there was a violation, it may also (in the same or a later judgment) award you 'just satisfaction' (i.e. damages and reimbursement of your legal costs). The Court's judgment is binding on the government but it can only declare that the Convention has been breached and that damages or costs should be paid. The Court cannot require the government to take any particular action to prevent similar breaches happening again. In other words, it will not automatically overturn the legislation or decision against which you have been complaining – those matters are for the government to decide. The government must, therefore, decide what steps are necessary to implement the judgment and the Committee of Ministers is responsible for ensuring that this is done.

If the case is not referred to the Court, it will be dealt with by the Committee of Ministers. It is unlikely to require any submissions (written or oral) in addition to those already made to the Commission. The Committee can only decide that there has been a violation of the Convention by a vote of at least two-thirds of its members; in a few instances this has not been possible and the case must be left unresolved. Where it decides that the Convention has been breached, the Committee can also decide what measures the government concerned should take and may ask the Commission to make proposals regarding an award of 'just satisfaction'.

The future

Protocol 11 to the Convention (which the UK has ratified) provides for the reorganisation of the Commission and Court. The proposals are that the current part-time Commission and Court will cease to exist and a new permanent Court will take their place. The Committee of Ministers will no longer decide on the merits of cases but will continue to supervise the compliance of states with the Court's judgments.

Individuals will have direct access to the Court, which in the vast majority of cases will sit in chambers of seven judges. Inadmissible and unmeritorious applications will be sifted out by committees of three judges. The friendly settlement option will be dealt with by the Court. In exceptional cases the chamber will relinquish jurisdiction in favour of a Grand Chamber which will decide the more important issues. All interstate cases will be heard by the plenary Court.

At the time of writing it is expected that the reorganisation will take effect in the autumn of 1998.

The value of the Convention

It is often assumed by people whose civil liberties are being infringed that 'going to Strasbourg' will provide a ready solution. In fact there are many hurdles to be overcome before a case can even be considered, the procedure is slow (it may take five years from application to judgment and a further two before its implementation by the government), and the Convention does not provide a guarantee against all infringements of civil liberties. None the less, cases brought against the UK under the Convention have led to the setting aside of repressive measures and have secured important reforms in the following areas: freedom of expression, immigration, inhuman and degrading treatment, mental patients' rights, parental rights, prisoners' rights, privacy, workers' rights and the rights of gay men. It is clear that without the Convention (and the right of individuals to complain) the UK would lack a valuable safeguard for its civil liberties.

The rights and freedoms protected by the Convention and which are binding on the UK (Articles 2 to 18 and Protocol 1) are set out below. The full text of the Convention and Protocols, together with the rules of procedure of the Commission, Court and Committee of Ministers can be obtained directly from the European Commission at the address given above.

Article 2

1. Everyone's right to life shall be protected by law. No one shall be deprived of his life intentionally save in the execution of a sentence of a court following his conviction of a crime for which this penalty is provided by law.
2. Deprivation of life shall not be regarded as inflicted in contravention of this article when it results from the use of force which is no more than absolutely necessary:

    (a) in defence of any person from unlawful violence;
    (b) in order to effect a lawful arrest or to prevent the escape of a person lawfully detained;
    (c) in action lawfully taken for the purpose of quelling a riot or insurrection.

Article 3
No one shall be subjected to torture or to inhuman or degrading treatment or punishment.

Article 4

1. No one shall be held in slavery or servitude.
2. No one shall be required to perform forced or compulsory labour.
3. For the purpose of this article the term 'forced or compulsory labour' shall not include:

    (a) any work required to be done in the ordinary course of detention imposed according to the provisions of Article 5 of this Convention or during conditional release from such detention;

(b) any service of a military character, or, in the case of conscientious objectors in countries where they are recognised, service exacted instead of compulsory military service;

(c) any service exacted in case of an emergency or calamity threatening the life or wellbeing of the community;

(d) any work or service which forms part of normal civic obligations.

Article 5

1. Everyone has the right to liberty and security of person. No one shall be deprived of his liberty save in the following cases and in accordance with a procedure prescribed by law:

   (a) the lawful detention of a person after conviction by a competent court;

   (b) the lawful arrest or detention of a person for non-compliance with the lawful order of a court or in order to secure the fulfilment of any obligation prescribed by law;

   (c) the lawful arrest or detention of a person effected for the purpose of bringing him before the competent legal authority on reasonable suspicion of having committed an offence or when it is reasonably considered necessary to prevent his committing an offence or fleeing after having done so;

   (d) the detention of a minor by lawful order for the purpose of educational supervision or his lawful detention for the purpose of bringing him before the competent legal authority;

   (e) the lawful detention of persons for the prevention of the spreading of infectious diseases, or persons of unsound mind, alcoholics or drug addicts or vagrants;

   (f) the lawful arrest or detention of a person to prevent his effecting an unauthorised entry into the country or of a person against whom action is being taken with a view to deportation or extradition.

2. Everyone who is arrested shall be informed promptly, in a language which he understands, of the reasons for his arrest and of any charge against him.

3. Everyone arrested or detained in accordance with the provisions of paragraph 1(c) of this article shall be brought promptly before a judge or other officer authorised by law to exercise judicial power and shall be entitled to trial within a reasonable time or to release pending trial. Release may be conditioned by guarantees to appear for trial.

4.   Everyone who is deprived of his liberty by arrest or detention shall be entitled to take proceedings by which the lawfulness of his detention shall be decided speedily by a court and his release ordered if the detention is not lawful.

5.   Everyone who has been the victim of arrest or detention in contravention of the provisions of this article shall have an enforceable right to compensation.

Article 6

1.   In the determination of his civil rights and obligations or of any criminal charge against him, everyone is entitled to a fair and public hearing within a reasonable time by an independent and impartial tribunal established by law. Judgment shall be pronounced publicly but the press and public may be excluded from all or part of the trial in the interests of morals, public order or national security in a democratic society, where the interests of juveniles or the protection of the private life of the parties so require, or to the extent strictly necessary in the opinion of the court in special circumstances where publicity would prejudice the interests of justice.

2.   Everyone charged with a criminal offence shall be presumed innocent until proved guilty according to law.

3.   Everyone charged with a criminal offence has the following minimum rights:

   (a)   to be informed promptly, in a language which he understands and in detail, of the nature and cause of the accusation against him;
   (b)   to have adequate time and facilities for the preparation of his defence;
   (c)   to defend himself in person or through legal assistance of his own choosing or, if he has not sufficient means to pay for legal assistance, to be given it free when the interests of justice so require;
   (d)   to examine or have examined witnesses against him and to obtain the attendance and examination of witnesses on his behalf under the same conditions as witnesses against him;
   (e)   to have the free assistance of an interpreter if he cannot understand or speak the language used in court.

Article 7

1.   No one shall be held guilty of any criminal offence on account of any act or omission which did not constitute a criminal offence

under national or international law at the time when it was committed. Nor shall a heavier penalty be imposed than the one that was applicable at the time the criminal offence was committed.

2. This article shall not prejudice the trial and punishment of any person for any act or omission which, at the time it was committed, was criminal according to the general principles of law recognised by civilised nations.

Article 8

1. Everyone has the right to respect for his private and family life, his home and his correspondence.
2. There shall be no interference by a public authority with the exercise of this right except such as is in accordance with the law and is necessary in a democratic society in the interests of national security, public safety or the economic wellbeing of the country, for the prevention of disorder or crime, for the protection of health or morals, or for the protection of the rights and freedoms of others.

Article 9

1. Everyone has the right to freedom of thought, conscience and religion; this right includes freedom to change his religion or belief, and freedom, either alone or in community with others and in public or private, to manifest his religion or belief in worship, teaching, practice and observance.
2. Freedom to manifest one's religion or beliefs shall be subject only to such limitations as are prescribed by law and are necessary in a democratic society in the interests of public safety, for the protection of public order, health or morals, or for the protection of the rights and freedoms of others.

Article 10

1. Everyone has the right to freedom of expression. This right shall include freedom to hold opinions and to receive and impart information and ideas without interference by public authority and regardless of frontiers. This article shall not prevent states from requiring the licence of broadcasting, television or cinema enterprises.
2. The exercise of these freedoms, since it carries with it duties and responsibilities, may be subject to such formalities, conditions, restrictions or penalties as are prescribed by law and are necessary

in a democratic society, in the interests of national security, territorial integrity or public safety, for the prevention of disorder or crime, for the protection of health or morals, for the protection of the reputation or rights of others, for preventing the disclosure of information received in confidence, or for maintaining the authority and impartiality of the judiciary.

Article 11

1. Everyone has the right to freedom of peaceful assembly and to freedom of association with others, including the right to form and to join trade unions for the protection of his interests.
2. No restrictions shall be placed on the exercise of these rights other than such as are prescribed by law and are necessary in a democratic society in the interests of national security or public safety, for the prevention of disorder or crime, for the protection of health or morals or for the protection of the rights and freedoms of others. This article shall not prevent the imposition of lawful restrictions on the exercise of these rights by members of the armed forces, of the police or of the administration of the state.

Article 12
Men and women of marriageable age have the right to marry and to found a family, according to the national laws governing the exercise of this right.

Article 13
Everyone whose rights and freedoms as set forth in this Convention are violated shall have an effective remedy before a national authority notwithstanding that the violation has been committed by persons acting in an official capacity.

Article 14
The enjoyment of the rights and freedoms set forth in this Convention shall be secured without discrimination on any ground such as sex, race, colour, language, religion, political or other opinion, national or social origin, association with a national minority, property, birth or other status.

Article 15

1. In time of war or other public emergency threatening the life of the nation, any High Contracting Party may take measures derogating from its obligations under this Convention to the extent strictly required by the exigencies of the situation, provided

that such measures are not inconsistent with its other obligations under international law.

2.   No derogation from Article 2, except in respect of deaths resulting from lawful acts of war, or from Articles 3, 4 (paragraph 1) and 7 shall be made under this provision.

3.   Any High Contracting Party availing itself of this right to derogation shall keep the Secretary General of the Council of Europe fully informed of the measures which it has taken and the reasons therefor. It shall also inform the Secretary General of the Council of Europe when such measures have ceased to operate and the provisions of the Convention are again being fully executed.

Article 16
Nothing in Articles 10, 11 and 14 shall be regarded as preventing the High Contracting Parties from imposing restrictions on the political activity of aliens.

Article 17
Nothing in this Convention may be interpreted as implying for any state, group or person any right to engage in any activity or perform any act aimed at the destruction of any of the rights and freedoms as set forth herein or at their limitation to a greater extent than is provided for in the Convention.

Article 18
The restrictions permitted under this Convention to the said rights and freedoms shall not be applied for any purpose other than those for which they have been prescribed.

Protocol 1

Article 1
Every natural or legal person is entitled to the peaceful enjoyment of his possessions. No one shall be deprived of his possessions except in the public interest and subject to the conditions provided for by law and by the general principles of international law.

The preceding provisions shall not, however, in any way impair the right of a state to enforce such laws as it deems necessary to control the use of property in accordance with the general interest or to secure the payment of taxes or other contributions or penalties.

Article 2
No person shall be denied the right to education. In the exercise of any functions which it assumes in relation to education and to teaching,

the state shall respect the right of parents to ensure such education and teaching in conformity with their own religious and philosophical convictions.

Article 3
The High Contracting Parties undertake to hold free elections at reasonable intervals by secret ballot, under conditions which will ensure the free expression of the opinion of the people in the choice of the legislature.

5.13 Other international treaties

Other international treaties also impose minimum standards in relation to human rights. For example, in the Council of Europe there are conventions or directives on the prevention of torture, inhuman and degrading treatment and on data protection. In the United Nations (UN) there are others on the rights of the child, discrimination, torture and refugees. These treaties do not usually allow the right of individual complaint but impose a duty on a government to report on its human rights record. In some cases they can involve spot checks.

The International Covenant on Civil and Political Rights is another important UN treaty which is binding on the UK and which is modelled on the ECHR but is more wide-ranging. The UK government has to report on its record under this treaty every five years and the United Nations Human Rights Committee most recently examined the UK's record in 1995. Unfortunately the government has refused to allow the right of individual petition, to allow complaints about breaches of the Covenant to be made directly to this Committee.

5.14 The Citizen's Charter

Areas covered by the Citizen's Charter have now set standards which organisations must meet. You can check whether you have a valid complaint by ringing the Citizen's Charter telephone line if there is one in your area.

5.15 Further information

Useful organisations
It is vital to get advice on complaints which have legal implications. If you cannot find advice locally, the following organisations will be able to put you in contact with their nearest affiliate:

Federation of Independent Advice Centres
13 Stockwell Road
London SW9 9AU
Tel: 0171 274 1839

The Law Centres' Federation
Duchess House
18–19 Warren Street
London W1P 5DB
Tel: 0171 387 8570

National Association of Citizens' Advice Bureaux
Middleton House
115–123 Pentonville Road
London N1 9LZ
Tel: 0171 833 2181

Bibliography

The following books may provide useful information about the European Convention on Human Rights:

Luke Clements, *European Human Rights – Taking a case under the Convention*, Sweet & Maxwell, 1994.

European Human Rights Law Review, Sweet and Maxwell (bi-monthly).

S. Farran, *The UK before the European Court of Human Rights: Case Law and Commentary*, Blackstone Press, 1996.

D.J. Harris, M. O'Boyle and C. Warbrick, *Law of the European Convention on Human Rights*, Butterworths, 1995.

P. Leach, *Recent Developments in European Convention Law, Legal Action* (regular round up of European Convention decisions, every January and July).

P. Van Dyk and G.J.H. Van Hoof, *Theory and Practice of the European Convention on Human Rights*, Kluger, 1990.

6

The rights of suspects

This chapter deals with the rights of suspects up to the point when they are either released by the police without charge, bailed by the police, or brought before a court. Other people, like customs and excise (see p. 67), have similar powers but the differences cannot be detailed here. In particular this chapter deals with:

- Police powers to stop and search persons and vehicles (without arrest).
- Police powers to search premises.
- Police powers of arrest.
- Police detention.
- The rights of suspects in the police station.
- Special powers under the Prevention of Terrorism Act.
- Further information.

This chapter uses expressions like 'reasonable grounds' or 'reasonable suspicion'. The use of the word 'reasonable' implies that what is or is not reasonable is a decision for the courts. The fact that the police believe that they have reasonable suspicion, for instance, is not sufficient. It implies, therefore, an objective test and not a subjective one. Unfortunately, it is difficult to define it more accurately.

Most of the police powers and corresponding rights for suspects are to be found in the Police and Criminal Evidence Act 1984 – known as PACE – and in the Codes of Conduct issued by the Home Secretary under PACE and approved by Parliament. PACE was the product of years of discussion about police powers. It was based on the recommendations in the *Report of the Royal Commission on Criminal Procedure* (published in 1981 – HMSO Cmnd 8092), a body which had been directed in its terms of reference to strike a balance between the interests of the community on the one hand and the rights and liberties of the individual suspect on the other. Another Royal Commission set up in March 1991 – this time on Criminal Justice – and some of its recommendations along with other ideas suggested by the government, were enacted in the Criminal Justice and Public Order Act 1994 which made some significant changes to the 1984 Act.

The most notable of these changes is the effective curtailment of the suspect's 'right of silence' (see p. 182). The Codes of Practice are now in their third edition.

The police have special powers under the Prevention of Terrorism legislation and these are described below on pp. 187–93.

If any of these police powers are abused:

- The abuse may make evidence obtained inadmissible in court.
- You may make an official police complaint (see p. 122).
- You may be able to sue the police (see p. 128).

STOP PRESS

The new government proposes to incorporate the European Convention on Human Rights into domestic law. The rights in the Convention are set out in Chapter 5. A Bill to incorporate the Convention is due to be published in the autumn of 1997 and this is likely to become an Act by July 1998 and to come into force not before January 1999. It is not clear at the time of writing exactly what effect this will have on our laws. It is likely that the Convention will be able to be used to challenge some of the existing procedures and judge-made law although whether the Convention will be given a higher status than statute is not so clear. Nevertheless the rights set out in this book may be enhanced by the Convention and in future the rights in the Convention will have to be considered much more seriously than they have been in the past.

6.1 Police powers to stop and search persons and vehicles (without arrest)

Part 1 of the Police and Criminal Evidence Act (PACE) empowers any constable acting with reasonable grounds for suspicion to stop, detain and search you or your vehicle, or anything in or on your vehicle for certain items, which may be seized. The provisions of the Act are supplemented by a Code of Practice on stop and search. The contents of the Code must be observed by the police, although the remedy for failure to observe it is usually to make a police complaint (or if prosecuted to raise an objection in court) rather than to take legal proceedings against the police.

PACE also provides some safeguards for other police powers of search. These relate, for instance, to drugs (on reasonable suspicion of being in unlawful possession), evidence of liability to arrest under the Prevention of Terrorism legislation, suspected possession of firearms, animal conservation and evidence of offences under the Sporting Events (Control of Alcohol etc.) Act 1985. The safeguards also apply in a limited way to the controversial powers of stop and search introduced by the Criminal Justice and Public Order Act 1994 when it is feared that an incident involving serious violence may take place (see below p. 161). For search powers on arrest, see p. 166.

Stolen or prohibited articles or knives
The power to stop and search in PACE enables a constable to search for stolen or 'prohibited articles' or knives (except short-bladed penknives,). PACE defines two categories of prohibited article:

- An offensive weapon.
- An article made or adapted for use in connection with one of a list of offences including burglary, theft, taking a conveyance without authority (or being carried in one) and obtaining property by deception.

Virtually any article could come within this second definition but there would have to be some evidence of the use of the article or the intention of the person making, adapting or carrying it, otherwise a constable would not have reasonable grounds to search.

Where the search may take place
The PACE power of stop and search may be used by the police in most public and some private places. In law the power is limited to one of the following types of place:

- A place to which, at the time of the proposed stop and search, the public (or any section of the public) has access as a matter of legal right or because there is permission.
- Any place (other than a dwelling) to which people have ready access at the time of the proposed stop and search.

These categories are obviously very wide and can include much private property, including front gardens and car parks. Whether you have ready access might depend on whether a gate or door is locked, or whether a plot of land is fenced.

However, a constable may not search you or your vehicle if you are on land which is used for the purpose of a dwelling, without having reasonable grounds for believing that you do not reside in the dwelling and are not in the place with the express or implied permission of a person who does reside in the dwelling. There is clearly a heavy duty on the constable in such cases, since the reasonable grounds must be justified objectively. These provisions should protect people behaving normally: window cleaners, post and milk deliverers and casual visitors.

Reasonable grounds for suspicion

The power of stop and search under PACE can only be exercised if the constable has reasonable grounds for suspecting that stolen or prohibited articles or knives will be found. The Code of Practice elaborates this requirement. There must be some concrete basis for the officer's belief, related to you personally, which can be considered and evaluated by an objective third person. Mere suspicion based on hunch or instinct might justify observation but cannot justify a search.

Reasonable grounds for suspicion cannot be based on attitudes or prejudices towards certain types of people, such as membership of a group within which offenders of a certain kind are relatively common (for example, young football fans). Nor can it be based on your skin colour, age, hairstyle, mode of dress, or previous convictions for possessing an unlawful article.

Stopping and detaining

Any police officer, whether or not in uniform, may search you personally, but usually only a constable in uniform may stop a vehicle. A police officer may detain you or your vehicle for a search, but not in order to find grounds to justify a search. The reasonable grounds must already exist.

The detention may only last for as long as it is reasonably required to permit a search to be carried out at the place of detention or nearby. You cannot be compelled to remain with your vehicle while the vehicle is searched, but you may wish to do so. Police officers have other powers to stop a vehicle, for example to check whether it is roadworthy or stolen, but not to search it.

Searching

In carrying out a search the police may not force you (but may request you) to remove any clothing in public (even if the street is empty) other than an outer coat, jacket or gloves. A more thorough search, involving the removal for instance of a hat or shoes, or a strip search (but not an intimate search: see below) may take place in private, but it must be near to where you were stopped. Thus it could take place, for example, in a police van. The Code states that such searches must be by a police officer of your sex and must be in the absence of any officer of the opposite sex.

The power to search a vehicle includes a power to search anything in or on it. If an unattended vehicle is searched, a notice to this effect must be left behind (inside the vehicle if reasonably practicable) stating the police station to which the constable is attached, that any claims for compensation should be made to that police station, and that you are entitled to a copy of the search record if requested within twelve months of the search. A constable may use reasonable force, if necessary, in the detention and conduct of the search, but force can only be necessary if you are first given the opportunity to cooperate and refuse.

A constable who discovers an article reasonably suspected to be stolen or prohibited may seize it.

It should be noted that the safeguards in PACE and in the Code of Practice do not apply to the routine searching of those entering sports grounds or other premises with their consent or as a condition of entry. Likewise, nothing in PACE or in the Code affects the ability of an officer to search you in the street on a voluntary basis provided that you are capable of understanding to what it is you are consenting. Juveniles and people suffering from a mental handicap or disorder are deemed by the Code incapable of consenting to a search.

Information to be given

A constable contemplating a search under any power to search (before or without arrest) must take reasonable steps to bring the following to your attention:

- If the constable is not in uniform, proof that he or she is a constable, which the Code says must be by showing a warrant card.
- The constable's name and police station.
- The object of the proposed search.
- The constable's grounds for proposing to search.
- The availability of a search record (see below) if it is practicable to make one.

The search may not be commenced until the constable gives you such information, and the information must be given even if not requested.

Search records

A constable who has carried out a search under any power to search (without or before making an arrest) must make a written record on the spot, or later if impracticable on the spot, unless it is totally impracticable to make a record at all because of the numbers involved or for some other operational reason.

The Code requires the search record to include your name, or if the police do not know your name, a description of you and a note of your ethnic origin. The record must identify the person making it and state the object of the search, the grounds for making it, the date, time and place, whether anything – and if so what – was found, and whether any – and if so what – injury or damage resulted from the search.

You are entitled to get a copy of any record made, on request, within twelve months of the date of the search.

Roadblocks

Police powers to set up roadblocks (referred to in section 4 of PACE as roadchecks) do not derive from PACE but from other sources: road traffic legislation (section 163 of the Road Traffic Act 1988) and case law. If a roadblock is for certain purposes, PACE provides that the police must follow certain procedures.

Search powers when an incident involving serious violence may take place.

Under the Criminal Justice and Public Order Act 1994, a senior police officer may issue a written authorisation for additional search powers, relating to pedestrians and vehicles, on the basis of a reasonable belief that serious violence is imminent. The powers will be limited to a specified locality and should only be for short periods at a time.

Where an authorisation has been issued any constable in uniform may stop and search any pedestrian or anything carried by the pedestrian, or any vehicle or anyone in it, for offensive weapons and dangerous instruments and may seize any such items which are found. Very importantly, under these powers, the police do not need to have any suspicion that they will find the items for which they may search. Code A applies (but not the provisions on reasonable suspicion) and the provisions on where searches may take place and the minimisation of embarrassment are particularly significant. It is unclear whether these powers to stop and search may be exercised on private premises. The stops and searches are subject to the same safeguards concerning provision of information, the nature of the search and record keeping as the powers under the 1984 Act described above. In addition, a pedestrian or driver of a vehicle who has been stopped is entitled to a written statement to that effect if an application is made within twelve months.

Failure to stop when required to do so under these new powers is a summary offence, with a maximum sentence of imprisonment of one month. In addition, it would of course amount to an offence of obstructing a police officer in the exercise of his or her duty.

The Knives Act 1997 amends the Criminal Justice and Public Order Act 1994 to allow the police to authorise stopping and searching for twenty-four hours in a particular locality if it is reasonably believed that people are carrying dangerous instruments or offensive weapons without good reason. Following such an authorisation, the police will not need to have any particular reason to search an individual. In addition, in 1997 the Home Office published revisions to Code of Practice A to PACE concerning stop and search powers. Which now allows for searches (for knives and drugs) of people suspected of being a member of a particular gang or group, on the basis of what is known about that group (rather than the individual).

'Statutory undertakers' – other police forces

'Statutory undertakers' are bodies authorised by statute to carry on a railway, transport, dock or harbour undertaking, the larger of which employ their own police forces (for example, the British Transport Police) whose members have the powers of constables within a geographically limited area. Members of these forces have many of the same powers as members of regular police forces, subject to certain limitations. These are not the same as private security organisations which enjoy no special 'policing' powers.

A constable employed by a statutory undertaker may stop, detain and search any vehicle (but not a person) before it leaves a goods area on the premises of the statutory body. Such stops are carried out routinely and need not be justified by any suspicion nor recorded. There is no statutory limitation on what may be searched for and the Code of Practice does not apply to these searches.

The Ministry of Defence has its own police force, who have the same powers as civilian police officers and are regulated by the Ministry of Defence Police Act 1987.

6.2 Police powers to search premises

The police have powers to enter and search your premises for many reasons. Some of these powers are set out in the Police and Criminal Evidence Act 1984 (PACE) but the police also have power to enter and search under other statutes, for instance the Theft Act 1968. It should be noted that the police do not always need to have a search warrant, although they must always have a reason for the search. There is a Code of Practice stating how the police should conduct searches. (For what you should do if the police do not follow the Code see p. 129.)

Search with your consent

The police may search your premises if you consent. However, the Code of Practice on searching premises provides that before seeking your consent the officer in charge should state the purpose of the proposed search, inform you that you are not obliged to consent and inform you that anything seized may be used in evidence. For the search to be lawful you must consent in writing. If you live in rented accommodation the police should not search the premises solely on the basis of your landlord's consent unless you are unavailable and the matter is urgent.

Search of premises under a magistrate's warrant

Magistrates have the power to issue search warrants under many Acts of Parliament – for example, to search for stolen goods under the Theft Act 1968, Misuse of Drugs Act 1971 and for racially inflammatory material under the Public Order Act 1986. More importantly, they have a power under the Police and Criminal Evidence Act to issue a warrant authorising the police to enter and search premises for evidence of a serious arrestable offence (see p. 169). Magistrates should only issue warrants under this section if there are reasonable grounds for believing that the police will not be able to obtain access to the evidence without a warrant, for example, if consent will not be forthcoming. In addition, magistrates should be satisfied that there are reasonable grounds for believing:

- The material is likely to be of substantial value (whether by itself or together with other material) to the investigation of the offence.
- That it is likely to be 'relevant evidence', that is, anything which would be admissible as evidence at a trial.
- That it does not consist of or include items subject to legal privilege, 'excluded material' or 'special procedure material' (see below).

This power clearly applies to premises owned or occupied by someone who is not implicated in the alleged offence.

The Police Act 1997 will for the first time give statutory authority to police 'bugging' and will allow the police with the prior authority of a Commissioner (a serving or retired High Court Judge) to go onto private property to plant surveillance devices and probably also to search and seize evidence. In order to use such powers the police would have to be satisfied that the action is necessary because it is likely to be of substantial value in the prevention or detection of serious crime, and that what the action seeks to achieve cannot reasonably be achieved by other means.

Material which has special safeguards

PACE gives special protection from search (but not necessarily from seizure) to some types of material felt to be sensitive. These categories are 'excluded material', 'special procedure material' and legally privileged material.

Excluded material

There are three kinds of 'excluded material':

* Personal records – examples of material which should normally be excluded are medical and psychiatric records, records kept by priests, the Samaritans, possibly school and college records, records of advice given by law centres and Citizens' Advice Bureaux.
* Human tissue or tissue fluid.
* 'Journalistic' material – i.e. material acquired or created for the purposes of journalism. There is no need for the holder of such material to be a professional journalist.

In order to qualify as 'excluded material' the items must have been held in confidence. This is a concept which can be legally complex.

The police cannot easily obtain a warrant to search for this material. They must follow a set procedure which will normally involve a hearing before a judge who will decide, amongst other things, whether it would be in the public interest to allow the police access to the material. Only the person in possession of the material, who will not necessarily be the suspect, and the police, have a right to make representations at the hearing. If the judge permits it, however, the suspect may make representations. If the judge considers it appropriate, he or she will make an order compelling production of the material to the police.

If the person in possession fails to produce the material, he or she may be in contempt of court (see p. 55) and the judge may be able to issue a warrant to the police to search his or her premises.

In some circumstances, if the police can convince the judge that the situation is urgent, they may be able to obtain a warrant from the judge without the party in possession of the material knowing.

Special procedure material

There are two categories of special procedure material:

* Material which is not excluded material but is held in confidence by certain persons.
* Journalistic material which is not excluded material, either because it is not held in confidence or does not consist of documents.

Examples of special procedure material are company accounts or stock records held on behalf of a client by a bank, solicitor or accountant. The procedure enabling the police to obtain this material is broadly the same as for 'excluded material' (see above).

Legally privileged material

The definition of items subject to legal privilege is crucial, since these items are exempt from most powers of search. The police have no power at all to seize material which they have reasonable grounds for believing to be legally privileged. There are three categories of legally privileged material:

- Communications to do with giving legal advice.
- Communications to do with legal proceedings.
- Items connected with either of the above communications.

In each category the definition hinges on the term 'professional legal adviser', which clearly includes barristers, solicitors and solicitors' clerks. There is no requirement that the adviser should work for a firm of solicitors and, therefore, the adviser may come from a law or advice centre. Although the advice of an unqualified person will not be privileged unless acting as an agent for a solicitor or barrister, it will in most cases be 'excluded material'. This would not protect it from seizure, however (see below).

Items held with the intention of furthering a criminal purpose are not legally privileged, but clearly a letter from a solicitor advising a client of potential criminal liability if a particular course of conduct were pursued would be privileged.

Entry and search without a search warrant

The police are given powers to enter premises without a warrant by many Acts of Parliament, for example, under the Gaming Act 1968 they have power to enter licensed premises to carry out inspections. Other powers include searches for drugs under the Misuse of Drugs Act 1971, and for firearms under the Firearms Act 1968. In addition, they may have the right to enter premises without a warrant to deal with or prevent a breach of the peace (see p. 34). The Police and Criminal Evidence Act provides them with several other powers:

- To execute a warrant of arrest or commitment.
- To arrest someone for an arrestable offence.
- To arrest someone for various offences under the Public Order Acts 1936 and 1986 (such as riot, violent disorder, affray, threatening behaviour and disorderly conduct); the Criminal Law Act 1977

(offences relating to trespass) and the Criminal Justice and Public Order Act 1994 (failure to comply with an interim possession order).

* To recapture a person who has escaped from lawful custody.
* To save life or limb or prevent serious damage to property.

The police officer need not be in uniform unless entering in connection with the Public Order Acts or the Criminal Law Act. He or she has a power to search the premises but this is only to the extent that is reasonably required for the purposes of entry. Any further search may be unlawful and may be the subject of a complaint or civil action (see Chapter 5).

Search of premises on arrest

The Police and Criminal Evidence Act 1984 (PACE) provides the police with clear authority to enter and search premises after an arrest. If you have been arrested for an 'arrestable offence' (see above) the police may search premises occupied or controlled by you for evidence of that offence or of some other arrestable offence connected with or similar to that offence. The police officer conducting this search should normally have with him or her written authorisation on the Notice of Powers and Rights (see below) for the search by an officer of at least the rank of inspector.

If you have been arrested for any offence (not just an 'arrestable offence') the police may enter and search any premises you were in at the time of the arrest or immediately before it for evidence of the offence for which you were arrested. Again, in both cases the police are only permitted to search to the extent reasonably required to find the evidence sought and if the search is excessive you may have the remedy of a police complaint or a civil action against the police.

Conduct of searches of premises

The conduct of searches is governed by the Police and Criminal Evidence Act and the Code of Practice (see p. 156). A search warrant may authorise anyone to accompany the constable who is executing it. Entry and search must be within one month from the date of the warrant's issue. You have a right to see the warrant and to be supplied with a copy. You also have a right, unless it is impracticable, to a notice in the standard form setting out police powers and occupiers' rights (Notice of Rights and Powers). You are also entitled to see the police officer's warrant card as a means of identification if he or she is not in uniform and in any case, the police officer should identify him- or herself. If you are not present but someone else who appears to the police to be in charge of the premises is available then they have the same rights as you. A warrant authorises entry on one occasion only.

The police have a right to use force if necessary to effect an entry or search, but only such force as is reasonable. All searches should take place at a reasonable hour, unless the constable conducting the search believes that the purpose of the search would be frustrated by waiting until such time. You are entitled to have a friend or neighbour to witness a search (although you do not have a right to delay a search unreasonably while you find a witness) unless the officer in charge has reasonable grounds for feeling this would seriously hinder the investigation.

The warrant must be endorsed afterwards by the police to show the following:

- Whether articles or persons specified in the warrant were found.
- Whether any other articles were seized.
- The date and time of the search's execution.
- The names of the officers who executed it except where the investigations are linked to terrorism in which case warrant numbers and duty stations should be shown.
- Whether a copy of the warrant, together with a notice of powers and rights, was handed to the occupier or left at the premises.

The occupier of the premises which have been searched has a right to inspect the search warrant (which should have been returned to the magistrates' court) within twelve months.

Seizure of property

When the police are lawfully on any premises (which includes being there with your consent) they have wide powers to seize anything on the premises if they have reasonable grounds for believing that:

- It has been obtained as a consequence of the commission of an offence.
- It is evidence in relation to any offence.
- It is necessary to seize it in order to prevent it being seized, lost or damaged, altered or destroyed.

'Anything' includes fingerprints. The police may require computerised information which comes within these categories to be produced in a form in which they can remove it. 'Excluded material' and 'special procedure material' (see above) are not protected from seizure once the police are lawfully on the premises. No power of seizure, however, authorises the seizure of material reasonably believed by a constable to be legally privileged.

If you request it, the police must provide a record of seized items within a reasonable time. Lawfully seized articles may be retained so long as is necessary, for example, for production in court, but the articles cannot be kept for use as evidence in a trial or for forensic examination if a photograph or copy would suffice.

6.3 Police powers of arrest

The police may arrest with or without a warrant. There are many powers of arrest under a warrant issued by a justice of the peace or judge and the rules governing each of them is set out in the statute creating the power. This section deals with police powers of arrest without a warrant.

The powers of arrest without a warrant are governed by the Police and Criminal Evidence Act 1984 and can be grouped into the following categories:

- Arrest at common law for breach of the peace.
- Summary arrest for an 'arrestable offence'.
- Arrest subject to conditions.
- Arrest under specific powers.
- Arrest for the purpose of fingerprinting.
- Arrest for failure to answer police bail.
- Arrest to have a sample taken.
- Arrest of a young person for breaking conditions of remand.

Arrest at common law for breach of the peace
A breach of the peace is not in itself a criminal offence but the police and any other person have a power of arrest where there are reasonable grounds for believing a breach of the peace is taking place or is imminent. The Court of Appeal has defined a breach of the peace as being 'an act done or threatened to be done which either actually harms a person, or in his presence his property, or is likely to cause such harm being done' (*R* v. *Howell*).

Summary arrest for 'arrestable offences'
PACE uses the phrase 'summary arrest' to mean arrest without a warrant and lists the arrestable offences for which the police can arrest without a warrant. The following are arrestable offences:

- Offences for which the sentence is fixed by law (including murder – life imprisonment).

- Offences carrying a maximum sentence of imprisonment for five years or more (these include serious offences of violence and dishonesty, but also some relatively minor offences such as shoplifting and minor criminal damage).
- Various statutory offences including offences under the Customs and Excise Management Act 1979, under the Official Secrets Acts 1920 and 1989, under the Sexual Offences Act 1956 and under the Theft Act 1968 (including taking a motor vehicle without the consent of the owner and going equipped for theft) and under the Football (Offences) Act 1991, the Public Order Act 1986 and Criminal Justice and Public Order Act 1994.

This power of arrest may be carried out by anyone – either a police officer or any other person (a citizen's arrest) – in the following circumstances:

- Anyone actually committing or whom he or she reasonably suspects to be committing an arrestable offence.
- Where an arrestable offence has been committed, anyone who is guilty or whom he or she reasonably suspects to be guilty of the offence.

A police officer may arrest in the same circumstances as any person (above), and also:

- Anyone who is or whom he or she reasonably suspects to be about to commit an arrestable offence.
- Where he or she reasonably suspects an arrestable offence has been committed, anyone whom he or she reasonably suspects to be guilty of the offence.

'Serious arrestable offences'

There is a further concept in PACE described as the 'serious arrestable offence'. The definition of a 'serious arrestable offence' does not affect the powers of arrest, but the more draconian police powers under PACE relating to the detention of a subject can be invoked where the offence is a 'serious arrestable offence' – such as detention without charge for up to ninety-six hours, denial of access to a solicitor and delaying notification of detention to a friend for up to thirty-six hours, the authorisation of roadchecks, etc.

The following are serious arrestable offences:

- Treason, murder, manslaughter, rape, kidnapping, incest or intercourse with a girl under thirteen, buggery with a boy under sixteen or a person who has not consented, indecent assault constituting gross indecency, causing an explosion likely to endanger life or property, certain offences under the Firearms Act 1968, causing death by dangerous driving, hostage taking, torture and many drug-related offences, ship hijacking and Channel Tunnel train hijacking, taking indecent photographs of children, publication of obscene matter.

- Any other arrestable offence if its commission has led or is intended to, is likely or threatened to lead to any of the following consequences: serious harm to the security of the state or to public order, serious interference with the administration of justice or with the investigation of offences, the death or serious injury (including disease and impairment) of any person, or a substantial financial gain or serious financial loss to any person.

- For the purposes of denial of access to a solicitor and notification of detention, certain offences under the prevention of terrorism legislation.

Arrest subject to conditions

Often, in a minor case, an arrest should be unnecessary. The alleged offender can be summonsed by post to attend court on a particular date and there is no need to go to a police station at all.

However, PACE also gives the police a power of arrest for all offences, no matter how trivial, petty or minor, which do not carry a power of arrest under the previously discussed powers. The power of arrest can only be used where:

- A constable has reasonable grounds for suspecting that you have committed or attempted, or are committing or attempting to commit an offence (but not where it is suspected that an offence will be committed in the future).

- It appears to the constable that service of a summons is impracticable or inappropriate because any of the general arrest conditions (see below) is satisfied.

Thus, the assumption is that the police should proceed by way of summons for minor offences and the power of arrest ought to be used only if this is impracticable or inappropriate. The impracticability or inappropriateness of the summons must arise from one of the general arrest conditions, which are as follows:

Name and address

- If your name is unknown to, and cannot be readily ascertained by, the police. (You cannot be made to wait while your name is ascertained or confirmed, but might agree to do so to avoid being arrested.)

- If the police have reasonable grounds for doubting that you have given your real name.
- If you have failed to furnish a satisfactory address for the service of a summons (i.e. one at which, it appears to the constable, you will be for a sufficiently long period to be served or at which some other specified persons will accept service of a summons).
- If the police have reasonable grounds for doubting whether an address furnished is satisfactory.

Prevention

- If the police have reasonable grounds for believing that an arrest is necessary to prevent you causing physical injury to yourself or to somebody else, or suffering physical injury, or causing loss of or damage to property (including your own), or committing an offence against public decency, or causing an unlawful obstruction of the highway (see p. 32).

Protection

- If the police have reasonable grounds for believing that arrest is necessary to protect a child or other vulnerable person (undefined) from you.

If you have been arrested under this power and are on the way to the police station, you must be released if a constable is satisfied that there are no longer any grounds for keeping you under arrest – for example, if you suddenly find some kind of identification or if there is no longer any risk of damage or injury.

Arrest under specific powers

The specific statutory powers are listed in PACE and some subsequent legislation and relate mainly to the armed forces, animals, absconders, children and offences under legislation concerning immigration, emergency powers, public order, trespass and the prevention of terrorism. They are not subject to the general arrest conditions (set out above), but many of them carry other conditions (for example, that the arresting constable must be in uniform). These powers of arrest include, for example, powers under the Road Traffic Act 1988 to arrest motorists for drink-driving offences.

Arrest for the purpose of fingerprinting

This power of arrest is designed to apply to somebody who appears at court after receiving a summons and who has not been taken to a police station under arrest. A constable may make an arrest without a warrant in order to have fingerprints taken at a police station. The following conditions must apply:

- You must have been convicted of a recordable offence (i.e. most offences other than trivial or traffic offences).
- You must not have been fingerprinted in the course of the police investigation (or in connection with any matter since conviction).
- You must have failed to comply, within seven days, with the requirement made within one month of the date of conviction to attend a police station for fingerprinting.

Arrest for failure to answer police bail

Under a power inserted into PACE by the Criminal Justice and Public Order Act 1994 the police can arrest you without warrant if you are released on bail from police detention, subject to a duty to attend at a police station and you fail to attend at the appointed time. You must be taken as soon as practicable after the arrest to the police station to which you should have reported.

Arrest to have a sample taken

Under another new power inserted into PACE by the Criminal Justice and Public Order Act 1994 the police may arrest you in order to take samples which could have been taken whilst you were in detention for a recordable offence (see below p. 184). The following conditions must apply:

- You must either have been charged or convicted of the offence and either not have had a sample taken or the sample was unsuitable or insufficient.
- You must have failed to comply with a request to attend a police station in order to have a sample taken.

Arrest of a young person for breaking conditions of remand

The Criminal Justice and Public Order Act 1994 inserted a provision into the Children and Young Persons Act 1969 whereby the police may arrest you in the following circumstances:

- You are a person who has been remanded or committed to local authority care.

- Conditions under the latter legislation have been imposed.
- The police have reasonable grounds for believing you have broken any of the conditions.

You must be taken as soon as practicable before a JP and in any event within twenty-four hours. The JP must decide whether a condition has been broken. If it has then the JP must remand you and the Children and Young Persons Act 1969 applies as though you were charged with or convicted of the offence for which the original remand or committal had been made. If a condition has not been broken, then the remand or committal continues subject to the same conditions as previously.

Information to be given on arrest

An arrest is unlawful unless you are told that you are under arrest and the grounds for the arrest at the time. Such an unlawful arrest will become lawful when the police tell you the reason for the arrest. This information must be given at the time of the arrest or as soon as is practicable afterwards. The information need not be given if it was not reasonably practicable to do so because of your escape from arrest before it could be given. If you attend voluntarily at a police station (or any other place with a constable) without having been arrested you are entitled to leave at will unless placed under arrest.

Arrest other than at a police station

After arrest, a constable must take you to a police station as soon as is practicable (subject to certain exceptions and the power to release you en route). However, a constable may delay taking you to a police station if your presence elsewhere is necessary in order to carry out such investigations as it is reasonable to carry out immediately, such as a search of premises.

Search of a person on arrest (other than at a police station)

A police officer may search you to the extent reasonably required if there are reasonable grounds for believing that:

- You may present a danger to yourself or to somebody else.
- You may have concealed on you anything which might be used to assist an escape from lawful custody or which might be evidence relating to any offence.

There are similar restrictions on searching in public to those discussed above (see p. 57).

6.4 Police detention

The circumstances in which an arrested person may be kept in police detention are set out in the Police and Criminal Evidence Act 1984. The detention is now unlawful unless the provisions of PACE are complied with. A key figure in the scheme is the 'custody officer', a police officer of at least the rank of sergeant.

Normally, the period of detention without charge should not exceed twenty-four hours, although in some cases the maximum period, with extensions, is as long as ninety-six hours. There are a number of stages at which continuation of custody must be authorised – in the early stages by police officers and in the later stages by magistrates. Provision is made for the appointment of custody officers and the performance by them (and any other constable in charge of the prisoner) of important duties. In particular, if the custody officer becomes aware at any time (perhaps after representations from a solicitor) that the grounds for the detention have ceased to apply and that there are no other grounds for continued detention, it is the duty of the custody officer to order your immediate release from custody. Conversely, you may not be released except on the authority of a custody officer at the police station where detention was last authorised. The custody officer is also responsible for keeping a 'custody record' in which all information required to be lodged by PACE and the Codes of Practice is recorded. You or your legal representative are entitled to a copy of this very important document on leaving police detention or appearing before the court. This entitlement lasts for twelve months after release.

On arrival at or after arrest at the police station

The custody officer must, as soon as is practicable after your arrival at the police station or answering to bail (or after arrest at the police station), determine whether there is sufficient evidence to charge you with the offence for which the arrest was made. He or she may detain you for as long as is necessary to make such a determination. If the custody officer decides that there is sufficient evidence to charge you, then you should be charged and must be released unless one of the post-charge detention conditions applies (see p. 177).

Detention without charge

If the custody officer decides that there is insufficient evidence to charge you, then you must be released, unless he or she has reasonable grounds for believing that detention without charge is necessary to secure or preserve evidence relating to an offence for which you are under arrest, or to obtain such evidence by questioning you. In such a case he or she may order further police detention, but the grounds for the detention must be recorded in writing on the custody record. You must be given these reasons.

Detention without charge cannot be authorised in your own interest, or to prevent the repetition or continuation of an offence, or to authorise police 'fishing trips' (since the evidence must relate to an offence for which you are under arrest). If the custody officer has reasonable grounds to believe that you will not answer questions (for example, because your solicitor has said so) detention cannot be necessary to obtain evidence by questioning and detention for questioning in such circumstances may well be unlawful.

There are special rules relating to those who appear to be younger than seventeen. The Code of Practice on detention, treatment and questioning prohibits the placing of any juvenile in police cells, unless no other secure accommodation or practicable supervision is available. In any event, the juvenile may not be placed in a cell with an adult. There are also rules as to the identifying of and giving information to those responsible for the juvenile's welfare. A juvenile who is not released after being charged should, if practicable, be transferred to the care of a local authority.

Review of detention
Periodic reviews of detention must be carried out for all persons in police custody pending the investigation of an offence. If you have been charged, the review is carried out by the custody officer. If you have not been charged, it is carried out by an officer of at least the rank of inspector who has not at any stage been directly involved with the investigation. The general rule is that the first review must be not later than six hours after the detention was first authorised, and subsequent reviews must take place at intervals of not more than nine hours.

Before deciding whether to authorise your detention, the review officer must give you (unless asleep) and your solicitor (or the duty solicitor) an opportunity to make oral or written representations. Representations by a solicitor may be made over the telephone. The representations might relate, for example, to the amount of evidence already obtained or to your refusal to answer questions, these matters being connected with the grounds on which continued detention can be authorised.

The detention clock
PACE limits the length of time for which you can remain in police detention. Such limitations are based on the passage of time from a particular point.

The general rule is that the time starts on your arrival at the first police station to which you are taken after arrest. If arrest takes place at the police station the time starts when you are arrested. There may be some delay between arrest and arrival caused by necessary investigation, but there is a general provision that an arrested person must be taken to a police station as soon as is practicable after arrest.

There are special rules if the arrest takes place outside England and Wales or in a different police area from the one in which you are questioned. You should not be interviewed except at a police station, unless there are special circumstances, for instance that a delay may lead to interference with evidence or harm to other people.

Detention limits and police extensions

The general rule is that you may not be kept in police detention for more than twenty-four hours without being charged. This period can be extended by a maximum of twelve hours on the authority of an officer of the rank of superintendent or above after giving opportunity for representations to be made. The extension can only be authorised where:

- The officer has reasonable grounds for believing that the offence is a serious arrestable offence.
- The investigation is being conducted diligently and expeditiously.
- Detention without charge is necessary to secure or preserve evidence of an offence for which you are under arrest or to obtain evidence by questioning.

The authorisation cannot last beyond thirty-six hours from when the detention clock began.

Detention limits and magistrates' extensions

You must be released by the end of thirty-six hours from the starting point, unless an application is made to a magistrates' court sitting in private. The application is made on oath by a police officer and supported by a written 'information' which must state the nature of the offence, the general nature of the evidence for the arrest, what enquiries have been made and are proposed, and the reason for believing the continued detention is necessary.

You are entitled to a copy of the information and to be legally represented (you can have an adjournment to obtain legal representation). The police officer will be at court to be cross-examined and representations may be made to the magistrates(s). These might be directed, for example, towards any delay in the investigation or in making the application, whether there is a serious arrestable offence involved, whether detention is necessary, and whether there is sufficient evidence for you to be charged.

The court may only authorise further detention if:

- The offence is a serious arrestable offence;
- The investigation is being conducted diligently and expeditiously; and
- Further detention is necessary to secure or preserve evidence relating to the offence or to obtain such evidence by questioning you.

The court may authorise further detention for up to thirty-six hours from the time that the application is granted. A further extension of up to thirty-six hours may be granted if the same procedure is followed. The total maximum period of detention is ninety-six hours from the original starting point (except under the Prevention of Terrorism Act where the maximum is seven days).

Detention after charge

After you have been charged, the custody officer must order your release unless one of the following post-charge detention conditions applies:

- Your name or address is unknown or doubted.
- Detention is necessary to prevent you committing an offence (if you were arrested for an imprisonable offence) or from causing physical injury to any other person or damaging property (if you were *not* arrested for an imprisonable offence).
- Detention is necessary to prevent you failing to appear in court to answer bail.
- Detention is necessary to prevent you interfering with the administration of justice or with the investigation of offences.
- Detention is necessary for your own protection.
- A juvenile needs to be detained in his or her own interest (this is additional to the other grounds which may apply equally to juveniles).

A person who has been detained after charge must be taken to court as soon as practicable and not later than the first sitting after charge. The police are now also able to impose bail conditions.

6.5 The rights of suspects in the police station

The rights of suspects after arrest are contained principally in the Police and Criminal Evidence Act 1984 and in the Code of Practice on the Detention, Treatment and Questioning of Persons and the Code of Practice on Identification of Persons by the Police (Codes C and D).

It is in this area that the provision of the Codes are most important. Any breaches by the police may result in disciplinary action against them and, if the breaches are sufficiently serious, any confession you make may not be admitted as evidence in a trial (see p. 56). The Codes contain detailed provisions governing the conditions of detention, for instance, on the right to legal advice and the right not to be held incommunicado, as well as on searches, exercise and medical treatment. The Codes also provide that if you are classed as a vulnerable person, for example, if you are mentally handicapped or a juvenile, an appropriate adult (not a police officer) should be present to look after your interests.

Personal searches at the police station

The custody officer (see p. 74) is under a duty to list all the property you have with you on your custody record. You may be searched, using reasonable force if necessary if you refuse to cooperate, by a police officer of the same sex, and you should be told the reasons for the search. You are allowed to check the list of property and you should only sign if it is correct.

Clothes and personal effects (not including cash) may only be seized if the custody officer believes you may use them to cause physical injury to yourself or to somebody else, to damage property, to interfere with evidence, to assist an escape, or if he or she has reasonable grounds for believing that they may be evidence relating to an offence. You should be given the reasons for the seizure.

Strip searches

A strip search may take place if the custody officer considers it necessary, but he or she has no power to authorise an intimate body search (see below). The courts have recognised that strip searches may be deeply humiliating and that the removal of a brassiere, for instance, would require considerable justification. No person of the opposite sex except for an 'appropriate adult' who has been specifically requested by the person being searched, may be present at such a search, nor anyone whose presence is unnecessary. Except in cases of urgency there must be two people present other than the person being searched, when the search involves exposure of intimate parts of the body. One of these may be the 'appropriate adult', if relevant. Reasons for a strip search and the results of the search must be recorded on the custody record.

Intimate body searches

An intimate body search consists of the physical examination of any one or more of a person's bodily orifices, including the anus, vagina, mouth, ears and nose. The police can only carry out an intimate body search in limited circumstances. They can search you if a police officer of at least the rank of superintendent has reasonable grounds for believing that:

- You may have concealed on you something that you could use to cause physical injury to yourself or to others, and that you might so use it while you are in police detention or in the custody of a court.
- You have concealed Class A drugs (such as heroin and cocaine, but not cannabis or amphetamines) on yourself and that you are in possession of the drugs either with intent to supply them to somebody else or with a view to committing a customs offence.

A search for drugs (Class A drugs only) may only be carried out by a registered medical practitioner or a registered nurse. It should only be carried out at a hospital, at a registered medical practitioner's surgery or at some other place used for medical purposes. An intimate search for potentially harmful items should also be carried out by a doctor or nurse, but may be conducted by a police officer if an officer of at least the rank of superintendent believes that it is not practicable for it to be carried out by a doctor or nurse. The search may be carried out at a police station.

The right to decent conditions
The Code says that there should only be one person in each cell, but only 'so far as is practicable'. Police cells must be adequately heated, cleaned, ventilated and lit. Bedding should be clean. Access to toilet and washing facilities must be provided.

The police should check on persons in cells once an hour, or every half-hour on those who are drunk. At least two light meals and one main meal should be offered in any period of twenty-four hours. Brief outdoor exercise should be offered daily 'if practicable'. For conditions for juveniles see above (p. 175).

The right to medical treatment
A detained person is entitled to a medical examination by a police surgeon on request (but not for minor ailments – although the benefit of the doubt should be given to the suspect). He or she may also be examined by a GP of his or her own choice at his or her own expense. He or she is entitled to have medication where appropriate.

The custody officer must also call the police surgeon if a detained person is injured, or appears to be suffering from physical illness or mental disorder, or otherwise appears to need medical attention.

All of this must be recorded on the custody record and, when a doctor is called, he or she must also make a record.

The right to legal advice

If you are arrested and held at a police station or other premises you have a statutory right to consult a solicitor (if you wish) in private and free of charge at any time. A duty solicitor scheme is in operation at every police station in England and Wales, so that free telephone advice or a free visit from a solicitor is available. On arrest you should be informed by the custody officer, orally and in writing, of this right, as well as the right to have someone informed of the arrest (see below), and your right to consult the Codes of Practice, and that these are continuing rights – if you do not take advantage of them when offered you can do so at any time you are in the police station. The police must remind you of your right to see a solicitor at many points during your detention: for instance, before the beginning or recommencement of any interview or before a review.

Access to legal advice may be delayed by the police, however, if you are detained for a 'serious arrestable offence' (see p. 169), a drug-trafficking offence, or certain other specified offences where the police are attempting to recover property and you have not yet been charged with an offence for up to thirty-six hours from the relevant time or for up to forty-eight hours in the case of a person detained under the Prevention of Terrorism legislation. Delay may be authorised only by an officer of at least the rank of superintendent if he or she has reasonable grounds (which must be recorded in writing) for believing that the exercise of the right to legal advice would lead to any of the following:

- Interference with evidence of a 'serious arrestable offence'.
- Harm to others.
- The alerting of accomplices.
- Hindering the recovery of property.

There are further grounds where a person is detained under the Prevention of Terrorism legislation. Once the reason for authorising the delay ceases to exist, there may be no further delay in permitting access. Delays are rare and even then they often will not be justified.

The Code provides that if you ask for legal advice you should not be interviewed until you have received it, unless:

- Delay is authorised (as above); or

- An officer of at least the rank of superintendent reasonably believes that delay caused by waiting for a solicitor involves risk or harm to persons or property; or
- This would unreasonably delay the investigation; or
- The solicitor cannot or will not attend and you do not want to use the duty solicitor scheme or the duty solicitor is not available; or
- You consent in writing or on tape to the interview going ahead.

You may consult your solicitor in person, on the telephone or in writing. If you are not allowed to see a solicitor you should think very carefully indeed before answering any questions or making a statement. This is a very difficult decision considering the curtailment of the right of silence (see below).

The right not to be kept incommunicado
If you are detained in a police station or other premises, you are entitled to have one friend, relative or person who is known to you or likely to take an interest in your welfare notified of your whereabouts as soon as is practicable, at public expense. The right is subject to the same delay as consultation with a solicitor (see above). You may exercise this right each time you are transferred to another police station. If the person cannot be contacted you may try two others and after that the police have a discretion as to whether you can try to contact any others.

The police should caution you that what is said in any letter, call or message may be given in evidence, except that the police should not listen to a call or read a letter to a solicitor.

With juveniles, the police have an additional duty to inform the person responsible for their welfare as soon as is practicable and to request their attendance at the police station. There are no provisions permitting delay.

The conduct of interviews
The conduct of interviews is covered by the Code of Practice. The overriding principle is that all persons in custody must be dealt with expeditiously and released as soon as the need for detention has ceased to apply. Except in very limited circumstances interviews should only take place in police stations. At the beginning of an interview at a police station the interviewing officer, after cautioning you, should put to you 'any significant statement or *silence*' which occurred before your arrival at the police station and you should be asked to confirm, deny or add to it. A 'significant' statement or silence is one which is capable of being used in evidence against the suspect or of giving rise to an 'inference'

under the Criminal Justice and Public Order Act 1994 (see below). An accurate written record should be made of each interview (whether or not it takes place at a police station) unless the interview is tape-recorded. You have a right to see the interview record and you should sign it only if it records exactly what you have said.

Virtually all interviews are now tape-recorded and procedures must follow the Code of Practice for tape-recording. You may find that your interview is video-recorded. But less formal interviews which are subsequently written up by police officers in their notebooks are still quite common and you usually have no chance to check the accuracy of their notes. The use of prolonged or oppressive questioning, or the denial of access to a solicitor, or other breaches of the Codes or the Act (so long as they are not merely technical) may render confessions inadmissible in evidence at court.

Questioning should cease as soon as the interrogating officer believes that there is sufficient evidence for a prosecution to be brought successfully. You should then be taken before the custody officer and charged or informed that you may be prosecuted.

Curtailment of the right of silence

The 'right of silence' long considered the most fundamental right of a suspect, has been curtailed by the Criminal Justice and Public Order Act 1994. The Act permits the court hearing the charge against you to draw such 'inferences as appear proper' from the fact of your silence in the following circumstances:

- Failure to mention a fact when questioned under caution *before charge* which is relied on in your defence.
- Failure on being charged with an offence or informed of likely prosecution, to mention a fact which it would have been reasonable for you to mention at the time.
- Failure or refusal to account for objects, substances or marks found on your person, in or on your clothing or otherwise in your possession, in the place where you were arrested.
- Failure or refusal after your arrest to account for your presence at a place at or about the time the offence is alleged to have been committed.

Before inferences can be drawn in the last two cases the officer should first have explained in ordinary language, amongst other things, the nature of the offence, the possibility of adverse inferences being drawn and that a record is being made of the interview which could be used in the trial. This is in additon to the caution which is now worded as follows:

You do not have to say anything. But it may harm your defence if you do not mention when questioned something which you later rely on in court. Anything you do say may be given in evidence.

This caution must be given before any questioning of someone who is suspected of committing an offence about his or her involvement in the offence. You should normally be cautioned on arrest and before any interviewing or continuation of an interview. If you are charged you should be cautioned in the same way but if you are questioned after charge the caution is simply that anything you say may be used in evidence but that you do not have to say anything. This is because there is no provision in the 1994 Act for inference to be drawn from silence after charge.

You cannot be convicted of an offence solely on the basis of your failure or refusal to answer questions or furnish information. Because the rules are more complicated it is of crucial importance that legal advice is sought before answering questions.

Fingerprints
Fingerprints (the term includes palmprints) may be taken from anyone over the age of ten without consent and without a court order in any of the following circumstances:

- If an officer of the rank of superintendent or above believes that fingerprints will confirm or disprove involvement in an offence and authorises the fingerprinting.
- If you have been convicted for a recordable offence.
- If you are charged with a recordable offence or informed that you will be reported for such an offence and fingerprints have not already been taken in the course of the investigation.

Recordable offences are specified in regulations and include all but the most trivial offences.

Where fingerprints are taken without your consent, reasons must be given before they are taken and those reasons must be recorded. Reasonable force may be used. If the police obtain your consent to fingerprinting, it must be in writing if given at a police station. Consent in the case of a child (aged ten to fourteen) is the consent of his or her parents alone and in the case of a young adult (aged fourteen to seventeen) of the parents and him- or herself.

Before your fingerprints are taken, with or without your consent, you should be told that they may be the subject of 'speculative search'. This means that they can be checked against other fingerprints held in records by or on behalf of the police.

Photographs

Your photograph may not be taken without your written consent unless you have been charged, reported for or convicted of a recordable offence and your photograph is not already on record, unless you were arrested along with others, or others are likely to be arrested and a photograph is necessary to establish who was arrested, when and where. A senior officer may also authorise the taking of your photograph where he reasonably believes that you were involved in an offence and there is other identification evidence.

The police may not use force to take a photograph and therefore if you do not cooperate – by turning your face away – the police cannot force you to do so.

Intimate and non-intimate samples

An intimate sample is a sample of blood, semen or any other tissue, fluid, urine, saliva, pubic hair or a swab taken from a bodily orifice other than the mouth. An intimate sample (other than urine) may only be taken by a medical practitioner and dental impressions by a registered dentist, and only if an officer of at least the rank of superintendent authorises it and you consent in writing (consent for juveniles is the same as for fingerprinting). The authorisation may only be given if the officer has reasonable grounds for believing the sample will confirm or disprove your involvement in a recordable offence or even if you are in police detention, if the police previously took from you in the course of investigating an offence, at least two non-intimate (see below) samples for the same means of analysis (often DNA) which prove to be insufficient. (See above p. 172 for powers of arrest to provide fingerprints and samples.)

If you refuse to consent 'without reasonable cause' the court or jury may (in committal proceedings or at a trial) draw such inferences from the refusal as appear proper, and the refusal may be treated as corroboration of any evidence against you to which the refusal is material. You must be warned of this before being asked to provide such a sample. This provision was inserted with rape suspects in mind. The provisions for breath tests and blood or urine samples in cases of drunk-drivers are quite separate. A non-intimate sample is a sample of hair other than pubic hair, a sample taken from a nail or from under a nail, a swab taken from any part of a person's body other than an orifice, and a footprint or a similar impression of any part of a person's body other than a part of the hand (except dental impressions – see above). Non-intimate samples may be taken with your written consent (consent for juveniles is the same as for fingerprinting) or without consent if:

- You are in police detention or being held in custody on the authority of a court and an officer of at least the rank of superintendent authorises it. He or she may do this if there are reasonable grounds for believing the sample will confirm or disprove your involvement in a serious arrestable offence. Reasons for taking the sample must be provided to you and recorded.
- You have been charged with or informed you will be reported with a view to summons for a recordable offence and either have not had a non-intimate sample taken in the course of investigation of the offence or such a sample was taken but it was not suitable or was insufficient for the same means of analysis (often DNA).
- You have been convicted of a recordable offence.

Speculative searches

As described above under 'fingerprints' and 'samples', the police have powers to take fingerprints and samples to compare with any on their databases. Before such fingerprints and samples are taken, you should be informed that they may be used for such a 'speculative search'. Any such search should be conducted before the police are required to destroy the fingerprints and samples.

Destruction of fingerprints, photographs and samples

If you are prosecuted for an offence and acquitted, or if you are not prosecuted or cautioned, all samples, fingerprints, photographs, copies and negatives must be destroyed as soon as is practicable (including the computer representation of your DNA profile). You are entitled to be present to witness the destruction of your photographs and fingerprints and either to witness the destruction of your photographs or be provided with written confirmation of the destruction. Samples should be destroyed also, except in very restricted circumstances, and there is no right to witness their destruction.

Fingerprints and samples taken under the Immigration Act or the Prevention of Terrorism Act may, however, be retained.

Identification by witnesses

Procedures for identification parades or other group identifications, video identifications with others (group identifications), confrontation by witnesses and the showing of photographs to witnesses are set out in detail in a Code of Practice and you should consult these and where possible have a solicitor present.

You are entitled to have a solicitor or friend present at an identification parade which should have at least eight persons (in addition to the suspect) who, so far as possible, resemble the suspect in age, height, general appearance and position in life. Two suspects should not be on the same parade unless they are of roughly similar appearance.

Making notes

If you have been involved in any incident with the police or you have witnessed an incident, it is advisable to make and keep full notes as soon as possible after the events in question.

The police are allowed to refer to notes in court. This happens not because police officers have some special status as witnesses – they do not – but because the notes are contemporaneous, that is, notes which are made at the time or as soon as reasonably practicable thereafter. Contemporaneous notes are not in themselves evidence, but they can be used to refresh the witness's memory.

You have the same right to use notes. A delay in writing the notes of several hours or even a day or so may not prevent you from using the notes. Even if you cannot use them at court they will be a helpful record of the events.

If you are detained at a police station the Codes of Conduct provide that you should be supplied on request with writing materials. (This may be delayed in certain circumstances.) When making notes:

- Write out a full and legible note of everything that happened in the correct sequence of events.
- Write down everything that was said, word for word if possible, particularly any conversation you had with police officers.
- Record the names and numbers, if you know them, of the police officers involved.
- Sign the notes at the bottom and put the time and date.
- If you see a solicitor, hand over the notes and make sure you get a copy to keep for yourself.
- If you are going to court take the notes with you.

If there are witnesses to the incident, take their names and addresses if possible and ask them to make notes.

If you have been injured (for example, by the use of excessive force by the police during your arrest) you must:

- Have photographs taken if there are any visible injuries.
- See a doctor so that your injuries are recorded.

The photographs and medical evidence may be of great value to you if you are charged with a criminal offence or if you wish to make a police complaint or sue the police.

6.6 Special powers under the Prevention of Terrorism Act

The Prevention of Terrorism (Temporary Provisions) Act 1989 (PTA) covers the whole of the UK. It is based on three earlier Acts, the first of which was rushed through Parliament after the Birmingham pub bombings in November 1974. The 1974 and 1976 Acts mainly covered activities associated with affairs in Northern Ireland. The PTA 1984, however, extended the power of arrest for questioning to cover anyone suspected of being involved with international terrorism. The 1989 Act created new offences and court powers of restraint and forfeiture relating to terrorist funds. It also created new powers of investigation into terrorist activities. The Prevention of Terrorism (Additional Powers) Act 1996 (the 1996 Act) completed a very speedy passage through Parliament (twelve hours in total in the House of Commons) giving police powers to designate areas at risk from bombing and implement additional stop and search procedures, searches of premises and parking restrictions.

The PTA does not deal directly with acts of violence usually associated with the word 'terrorism', such as bombings and killings. These are crimes under ordinary criminal law. It is essentially a law that increases the power of the police to detain and interrogate anyone who may have information about 'terrorism', whether or not they are personally involved. 'Terrorism' is defined as 'the use of violence for political ends'. It includes 'any use of violence for the purpose of putting the public or any section of the public in fear'. The PTA is also intended to discourage support for certain Irish organisations.

This section covers the provisions of the Act as they apply to acts of political violence related to Irish or international affairs. Great Britain includes England, Scotland and Wales. The United Kingdom includes Great Britain and Northern Ireland.

If you are arrested or detained under the PTA, it is essential that you obtain expert legal advice as soon as you can.

Arrest and questioning
Under the PTA a police officer can arrest you without a warrant if he or she has 'reasonable' grounds to suspect many activities, some of which are listed below:

- You are involved in the 'commission, preparation or instigation of acts of terrorism' connected with Northern Ireland or any foreign country. Any act connected solely with Great Britain or any part of the UK but unconnected with the conflict in Northern Ireland is not covered by the PTA; or

- You belong to or support any section of the Provisional or Official IRA, or the INLA (see 'banned organisations', p. 159); or
- You have solicited, lent, given or received money or other property for use in connection with acts of terrorism, or you have been involved with the movement of terrorist funds.
- You are subject to an exclusion order and enter a territory forbidden to you, or you have helped or given accommodation to any excluded person while they were in a territory forbidden to them (see 'Exclusion orders', p. 90).

If you are unsure that you are being arrested under the PTA, ask the police officer making the arrest which power is being used. Once arrested, the police can detain you for up to forty-eight hours and then for up to a further five days with the consent of a Secretary of State (in England and Wales the Home Secretary). During this time they do not have to charge you or take you before a court.

During your detention, the police (or prison officer) can take any 'reasonably necessary' steps to identify you, including photographing, fingerprinting and measuring you without your consent or a court order and with reasonable force if you refuse. It is a criminal offence not to give the police, or the army if you are in Northern Ireland, specific information you may have about people or events concerned with acts of political violence connected with Irish affairs. You should always be careful not to pass on anything based on rumour, and you are not obliged to pass on any information at all if you have a reasonable excuse, for example, if the information incriminates you personally or if you would have reason to fear for the safety of either yourself or your family. You can be fined and/or imprisoned if convicted. Although very few have actually been charged or convicted of this offence, people have been threatened with this during interrogation. This offence does not apply to information relating to acts of international terrorism. Other than the offence of 'withholding information', the general principle of the 'right to silence', in its curtailed form, prevails (see above, p. 182), and you are therefore not obliged to answer any other type of question (except about your identity). Because of the inferences which may be drawn by a court from your failure to answer questions during interviews you must consider the consequences of remaining silent extremely carefully.

Your rights under the PTA are, in certain other respects, more limited than those of other suspects. For example, in England and Wales, the 'safeguards' provided in the Police and Criminal Evidence Act (see p. 156) do not apply to limit the circumstances in which you can have your fingerprints taken or provide circumstances under which they will be destroyed – so records can be kept indefinitely. Also, you do not have an absolute right to legal advice until after forty-eight hours and then, under certain circumstances, a senior officer can decide that you can only consult your solicitor in the sight and hearing of a police officer unconnected with your case. You do not have an absolute right to have someone informed of your detention until after forty-eight hours. The Code of Practice under PACE provides for the physical conditions of your detention and your heating, meals, lighting, etc., should therefore be the same as for other suspects, as should those concerning medical treatment.

Always obtain legal advice in any case as soon as possible and before answering any questions.

Examination or detention at ports or airports

Under the PTA, you can be stopped, questioned and detained by an examining officer while entering or leaving Great Britain or Northern Ireland to find out whether you have any connection with or information about the use of violence in relation to Irish or international affairs, or whether you have breached an exclusion order or assisted someone else to do so.

Examining officers can be police, immigration or certain Customs and Excise officers and, in Northern Ireland, soldiers. They can require you to fill in a Landing or Embarkation Card which asks for your name and the details of your address, occupation, name of your employer, address where you will be staying and the purpose of your trip. They can also require you to produce a passport or other papers establishing nationality and identity, or produce any other papers establishing nationality and identity, or produce any other documents considered relevant.

They can search any baggage and keep anything which they consider could be relevant in a court case or in considering an exclusion order. You can be asked any reasonable question.

You can be detained for up to twelve hours in the absence of any suspicion; after this the officer must have 'reasonable suspicion' to continue your detention and you should receive a Notification of Further Examination. As with PTA arrests elsewhere, you cannot be held beyond forty-eight hours without the authority of a Secretary of State and, with the appropriate authority, you can be held for up to a total of seven days.

It is an offence to refuse to comply with directions from an examining officer and you can be fined and/or imprisoned if convicted.

Search of persons or premises

Under the PTA you can be stopped and searched without a warrant if the police suspect you of being involved in terrorism and need to establish if you are carrying anything which makes you liable for arrest. You can also be stopped and searched if you are suspected of supporting a banned organisation or of breaking an exclusion order.

There is a new power inserted by the Criminal Justice and Public Order Act 1994 whereby a senior officer may issue an authorisation covering a specific locality for a specific period that the police may stop and search any vehicles, their drivers and passengers for articles which could be used in connection with terrorism. The police do not need to have any suspicion in relation to the person or vehicle searched. In other respects Code A and the other safeguards in the Police and Criminal Evidence Act 1984 apply. The 1996 Act inserts the same power into the PTA to issue an authorisation for searches of pedestrians. Again the police need not have any suspicion in relation to the person searched.

The police can apply to a magistrate for a warrant to search premises in the usual way (see p. 162). However, they can also carry out a search with a note signed by a superintendent (or officer of higher rank) if he or she considers the case to be one of great public emergency. Using these powers of search the police can seize anything considered to be evidence of an offence relating to a proscribed organisation or an exclusion order, or which would justify the Home Secretary exercising powers of proscription or exclusion.

Exclusion orders

Under the PTA, an exclusion order can be used to expel you from either Great Britain or Northern Ireland or from the whole of the UK. This process does not happen through the courts. Instead, the Secretary of State – usually the Home Secretary or the Secretary of State for Northern Ireland – signs an order when satisfied that:

*   It appears expedient, in order to prevent acts of terrorism intended to influence government policy or public opinion with respect to Northern Ireland affairs;
*   You are or have been concerned in the 'commission, preparation or instigation of acts of terrorism'; or
*   You are attempting to enter Great Britain or Northern Ireland with a view to being concerned in the 'commission, preparation or instigation of acts of terrorism'.

Terrorism in this context is defined as the use of violence designed to influence public opinion or government policy with respect to affairs in Northern Ireland. This includes any use of violence intended to put the public or any section of the public in fear. You cannot, therefore, be excluded if you are believed only to be involved in international terrorism. It is possible, however, that you could be deported under the Immigration Act (see p. 283). 'Commission, preparation or instigation' covers any type of involvement.

Restrictions on exclusion

The type of exclusion order depends on whether or not you are a UK citizen. If you are a UK citizen you cannot be completely excluded from the UK. You can, however, be forbidden to enter (or be in) either Great Britain or Northern Ireland unless you are already excluded from one of these areas or you have been living in the area from which you are to be excluded for the previous three years (not including time spent in prison in the UK, Channel Islands or Isle of Man). If you are excluded you will be removed to the part of the UK you are allowed to be in.

If you are not a UK citizen, you can be forbidden to enter or be in the UK or any part of it. Before excluding you, the Home Secretary should consider whether you have connections which would make it appropriate to send you to another country. You can be excluded irrespective of the length of time you have been living in the UK.

Challenging exclusion

If you are excluded, you should be given a written order that says this and tells you about your right to object as soon as possible. If you want to object, you must write to the Home Secretary within seven days and try to prove your case. If you ask, you also have the right to a private interview with a government adviser appointed by the Home Secretary. You can have a solicitor with you at this interview if the adviser agrees. You will remain in custody while the Home Secretary considers your arguments against exclusion. If you do not make representations within seven days you will be removed whether you agree to this or not. If you agree to being removed before making representations, you must write making your case against exclusion and asking for an interview, if you want one, within fourteen days of your removal. By making representations after you are removed, you lose your absolute right to an interview since you can only have one if the Home Secretary considers it 'practicable'.

If you use either procedure the Home Secretary must consider whether or not to cancel the order, taking into account the report of any interview with the adviser, the adviser's opinion and anything else considered relevant. You can ask people to write supporting your case. However, you cannot call a witness or appeal to a court. The procedure also denies you your right to know what evidence has satisfied the Home Secretary that you should be excluded or the reasons why your representations against the order are successful or not. You cannot, therefore, be confident of being able to provide the evidence necessary to challenge the decision adequately. It is, nevertheless, worth making representations since a number of orders are cancelled as a result.

If your exclusion is not cancelled after you make representations it will last for three years. The Home Secretary can then make a new order excluding you for another three years after reviewing your case. This is done by the Home Office which writes to you at your last known address asking you to fill in a form or write if you want to take part in that review. You may also be offered an interview with the police and you can ask to take a solicitor to this. If you do not hear from the Home Office, you can write asking if you are still excluded and, if necessary, asking for a review. If you are excluded for another three years you can write making representations against this within fourteen days. In any exclusion order case you should obtain expert legal advice to help you with the representations and to consider any possible legal remedies.

Related criminal offences

You can be arrested and charged if you disobey an exclusion order or if you help anyone else to do so. You can be fined and/or imprisoned if convicted. The consent of the Attorney General is necessary before you can be prosecuted.

Banned organisations

Any organisation in Britain can be banned ('proscribed') under the PTA if it appears to the Home Secretary to be involved in terrorism in the UK that is connected to affairs in Northern Ireland, or appears to be promoting or encouraging it. Organisations in Northern Ireland are banned under the Emergency Provisions Act. Organisations which appear to be connected with international terrorism cannot be banned. An organisation is defined as any association or combination of people. The Provisional and Official IRA were proscribed in 1974, the INLA in 1979 and the UDA in 1992.

Related criminal offences

It is a criminal offence:

- To belong or to say you belong to a proscribed organisation, except where you prove that you were a member before the organisation was banned and that you have not been a member since.
- To raise or receive money or goods on behalf of a banned organisation or to encourage any other form of support for it,

except where you can prove that you did not know the money or goods were for this purpose.

- To help organise a public or private meeting of more than three people in support of a banned organisation, or where a speaker belongs or says he belongs to one of these organisations, except where you prove that you did not know this was the case.
- To display, carry or wear in public anything which gives rise to a reasonable fear that you are a member or supporter of a banned organisation, even if you are not.

Apart from the IRA, the INLA and the UDA, it is not illegal to belong to any other group or party in Great Britain, and provided you do not call for support for a banned organisation or for political violence, you can express any views you like about the situation in Northern Ireland. The IRA, INLA and UDA are also illegal in Northern Ireland under the Emergency Provisions Act, as are certain other organisations and groups.

6.8 Further information

Useful organisations

Consult your local telephone directory for the addresses and telephone numbers of the following organisations:

- Citizens' Advice Bureaux
- Law Centres

Bibliography

E. Cape, *Defending Suspects at Police Stations*, Legal Action Group, 1995.

J. Harrison and S. Cragg, *Police Misconduct*, Legal Action Group, 1995.

H. Levenson and F. Fairweather and Ed Cape, *Police Powers: A Practitioner's Guide*, Legal Action Group, 1996.

Ken Lidstone and Clare Palmer, *The Investigation of Crime: A Guide to Police Powers*, Butterworths, 1996.

N. Zander, *PACE 1984*, Sweet and Maxwell, 1996.

7

The rights of defendants

This chapter deals with:

- Principles and procedures.
- Representation and legal aid.
- Trial by jury or trial by magistrates.
- Committal proceedings.
- The right of appeal.
- The right to bail.
- Further information.

7.1 Principles and procedures

If the police suspect that you have committed a crime, they can arrest you or they can stop you to request information (for example, concerning a motoring matter) or they can ask you to come to the police station voluntarily. If you are arrested and questioned at a police station, you may at the end of the police enquiries be charged there and then, and given a charge sheet which will set out the details of the offence and provide you with the date and time that you have to attend court. Alternatively, you may simply be released and in due course find that you are served, by post, with a summons – again a document setting out the nature of the offence you are charged with, and with the date and time that you must attend court. If you fail to turn up in court either in response to police bail following a charge at the police station or in response to a summons, a warrant may be issued for your arrest. Often the police will use the arrest and charge procedure instead of using a summons even though there is no need to do so. As well as the police, other bodies such as the DSS or Customs and Excise can bring criminal proceedings.

There are a number of fundamental principles which are at the heart of our criminal justice system:

- The accused is presumed innocent until proved guilty.

- The prosecution must show beyond reasonable doubt that you have committed the offence. This means that if there is doubt as to guilt, then there must be an acquittal.
- You will be tried on the evidence in the case, not as a result of your previous convictions; the court will not be told of any 'record' since that might create prejudice. You will lose the protection of this rule if you falsely tell the court that you do not have convictions (or that you are of good character) or you attack the character of the prosecution witnesses.
- The trial is based on the spoken evidence of witnesses; generally, written evidence is not allowed since there is no opportunity for the maker of the statement to be cross-examined; it is allowed however when the contents of the evidence are agreed by both sides. The evidence of a witness must be of what he or she saw or heard and not hearsay (i.e. second-hand evidence).
- There are other safeguards that protect you in your dealings with the police when you are a suspect.
- You can still if you wish remain silent in the police station, but, in the words of the caution 'it may harm your defence if you do not mention when questioned something which you later rely on in Court'. For example, the police may have evidence that you were at a particular place involved in an incident of disorder. If you were not there at all, it may be in your best interests to explain immediately where you really were and who you were with, as if you say nothing about your whereabouts or alibi, but introduce this explanation months later at your trial, the court can

---

STOP PRESS

The new government proposes to incorporate the European Convention on Human Rights into domestic law. The rights in the Convention are set out in Chapter 5. A Bill to incorporate the Convention is due to be published in the autumn of 1997 and this is likely to become an Act by July 1998 and to come into force not before January 1999. It is not clear at the time of writing exactly what effect this will have on our laws. It is likely that the Convention will be able to be used to challenge some of the existing procedures and judge-made law although whether the Convention will be given a higher status than statute is not so clear. Nevertheless the rights set out in this book may be enhanced by the Convention and in future the rights in the Convention will have to be considered much more seriously than they have been in the past.

infer that your account is something that you made up at a later date because, if true, it would have been reasonable to give the details at once. There must be other evidence against you for an adverse inference to be drawn from silence and there is also a range of situations in which failing to mention relevant facts would not be considered unreasonable, depending on age, mental state, etc. You will need legal assistance to help you decide what to do.

Ninety per cent of prosecutions are brought by the Crown Prosecution Service but individuals themselves can also bring criminal cases. Usually these will start by summons. The Director of Public Prosecutions can take over such proceedings in order to continue them or to put a stop to them. Legal aid is not available in such cases and there may be other cost implications. Some other institutions like local councils also prosecute, as do some individual shop owners.

7.2 Representation and legal aid

Whoever brings the proceedings and whether you receive a summons or are charged at a police station, it is advisable to have advice from a lawyer as soon as possible. You may think that your innocence will be obvious to the court, but you cannot be sure that you will be believed. Court procedures can be confusing and the rules of evidence which govern what you can and cannot say are complicated. Even if you do decide to plead guilty, a lawyer can tell the court about any special circumstances which might help to reduce the penalty you receive.

If you are charged by the police or receive a summons, you can go to a solicitor or a law centre for advice upon whether to plead guilty or not guilty and to obtain information as to what penalty you are likely to receive if found guilty. Advice will be free from a law centre, and will be free from a solicitor if you are in receipt of income support. If you are working but on a low wage you may have to make a contribution by weekly sum to your legal aid. You are entitled to receive advice in person from a solicitor in the police station if you are detained there and that assistance is always free no matter what your income is.

The police must tell you of your right to contact a solicitor. You can nominate one of your own choice, or if you do not know of one, you can request the duty solicitor. The duty solicitor is not some kind of a second-class solicitor chosen by the police – most legal aid solicitors in any geographical area are part of a duty rota and take it in turns to cover particular days and nights to give emergency help to those who need them. Duty solicitors are also provided in the court as well as the police station. They can apply for bail for you, help you with legal aid and will speak to the court for you if you decide to plead guilty. While acting as duty solicitor, they cannot represent you at a contested trial.

If your case is to progress through the courts, your solicitor will provide you with an application form for legal aid as will the court itself. The application must be granted if you are below the appropriate financial threshold *and* if it is in the interests of justice that you should be defended. Refusals of legal aid vary from court to court but are rare, except on financial grounds, if the offence is a serious one or there are complicating factors in the case. If the application is granted, the legal aid order is sent to your solicitor if you have one or to a solicitor you can choose from a list kept at the court.

In any case that can be tried in the Crown Court (see below) there is a right of appeal if legal aid is refused (unless the refusal is only on financial grounds). In other cases it is possible to ask the court to review the decision to refuse legal aid by writing to the court or by making representations in person.

Using a McKenzie adviser

If you are refused legal aid and cannot afford to pay a lawyer privately, or if you prefer to defend yourself, you are entitled to have a friend – known as a McKenzie adviser – with you in court. This friend cannot speak openly to the court but can sit beside you, take notes and give you advice as to what to do and what questions to ask. The reason this friend is known as a 'McKenzie' is because of the case in which this right was first established.

As soon as possible after the case begins you should say to the court, 'I would like to have a friend as a McKenzie adviser to sit beside me to help me in representing myself.' If the application is refused, you should ask for an adjournment to obtain legal advice because the High Court can compel magistrates to accept the presence of a McKenzie adviser and you can apply for civil legal aid for your application to the High Court.

7.3 Trial by jury or trial by magistrates

All criminal cases start in the magistrates' court and most (93 per cent) are finally dealt with there. Others go to higher courts, the Crown Courts, where the cases are heard by a judge and jury. The question of 'venue', or where the case is to be finally disposed of, depends upon the type of offence with which you are charged:

- Some relatively trivial offences such as minor public order charges and most motoring matters can only be dealt with in the magistrates' court and are called 'summary' offences.

- Serious matters such as murder, rape and wounding with intent can be dealt with only in the Crown Court and these are called 'indictable offences'.
- Some offences can be dealt with at either court and these are called 'either way' offences.

Note that in many summary only cases there will be a time limit on bringing proceedings. Usually prosecutions have to be brought within six months of the incident. Such limits do not apply in more serious cases.

Where offences are triable either way, the magistrates will themselves express a view as to where they feel the case should proceed. If they decide the case must go to the Crown Court, you do not have any choice. If you want to be tried in the magistrates' court, you should explain this to them before they decide. However, even if they say that they will deal with the matter at magistrates' level, you will have the right if you wish to choose trial by jury. Making this decision really requires legal advice and discussion with your family or friends. Amongst the things to bear in mind when making your decision are:

- The case is likely to be heard more quickly in a magistrates' court than a Crown Court.
- The chances of acquittal by a jury are usually greater than by magistrates.
- Penalties are generally lighter in a magistrates' court, although the magistrates can still send a defendant to the Crown Court for the purpose of sentencing if they think it is appropriate to do so.
- Costs will be lower in the magistrates' court which is important for those people not entitled to legal aid (although it is more likely that legal aid will be granted for Crown Court trials).
- If evidence needs to be challenged, for instance that a confession was made to the police under duress, this can usually be best handled by the Crown Court because, despite any ruling on whether evidence can be used in the magistrates' court, the magistrates will have heard the evidence anyway!

7.4 Committal proceedings

If you are charged with an indictable offence or an either way offence which is going to the Crown Court, the magistrates have to decide whether there is enough evidence to send you for trial to the Crown Court. This is done at a hearing called a 'committal'. Often the written statements of the prosecution's witnesses can be accepted without any live evidence being called and the hearing will be brief and uneventful. In certain circumstances, the defence may want to insist that witnesses be called to give evidence in court at the committal hearing – again you need legal advice as to whether this would be appropriate in your case. At a committal hearing, the magistrates are not deciding if you are guilty or not, but only if the prosecution evidence shows that there is at least a case for you to answer.

Trial in the magistrates' court

With a few exceptions for traffic offences where it is possible to plead guilty by post, you have to attend at court regardless of whether you wish to plead guilty or not guilty. If you do not attend a warrant for your arrest is likely to be issued. It is often necessary for you to attend on a number of occasions before the trial itself as well.

You or your lawyers should have received a copy of all of the evidence (in the form of statements) before the trial and you should know something of what is going to be said and what prosecution witnesses are to be called. If you have decided to plead guilty you should have decided this in advance so that you can notify the prosecution to avoid them having to bring all their witnesses to court (and avoid extra costs for yourself). It is likely that your sentence will be lighter (and there may be fewer costs) if you plead guilty than if you fight the case, although you should be aware of the consequences of doing so. In particular, once the court has sentenced you it is virtually impossible to undo your conviction and subsequent record.

It is important if you are to defend yourself to be aware of the procedure in the court. Once you have said you will plead not guilty the trial will usually be adjourned to another date because the court will have to allow more time for the hearing. On the day of the trial the prosecution begins by giving a brief account of the case and then calls its witnesses. Each witness is asked questions by the prosecution and then you or your lawyer are given a chance to cross-examine them. Any matters of dispute must be put to the witnesses otherwise the court will assume that what they have said is accepted by you.

The prosecution can then re-examine the witnesses but only to 'clear-up' matters raised during the cross-examination. When all of the prosecution's witnesses have been heard you can then submit that there is 'no case to answer' if the evidence given so far does not demonstrate your guilt. If this submission is not successful you then call your witnesses, only this time of course you begin the questioning. If you intend to give evidence yourself you will be the first defence witness. After all the witnesses have been heard both the prosecution and defence make short speeches outlining why the magistrates should convict (or not!).

You do not have to call any witnesses or give evidence yourself. The prosecution has to prove its case and you can merely attack its evidence although your case is very likely to be much stronger if you give your side of the story. Because of the prosecution's duty to prove the case beyond reasonable doubt you only need to create a doubt to be acquitted.

After giving their verdict the magistrates will release you if they decide you are not guilty. You should be able to get any legal costs back if you are acquitted and you should consider whether you would be able to sue the police for assault (on arrest), false imprisonment and malicious prosecution (see p. 128).

If the court decides you are guilty they will then hear from the prosecution about your character and any convictions. You can then make a speech in mitigation pleading for a lenient penalty. You can call character evidence and if you are concerned that you might be imprisoned, you or your lawyer can explain and produce evidence of why it would be wrong to put you in prison (family needs, employment prospects, etc.). Before passing sentence the magistrates may wish to obtain reports from the probation service or doctors and as a result the sentence decision must be postponed.

Trial in the Crown Court

After the case is committed for trial a date will eventually be fixed (although often you will be given very little notice of this). There are some differences between trial in the Crown Court and the magistrates' court. One difference is that you must disclose any evidence of alibi or of experts that you intend to give at the trial before the trial occurs.

Otherwise the trial follows very much the same pattern as described above for the magistrates' court. Of course in Crown Court trials the jury decides on guilt or innocence and the judge decides on matters of law, whether evidence can be heard or not (an argument heard in the absence of the jury) and on sentence. One other difference is that after the prosecution and defence have made their speeches to the jury, the judge then sums up the evidence and explains the law.

Although the judge will expect the jury to reach a unanimous verdict, if they cannot do so after two or three hours the judge will tell them that they can reach a majority verdict (of at least ten of them).

7.5 The right of appeal

After conviction and sentence in the magistrates' court of a summary offence or an either way offence, you can appeal to the Crown Court against your conviction or, if you pleaded guilty, against the sentence you received. An appeal must be made within twenty-one days of the magistrates' court hearing. Appeal forms are available from the magistrates' court or the Crown Court and there are further forms to be filled in for legal aid for the appeal. If the sentence of the magistrates was one of custody, you can apply for bail to be granted until the appeal is heard, and if bail is refused at this stage it may still be possible to speed up the hearing of the appeal so that you are not detained for long before the matter is reviewed.

The hearing of the appeal against conviction does not involve a jury even though there is a complete rehearing of the case. It is heard by a judge sitting with two magistrates other than those who have already dealt with you. The Crown Court can confirm, reverse or change the decision of the magistrates' court.

Appeals on a point of law

If you think that the magistrates made a mistake in law, you can appeal to the Divisional Court of the Queen's Bench Division of the High Court, again within twenty-one days of the decision, asking the magistrates to 'state a case' for the opinion of the High Court. This is a complicated procedure and again you should consult a solicitor and may well qualify for legal aid.

Appeals from the Crown Court

An appeal against conviction or sentence at the Crown Court itself is made to the Court of Appeal (Criminal Division); the necessary forms are obtained from the Crown Court that dealt with you and should be sent back there. You are entitled as of right following any Crown Court proceedings to have written advice from the lawyer who dealt with your case as to whether you have grounds for appeal. Even if your lawyer does not recommend an appeal and therefore does not put his or her name to any appeal, you can still appeal yourself. If you are in prison, the legal aid office within the prison will provide you with the necessary forms.

The prosecution can only appeal against sentence (if it is unduly lenient) but not against an acquittal.

When an appeal is lodged, it is first of all considered by a single judge. If the single judge sees no merit in your appeal and says so you can still appeal against that decision to the full Court of Appeal of three judges. You may be warned that if you do this, time may be added to any custodial sentence you have been ordered to serve. In fact, in practice this scarcely ever happens. However, if leave is refused you are very unlikely to be granted legal aid and you may have to represent yourself without the help of lawyers.

Appeals to the House of Lords

An appeal from the Court of Appeal to the House of Lords is only possible if it is on a point of law which is of 'general public importance'.

Permission to pursue this course must be given either by the Court of Appeal or the House of Lords itself. Very few criminal appeals reach this stage – the procedure is complicated and again legal advice is essential.

7.6 The right to bail

'Bail' means that you are released from custody either by the police or by a court, but with a duty to appear either at a police station or a magistrates' court or Crown Court as and when specified. Failure to appear without a reasonable excuse is an offence. Bail can be granted by a police station or court subject to conditions, such as living at a particular address, reporting on particular days to a local police station, staying indoors at night between certain hours, not approaching a particular prosecution witness, surrendering your passport, or providing one or more sureties.

Sureties

A surety is somebody who undertakes to forfeit a sum of money if you do not appear in court for your trial. The exact sum is fixed by the court when granting bail and the court decides if a person is a suitable surety by considering their financial position, their character – in other words their lack of any criminal convictions themselves – and how likely the person is to be able to influence you to attend court.

Bail at a police station

After you have been charged at a police station, you must be given bail unless:

- Your name and address are unknown or doubted on reasonable grounds;
- The custody officer reasonably believes detention is necessary for your own protection or protection of others or their property; or
- The custody officer reasonably believes that you will fail to appear at court or that detention is necessary to avoid interference with the investigation or the administration of justice.

If you are detained by the police in this way, you must be brought before the next available magistrates' court, which, hopefully, would be no later than the following morning. If you are arrested on a Saturday, you may be held until the following Monday morning before being taken to court.

Bail at the magistrates' court

An accused person is entitled to bail unless certain exceptions apply. You are not allowed to make bail applications each and every time that you appear before the court, though if the first bail application is made in somewhat hurried circumstances and before your solicitor has had a chance to look into every aspect of the case, you will normally be allowed a further bail application one week later if bail is at first refused. If bail is refused, then you will normally not be allowed further applications unless there is a real change in your circumstances.

If the offence you are charged with does not carry a prison sentence, bail must be granted unless:

* You have previously been given bail and failed to come to court; or
* The court believes you should be kept in custody for your own protection; or
* You have been granted bail in connection with the present charge and have broken the conditions of your bail.

If the offence does carry a prison sentence, bail must still be granted unless the court believes that:

* Any of the above three factors apply; or
* You will probably not turn up for your trial; or
* You will probably commit an offence whilst on bail; or
* You will probably interfere with witnesses or in some other way obstruct the course of justice.

In deciding whether or not to give you bail, the court considers your own character, background, associations and connections in the community, any previous record on your part in turning up for trial after being bailed, the strength of the evidence against you, and anything else which it thinks relevant. If you are already on bail for an offence and find yourself arrested for a new offence, further bail will not readily be granted.

Bail at the Crown Court

If you are refused bail by the magistrates, you can appeal against their decision by applying for bail to a Crown Court judge. This hearing will normally be dealt with by your solicitor 'in chambers' which means that the application is heard in the judge's private room rather than in open court. You will not normally be present, but simply notified at the prison where you are held of the outcome of the application.

Bail from the High Court

If a Crown Court judge refuses you bail, you can apply to a High Court judge in chambers. Legal aid is not available for this particular step, so you would have to find out whether your solicitor would be prepared to deal with the application without charge or try to raise the necessary money through your family.

Reasons for bail decisions

Normally a court must give reasons for refusing to grant bail – and in certain cases must give reasons for granting bail, for example in cases of murder, manslaughter and rape where the prosecution have opposed the grant of bail.

Appeals by the prosecution

The prosecution now has a new right to appeal against the decision of the court to grant bail. The appeal has to be lodged quickly but you will be kept in custody pending the decision. It is very important to obtain legal advice if this happens to you. The right to appeal by the prosecution only applies where the offence charged carries a maximum penalty of five years or more and only where the defendant has previously committed an offence whilst on bail in the last ten years.

7.9 Further information

Useful organisations

Consult your local telephone directory for addresses and telephone numbers of the following organisations:

- Citizens' Advice Bureaux
- Law centres

Bibliography

Archbold, *Criminal Pleading, Evidence and Practice*, Sweet & Maxwell, published every year.
J. Smith and B. Hogan, *Criminal Law*, Butterworths, 1993.
Stone's Justices' Manual, Butterworths, published every year.

8

The rights of prisoners

This chapter sets out the rights that prisoners have. It deals with:

- Reception.
- Complaints and requests and the Prisons Ombudsman
- The courts.
- Access to lawyers.
- Visits and letters.
- Telephones.
- Marriage and founding a family.
- Women prisoners.
- Categorisation and allocation.
- Discipline, adjudication and punishment.
- Segregation and transfer.
- Medical treatment.
- Work, exercise and education.
- Parole.
- Further information.

Prisoners retain certain basic rights which survive despite imprisonment. The rights of access to the courts and of respect for one's bodily integrity (i.e. not to be assaulted or treated medically against one's will) are such fundamental rights. Others may be recognised as the law develops. Prisoners lose only those civil rights that are taken away either expressly by an Act of Parliament or by necessary implication. (One right taken away by statute is that prisoners detained following conviction do not have a right to vote.) The test in every case is whether the right is fundamental and whether there is anything in the Prison Act 1952, the Prison Rules 1964 or elsewhere which authorises the prison authorities to limit such a right. In law, the Prison Rules have legal force only insofar as the Prison Act gives authority for the Rule: legal challenges to the Rules have been successful in cases where the courts have held that the Act does not authorise the scope of a particular Rule. The Prison Rules provide a structure and framework for the regulation of prison life. Breach of the Rules by the prison authorities does not of itself give prisoners the right to sue in the courts for damages.

STOP PRESS

The new government proposes to incorporate the European Convention on Human Rights into domestic law. The rights in the Convention are set out in Chapter 5. A Bill to incorporate the Convention is due to be published in the autumn of 1997 and this is likely to become an Act by July 1998 and to come into force not before January 1999. It is not clear at the time of writing exactly what effect this will have on our laws. It is likely that the Convention will be able to be used to challenge some of the existing procedures and judge-made law although whether the Convention will be given a higher status than statute is not so clear. Nevertheless the rights set out in this book may be enhanced by the Convention and in future the rights in the Convention will have to be considered much more seriously than they have been in the past.

More detailed instructions are given in the Standing Orders and Advice and Instructions to Governors (which replaced Circular Instructions), the internal directives which govern the conduct of prison life issued to prison governors and prison officers. A number of the Standing Orders are now published by the Home Office. They are a vital source of information about prisoners' rights and entitlements.

8.1 Reception

On reception into prison a prisoner will be searched and may be photographed. Any property which he or she is not allowed to have with him or her in prison will be kept by the prison authorities. A list will be made on arrival of all property and the prisoner must be given the opportunity to check it is correct before signing it. All cash must be paid into an account which is under the governor's control. All prisoners should be issued on arrival with a copy of the Prisoners' Information Handbook. A copy of the Prison Rules must be made available to any prisoner who requests it.

8.2 Complaints and requests

Within prison, complaints and/or requests may be made in person or in writing to a governor, or to the Board of Visitors. A governor must be available each day to hear complaints or requests. The prisoner need not give the reason for his or her application to see the governor and an application may be made direct in writing and in confidence to the governor or chair of the Board of Visitors. Prisoners will have to give the reason why they wish the complaint to be dealt with in confidence, but it may be that the person complained about will be told of the complaint – which rather discourages complaints of this nature. If a complaint is made to the governor a written reply should normally be received within seven days.

If the prisoner is not satisfied with the decision, he or she may appeal to the casework unit, a department under the control of the area manager at Prison Service Headquarters.

Some issues – called 'reserved subjects' – may only be dealt with by Prison Service Headquarters. These include parole, transfer to or removal from mother and baby units, Category A status, life sentence prisoners, transfers and deportation. Complaints on these issues will be dealt with by the relevant department and should also be replied to within six weeks. The booklet 'How to Make a Request or Complaint: Information for Prisoners' which gives details of the procedures should be available in prison libraries.

If a prisoner is not satisfied with the response received from this system, it is possible to make a complaint to the Prisons Ombudsman. The Ombudsman can investigate complaints only when the internal request/complaints system has been exhausted and the complaint must be made within one month of the reply received from Prison Service Headquarters. The complaint must be made personally by the prisoner (or with his/her signed authority). The Ombudsman will normally take around twelve weeks to investigate the matter and will then issue a report either upholding or rejecting the complaint. If it is upheld, recommendations will be made to the Prison Service about the individual case and any general issues that it raises. The Ombudsman cannot investigate decisions concerning release on parole licence, decisions made personally by Ministers or clinical judgements made by medical staff.

Prisoners may also raise complaints with any outside organisation or person, for example, their MP, the Parliamentary Commissioner for Administration, the European Parliament, the European Commission of Human Rights (ECHR), the police; petitions may also be made to the Queen and Parliament. For a complaint to be admissible with the ECHR it must be made within six months of the alleged breach or from the time that all effective remedies that exist in this country have been exhausted. It is important to remember that the request/complaint system is not considered a suitable remedy when calculating this time limit. Again, details of how to petition the ECHR should be available in the prison library (see Chapter 5).

8.3 The courts

Prisoners have the absolute right to commence legal proceedings in the courts either in person or through a solicitor. Prisoners can conduct:

- Normal civil proceedings such as divorce or breach of contract.
- Cases where the prisoner is suing the prison authorities, for example, for assault or medical negligence.
- Judicial review in the High Court of an administrative or disciplinary decision which affects him or her.

The High Court will only intervene by way of judicial review when it can be shown that a decision has been taken which is wrong in law (for example, where the prison authorities had no power to do what they did) or the decision was flawed by procedural unfairness. The High Court has reviewed a wide range of decisions by the prison authorities, including parole and parole revocation, security categorisation, transfer, censorship, segregation and the separation of a mother from her baby.

The Race Relations Act applies to prisons and discrimination (for example, in the allocation of jobs) would be actionable in the courts.

A breach of the Prison Rules does not give a prisoner grounds by itself to sue the prison authorities for their failure to comply with the Rules. In such cases, the prisoner will need to establish some form of loss or damage resulting from the breach of the Rules.

At present, a prisoner acting without a solicitor who wishes to be produced at court to present his or her case in person must apply to the Home Office by completing the relevant request form, which includes a requirement that he or she undertakes to pay the costs of his or her production. These costs should be limited to production from the prison nearest to the court and the level at which they are set should have regard to what the prisoner can actually afford to pay. The courts have recognised that there may be an appearance of bias if the Home Office refused to produce at court a prisoner who was unable or who had refused to give an undertaking as to costs in an action when the Home Office is the defendant to the action. A prisoner faced with this difficulty should apply to the court which is to hear his or her action for guidance.

8.4 Access to lawyers

Prisoners have an absolute right to have visits from and correspond with their solicitor. They do not have to tell the prison authorities why they wish to contact a solicitor, nor make any complaint about prison treatment to the authorities before contacting a solicitor for legal advice.

8.5 Differentiated regimes

All prisoners, including unconvicted and civil prisoners, are required to be classified to one of three regimes: basic, standard or enhanced. This decision is taken by the governor based on the prisoner's performance in custody (for example, their disciplinary record). Each regime offers a different level of incentives and privileges and commonly, prisoners on the basic regime will receive the bare legal minimum in terms of visits or access to private cash and wages. Those on the standard and enhanced regimes will receive progressively more favourable facilities, although the precise nature of these will vary according to each prison's security category. These regulations also require a number of key items such as phonecards, cigarettes and stamps to be purchased from the private cash allowance.

8.6 Visits and letters

There are detailed regulations on communications which are set out in Standing Order 5 which is publicly available from HMSO and which should also be available in the prison library.

Visits

Convicted prisoners are entitled to a visit on reception to prison and then a minimum of two visits every four weeks. Governors should allow more visits if facilities and staffing make this possible and many prisons do so for prisoners on the standard and enhanced regimes. Prisoners will be issued with visiting orders (VOs) which must be sent out, with the visitors' names on them. Visitors then present the order on arrival at prison. Up to three adults and four children are normally allowed at once. Most prisons now require visitors to telephone in advance of their visit to ensure that there is sufficient space for it to take place.

Unconvicted prisoners may have daily visits. These should total at least one and a half hours a week, though in practice such visits are likely to be limited to short daily visits.

Visits from legal advisers, probation officers, etc., do not count against a prisoner's visits' entitlement. Nor is there a restriction on the number of visits allowed from a legal adviser.

The Assisted Prison Visits Scheme exists to help close relatives with the costs of travel. All prisoners, convicted and unconvicted, are eligible for assisted visits if the relative(s) qualify because of their low income.

The governor or Board of Visitors may grant extra visits if they are considered necessary for the welfare of the prisoner or his or her family. A prisoner who is located far from home may save up to twenty-six visits a year and then be transferred temporarily to a prison near his or her family to have these accumulated visits. The prisoner must have served at least six months since he or she was allocated to a prison to be eligible for accumulated visits.

It is a criminal offence to pass items to a prisoner during a visit, for which the visitor can be fined or imprisoned. Most prisons will allow certain items to be handed in through official channels. The governor has power to refuse or restrict visits on the grounds of security, good order and discipline, or if he or she believes it will prevent or discourage crime, by either:

- Refusing visits from certain people.
- Ordering closed visits, i.e. in a small room with a prison officer present.
- Ordering screened visits where there is a glass partition between prisoner and visitor.

There is power to search and strip search visitors entering or leaving prisons providing that no more than reasonable force is used, that the decision to search is not perverse and that the search is conducted in a seemly and decent manner and only by members of the same sex as the visitor.

Police officers may interview an inmate in prison, but only if the prisoner is willing to be interviewed. The provisions of the Police and Criminal Evidence Act and the Codes of Practice do not generally apply to interviews in prison but instructions to the prison authorities say that the spirit of the provisions must be observed as though the interview were at the police station. Copies of the Codes of Practice must be made available in the prison library. The prisoner of course has the right to consult a legal adviser before any interview takes place.

Letters

Convicted prisoners may send one letter a week on which the postage will be paid (the 'statutory' letter) and at least one 'privilege' letter, the postage for which must be paid for out of the private cash allowance. The statutory letter may not be withdrawn or withheld as part of punishment for a disciplinary offence. In addition, prisoners may be granted 'special' letters which do not count against the statutory or privilege letter allowance. A special letter should be granted, for example, after conviction to allow a prisoner to settle his or her business affairs, when transferred to a different prison, or to make arrangements regarding employment and accommodation on release.

In practice, prisoners in many prisons may send and receive more letters than this minimum allowance. Prisoners in open prisons have no restriction on the volume of their correspondence.

Unconvicted prisoners may send as many letters as they wish at their own expense and will be allowed two second-class letters per week on which the postage will be paid by the prison authorities.

Censorship

Mail is censored in dispersal prisons (those designed to accommodate high-risk prisoners) and for all Category A prisoners, but otherwise letters will not routinely be read. There is power for the governor to return an 'excessive' number of letters from a correspondent, and if they are 'overlong' the governor may request letters be limited to four sides of A5 paper. Letters may be returned to the sender if these requests are ignored. Complaints about prison treatment are no longer prohibited and letters – whether to family or to MPs, the ECHR, etc. – may not be stopped on this ground.

Letters between a prisoner and his or her legal adviser are protected from interference and may not be read nor stopped, whether or not legal proceedings have been issued. There may be examination of such correspondence only to the minimum extent necessary to check that it is *bona fide* legal correspondence. If a letter is to be inspected it must be done in the presence of the prisoner.

8.7 Telephones

Card-operated telephones for the use of prisoners are being installed in all prisons so that closer links with family and friends can be maintained by those in prison. For security reasons all calls will be recorded and all calls may be monitored and recorded, except those to legal advisers, the Samaritans and other 'reputable organisations'. Use of the telephone may be limited by the governor, but should not be restricted as part of a disciplinary punishment unless the offence was directly related to the misuse of the cardphone or phone card.

Contacting the media

Prisoners are not allowed to telephone the media from cardphones and must make an application for permission from the governor. Letters sent to the media can be stopped if they contain information about the past criminal offences of the prisoner or others, identify members of staff or are sent in return for payment. Serious comment on the criminal justice system is allowed. It used to be policy for journalists visiting prisons to be asked to sign an undertaking stating that any material obtained would not be used for publication or professional purposes. This policy was ruled to be unlawful by the High Court in December 1996 and journalists should now be allowed to visit in the same manner as other social visitors. At the time of writing, an appeal against the decision is in process.

8.8 Marriage and founding a family

High-risk prisoners who wish to get married will have to make arrangements with the prison authorities for a service to take place within the prison. Low-risk prisoners may be given escorted leave or temporary release to marry outside prison.

Prisoners, especially those serving long sentences, may wish to start a family with their partner by artificial insemination. Prison Department policy is that this should only be allowed where there are 'exceptionally strong reasons', and where the applicant couple are legally married. Article 12 of the European Convention on Human Rights guarantees the right to marry and found a family: a refusal by the Prison Department to allow artificial insemination could be challenged in the ECHR.

8.9 Women prisoners

Male and female prisoners will be held completely separately from each other, though this may be in the same prison. As a matter of practice, women prisoners are allowed to wear their own clothes and do not have to wear prison uniform.

There are a limited number of mother and baby units within the prison system. A baby may be kept up to the age of nine months in Holloway, eighteen months at Styal (both closed prisons) and eighteen months at Askham Grange. If the baby has reached these age limits before the mother has served her sentence, the mother may be forced to give up looking after her baby either then or at an earlier stage.

8.10 Categorisation and allocation

There are broadly five categories of prison:

- local prisons for unconvicted and short-term prisoners,
- dispersal prisons for high security prisoners,
- training prisons for long-term prisoners who do not need the highest security,

- category C prisons, which are closed but have less internal security and
- open prisons for prisoners not believed to be a risk to the public or in danger of escaping.

Immediately after conviction, a male prisoner will be held at a local prison while his security categorisation and allocation is decided. Because there are fewer young offenders and women prisoners and prisons, the arrangements are not exactly the same. Women's prisons and young offender's institutions are simply divided into open and closed establishments.

Categorisation

There are four security categories:

- Category A: prisoners whose escape would be highly dangerous to the public, police or security of the state no matter how unlikely their escape may be.
- Category B: prisoners who do not need the highest conditions of security but for whom escape must be made very difficult.
- Category C: prisoners who cannot be trusted in open conditions but who do not have the ability or resources to make a determined escape attempt.
- Category D: prisoners who can reasonably be trusted to serve their sentences in open conditions.

Women prisoners and young offenders may be made Category A but normally, they will either be allocated simply to open or closed conditions. Categorisation decisions are made by the governor and these can be reviewed by the prisoner casework unit through the complaints or requests procedure. A prisoner can then either make a complaint to the Ombudsman if the decision is considered to be unfair or, alternatively, could apply to the High Court for judicial review of his or her categorisation if there were evidence that it had been arrived at unlawfully, for example, by taking account of irrelevant information or applying the wrong criteria.

Category A prisoners have greater restrictions upon them for security reasons, and their visitors will be vetted by the police on behalf of the prison authorities. These prisoners are entitled to a formal, annual review of their security categorisation during which the gist of reports prepared on them will be disclosed and the prisoner invited to make written representations to the decision-making committee. Legal advice and assistance can be sought in making these written representations.

Allocation

Prisoners may be allocated to any prison in England and Wales according to the offence, sentence, security category and individual circumstances of the prisoner. There is no right to be located close to home, but the prisoner can apply for transfer (as can his or her family, who might wish to put in evidence, for example, from a GP about the difficulties illness causes in travelling long distances). Again, the Ombudsman could intervene in an allocation decision if it could be shown to be unfair or, an application can be made to the High Court if the decision is, for example, wrongly motivated, especially if it deprived an unconvicted prisoner of access to his or her lawyers and family.

8.11 Discipline, adjudication and punishment

The Prison Rules create a number of offences against discipline which can be punished by the governor. The Board of Visitors no longer has any powers in relation to disciplinary matters. If the alleged offence is too serious for the governor to deal with, it will be referred to the police for prosecution in the criminal courts. If there is to be a referral to the police, a disciplinary charge should still be laid against the prisoner and, if the governor is satisfied that there is a case to answer, he or she should adjourn the hearing pending the outcome of the police investigation. If the police decide not to proceed in the outside courts, the governor may continue the proceedings. However, a prisoner cannot be tried for the same offence in both the criminal courts and before the governor.

There is a new offence of prison mutiny which can be punished with imprisonment up to ten years, a fine or both. It is committed if two or more prisoners engage in conduct intended to 'further a common purpose of overthrowing lawful authority' in a prison. Prisoners may be regarded as taking part in a mutiny if they fail to leave when there is a reasonable opportunity to do so.

Offences under the Prison Rules range from the more serious which are also criminal offences (such as assault), to more minor offences, for example, refusing to work or the catch-all 'in any way offending against good order and discipline'. If the governor is to deal with the alleged offence then the procedure as set out in the *Discipline Manual* should be followed (a copy of this should be available to prisoners on request or can be purchased from the Home Office at a price of £2.50). The essential points are:

- A charge must be laid as soon as possible and, 'save in exceptional circumstances', within forty-eight hours of the discovery of the offence.
- Pending enquiry by the governor a prisoner who is to be charged may be segregated. After the governor's first enquiry, segregation is only permissible under Rule 43 (see below).
- The charge must be in sufficient detail for the prisoner to know exactly what is alleged against him or her.
- The governor must ask if the prisoner understands the procedure and if he or she wishes to be legally represented or assisted, but is not obliged to grant a request for legal representation; as an alternative, the prisoner can ask for the assistance of a 'McKenzie friend'.
- If legal representation is refused, the prisoner may still request an adjournment in order to get legal advice from a solicitor.
- The prisoner may request copies of statements or other written material which is to be used in evidence and the governor should usually allow this.
- At the hearing the prisoner must be allowed to put questions to witnesses who give evidence against him or her and to call witnesses who are relevant to his or her defence.
- The case must be proved to the criminal standard of proof, i.e. beyond a reasonable doubt.

The maximum number of additional days which a governor may order to be served as punishment for an offence is forty-two. If found guilty of more than one offence arising from the same incident, punishment may be ordered to run consecutively, but the total period may not exceed forty-two days. Other punishments include forfeiture of facilities (maximum forty-two days), stoppage of earnings (maximum forty-two days), cellular confinement (maximum fourteen days) or exclusion from work (maximum twenty-one days).

A prisoner may ask the prisoner casework unit to review a finding of guilt or the punishment imposed. Before doing so, the prisoner should always request a copy of the record of the disciplinary hearing which must be provided free of charge. Governors' disciplinary hearings can also be reviewed by the Ombudsman or the High Court if the governor made a mistake in law or adopted a procedure which was unfair.

Prisoners can apply to the governor for cancellation of additional day awards if they have had a period of six months without further awards being made. Neither the seriousness of the original disciplinary offence, nor the criminal offence for which the prisoner is serving his or her sentence are relevant to the question of whether an award of additional days should be reduced in whole or part. The question is whether the prisoner's behaviour and attitude have shown an improvement. The guidelines state that normally no more than half of additional days awarded should be returned on any one application.

Mandatory drugs tests

All prisoners can be required to undertake a mandatory drugs test, either on a random selection or if the governor has reasonable suspicion that an individual is using or supplying controlled drugs. It is a disciplinary offence to refuse a test or to test positive for a controlled drug. There are statutory defences that the prisoner had lawful excuse to take the drug (e.g. as prescribed medicine) or that it was administered to the prisoner without his/her knowledge or consent.

8.12 Segregation and transfer

Prisoners can be segregated either as punishment following adjudication (maximum fourteen days), 'for the maintenance of good order and discipline', or at the prisoner's request for his or her own protection. Prisoners segregated as a punishment must first be certified fit for such punishment by the medical officer, who should also see the prisoner daily during segregation and may order a return to normal location on medical grounds.

Prisoners segregated in the interests of good order and discipline (GOAD) may not be segregated for more than three days without the authorisation of either a member of the Board of Visitors or the Home Secretary. This authorisation may be for a maximum of one month, but may be renewed from month to month. Reasons for the segregation must be given as soon as possible and 'as far as practicable' in writing if the prisoner so requests.

Additionally, prisoners considered to be seriously disruptive or subversive may be transferred on a temporary basis to another prison for a period of up to one month for a 'cooling off' period. Inmates must be told of the reason for transfer in writing within twenty-four hours of the action being taken. A prisoner transferred under this provision must not be automatically segregated at the new prison, but only if the governor of the new prison considers it necessary and the same rules concerning segregation as detailed above will apply.

Temporary confinement and restraints

Prison officers are instructed not to use force 'unless absolutely necessary' and when necessary to use no more force than is 'absolutely necessary' to achieve the required objective.

A violent or unmanageable prisoner may be placed temporarily in a special or strip cell, but not as punishment, nor may he or she be held in such a cell after he or she has ceased to be violent. The cell will be stripped of furniture except for a mattress or have cardboard furniture which cannot cause injury. This can only be done on the authority of the governor. Furthermore, the governor may order a prisoner be put in physical restraints where necessary to prevent injury to him- or herself, others, damaging property or creating a disturbance. Body belts, which are made of a leather belt around the waist with handcuffs attached to restrain movement, may be used for this purpose.

Physical restraints should only be used in rare and extreme cases. If restraints are used, the medical officer and a member of the Board of Visitors must be informed without delay. If the medical officer disagrees with the order to put the prisoner under restraint the governor must comply with his or her recommendation.

Prisoners put into a special cell or mechanical restraint must be observed every fifteen minutes and be visited by the governor and medical officer twice every twenty-four hours. A prisoner may not be held for longer than twenty-four hours in mechanical restraints without the written authorisation of a member of the Board of Visitors or an officer of the Home Office (who is not an officer of the prison). If a prisoner is held wrongly – either unnecessarily or for too long – in a body belt or other restraint, he or she will be entitled to claim damages in the court for assault.

8.13 Medical treatment

Convicted prisoners are in the care of the Prison Medical Service, which is not part of the National Health Service; they therefore have no right to consult the doctor or dentist of their choice for treatment. Unconvicted prisoners, if willing to pay any expenses involved, may be visited and treated by the doctor or dentist of their choice. However, a prisoner who is party to legal proceedings may be visited by an independent doctor where examination is relevant to those proceedings.

The Access to Health Records Act 1990 gives the prisoner the right to see (and have copies made on request) their medical records since 1 November 1991 (though disclosure can be refused on the basis that it would cause serious harm to the physical or mental health of the patient or any other individual). All medical information on a prisoner should be treated in confidence and is not to be disclosed except for 'specifically defined purposes'.

The same confidentiality applies to prisoners who are HIV positive. The prison guidelines say, 'If it seems desirable in the inmate's interest to inform a third party [that he or she is HIV positive] a member of staff must consult the prisoner and must obtain the prisoner's consent before disclosing the information.' The prison authorities may be liable in damages if they negligently reveal confidential information (for example, that a prisoner has committed sexual offences) as a result of which he is assaulted.

8.14 Work, exercise and education

Work

All convicted prisoners may be required to work unless the medical officer has certified the prisoner unfit for all or a specific type of work. It is a disciplinary offence to refuse to work or intentionally to fail to work properly. Account should be taken of a prisoner's religion so that he or she is not required to work on recognised days of religious observance.

The Prison Rules give the maximum working day as ten hours, but do not give a minimum working day. Prison workshops are exempt from the provisions of the Factories Act: if injured at work prisoners must rely upon a civil claim of negligence in order to claim damages for their injury. In practice, governors are required to observe the requirements of the Factories Act and the Health and Safety at Work Act 1974; governors are also instructed to give Health and Safety Executive inspectors access to all areas of the prison.

If found guilty of a disciplinary offence a prisoner may be excluded from working with other prisoners as part of his punishment for a maximum of twenty-one days and/or have his earnings stopped or reduced. Wages can only be stopped to their full value for a period of forty-two days, but the length of this punishment can be spread out over eighty-four days (e.g. the loss of half of one's earnings over this period of time).

Exercise

Convicted prisoners no longer have a statutory right to one hour's exercise each day. There is a right to one hour's physical exercise a week and it is aimed to allow one hour's exercise in the open air per day if circumstances permit. Health care advice is that this period should not normally be reduced to less than half an hour a day.

Education

The prison department is under a general duty to provide evening classes at every prison and to encourage prisoners to 'profit' from the educational facilities provided. This does not mean that every prisoner has a right to the educational course of his or her choice, and the prison authorities have a wide discretion as to what educational facilities they provide and who is to benefit from them.

Local education authorities provide a programme of evening classes in all prisons but classroom space is often limited. Facilities for daytime study and remedial teaching vary. The governor is responsible for assessing a prisoner's needs and suitability for further study. He or she can release individuals from work duty for study. Permission from the prison authorities can be obtained to take a correspondence course and long-term prisoners often study Open University courses leading to a degree. All prisons have at least one library.

Governors are instructed that prisoners of compulsory school age should have educational and vocational training for at least fifteen hours per week and should be denied education only as a last resort.

The governor may suspend or end attendance at educational classes if he or she believes it necessary to prevent disruption or for security reasons, or if a disciplinary punishment, for example segregation, prevents it, but removal from education may not in itself be ordered as a punishment.

Reading and writing materials

Prisoners are entitled to have supplied to them at their own expense 'books, newspapers, writing materials and other means of occupation' except those which appear objectionable. Generally, material should only be denied if it includes matter which incites or involves criminal or disciplinary offences. While it may be permissible to withhold a particular issue of a publication, a blanket ban may be challengeable in the courts.

8.15 Parole

The rules regarding release from custody changed in October 1992 and a different scheme applies to all those sentenced on or after 1 October 1992.

Sentence prior to 1 October 1992

Prisoners serving more than twelve months will be eligible for release on parole one-third of the way through the sentence. Release will be automatic at the two-thirds stage (subject to any loss of remission for disciplinary offences). Consideration for parole happens automatically but after October 1994 all prisoners will be considered under the new system described below.

Sentence on or after 1 October 1992

Those serving less than four years will automatically be released halfway through their sentence. For those serving twelve months or less release is unconditional. Those serving over twelve months will be released on licence until the three-quarters point of their sentence and will be subject to compulsory supervision by the probation service. Conditions may be attached to the licence, for example, to attend medical or psychiatric treatment, not to undertake certain types of work, not to communicate with named persons. For short-term offenders only, failure to comply with licence conditions is an offence which can be tried and punished at the magistrates' court.

If the released prisoner commits any offence punishable by imprisonment between the time of his or her release and the date when his or her original sentence runs out, then he or she will be liable to serve the balance of the original sentence which is outstanding at the time of the fresh offence.

For those serving four years or more, the system of parole remains and is as follows: prisoners will be eligible for release on parole once half of the sentence has been served; at the two-thirds stage of the sentence the prisoner will be released automatically. Recommendations by the Parole Board to release prisoners serving seven years or more must be approved by the Secretary of State.

Between the two-thirds automatic release point and the three-quarters point in the overall sentence, the 'at risk' provisions with regard to further offences which are imprisonable apply as they do for short-term prisoners.

Long-term prisoners who are in breach of parole licence conditions may be recalled to prison and if recalled may remain in prison until the three-quarters point of the original sentence. If recalled, the prisoner must be told of the reasons for recall and can appeal against the decision in writing to the Parole Board.

The parole process for all prisoners will begin six months before the prisoner is first eligible for release on parole. A dossier will be compiled of all the material to go before the Board. The prisoner will be shown all such reports (unless it is considered some material should not be shown: any proposal to withhold material must be referred to the chair of the Parole Board) and his or her comments and representations will go before the Board when the case is considered. An interview is then arranged with a member of the Parole Board and the record of this interview is disclosed to the prisoner and then placed with the other papers. The prisoner should be told whether parole has been granted three weeks before he or she is eligible for release and reasons for the decision will be given. The release dates of long- and short-term prisoners will be subject to postponement if 'additional day awards' have been made as punishment for disciplinary offences.

The Home Secretary has power to release any prisoner on compassionate grounds 'in exceptional circumstances'. This power is normally reserved for prisoners who are in the advanced stages of a terminal illness. A prisoner so released will be subject to supervision up to the three-quarters point in the sentence (or, for those serving less than twelve months, the halfway point).

Life sentence prisoners

There are two categories of life sentence: a life sentence is mandatory if convicted of murder. For other offences (for example, rape, grievous bodily harm), the court may impose a life sentence. This is referred to as a discretionary life sentence.

Discretionary lifers

The trial judge will usually, when sentencing, fix the punishment period – the tariff – to be served before release can be considered. The length of this tariff may be appealed as with a determinate prison sentence. At the end of this period there will be a hearing before a panel of the Parole Board to decide whether the prisoner should be released. The Discretionary Lifer Panel will meet at the prison where the prisoner is located to consider the case. The prisoner is entitled to legal representation (and legal aid is available for this) to prepare and conduct his or her case. The prisoner is entitled to see all reports which go before the Panel except those which would 'adversely affect the health or welfare of the prisoner or others'; in such a case the reports must still be shown to the legal representative.

If the Panel is satisfied that it is no longer necessary for the protection of the public that the prisoner be detained, then he or she will be released. If the Panel does not direct release, the prisoner is entitled to have his or her case considered again by the Panel at two-year intervals.

Mandatory lifers

Those serving a sentence for murder will have a tariff set by the Home Secretary following recommendations by the trial judge and the Lord Chief Justice. The decision is that of the Home Secretary, but the prisoner must be given:

- Information as to the period the judges have recommended should be served for the purpose of deterrence and retribution.
- The opportunity to make written representations to the Home Secretary as to how long he or she should serve before he or she can be considered for release.
- Reasons for any decision of the Home Secretary not to follow the recommendation of the judges as to how long should be served for the purposes of retribution and deterrence.

Once the tariff period has expired, life sentenced prisoners may be released if the Parole Board recommends release to the Home Secretary and the Home Secretary, after consultation with the Lord Chief Justice and the trial judge (if available), accepts that recommendation. The first review takes place three years before the tariff expires and subsequent reviews at intervals set by the Home Secretary (normally two years). The prisoner will be given a dossier containing details of the offence, progress in custody and up-to-date reports from a range of prison and probation staff. Lifers are normally expected to progress to open prison conditions before release will be authorised.

Release will only be authorised if it is felt that the prisoner no longer poses a risk of committing further offences and if there is a satisfactory release plan. Life sentenced prisoners can be detained on these grounds (the risk factor) after the tariff has expired. Once a life sentenced prisoner is released, he or she will remain on life licence and can be recalled to prison by the Home Secretary or the Parole Board if the terms of the licence are breached or if his/her behaviour causes concern. If a prisoner in this position is recalled, a further review will be conducted by the Parole Board to decide on the fairness of the recall.

Her Majesty's Pleasure

People convicted of murder who were under the age of eighteen at the time the offence was committed are sentenced to be detained at Her Majesty's Pleasure. This sentence used to be administered in the same way as the mandatory life sentence but following a judgment in the European Court in February 1996, is now a mixture of the discretionary and mandatory life sentence. The tariff is fixed in the same manner as for mandatory lifers by the Secretary of State. The House of Lords are due to hear an application on this point in the near future.

Since August 1996 the release procedure for these prisoners is to be the same as for discretionary lifers (i.e. an oral hearing before a panel with legal representation). At the time of writing, these new procedures have not yet been provided for in legislation and it is likely that there will be some minor procedural discrepancies until this has been resolved.

Crime (Sentences) Act 1997

People sentenced under this Act are no longer eligible for parole and a whole new scheme will apply.

People who receive an automatic life sentence for a second violent or sexual offence will be subject to the same release scheme as discretionary life sentenced prisoners (see above).

Prisoners who receive a determinate sentence are no longer entitled to parole and are required to serve the full length of their sentence. For those serving a sentence of more than two months, remission can be earned at a rate of six days for every month served. This is subject to a maximum of 20 per cent of the total sentence. Remission can be earned on time served on remand for people who subsequently receive a prison sentence. The decision about earned remission is made by the prison governor and is based on custodial behaviour, including compliance with sentence planning targets such as attending offending behaviour courses. Prisoners who receive additional days for disciplinary offences (see above) cannot be held beyond the end of their sentence and these additional days can only be offset against earned remission.

On release, people who received a sentence of twelve months or more will be subject to supervision for 25 per cent of their sentence. For example, a person who received a sentence of two years will be supervised for six months on release.

Temporary release

Prisoners may be released for a set period, usually between two and five days) on the authority of the prison governor. This can be for compassionate reasons, such as attendance at a funeral or for medical treatment, or on resettlement licence. Before temporary release can be granted, all prisoners must pass a risk assessment carried out in the prison. Compassionate temporary release can be granted at any point in the sentence. Resettlement licence can be granted after a prisoner has reached his/her parole eligibility date, but if parole is refused, the application will be suspended for a period of six months. For prisoners serving less than four years, an application can be made after they have served one-third of their sentence. Certain groups are ineligible for any form of temporary release, such as high-risk prisoners, or those who are to be deported at the end of their sentence.

Discharge

On release, personal clothing and belongings are returned. Suitable clothing will be provided if the prisoner's clothing is inadequate. Money received on reception will be returned and most prisoners will be eligible for a discharge grant. Those serving under fourteen days are not entitled to the discharge grant, though the prison authorities may give a subsistence allowance to enable the prisoner to get to the local DSS office. A travel warrant to an address in the United Kingdom will also be given.

8.15 Further information

Useful organisations

Justice
59 Carter Lane
London EC4V 5AQ
Tel: 0171 329 5100

NACRO (National Association for Care and Resettlement of
Offenders)
169 Clapham Road
London SW9 0PU
Tel: 0171 582 6500

POPS (Partners of Prisoners and Families Support Group)
St Marks Cheetham
Tetlow Lane
Cheetham
Manchester M8 7HF
Tel: 0161 740 8600

People's Place
388 Old Street
London EC1V 9LT
Tel: 0171 729 5050

Prison Reform Trust
2nd Floor, Old Trading House
15 Northburgh Street
London EC1V 0PR
Tel: 0171 251 5070

Prisoners' Advice Service
Unit 305
Hatton Square
16/16a Baldwin Gardens
London EC1N 7RJ
Tel: 0171 405 8090

Women in Prison
Unit 3b, Aberdeen Studios
22 Highbury Grove
London N5 2EA
Tel: 0171 226 8180

Inquest (Deaths In Custody)
Ground Floor, Alexander National House
330 Seven Sisters Road
London N4 2JP
Tel: 0181 802 7430

Bibliography

S. Creighton and V. King, *Prisoners and the Law*, Butterworths, 1996.
M. Leech, *The Prisons Handbook*, Pluto Press, 1997.
S. Livingstone and T. Owen, *Prison Law*, Oxford University Press, 1997.

9

The right not to be discriminated against

This chapter deals with:

- Race discrimination.
- Sex discrimination.
- Sexual minority discrimination.
- Disability discrimination.
- Further information.

9.1 Race discrimination

The Race Relations Act 1976 deals with race discrimination in employment and training; education; housing; the provision of goods, facilities and services, and advertising. It also set up the Commission for Racial Equality (CRE). The Act applies to England, Wales and

---

STOP PRESS

The new government proposes to incorporate the European Convention on Human Rights into domestic law. The rights in the Convention are set out in Chapter 5. A Bill to incorporate the Convention is due to be published in the autumn of 1997 and this is likely to become an Act by July 1998 and to come into force not before January 1999. It is not clear at the time of writing exactly what effect this will have on our laws. It is likely that the Convention will be able to be used to challenge some of the existing procedures and judge-made law although whether the Convention will be given a higher status than statute is not so clear. Nevertheless the rights set out in this book may be enhanced by the Convention and in future the rights in the Convention will have to be considered much more seriously than they have been in the past.

Scotland, but not to Northern Ireland. Complaints by individuals who believe they have been discriminated against must be made either to the industrial tribunal (for employment-related matters) or to the County Court (in Scotland, the Sheriff Courts).

What is discrimination?

The Act sets out the circumstances in which discrimination on the grounds of race is unlawful. It defines three types of discrimination: direct discrimination, indirect discrimination and victimisation. The Act defines racial grounds as being on the grounds of colour, race, nationality or ethnic or national origins. Most people think of race discrimination as being less favourable treatment on the grounds of colour or race. However, discrimination on the grounds of nationality, ethnic or national origins is equally unlawful. Thus if a workplace contains Afro-Caribbean and African employees and the employer treats the African employees less favourably by allocating them the menial or less interesting work, that could amount to less favourable treatment on racial grounds. Similarly, if a Japanese bank offered its services to Korean customers on less favourable terms than those offered to other customers, the bank's actions could constitute less favourable treatment on racial grounds.

Direct discrimination

Direct discrimination occurs when a person treats another less favourably on racial grounds than he or she would treat, or treats, some other person. Sometimes direct discrimination is very obvious (for example, 'no blacks here'), but it may be more subtle. For example, quotas are sometimes operated by some clubs or pubs to prevent their black members or customers from exceeding a specific number or proportion. Or a person might be refused a job or promotion on the grounds that customers would not like it. Both of these situations are examples of direct discrimination. Intention and motive are irrelevant to the question of whether a person has been subject to unlawful direct discrimination on the grounds of race.

Segregation

Segregation on racial grounds is defined by the Act as direct discrimination. Providing separate washing facilities for white and Asian employees, even if the facilities are of the same standard, might be an example of segregation on racial grounds.

Indirect discrimination

Indirect discrimination occurs when a racial group is unjustifiably at a disadvantage in its ability to comply with a specific requirement or condition. For example, a job that requires the employee to be clean-shaven would put Sikhs in general at a disadvantage. Excluding job applicants who live in a certain area of a city, where that area is occupied by a higher proportion of ethnic minority people would put ethnic minority candidates at a disadvantage. If the requirement cannot be objectively justified with reference to criteria other than race, a claim for indirect discrimination would lie. Only people who experience this disadvantage themselves can bring a complaint.

The concept of indirect discrimination is not user-friendly. The legal definition and the case law it has generated are complex and abstruse. Perhaps as a result, this provision of the Act is greatly underused. If you consider you unjustifiably suffer a disadvantage because you cannot comply with a requirement or condition you should consider seeking specialist help (see p. 266).

Intention is a relevant question in a claim based on indirect discrimination. The motive of the alleged discrimination is not considered when the tribunal or court is deciding whether, in fact, you have been discriminated against. However, once a finding of indirect discrimination has been made, a tribunal or court can decide not to make an award of compensation to you because it is satisfied that the discrimination was unintentional.

Victimisation
Victimisation occurs when one person treats another less favourably than he or she treats, or would treat, someone else in those particular circumstances because the person victimised has done any of the following:

- Brought proceedings against the discriminator or any other person under the Act; or
- Given evidence or information in connection with proceedings brought by any person against the discriminator or any other person under the Act; or
- Otherwise done anything under or by reference to the Act in relation to the discriminator or any other person; or
- Alleged that the discriminator or any other person has committed an act which (whether or not the allegation so states) would amount to a contravention of the Act; or
- The discriminator knows that the person victimised intends to do any of those things or suspects that the person victimised has done, or intends to do, any of them.

A person making allegations of discrimination must make those allegations in good faith in order to be protected by the victimisation provisions of the Act. An example of a situation in which a claim of victimisation might arise is where another employee accuses his or her boss of discriminating against him or her on the grounds of race and as a result of the complaint is demoted or disciplined.

Responsibility for acts of discrimination

The Act makes unlawful certain types of discrimination which are considered below. It also makes it unlawful to instruct someone to carry out an unlawful act of discrimination or to induce or attempt to induce, directly or indirectly, such an act. Only the CRE may bring proceedings in respect of such unlawful instructions and/or inducements.

Employment and training

This is dealt with in Part II of the Act. Employers are made responsible for the unlawful acts of their employees which are acts done during the course of employment. The employer can avoid liability for the unlawful acts of employees if it can be shown that the acts complained of fell outside the scope of employment. Employers can also avoid liability if they can show that they took such steps as were reasonably practicable to prevent their employees from doing such unlawful discriminatory acts.

It is also unlawful for a person, including an employee, to aid another to do an unlawful act of discrimination. Thus where an employee devises a plan to send a racially offensive card to an employee who is a member of a racial group and enlists the help of a colleague to carry out that plan, both the originator of the plan and the colleague may be guilty of unlawful discrimination on the grounds of race.

It is unlawful for an employer to discriminate against you on grounds of race in any of the following ways:

- Refusing to hire you or consider you for a job.
- Offering you a job on less favourable terms than other people.
- Refusing to promote you or transfer you to another job.
- Refusing to make provision for you to be trained.
- Giving you less favourable fringe benefits.
- Putting you on short-time work, dismissing you or making you redundant.

As the law stands at the moment, if you are discriminated against or victimised by your former employer after your employment has terminated, for example in the conduct of an appeal hearing, you have no remedy under the Act.

In order to win a case of race discrimination (see p. 347 for more information about making a complaint of race discrimination), you must show that you were being treated less favourably than someone of different racial or national origins would be treated and that the treatment you received was because of or on the grounds of your race. It is also necessary to show that you suffered some detriment or disadvantage as a result of this differential treatment. Injury to feelings is a detriment or disadvantage recognised by industrial tribunals and the courts for which compensation may be awarded. A court or tribunal can also make an order for the payment of compensation if you have suffered financial loss as a result of the discrimination you are complaining about. It is important to remember that the burden of proof is on you. This means that you must provide the industrial tribunal or court with enough evidence to prove your claim.

The Act covers both permanent and temporary jobs, whatever the size of the firm. It covers apprentices and trainees as well as other employees; partners in a firm of six or more partners (such as a solicitors' firm); the police (who are not technically employees); sub-contracted workers (such as the 'lump' building workers or night cleaners), and employment agencies.

It is unlawful for the government to discriminate on race grounds in appointing people to serve on public bodies. It is also unlawful for trade unions and professional associations to discriminate in any of the following ways:

- Deciding who to admit to membership.
- Refusing to let you join.
- Only allowing you to join on less favourable terms.
- By giving you fewer benefits, facilities or services or refusing to let you have any of these benefits (for example, legal services, representation in a dispute).
- Expelling you or subjecting you to any other disadvantage.

Similarly, it is unlawful for any licensing body (for example, the Law Society, which licenses solicitors; the Director General of Fair Trading, who licenses credit and hire businesses or the police, who license taxi-drivers) to discriminate on racial grounds in deciding who can have a licence. Furthermore, whenever one of these bodies has to consider an applicant's 'good character' before giving a licence, they will be able to take into account any evidence about previous unlawful race discrimination. So, for instance, magistrates who are renewing a publican's licence should take account of any evidence that the publican or his or her employees had previously refused to serve black people.

The Courts and Legal Services Act 1990 extended the non-discrimination provisions of the Act to the legal profession.

Racial abuse and harassment at work

If you are subjected to racial abuse and/or racial harassment at work you may be able to bring a claim under the Act. Racial abuse or harassment is characterised as direct discrimination on racial grounds. However, you will have to prove on a balance of probabilities that as a result of the insult, abuse or harassment you are disadvantaged at work, in order to succeed in your complaint.

A complaint about race discrimination in employment must be brought to an industrial tribunal (see p. 347) within three months of the act or failure to act being complained of. The tribunal has a discretion to extend the time for bringing a complaint of race discrimination if, in all the circumstances of the case, it considers it just and equitable to do so.

Exceptions

It has already been noted that not all race discrimination is made unlawful by the Act. Racial discrimination is still lawful in any of the following situations:

- Employment in a private household.
- If an employer wants to employ someone who is not ordinarily resident in Great Britain, but who will be trained here before going to work abroad.
- Employment of workers on ships who were recruited outside Great Britain.
- Employment outside Great Britain.
- Employment in dramatic performances, or for artists' or photographic modelling, where someone of a particular racial group is needed for reasons of 'authenticity'.
- Employment in restaurants, etc., with a particular setting where someone of a particular racial group is needed for reasons of authenticity (for example, Chinese waiters or waitresses in a Chinese restaurant).
- Employment of someone to provide personal services to a particular racial group, where someone of the same racial group can do the job most effectively.

The last three exceptions are known as 'genuine occupational qualification' exceptions. If race is genuinely an occupational qualification, then the employer may legitimately discriminate in the last three ways described above. In any of these cases, the employer must try to fill a vacancy from existing workers before discriminating on racial grounds. The CRE has published a Code of Practice for the elimination of racial discrimination and the promotion of equality of opportunity in employment which is obtainable from the CRE (see p. 266). The Code sets out guidelines of good race relations practice although it is not enforceable in law.

Training

It is unlawful for any of the following training organisations to discriminate on race grounds:

- Industrial training boards.
- Employment Services Agency.
- Training Services Agency.
- Employers' organisations which provide training.
- Any other organisation designated by the Home Secretary.

These organisations are, however, allowed to practise 'positive discrimination' where there have been no people of a particular racial group, or very few, doing a particular kind of work, either in the whole of Great Britain or in a region, in the previous twelve months. In this case they will be allowed to run training courses or provide facilities for that racial group only, or to encourage people from that group to take up a particular kind of work.

Employers will also be allowed to run training courses for a particular racial group only, or to encourage them to take up a particular kind of work, where there have been no people of that racial group, or very few, doing that kind of work in the firm during the previous twelve months.

Trade unions and professional organisations are also allowed to organise special training courses to encourage people from a particular racial group to hold posts within the organisation (for example, as shop stewards or officials) where there have been very few or no people from that group holding such posts in the previous twelve months.

Education

Part III of the Act deals with discrimination in the field of education. The Race Relations Act applies to schools or colleges maintained by a local education authority (LEA), independent ('public' or fee-paying) schools, or colleges, special schools, grant-maintained 'opted-out' schools and universities. The Home Secretary can also designate other establishments to be covered by the law.

It is unlawful for any educational body (including the governors of a school or college and an LEA) to discriminate on race grounds in any of the following ways:

- The terms on which they admit you.

- Refusing to admit you.
- Providing more facilities or better facilities for particular racial groups.
- Expelling you or in any other way putting you at a disadvantage.
- Acting in any other way which involves race discrimination.

If you or your child has been discriminated against, you will have to make a complaint to the Secretary of State for Education (this does not apply to complaints against independent schools or universities where you apply to the institution directly). The Minister will have two months in which to do something about your complaint. If the Minister rejects your complaint, or the two months run out, you can make a complaint to the County Court. A County Court action must be brought within six months (or eight months if the complaint has first gone to the Minister).

The Act also puts a general duty on LEAs to ensure that educational facilities are provided without race discrimination. This duty is a general duty and cannot be enforced by you directly. You can, of course, draw the attention of local councillors and school governors to it. The general duty can only be enforced by the Secretary of State for Education ordering the LEA to carry out its duties reasonably.

It is lawful for LEAs and other bodies to provide special facilities to meet the particular needs of a racial group (for example, for language classes).

Overseas students

There is only one exception to the education sections of the Act and this concerns overseas students. It is lawful for any organisation or individual providing education or training to discriminate on racial grounds against people who are not ordinarily resident in Great Britain and who do not intend to remain in Great Britain after their period of education or training. This means, for instance, that it is lawful for colleges or halls of residence to charge higher fees to overseas students.

Housing

Housing and premises, such as business premises, are also covered by Part III of the Act. In general, it is unlawful for someone to discriminate on race grounds, when selling, letting, subletting or managing property, in any of the following ways:

- In the terms on which you are offered the premises.
- By refusing to let you buy or rent the premises.
- By treating you differently from other people on a list of people wanting to buy or rent the premises.

- By refusing to agree to the transfer of a lease to you.
- By refusing you access to any benefits or facilities in the premises you occupy.
- By evicting you or subjecting you to any other disadvantage.

The law covers private landlords and owner-occupiers as well as local authorities.

Exceptions
There are three main exceptions. First, owner-occupiers selling or letting their property are excluded, provided that they do not advertise or use an estate agent.

Second, small residential premises (for example, small boarding houses or shared flats) are excluded. To qualify as 'small residential premises', the owner or occupier (or a near relative) has to live permanently in the house or flat; part of the house or flat, other than stairs or storage space, has to be shared with other people; and there must be only two households (other than the owner's or occupier's household) or not more than six people (other than the owner's or occupier's household) in the house or flat. A boarding house containing more than six lodgers, in addition to the landlord/lady's family, would not be allowed to discriminate, but a boarding house with fewer lodgers would be allowed to.

Third, charities and membership bodies whose main purpose is to provide benefits for a particular racial group are allowed to provide housing for that group only. But these organisations will not be allowed to discriminate on grounds of colour, only on grounds of race, nationality or national or ethnic origin.

Goods, facilities and services
Part III of the Act also covers any 'goods, facilities or services' which are offered to the public or a section of the public. This means, for instance, the services and facilities offered by hotels, boarding houses, pubs and restaurants, banks, insurance companies, credit houses and hire purchase firms, transport authorities and local authorities. Direct or indirect discrimination (see p. 226) by any such organisation will be unlawful.

If you have been discriminated against on racial grounds by someone offering goods or services to the public, you must bring your action in the County Court. An action must be brought within six months.

Any contract (for example, to buy goods or supply services) which includes a term which discriminates on racial grounds is void and can be amended by applying to the County Court to strike out that term formally.

Exceptions

There are a number of situations where race discrimination remains lawful:

- Any arrangement where someone takes a child, elderly person or someone needing special care and attention into his or her home to be looked after (for example, fostering children).
- Goods, facilities or services provided outside Great Britain, or insurance arrangements to cover a situation outside Great Britain. (But the services of, for instance, a travel agent in this country, even though it arranges foreign travel, will still be covered.)
- Charities and voluntary organisations whose main purpose is to provide benefits for a particular racial group (but these organisations will not be allowed to discriminate on grounds of colour, only on grounds of race, nationality or national or ethnic origin).
- Special arrangements can be made for members of a particular racial group who have particular needs for education, training, welfare, etc. (for example, language classes).
- Discrimination on grounds of nationality, place of birth or length of residence is permitted in:

  (1) selecting people to represent a particular place or country in a sport or game; or
  (2) deciding who is eligible to compete in any sport or game, according to the rules of the competition.

Prisons

The provisions prohibiting unlawful discrimination in housing and in relation to goods, facilities and services have been held to prevent the unlawful discrimination by prison officers in the allocation of work to prisoners. They also probably make unlawful other discrimination occurring in the prison regime (for example, more unfavourable withdrawal of privileges from, and more frequent strip searches of, black prisoners).

Clubs

Under the previous race relations laws, private clubs, such as political and working-men's clubs, were allowed to discriminate on race grounds. It is now unlawful for any club or society with twenty-five or more members to discriminate on race grounds in any of the following ways:

- Refusing to allow you to join.

- Offering you less favourable terms of membership.
- Giving you fewer benefits, facilities or services or refusing to let you use or have any of these benefits (for example, social facilities).
- Expelling you from the club or changing the terms of your membership.
- Putting you at a disadvantage in any other way.

But a club or society whose main purpose is to provide benefits for people of a particular racial group, whatever its size, will continue to be allowed to discriminate on race grounds (although not on grounds of colour).

Advertisements

It is unlawful to insert, publish or cause to be published an advertisement which indicates that an employer, a company or anyone else intends to discriminate unlawfully. The absence of an intention to discriminate is no defence.

Only the CRE (see p. 266) will be able to take legal action against discriminatory advertisements. If you see an advertisement which you believe breaks the law you should bring it to the Commission's attention. You can also make a complaint about the advertisement to the person displaying it yourself.

Discrimination is allowed where exceptions in the law exist, for example, advertisements for jobs to which the genuine occupational qualification applies, for employment outside the United Kingdom and for posts and training where positive action is permitted. But an advertisement for employment in a private household must not be racially discriminatory.

Commission for Racial Equality

The Commission for Racial Equality (CRE) was set up by the Race Relations Act 1976 with the duties of:

- Working towards the elimination of discrimination.
- Promoting equality of opportunity and good relations between persons of different racial groups generally.
- Keeping under review the working of the Act and, when required by the Home Secretary or when it otherwise thinks it necessary, to draw up and submit to the Home Secretary proposals for amending it.

In carrying out its duties, the CRE has the following powers:

- To undertake formal investigations into discriminatory practices which are unsuitable to be dealt with on an individual basis.

- To support, including financially, individuals taking up complaints of discrimination.
- To issue Codes of Practice on employment. The first Code was approved by Parliament in 1984. It is not legally binding but can be used in evidence at an industrial tribunal.
- To examine areas of policy outside the scope of the Act.
- To issue non-discrimination notices. This happens if the CRE decides, as a result of a formal investigation, that the law has been broken.
- To fund research and other projects.
- To apply for an injunction if it believes someone has broken the law and is likely to go on doing so. In the following circumstances, it is the CRE alone which can take action, such as applying for an injunction, if discrimination has taken place:

  (1) if an advertisement demonstrates an intention to discriminate unlawfully;
  (2) if someone instructs an employee or agent to discriminate unlawfully;
  (3) if someone puts pressure on anyone else to discriminate unlawfully.

Investigations

The CRE can conduct 'formal investigations' into any subject it chooses – for instance, employment patterns in a region, the recruitment policies of a firm, housing allocation policies in local authorities, and so on.

The CRE must give notice of its intention to hold a formal investigation and draw up terms of reference. If it is investigating a particular organisation or person and states in the terms of reference that it believes they are discriminating unlawfully, then it will be able to require them to give evidence or produce information. The power to take evidence and summon witnesses will also apply in other investigations with the consent of the Home Secretary, or if the aim of the investigation is to see whether a non-discrimination notice is being obeyed (see below).

Either during or at the end of an investigation, the CRE can make recommendations for changes which would promote equality of opportunity. These recommendations will not be legally binding, but could be used to bring pressure on the organisation or person, or as evidence in an individual case against them.

Non-discrimination notices

The CRE will be able to issue a non-discrimination notice if it decides, during a formal investigation, that an organisation or individual has discriminated unlawfully.

The non-discrimination notice requires the organisation or person named in it to stop discriminating unlawfully and, if necessary, to let the people concerned know what changes have been made in their procedures or arrangements in order to obey the non-discrimination notice. Before issuing the notice, the CRE must warn the organisation or person concerned that it is thinking of doing so, and give it or them twenty-eight days to make representations. Once the notice is issued, the organisation or person named can appeal to the industrial tribunal (in an employment case) or the County Court. The appeal must be made within six weeks of the issue of the notice.

If the appeal fails, or no appeal is made, the non-discrimination notice becomes final – in other words, it can be enforced. The CRE keeps a register of notices which have become final and anyone is entitled to inspect this register and take a copy of any notice in it.

Injunctions

A non-discrimination notice can only be enforced if the CRE goes to court and gets an injunction. It can do this at any time within five years of when the notice becomes final if it thinks that the organisation or person named in the notice will continue to discriminate unlawfully. An injunction is an order by a County Court or the High Court ordering someone to stop acting in a particular way. If the organisation or person does not obey the injunction, they will be in contempt of court and the CRE can apply to the court to have the people involved fined or imprisoned.

The CRE may also apply to the County Court for an injunction without issuing a non-discrimination notice in the following circumstances:

- If someone has successfully brought a complaint against an individual or organisation and the CRE considers that the individual or organisation will go on discriminating unlawfully.
- If the CRE considers that someone has discriminated unlawfully and is likely to go on doing so; in this case, the CRE must itself apply to the industrial tribunal or county court to get a finding that the person concerned has in fact discriminated unlawfully.
- If the CRE considers that someone has published an unlawful advertisement (see p. 235), instructed an employee or agent to discriminate unlawfully, or put pressure on anybody else to discriminate unlawfully. Only the CRE can take action on these kinds of unlawful acts.

Local authorities and race equality

The Act imposes a duty on every local authority to make appropriate arrangements with a view to seeing that their various functions are carried out with due regard to the following needs:

- To eliminate unlawful racial discrimination.
- To promote equality of opportunity and good relations between persons of different racial groups.

This duty affects every power and duty of a local authority.

Criminal acts to stir up racial hatred

The Public Order Act 1986 prohibits certain acts intended or likely to stir up racial hatred (see p. 53). No prosecution for these offences may be brought without the Attorney General's permission. The Act covers:

- The use of words or behaviour or displays of written material which are threatening, abusive or insulting and intended to stir up racial hatred. The acts do not have to be committed in public; however, such acts, if committed in a private dwelling, are outside the Act.
- Publishing or distributing to the public written material which is threatening, abusive or insulting and intended to stir up racial hatred or which, in the circumstances, is likely to stir up racial hatred. This will include racist graffiti as well as newspaper articles and other similarly offensive racist material which is threatening, abusive or insulting.
- The public performance of a play which involves the use of threatening, abusive or insulting words or behaviour intended to stir up racial hatred or which, in the circumstances, are likely to stir up racial hatred. There are defences to this offence which apply in very limited circumstances. The offence is primarily aimed at the presenter and director, but actors who alter their lines will be within the prohibition.
- Distributing, showing or playing a recording of visual images (including video recordings) or sound which is threatening, abusive or insulting and which is intended to stir up racial hatred or which, in the circumstances, is likely to stir up racial hatred.
- Broadcasting (including a programme in a cable programme service) which is threatening, abusive or insulting and which is intended to stir up racial hatred or which, in the circumstances, is likely to stir up racial hatred. (For further controls on broadcasting see Chapter 2.)

Inflammatory material

The Public Order Act 1986 also makes it an offence to have possession of written material which is threatening, abusive or insulting, or a recording of visual images or sound which is threatening, abusive or insulting with a view to use it, and with the intention that racial hatred will be stirred up or in circumstances in which it is likely to be stirred up. Powers of entry, search and forfeiture are given in respect of such material. Again, prosecutions may only be brought with the Attorney General's consent.

In the Public Order Act 1986, 'racial hatred' is defined as hatred against a group of persons in Great Britain defined by reference to colour, race, nationality (including citizenship) or ethnic or national origins. This definition does not include religion. It may also exclude travellers (see also p. 360).

The Criminal Justice and Public Order Act 1994

This renders racial, sexual and other forms of harassment in the street and at work a criminal offence punishable by imprisonment. The Act creates a new offence of causing intentional harassment, alarm or distress by the use of threatening, abusive or insulting words, behaviour, writing, sign or other visible representation. It also makes the publication of racially inflammatory material an arrestable offence.

9.2 Sex discrimination

This section deals with sex discrimination in education; housing; the provision of goods, facilities and services; advertising, and social security. The duties and powers of the Equal Opportunities Commission are also explained here.

Sex discrimination in pay and terms and conditions of work is dealt with in Chapter 13, as is information on maternity rights for working women. Sex discrimination as it relates to immigration and nationality is dealt with in Chapter 10.

What does the law cover?

The law relating to sex discrimination is heavily influenced by European Community law. Article 119 of the Treaty of Rome provides that 'Each Member State shall ... maintain the application of the principle that men and women should receive equal pay for equal work.' Article 119 is extended by additional Directives. The most relevant being the Equal Pay Directive (Directive 75/117) and the Equal Treatment Directive (Directive 76/207) (ETD).

The Sex Discrimination Act 1975, as amended by the Sex Discrimination Act 1986 (SDA), covers discrimination in the following areas:

- Employment.
- Education.
- Goods, facilities and services.
- Housing.

The Act covers discrimination against men and women. It also almost certainly protects against discrimination against transsexuals. The ETD has been interpreted to include within the definition of 'sex' protection for transsexuals (P *v.* S & Cornwall County Council [1996] ICR 795). In 1996 there were two decisions of industrial tribunals which held, following P *v.* S that the SDA applied to transsexual people. On the 27 June 1997 the Employment Appeals Tribunal held that the SDA does apply to transsexuals. Whether the ETD also protects against discrimination on the grounds of sexual orientation is presently under review. The argument being discrimination against gay men and lesbians is discrimination on the grounds of 'sex'. Two references have been made to the European Court of Justice to determine this point.

The Act also makes it unlawful to discriminate against married people in the fields of employment and training. But this does not apply to the other areas of the Act listed above. Discrimination against single people because of their marital status is lawful.

The SDA does not cover:

• Tax.
• Social security.
• Immigration.
• Nationality.

There are other exceptions within the areas that are covered by the law. These are mentioned below, under the relevant headings.

What is discrimination?
The Sex Discrimination Act 1975 defines discrimination in two ways: direct and indirect.

Direct discrimination
Direct discrimination is when you are or would be treated less favourably in the same circumstances than someone of the opposite sex, just because of your sex. For example, admitting only boys to a GCSE course in electronics at a mixed school would be direct discrimination. So would offering hire-purchase facilities only to men, or half-price entry to a disco only to women.

Indirect discrimination
Indirect discrimination occurs when a requirement or condition is applied to both sexes in any area covered by the Act with which, in practice, far fewer members of one sex than the other can comply. Indirect discrimination is unlawful if it cannot be shown to be justifiable irrespective of sex and if the aggrieved person can show that

the discrimination causes them detriment. For example, an after-school computer club open only to pupils taking an exam course in computer science could be against the law if hardly any girls took the exam course. Similarly, a housing association which excluded single parents from membership could be indirectly discriminating because the vast majority of single parents are women.

Victimisation

The Act also protects you against victimisation for taking action under either the Sex Discrimination Act or the Equal Pay Act. This provision makes it unlawful to treat you less favourably than anyone else because you have done any of the following:

- Made a complaint under either of the Acts.
- Helped someone else to make a complaint.
- Given evidence in a court or tribunal in a case under either of the Acts.
- Accused someone of breaking either of the Acts.
- Taken any other action in connection with either of the Acts.

Sexual harassment

The SDA does not contain any express provisions in relation to sexual harassment. However, sexual harassment is a form of direct discrimination. It is recognised as a serious issue and the source of much misery and distress for victims and their families. Sexual harassment can take a variety of forms. The term suggests a degree of repetition in the conduct or behaviour complained of, but this is not always necessary. A single incident can in some circumstances be properly described as sexual harassment. The European Commission Code of Practice on Measures to Combat Sexual Harassment provides a helpful outline definition. It states that sexual harassment includes unwanted conduct of a sexual nature, or other conduct based on sex, affecting the dignity of women and men at work. It can include unwelcome physical, verbal or non-verbal conduct. Sexual harassment may include ridicule, unwelcome comments about appearance, demands or requests for sexual favours and even actual physical assault. Men may also be subject to sexual harassment as some recent industrial tribunal decisions have acknowledged.

In order to succeed in a claim founded on sexual harassment, the complainant must show that the behaviour complained of is less favourable treatment on the grounds of sex and that she or he has suffered a detriment as a result.

The fact that industrial tribunal hearings, in particular, are public hearings and are often attended by the press has on occasion deterred individuals who have been subjected to harassment from pursuing their case to tribunal. Where cases involve allegations of sexual misconduct or conduct related to sex, gender or sexual orientation, an industrial tribunal has been able to make an order prohibiting publication of any matter likely to enable members of the public to identify an individual affected by or making the complaint. The tribunal will be able to make such an order either on the application of the parties or of its own motion. This power enables an industrial tribunal to produce written decisions which also exclude matters likely to assist in the identification of individuals involved in the proceedings. In addition an industrial tribunal now has the power to make a restricted reporting order either on application of the parties or of its own motion. Such an order, if made, prevents the reporting of the identity of specified individuals in the proceedings while the case is being heard.

Education

The SDA makes it unlawful to discriminate on grounds of sex, directly or indirectly, in any of the following areas:

- Admissions policies.
- Access to classes, courses or other benefits, facilities or services provided by the school or college.
- Any other unfavourable treatment.

The Act permits the continuation of single-sex schools, but also places a general duty on local education authorities to provide education without sex discrimination. This might mean, for example, that although a single-sex girls' school may not offer a design and technology course through its own curriculum, the LEA has to ensure that if boys in the same area have the opportunity to study this subject, arrangements are made to enable girls to take it, perhaps by attending a nearby mixed school for those lessons.

The following bodies can be held responsible for discrimination under the SDA:

- All schools, colleges and other educational establishments maintained by LEAs. Depending on the circumstances of the case, the LEA itself and/or the governors of the institution can be held responsible. Governors can be held responsible individually or collectively.
- Independent or private schools. The proprietors would be responsible.
- Universities. The governing body would be responsible.

- Other establishments designated by the Secretary of State for Education. These include other establishments in receipt of grants (such as grant-maintained schools) from the DES or the local authority. The governing body in each case is responsible for any discrimination.

Educational trusts
The SDA allows educational trusts to change their terms, with consent from the Secretary of State for Education, in order to apply their benefits to both sexes.

Exceptions

- Single-sex schools and colleges. A single-sex institution planning to turn co-educational can apply for permission to discriminate by admitting more members of one sex for a limited period.
- Co-educational schools which provide boarding accommodation for one sex only may continue to do so. If provided for both sexes, accommodation must be equal though it may be separate.
- Education provided by charities set up to benefit one sex only.
- Further education courses in physical training.
- In sport, single-sex competitive sport is allowed 'where the physical strength, stamina or physique of the average woman puts her at a disadvantage to the average man'. In practice, this has often been used to exclude girls from certain sports at school.

Housing
The SDA makes it unlawful to discriminate in renting, managing, subletting or selling accommodation. Owner-occupied properties, small boarding houses and flat-sharing, however, are excluded from the Act. Single-sex housing associations are also exempt.

Mortgages
Building societies, local authorities or any other body which grants mortgages are breaking the law if they treat women applicants any less favourably than they would treat a man in the same circumstances. For example, they may not apply different rules regarding earnings levels, age, dependants, and so on.

Goods, facilities and services
This covers a wide range of public and private services, including pubs, cafes, restaurants, hotels, transport, banking, insurance, hire purchase, recreation and entertainment.

The list of exceptions to this part of the Act, however, is just about as long as the list of situations it does cover. The exceptions are:

- Private clubs, such as working-men's clubs and sports clubs. (Note: these are covered by the equivalent section in the Race Relations Act 1976.)
- Political parties. Women's sections and conferences are still lawful.
- Religious bodies may continue to discriminate if necessary because of their doctrine or because not to do so would offend 'a significant number' of its members.
- Hospitals, prisons, hostels, old people's homes and any other places for people needing 'special care'.
- Competitive sport, if an average woman would be at a disadvantage because of her physical capacity compared to the average man.
- Charities and non-profit-making organisations set up to provide facilities or services for one sex only. This doesn't mean such organisations may discriminate across the board – for example, by restricting their office workers to one sex only – but they may discriminate in the provision of services, including who is employed in actually providing those services.
- Insurance companies and similar bodies. These may discriminate if it is on the basis of 'reasonable actuarial information'. For example, women can be offered cheaper car insurance than men because statistics show they are safer drivers.
- Facilities and services which need to be restricted to one sex only in order to preserve 'decency and privacy'. This covers toilets, saunas, changing rooms, and so on.
- Certain provisions in relation to death or retirement are also excluded. Occupational pension schemes and redundancy payment schemes are outside of the Act.

Discriminatory contractual terms
Contractual terms which conflict with the Act are void. This applies to any term of a collective agreement, rule made by employers, organisations of workers, professional organisations or regulatory bodies. Individuals affected by such terms or rules have the right to apply to the industrial tribunal to have the term or rule declared invalid.

Advertisements
If an advertisement for a job covered by the SDA states or implies an intention to discriminate against men or women applicants, a complaint could be made to an industrial tribunal under the

employment sections of the Act, as the advertisement would count as part of the arrangements made by the employer to fill a vacancy.

Advertising in other areas, for example, for accommodation, entertainment or services, is also covered by the SDA but complaints about discriminatory advertising may only be taken up by the Equal Opportunities Commission (EOC). If you see a discriminatory advertisement, you can report it to the EOC (the address is at the end of this chapter).

Sexism in advertising, through offensive images of women used to sell products for example, is not outlawed by the SDA. But complaints of sexism or anything else you consider to be illegal, indecent, dishonest or untruthful can be made to:

Advertising Standards Authority
15–17 Ridgmount Street
London WC1E 7AW
Tel: 0171 580 5555.

How to complain about sex discrimination

A complaint under the SDA must be taken to an industrial tribunal if it concerns employment, including cases of victimisation concerned with employment. However, it appears that if your complaint is about discriminatory treatment during the course of an appeal hearing following a summary dismissal you fall outside the scope of the Act. If your employer is a public body you may still be able to pursue a claim relying directly on the provisions of European law. Your complaint of discrimination must be lodged within three months of the discrimination complained of. Complaints of discrimination in education, housing, and the provision of goods, facilities or services must be made to the County Court. Complaints concerning education must first be made to the Secretary of State for Education. If the matter has not been resolved to your satisfaction within two months, you may then proceed with action in the County Court. Complaints about housing, goods, facilities and services must be made within six months of the discrimination taking place. There is a discretion to extend the time for the presentation of a complaint if the court or tribunal is satisfied that it would be just and equitable to do so having regard to all the relevant circumstances and the reasons for the late presentation of the claim.

The Equal Opportunities Commission (EOC)

The EOC was set up under the Sex Discrimination Act 1975 (SDA) with the following duties:

- To work towards the elimination of sex discrimination.
- To promote equality of opportunity between men and women generally.
- To keep the SDA and the Equal Pay Act under review and propose amendments to the Home Secretary.

In carrying out its duties, the EOC has the following powers:

- To undertake formal investigations into discriminatory practices which are unsuitable to be dealt with on an individual basis.
- To support, including financially, individuals taking up complaints of discrimination.
- To issue Codes of Practice on employment. The first Code was approved by Parliament in April 1985. It is not legally binding but can be used in evidence at an industrial tribunal.
- To examine areas of policy outside the scope of the Act, for example, social security, taxation, maternity rights.
- To issue non-discrimination notices. This happens if the EOC decides as a result of a formal investigation that the law has been broken.
- To fund research and other projects.
- To apply for an injunction if it believes someone has broken the law and is likely to go on doing so. In the following circumstances, it is the EOC alone which can take action, such as applying for an injunction, if discrimination has taken place:

  (1) if an advertisement demonstrates an intention to discriminate unlawfully;
  (2) if someone instructs an employee or agent to discriminate unlawfully; or
  (3) if someone puts pressure on anyone else to discriminate unlawfully.

Local authorities
Unlike the Race Relations Act, the Sex Discrimination Act does not impose a statutory duty on every local authority to carry out its functions with regard to eliminating unlawful discrimination and to promoting equal opportunity.

Social security
An EEC directive on equal treatment in social security has led to some changes in Britain's social security benefits in recent years. For example, men and women now have equal treatment in short-term, contributory benefits, such as unemployment benefit. Women may also claim

income support on behalf of their partners and dependants, although in practice this is rare. Discrimination against married women claiming the invalid care allowance (ICA) has now been outlawed following a successful test case under the European directive. Married and co-habiting women claiming ICA may also put in for back payments to December 1984, if applicable to their case.

9.3 Sexual minorities

Sexual orientation

There are no laws specifically criminalising sex between lesbians. As a general rule consensual sexual activity between men over eighteen in private is legal, although under specified circumstances. There is no statutory protection against discrimination on grounds of sexual orientation. Although recent decisions granting transsexuals protection under European Community law (see above sex discrimination 9.2) *may* also mean that the same protection is guaranteed to gay men and lesbians. However, if an individual is dismissed by reason of his/her sexual orientation and has sufficient qualifying service in that employment, he or she may be able to bring a claim in respect of unfair dismissal. However, broadly speaking, at present, there is little legal sanction against such discrimination in the fields of employment, housing, immigration, the provision of services and parental rights.

Criminal law

Women

There are no laws specially restricting lesbian behaviour, except in the armed forces where women can be charged with committing 'disgraceful conduct of an indecent or unnatural kind'.

Technically, lesbians can be prosecuted for the following acts, but they rarely are:

- Insulting behaviour (see below).
- Indecent assault on another woman who did not consent or who is under sixteen.
- Although there is no age of consent for lesbians, the Indecency with Children Act 1960 provides that a woman committing an act of gross indecency, i.e. having sex (see below) with a girl under fourteen, would be breaking the law.

Men

It is legal for two men over eighteen to have sex together, provided they are in private and both consent (this is now the law throughout the whole of the UK). In this context, sex means any form of sexual activity (subject to the potential restriction mentioned above) including intercourse (buggery). The following restrictions apply to sex between men:

- The age of consent is eighteen – two years older than the age at which heterosexuals can have lawful intercourse.
- 'In private' does not include places such as public lavatories (even if no one can see), nor when more than two people are present (even if they all consent). It is up to the prosecution to prove that the activity did not take place in private, and many courts have decided that particular places were 'in private', even if the public theoretically had access to them (for example, a dark lane, behind a clump of bushes, in an enclosed yard after normal working hours, etc).
- Meeting another man with a view to having lawful sex may itself be illegal. Because of the law of importuning or soliciting, it may be an offence for a man to chat up another man if done in a public place. Even just smiling at someone can be classified as importuning and, if a man 'persistently' importunes for an 'immoral purpose', that is an offence. It is up to the court to decide if lawful sexual activity amounts to an 'immoral purpose' in any particular case, but they can (and sometimes do) find men guilty of this offence even though the sexual activity would have been lawful, i.e. between two consenting men over eighteen and in private.
- Members of all branches of the armed forces are still denied the right to a homosexual sex life. All forms of lesbian or gay sex are illegal and can lead to a court martial and a dishonourable discharge, plus up to two years' imprisonment.
- It is illegal for merchant seamen to engage in gay sex on board a ship on which either of them is serving, though this does not apply to deep-sea oil rigs.
- Displays of affection in public by lesbians or gay men might be illegal on the ground of 'insulting behaviour' (see below).

Offences

Cruising/picking up men

A man making an approach to another man with a view to having sex may itself be a crime, even though it was intended to have sex in circumstances which would be legal. Under the Sexual Offences Act 1956, it is an offence persistently to importune in a public place for an immoral purpose. This law was enacted originally at the end of the nineteenth century to outlaw pimping for female prostitutes in the

Leicester Square music halls. Now it is used almost exclusively to stop men approaching other men with a view to sex – known as cruising, or more commonly, picking someone up. Usually the police arrest men for importuning (also called 'soliciting') outside or near gay pubs or clubs, or in parks, public lavatories or other places where it is likely that one man can pick up another. This law is not used primarily against men who are prostitutes, though male prostitution is covered by it. Importuning is any kind of approach to another person – a smile is enough – and either words or gestures will do. 'Persistently' means more than once to the same person, or to two or more people. If a man speaks to or gestures towards another man just once it is not an offence under this section, but it may still be caught by the offence of 'attempting to procure an act of gross indecency' (see below). Whether a purpose is an 'immoral purpose' depends entirely on the view of the court applying its own standards. Magistrates are known to convict of this offence much more frequently than juries. The higher courts have made it clear that a man can be convicted of this offence even though he was chatting someone up with a view to having perfectly lawful sex – i.e. both consenting, twenty-one (the age of consent at the time) or older and in private. Many juries have taken the view that picking up another man, even a stranger, for sex is not an 'immoral purpose' caught by this Act, and the majority of such cases result in acquittals if fought in the Crown Court.

Sentences vary widely from place to place. For most men convicted of this kind of offence, it is the publicity, social costs, exposure and humiliation that are far greater penalties than those imposed by the courts which are frequently in the form of a fine.

Sexual activity

Any kind of sexual activity involving a man under eighteen or taking place 'in public' is illegal. The law uses the term 'gross indecency' to describe all sexual activity between males other than buggery (anal intercourse). 'Gross indecency' includes sexual activity short of physical contact as well as touching. For example, two men masturbating in sight of each other, although separated by a wall, have been found guilty of gross indecency even though they were in adjacent locked cubicles of a public lavatory and no one else could see them (except police officers peering down from a hole in the ceiling). It is not 'gross indecency' to engage in sexual activity merely directed towards another man unless he too is a willing participant in the sense that he is aware of what is going on and cooperates in an 'indecent exhibition'. This offence was once used to prosecute the director of a play in which the actors simulated gay sex.

To commit 'gross indecency' the men involved in the act must be acting in concert and there must be at least some participation and cooperation by both, but actual physical contact between them is not necessary. It is a question for the court to decide as to whether the activity that was taking place amounts to 'gross indecency'. If either or both of the parties are under eighteen they can both be prosecuted, though in practice this is rarely done if both are under eighteen. The Director of Public Prosecutions must give his or her consent to a prosecution for an offence involving someone under eighteen.

In many cases sexual activity will only be illegal because it takes place in public. It is for the prosecution to prove that an act of gross indecency took place otherwise than in private. Whether a place is public or private is a question for the court. In the case of Reakes (1974), the Court of Appeal approved the following definition of 'in private': 'Look at all the surrounding circumstances, the time of night, the nature of the place including such matters as lighting and you consider further the likelihood of a third person coming upon the scene.'

As with cases of importuning, a majority of juries acquit on charges of gross indecency. There is a better chance of acquittal in the Crown Court than in the magistrates' court, which has no jury.

It can also be an offence to approach another man with a view to having sex, either by 'importuning' or by 'attempting to procure an act of gross indecency'. This means no more than making an approach to another man. It differs from importuning in two ways: there does not need to be any 'persistency' or repetition of the approach; but also, for it to be an offence, the prosecution must prove that the sexual activity sought would have been illegal, i.e. in public usually. Buggery between men is legal or illegal in the same circumstances as gross indecency, i.e. it depends on the ages of the parties and the place where it happens.

Displaying affection in public

Lesbians or gays who hold hands or kiss or fondle each other in public in the same way as heterosexuals may be committing an offence of 'insulting behaviour' under the Public Order Act 1986. Much will depend on the particular facts of the case and, as it is an offence which can only be tried in the magistrates' court, it will usually depend on the moral and political views of the magistrates as to whether the behaviour is regarded as insulting. The term 'insulting' is not defined by the law; it has to be given its ordinary meaning, but the higher courts have upheld a conviction under similar (though not identical) legislation where two men were fondling each other's genitals and buttocks over their clothes in the course of saying goodnight in a public place.

Policing and agents provocateurs

The police have a very wide discretion in the way they enforce the offences referred to above. In some areas of the country they are far more rigorous about seeking out gay offences than in others, and the attitudes of the same police force may change from time to time depending on the views of the senior officers responsible for operational decisions.

In some instances the police themselves try to lure men into committing offences, especially importuning. They do this by standing around, often dressed to attract an advance, usually outside gay pubs or in public lavatories, making it obvious that they are looking for a pick-up. A man who approaches a policeman who is acting as an agent provocateur will not thereby automatically have a defence to a charge of importuning or attempting to procure an act of gross indecency, despite the fact that police and Home Office regulations specifically prohibit this activity. However, a jury in such a case may well be more disposed to acquit the man on other grounds as an indication of their disapproval of the police behaviour.

Conspiracy to corrupt public morals

This is a rarely used but powerful criminal offence, invented by the judiciary rather than passed by Parliament. It has been used in particular to prohibit gay men advertising in the 'contact' pages of magazines. Essentially, it is an offence to conspire or agree to do some act which, in the opinion of a jury, is calculated to corrupt or debauch public morals. In 1973, the House of Lords upheld, by a majority, the conviction of a magazine containing explicit gay contact ads on the ground that encouraging homosexuality is the sort of thing a jury might properly consider to be a 'corrupt practice'. However, the people placing the advertisements were not prosecuted. Since 1973, there have been no further prosecutions of this kind and explicit advertisements are now commonplace. The law, however, has not been repealed so there is always the possibility of a prosecution in the future.

Young people

While the criminal law prohibits any kind of gay sex life for men under eighteen, lesbian and gay teenagers who assert their independence once they become sixteen could find themselves taken into care by the local authority on the grounds that they are in 'moral danger'.

If they are under seventeen they can be detained by the police or other agencies. This is quite rare, however there are a number of cases of young lesbians and gays who have been dealt with in this way simply because they wanted to live with other lesbians or gay men, even at an age when they were old enough to marry and live with another person of the opposite sex.

However, these possibilities are unlikely.

Civil law

There is no difference in the way in which the civil law affects lesbians and gay men. Both groups are treated in the same way in principle, though in practice there may be a difference if a man's civil rights are threatened as a result of a conviction for one of the consensual sexual offences referred to above which do not affect lesbians. There are no specific statutes protecting lesbians and gay men from discrimination on the grounds of their sexual orientation.

Employment

If the European Court of Justice interprets relevant Community law prohibiting sex discrimination as including discrimination on the grounds of sex discrimination, then the following will cease to apply (see Sex Discrimination 9.2).

Recruitment

At present, broadly speaking, there is no way a lesbian or gay man can challenge an employer who refuses to give her or him a job on the grounds of their sexual orientation. The Sex Discrimination Act 1975 prohibits discrimination on grounds of sex or marital status (see 9.2,) but has not yet been interpreted to include sexual orientation. However, in rare cases it might be possible to use this legislation when the real reason for the discrimination is sexual orientation.

An example is the Dan Air case. The airline company had a policy of only employing women cabin staff and not even considering for interview men who applied for posts on the grounds that, if any of them were gay, passengers might be exposed to the risk of becoming HIV positive.

The Equal Opportunities Commission investigated Dan Air's policy and found that there were no medical grounds for implementing it, with the result that the company was in breach of the Sex Discrimination Act. They issued a non-discrimination notice (see 9.1, p. 246) and subsequently Dan Air changed their policy.

The case illustrates the point that the company was discriminating against all men in their desire to exclude gay men, and so was breaking the law.

Existing workforce

Many employees suffer discriminatory treatment at work because they are known or believed to be lesbian or gay. There are even some cases of discriminatory treatment of gay men by colleagues and employers on the grounds that they may be HIV positive solely because they are gay.

The difficulty in challenging such treatment is that there is no specific law prohibiting it, and lesbian and gay workers have to depend on general employment laws which have not always proved of much use in these circumstances.

If an employer discriminates against a lesbian or gay worker (for example, by denying them promotion) or responds to hostile pressure by colleagues (for example, by moving the worker concerned to different duties or a different location), the only way that the worker can challenge the decision in law is by resigning and claiming 'constructive dismissal' (see Chapter 13) on the ground that the employer has acted in breach of contract. This is obviously a high-risk strategy. The European Commission Code on Measures to Combat Sexual Harassment, recognises that gay men and lesbians are vulnerable to harassment (see Sexual Harassment above).

Dismissal on grounds of sexual orientation

The response of the industrial tribunals and the Employment Appeal Tribunal (EAT) to dismissals on grounds of sexual orientation has varied from case to case and is difficult to predict, except that it is more often unfavourable to the employee than the employer. In one notorious decision in 1980, the EAT in Scotland upheld as fair the dismissal of a maintenance worker at a children's camp solely on the ground that he was gay. It was held reasonable for the employer to dismiss him on the basis of prejudice by parents whose children attended the camp, even though that prejudice was without any basis. Most of these cases come to the tribunals following a man's conviction for a gay offence.

In another of the few sexual orientation cases to be heard by the EAT, it was held fair to dismiss a teacher following his conviction for gross indecency outside working hours. The EAT went to some pains to emphasise that each case must be decided on its merits and it was neither automatically fair nor automatically unfair to dismiss in such cases.

Even in cases when dismissal has been found unfair, the tribunals often make remarks to the effect that no danger is posed because the worker concerned does not have contact in their job with young people, the public, etc. This fails to recognise the nature of the offences for which gay men are usually convicted, i.e. consenting acts with other adults.

Few cases involving lesbians have reached the tribunals, partly because of the different criminal laws. However, one of the best-known cases, Boychuk (1977), demonstrates the hazards of showing one's sexual orientation openly at work. Ms Boychuk wore a badge with the words 'Lesbians Ignite' in her job as a receptionist at an insurance company's office. She was dismissed for refusing to take it off and her dismissal was upheld as fair by the EAT.

There are a number of trade unions which have specific lesbian and gay sections or groups which have campaigned effectively within the workplace to prevent discrimination. They can be contacted through the lists of lesbian/gay organisations (see p. 268).

Housing

A lesbian or gay relationship is not treated as being equivalent to a heterosexual marriage in the eyes of the law. This has meant that in housing law lesbians or gay men have no right to succeed to a tenancy if their partner dies, regardless of how long-established their relationship was, and even though the surviving partner in a heterosexual couple living together 'as husband and wife' would be entitled to succeed to the tenancy. The Code of Guidance to the Housing Act 1996 has gone some way to remedy this discriminatory treatment and some local authorities will exercise their statutory discretion to extend tenancy rights to lesbian and gay partners.

Immigration

The same approach has been taken by the courts to lesbian or gay relationships in immigration law as in housing law, i.e. they cannot be compared to a heterosexual marriage. Lesbian and gay relationships are not recognised for immigration purposes though the Home Office has suggested that applications could be considered if there were exceptional circumstances such as the grave illness of the British partner. A case-by-case approach should be adopted. Also, foreign nationals would be entitled to apply for asylum (see p. 286) if they could demonstrate that they would be likely to be persecuted, for instance on the grounds of their sexuality, in the country that they would be returned to. Disturbingly, to date, the European Commission of Human Rights has consistently held that lesbian and gay relationships, regardless of their stability (and whether children are involved), are not protected by the right to family life. The European Court of Human Rights has not yet decided whether the right to family life does apply.

Parental rights

There is no law against lesbians or gays being parents and many lesbians and gays marry or live in heterosexual relationships before coming out and thus already have children. Lesbians sometimes have children using artificial insemination by donor or by other means.

Lesbians or gays who seek custody of or access to their children following a break-up may discover that the law treats them less favourably than heterosexuals in the same circumstances. Although there is a right to apply to the courts for a residence order (custody) or for access, this right is entirely at the discretion of the judges who have often been biased against lesbian or gay parents. For example, mothers are usually given a residence order in disputes between parents but if the court knows she is a lesbian her chances are then much less than that of the father. However, courts have granted custody to both lesbians and gays. Local authorities allow applications to foster from both single lesbians and gays and from those in couples and obviously the special needs of young people who are lesbian or gay should be considered.

Ban on promoting homosexuality

The most significant piece of legislation affecting homosexuals since the reforming 1967 Act is Section 28 of the Local Government Act 1988, which bars the 'intentional promotion of homosexuality' by local authorities. The section prohibits the intentional promotion of homosexuality, the publishing of material with the intention of promoting homosexuality or the promotion of teaching in any maintained school of 'the acceptability of homosexuality as a pretended family relationship'.

The section does not prohibit such activities if done for the purpose of treating or preventing the spread of disease. It is very likely that the section will be interpreted narrowly by the courts to prohibit only things done or publications which actively advocate a homosexual lifestyle or sexual experimentation to whose not otherwise so inclined. Nevertheless, many local authorities throughout Britain have reacted to its enactment by adopting policies of self-censorship and caution, in most cases probably unnecessarily. There have been examples of local authorities banning:

- The publication of a list of advice agencies for young people because a couple of the hundreds of entries were lesbian and/or gay organisations.
- The performance of a play by a 'theatre in education' group because it contained a scene involving a gay man.
- The publication of a cartoon in a Women's Unit newsletter because it was a lesbian parody of heterosexual attitudes.
- The confirmation by a gay teacher of his sexuality when asked about it by children in his class.
- The stocking in public libraries of the gay and lesbian weekly newspaper 'The Pink Paper'.

Expert legal opinion is of the view that none of those examples fell within the terms of Section 28 and all these local authorities misinterpreted the section by imposing such bans. These cases do, however, illustrate the real impact of the section, which is to inhibit, censor and undermine the legitimate functions of local government and schools.

The ban on promoting the teaching of the 'acceptability of homosexuality as a pretended family relationship' in maintained schools is, in strict legal terms, greatly weakened by two factors. First, it is school governors and not local authorities who are legally responsible for sex education in schools. School governors are not affected by Section 28. Second, it is highly unlikely on any interpretation of the section that discussion of and counselling about homosexuality would be prohibited or restricted by this law. However, as we noted, some local authorities have already acted as though they are prevented from discussing or offering advice and counselling about homosexuality, despite the fact that the law will not prohibit it.

Note that it is local authorities not individuals who are liable under this section. At the time of writing the new Labour Government suggested it might revoke section 28.

Transvestites

There is nothing in the law to stop anyone dressing in clothes traditionally worn by members of the opposite sex. Sometimes, however, transvestites have been arrested for 'insulting behaviour' (see p. 248) and in theory they could in some circumstances be convicted of this offence, but such situations are very rare. In 1996 the Employment Appeal Tribunal rejected an appeal from a local authority employee who claimed unlawful sex discrimination after he had been threatened with disciplinary proceedings for wearing at work what was conventionally regarded as female wear (*Kara* v. *London Borough of Hackney*, 13 May 1996).

Transsexuals and transgendered people

It is lawful to undergo gender reassignment (sex change) surgery but there is no consequent right in law to be regarded as a member of the opposite sex from that into which you were born. In practice, however, transsexuals are able to obtain most official documents except a birth certificate in their new name and sexual identity. Medical cards, driving licences, income tax forms, passports, etc., will be issued by the relevant authorities in the new identity.

There is no right to be married as a member of the opposite sex and for the purposes of the law any such marriage is void in this country. The European Court of Human Rights has ruled that refusal of an amended birth certificate and the right to marry is not a breach of the right to a private life contained in the European Convention on

Human Rights, although a case against France suggests that the Court may reconsider its position. A decision of the European Court of Human Rights against the UK is expected soon which will re-examine the earlier case law.

Sado-masochism

The House of Lords, in Brown [1993], has ruled that certain sado-masochistic sex which involves the infliction of injury which is more than merely 'transient and trifling' is a criminal offence. This is so even where there is express consent to the act or acts. Although the defendants in that case were gay men, it applies equally to the activities of heterosexuals and lesbians. Although the Court of Appeal in a later case involving a married couple (Wilson [1996]) distinguished that case from the Brown decision. The European Court of Human Rights has held that the UK was not in breach of the European Convention on Human Rights in prosecuting the defendants in the Brown case.

9.4 Disability discrimination

The Disability Discrimination Act 1995 is the first legislative attempt to address comprehensively the issue of discrimination against disabled people. The Act is divided into six parts. Part 1 defines the meaning of 'disability' and 'disabled persons'. Part 2 deals with discrimination in employment. Part 3 deals with discrimination in other areas, namely, the provision of goods, facilities and services. Part 4 deals with education. Part 5 deals with public transport. Part 6 establishes the National Disability Council.

The Act will be brought into force in stages. The provisions relating to employment and the provision of goods and services came into force in November 1996.

The framework of the Disability Discrimination Act 1995 differs from the framework of both the Sex and Race Discrimination Acts. The Disability Discrimination Act contains no general principle of equal treatment. It contains three separate definitions of discrimination. Under the Disability Discrimination Act, the notion of justification is incorporated into the definition of discrimination so that actionable discrimination only occurs when you are treated less favourably for a reason related to your disability which cannot be justified under the Act. As a result of this approach there are differing definitions of discrimination for the purposes of Part 2 and Part 3 of the Act.

A further difference from the Sex and Race Discrimination framework is that the Disability Discrimination Act does not recognise the concept of indirect discrimination. The scope of the Act is more limited than that of the Race and Sex Discrimination Acts. The education, police, prison and armed services are excluded from its provisions as are firms employing fewer than twenty people.

Section 1 of the Act establishes a new definition of 'disabled person' as a person who has 'a physical or mental impairment which has a substantial and long-term adverse effect on his/her ability to carry out normal day to day activities'. To benefit from the Act's protection, a person must either be a person who has a disability or be a person who has had such a disability.

The terms physical or mental impairment are to be interpreted in their broadest sense. However, mental impairment is further defined in Schedule 1 paragraph 1 (1) of the Act as 'suffering from a mental illness which is clinically well recognised'. An impairment will have the relevant adverse effect only if it restricts an individual's ability to carry out one of a prescribed and exhaustive list of normal day-to-day activities.

Like the Race and Sex Discrimination Acts, the Disability Discrimination Act involves the Complainant making comparisons. Under the Disability Discrimination Act the comparison which must be made is between a disabled person and a person to whom the less favourable treatment is not applied. This might be an able-bodied person or a person with a different disability or impairment from the Complainant.

Discrimination in employment

Discrimination in employment is dealt with in Part 2 of the Act. Section 4(1) sets out the less favourable treatment which is prohibited by the Act in relation to employment. This treatment is discrimination:

- in the arrangements made for appointing employees;
- in the terms on which employment is offered;
- by refusing to offer employment.

Further, Section 4(2) prohibits discrimination:

- in the terms of employment;
- in the opportunities offered for training, promotion, transfer or any other benefit of employment;
- by refusing to offer such opportunities;
- by dismissing a disabled person or subjecting him/her to any other detriment.

Less favourable treatment is defined in Section 5(1) of the Act. An employer discriminates against a disabled person if, for a reason which relates to the person's disability, he or she treats the disabled person less favourably than they would treat a person to whom the reason does not apply *and* they cannot show that the treatment is justified. Additionally, Section 5(2) provides that an employer discriminates against a disabled person if he or she fails to provide such reasonable adjustments to the working environment as are required by Section 6 of the Act *and* he or she cannot justify this failure. If the material reason for the less favourable treatment could be resolved by a reasonable adjustment to the working environment, then the employer's decision cannot be justified where the less favourable treatment puts the disabled person at a substantial disadvantage.

In the absence of case law, it is not yet clear how close a causal connection is required between the less favourable treatment complained of and the individual's disability. However, the Act uses the words 'for a reason which relates to' which suggests that a looser causal connection may be acceptable than that under the Race and Sex Discrimination Acts respectively.

Reasonable adjustments

Where any arrangements made by or on behalf of an employer, or any physical features of premises occupied by an employer, place a disabled employee at a substantial disadvantage in comparison with persons who are not disabled, then the employer must take such steps as are reasonable in all the circumstances to prevent the disadvantageous effect.

The duty to make reasonable adjustments is not limited to employers. It is relevant to trade unions and employers' associations as well as users of contract workers.

The duty to make reasonable adjustments is owed to individual disabled persons when the relevant circumstances arise and where the employer knows or could reasonably be expected to know that a person has a disability and as a result is placed at a substantial disadvantage by their working arrangements or premises: Section 6. The duty is not a general one. It arises in relation to a particular disabled job applicant or employee. If the employer does not know or could not reasonably be expected to know that an applicant or employee has a disability and is likely to be disadvantaged, then the duty is not imposed.

A failure to make reasonable adjustments is not actionable in itself. It is a failure to make reasonable adjustments without justification which amounts to unlawful discrimination under Section 5 of the Act.

The Act provides some illustrations of what might be a reasonable adjustment, e.g. an employer is not obliged to take steps to make adjustments, he or she is only required to take such steps as are reasonable in all the circumstances. The Act provides a list of factors which will be taken into account in assessing whether an employer has acted reasonably in refusing to make an adjustment. These are:

- the extent to which the step would prevent the effect in question;
- the extent to which it is practicable for the employer to take the step;
- the financial and other costs which would be incurred by the employer in taking the step and the extent to which it would disrupt any of the employer's activities;
- the extent of the employer's financial and other resources;
- the availability to the employer of financial or other assistance with respect to taking such a step.

The list is not exhaustive and there may be additional factors which should be considered in determining reasonableness.

Justification

Less favourable treatment can only be justified if the reason for it is both material to the circumstances of the particular case and substantial: Section 5(3). How the tribunals interpret the words 'material' and 'substantial' will clearly determine both the availability of the justification defence and the extent of the protection actually provided to disabled people by the Act.

Liability of employers and principals

An employer is responsible for acts of discrimination carried out by his/her employees in the course of their employment whether or not it was done with the employer's knowledge or approval: Section 58. This is so unless the employer can show that he/she has taken such steps as were reasonably practicable to prevent the employees from committing the acts of discrimination complained of.

Advertisements

The Act merely provides that where a discriminatory advertisement has appeared and a disabled person has applied for and been rejected for employment and lodges a complaint against that employer to the Tribunal, the Tribunal will assume unless shown otherwise that the decision is related to the Complainant's disability.

Aiding unlawful acts

A person who knowingly aids another person to do an act made unlawful by the Disability Discrimination Act is treated as if he/she had committed the acts of discrimination themselves. Such a person will have a defence if he/she has been told that the action is not discriminatory and it was reasonable for him/her to rely on such a statement.

Trade unions and trade associations

Section 13 makes unlawful discrimination by trade organisations which includes trade unions, organisations of employees, and organisations whose members carry out a particular trade or profession. The Act prohibits discrimination in the terms upon which such an organisation is prepared to admit a disabled person to membership, and the refusal to accept an application for membership from a disabled person. Section 13 (2) of the Act prohibits discrimination in the case of a disabled person who is already a member of the organisation concerned in:

- the way in which the organisation affords the disabled person access to any benefit, or by refusing or deliberately omitting to afford him access to the benefit;
- by depriving him/her of membership, or varying the terms on which he/she is a member; and
- by subjecting him/her to any other detriment.

Part 3: The provision of goods, facilities and services

Part 3 of the Act prohibits discrimination against a disabled person in the provision of goods, services or facilities. The provisions include services provided by public authorities as well as those provided by private agencies or individuals, irrespective of whether or not there is a charge for the services concerned. Examples of the types of activities covered by the provisions of this part of the Act include: communications, information services, hotels and boarding houses, financial and insurance services, entertainment facilities, training, employment agencies, and the use of any public place. Education and transport services are excluded from this part of the Act.

Discrimination under this part of the Act occurs when a service provider treats a disabled person less favourably for a reason which relates to that person's disability and which cannot be justified under the provisions of the Act: Section 20(1). The service provider also discriminates if he/she fails to provide the disabled person with a reasonable adjustment when required to do so under Section 18 of this Act and that failure cannot be justified.

Section 16 of the Act indicates that the following discrimination is unlawful:

- refusing service; or

- treating a disabled person less favourably than the standard of service or in the manner in which the service is provided; or
- providing the service on less favourable terms.

It is also unlawful for a person to fail to comply with the duty to make reasonable adjustments, the effect of which is to make it impossible or unreasonably difficult for the disabled person to make use of the goods, facilities or services.

Justification

Justifications for otherwise discriminatory treatment are set out at Section 20(3) and (4). These justifications are capable of excusing both a failure to provide a reasonable adjustment and a failure to provide equal treatment. They are as follows:

- if the less favourable treatment is necessary in order not to endanger the health and safety of any person, including the disabled person;
- if the disabled person is incapable of giving informed consent or of entering into an enforceable agreement and for that reason the treatment is reasonable in that case;
- where a person has been refused service, this must be necessary because the provider of services would otherwise be unable to provide the service to members of the public;
- where the less favourable treatment relates to the standard, manner or terms of which a service is provided, this must be necessary in order to provide the service either to the disabled person or to other members of the public;
- where there is a difference in the terms on which the service is provided to a disabled person this must reflect the greater cost to the provider of providing the service to the disabled person.

Reasonable adjustments

Section 18 requires service providers to take such steps as are reasonable in the circumstances to amend policies, procedures and practices; and to remove or alter physical features or provide a reasonable means of avoiding them or provide a reasonable alternative means of delivering the service where a disabled person would otherwise find it impossible or unreasonably difficult to use the service. The service provider is also under a duty to provide auxiliary aids or services wherever these would facilitate the use by disabled persons of such a service.

Where there are physical barriers to access, the service provider can respond in three specified ways: Section 21(2)

- by removing or altering the physical feature concerned;
- by providing a reasonable means of avoiding the physical barrier;
- by providing a reasonable alternative means of delivering a service.

There are no provisions in this part of the Act which set out the factors to be taken into account when determining the reasonableness of making adjustments. However, the Act reserves the right to set out such factors in Regulation form in due course. The Secretary of State has power to establish a financial ceiling on the extent of costs which it is reasonable for a service provider to incur in making adjustments. It is worth noting that nothing in the provisions of the Act requires a service provider to take any steps which would fundamentally alter the nature of the service, facility or business provided or conducted.

Purchase or rental of premises

Sections 22 and 24 of the Act make discrimination in the sale, letting, assignment, sub-letting or management of premises unlawful. The definition of premises extends to land, business and residential properties. The behaviour prohibited is:

- refusing to dispose of premises to a disabled person; or
- offering the said premises on less favourable terms to a disabled person; or
- in the less favourable treatment of a disabled person in relation to any list of persons in need of premises of that description.

These Sections further prohibit discrimination against a disabled person:

- in the way in which a disabled person is permitted to make use of any benefits or facilities;
- by refusing to allow that disabled person the use of such benefits or facilities; or
- by evicting that disabled person or subjecting him to a detriment.

The provisions for the justification of the less favourable treatment outlined above are very similar to those permitted in relation to the general provision of goods, facilities and services. Private sale and small dwellings are excluded from these provisions.

Part 5: Transport

Part 5 of the Act is concerned with access to certain public transport vehicles and to the infrastructure of transport.

Licensed Cabs

The Secretary of State has the power to define by Regulations standards of access which new taxis will be required to meet. It will be an offence for a taxi driver to fail to comply with any such requirement or to drive a vehicle which fails to conform to the said Regulations. The equivalent requirements can be imposed on vehicles used under a contract to provide hire car services at designated transport facilities.

Once the Regulations are in force, the licensing authority will not be able to grant licences to taxis unless vehicles comply with the accessibility provisions. The Secretary of State can grant a licensing authority exemptions from the above licensing restrictions provided that specified criteria are met. These are that, having regard to the circumstances in its area, it would be inappropriate to apply the access requirements and that the application of such standards would result in an unacceptable reduction in the number of taxis in the area.

Section 36(3) of the Act requires taxi drivers to carry the disabled passenger while he remains in his wheelchair; not to make any additional charges for doing so; if the passenger chooses to sit in a passenger seat, to carry the wheelchair; to take such steps as are necessary to ensure that the disabled passenger is carried in safety and reasonable comfort, and to give such assistance as may be reasonably required. Section 37 imposes comparable requirements on taxi drivers in relation to the treatment of disabled persons with guide dogs and hearing dogs.

Buses, coaches and other public service vehicles

Section 40 gives the Secretary of State power to make Regulations covering access to public service vehicles for disabled persons to ensure that disabled persons can get on and off buses and coaches in safety and without unreasonable difficulties and to be carried in such vehicles in safety and reasonable comfort.

Rail

Rail transport Regulations model those relating to public service vehicles. It will be an offence to operate a rail vehicle in public service which does not comply with the accessibility Regulations when they are promulgated.

Enforcement

A complaint of unlawful discrimination in relation to employment must be brought in the Industrial Tribunal. Proceedings should be started within three months of the allegation. The Tribunal does have discretion to hear a case presented outside the time limits if it considers it just and equitable to do so. In deciding whether or not to allow a complaint presented out of time to proceed, the Tribunal can take into account any relevant factors including the strength of the case, the reasons for the delay and the extent to which a person's disability has impeded the ability to bring a case within the prescribed time limits.

Claims in relation to unlawful discrimination in the provision of goods, facilities and services must be brought by civil proceedings in the County Courts. Claims must be brought within six months of the act of discrimination complained of. The Courts have a discretion to extend the time for bringing a complaint if it considers it just and equitable to do so. Also, where a disabled person has consulted the network of assistance agencies established under the Act before the end of the six-month period, the time limit will be extended by a further two months.

Remedies

The Industrial Tribunal can make such orders as it considers just and equitable including a declaration of the rights of the parties; compensation for foreseeable damages arising directly from the unlawful act of discrimination; damages for injury to feelings; and a recommendation that within a specified period of time the Respondent takes reasonable action to remove or reduce the adverse effects on the Complainant of any matter to which the complaint relates. In the County Court, injunctive relief is also available.

The Act provides for limits to be prescribed as to the maximum amount of damages that can be awarded as compensation for injury to feelings.

National Disability Council

The Act establishes the National Disability Council whose role is to advise the Secretary of State on the operation of the Act and on the elimination of discrimination on the grounds of disability. The National Disability Council is required to prepare an annual report on its activities and place the report before Parliament. In addition, the National Disability Council may prepare codes of practice providing specific guidance on specific aspects of the Act (other than employment matters) at the request of the Secretary of State. Before giving advice to the Secretary of State, the National Disability Council is obliged to consult and have regard to the responses of such persons as it considers appropriate. The members of the National Disability Council are appointed by the Secretary of State and must have knowledge or experience of the needs of disabled people or people who have been disabled, or be members of professional bodies or bodies which represent industry or other business interests. The Secretary of State must try to ensure that at least half of the members of the Council are disabled persons, persons who have had a disability or the parents or guardians of disabled people.

9.5 Further information

Race discrimination

Useful organisations

Liberty
21 Tabard Street
London SE1 4LA
Tel: 0171 403 3888

Commission for Racial Equality
10–12 Allington Street
London SW1E 5EH
Tel: 0171 828 7022

Community Race Equality Councils exist throughout the country.
You can get the address of your nearest CREC from a Citizens' Advice
Bureau, the town hall or the telephone directory.

Law Centres' Federation
Duchess House
18–19 Warren Street
London W1P 5DB
Tel: 0171 387 8570
Contact them to find out the address of your nearest law centre.

Runnymede Trust
133 Aldersgate Street
London EC1A 4JA
Tel: 0171 600 9666

Society of Black Lawyers
Unit 149
Brixton Enterprise Centre
442–444 Brixton Road
London SW9 8EJ
Tel: 0171 274 4000 ext. 290

Trade unions will often be able to help you if you suffer discrimination
at work.

Bibliography
The CRE publish a number of useful pamphlets on the workings of the Race Relations Act 1976, including a code of practice.
Paul Nichols, *Tolley's Handbook on Discrimination*, Tolley, 1990.

Sex discrimination

Useful organisations

Liberty
21 Tabard Street
London SE1 4LA
Tel: 0171 403 3888

Citizens' Rights Office
Child Poverty Action Group
1–5 Bath Street, 4th Floor
London EC1V 9PY
Tel: 0171 253 6569

Equal Opportunities Commission
Overseas House
Quay Street
Manchester M3 3HN
Tel: 0161 833 9244

Rights of Women (ROW)
52–54 Featherstone Street
London EC1Y 8RT
Tel: 0171 251 6577

The addresses of your local Citizens' Advice Bureau or Rape Crisis Centre can be found in the telephone directory.

Bibliography
S. Edwards, *Sex and Gender in the Legal Process*, Blackstone Press, 1996.
Equal Opportunities Review, IRS, 18–20 Highbury Place, London N1 1QP. Tel: 0171 354 5858.
C. Palmer, *Discrimination at Work: the law on sex and race discrimination*, Legal Action Group, 1992.

Transsexuals/Transgender and Transvestites

Useful organisations

Liberty
21 Tabard Street
London SE1 4LA
Tel: 0171 403 3888

Beaumont Society (for Transvestites and Transsexuals)
BM 3084
London WC1N 3XX
Information tel: 0582 412220
Advice tel: 0700 028 7878

Press for Change
BM Network
London WC1N 3XX
Tel: 0161 225 1915 or 0161 432 1915

Sexual orientation

Useful organisations

Liberty
21 Tabard Street
London SE1 4LA
Tel: 0171 403 3888

Bisexual Group Helpline
86 Caledonian Road
London N1
Tel: 0181 569 7500 or 0131 557 3620

Campaign for Homosexual Equality (CHE)
PO Box 342
London WC1X ODU
Tel: 0402 326151

GALOP (Gay policing project)
2G Leroy House
436 Essex Road
London N1 3QP
Tel: 0171 704 2040
LAGER (Lesbian and Gay Employment Rights)
21 St Margaret's House
Old Ford Road
London E2 9BL
Tel: 0171 704 6066

Lesbian and Gay Youth Movement
BM GYM
London WC1N 3XX
Tel: 0181 317 9690

Lesbian and Gay Christian Movement
Oxford House
Derbyshire Street
London E2 6HG
Tel: 0171 739 1249

London Friend (Counselling and advice organisations for lesbians
and gays)
86 Caledonian Road
London N1
Tel: 0171 837 3337 (gay help line)
Tel: 0171 837 2782 (lesbian help line)

London Lesbian and Gay Switchboard
BM Switchboard
London WC1X 3XX
Tel: 0171 837 7324 (twenty-four hours)

OutRage!
5 Peter Street
London WC1V 3RR
Tel: 0171 439 2381

Stonewall Group
16 Clerkenwell Close
London EC1R OAA
Tel: 0171 336 8860

Terrence Higgins Trust
BM/AIDS
London WC1N 3XX
Tel: 0171 242 1010
For advice and support on HIV and AIDS issues.

Immunity
1st Floor
32–38 Osnaburgh Street
London NW1 3ND
Tel: 0171 388 6776

Bibliography

Madeleine Colvin et al., *Section 28 – A Practical Guide to the Law*,
  Liberty, 1989.
Caroline Gooding, *Trouble with the Law*, Gay Men's Press, 1992.
Liberty, *Lesbians and Gay Men and the Criminal Law*, 1990.

April Martin, *Lesbian and Gay Parenting Handbook*, Harper Perennial, 1993.

Disability discrimination

Useful organisations

The British Council of Organisations for Disabled People (BCODP)
Litchurch Plaza
Litchurch Lane
Derby DE24 8AA
Tel: 01332 29551

The Disability Alliance
First Floor East Universal House
88–94 Wentworth Street
London E1 7SA
Tel: 0171 247 8776

Bibliography

Colin Barnes and BCODP, *Disabled People and Discrimination*, Hurst and Co, 1991.
Ian Bynoe, *Equal Rights for Disabled People*, Institute of Public Policy Research, 1991.
Disability and Work, Labour Research Department, 1993.
The Disability Rights Handbook, The Disability Alliance (published each year).
Bryan Doyle, *Disability Discrimination – The New Law*, Jordans, 1996.
Caroline Gooding, *Disability Discrimination Act 1995*, Blackstone Press, 1996.

10

The rights of immigrants

This chapter deals with:

- The framework of control.
- Coming to settle.
- Coming to work.
- Coming for temporary purposes.
- Enforcement of immigration controls.
- Refugees.
- Rights to British nationality.
- Further information.

10.1 Immigration control

The present laws on controlling the entry into, residence in and departure from the United Kingdom are governed mainly by the Immigration Acts of 1971 and 1988 which came into force on 1 January 1973 and 1 August 1988 respectively. These Acts lay down general principles about who is subject to immigration control and who is not.

In addition, a further two recent acts govern immigration control. The Asylum and Immigration Appeals Act came into effect on 26 July 1993. This Act placed certain restrictions on asylum seekers and their dependants and provided for a right of appeal to asylum seekers who applied to and were refused by a United Kingdom port. The 1993 Act also took away the right of appeal against refusal from visitors, short-stay students, prospective students and a range of others who did not meet certain mandatory requirements under the Immigration Rules.

The provisions of the 1996 Asylum and Immigration Act took effect in January 1997. The 1996 Act effectively denies the right to claim asylum to nationals of certain countries designated by the Home Secretary. It restricts and accelerates the appeals procedure in many cases. The Act increases the number of immigration offences, increases powers of search and arrest in relation to these and provides for increased penalties for immigration offences. In terms of the social protection of asylum seekers, the 1996 Act denies the most basic social

271

security benefits to any asylum seeker who does not make the claim for asylum on arrival at the port. The Act also severely restricts entitlement to public housing to all who are subject to immigration control.

The 1996 Asylum and Immigration Act represents a fundamental change in the regulation of immigration control, in that it markedly extends this control to beyond the port and into daily life. Proof of immigration status may have to be asked for by many public authorities. In some cases, such as the Benefits Agency dealing with a claim for social security benefits, a person's immigration status has first to be proved, before a person has access to any benefits. In the past, British governments had consistently stated that this country had 'firm but fair' immigration control at the port, but once allowed in, you could expect to be treated equally. This latest law makes it not just lawful to discriminate, but imposes a duty on employers, Benefits Agency staff, local authorities, doctors, hospital staff, teachers and others to determine someone's immigration status.

The Immigration Acts are the statutory basis for the control of immigration. However, the powers granted under the Immigration Acts are very general. How that power is to be exercised is set out in the Immigration Rules. These attempt to be wide-ranging and fairly precise, and try to cover every conceivable type of application and state the requirements for each, but are not exhaustive. They do not cover the many applications and grants of stay which are 'outside the rules': those allowed to remain permanently due to long residence; those fleeing civil war; those allowed to stay to care for a sick relative; those in same-sex relationships; those here as domestic workers, and others.

The Rules are both numerous and can change frequently, often without close parliamentary scrutiny. The main Rules currently in force are called House of Commons Paper No. 395 of 1994 (HC 395) which came into effect on 1 October 1994. Further Rules came into effect in October 1995, January 1996 and in November 1996 following the introduction of the 1996 Asylum and Immigration Act.

There are also detailed instructions to immigration officers on how they should operate the Rules; these instructions are not published and are secret. There are also Home Office policies ranging in subject from long residence in the UK, to matters to be taken into account in deportation cases. Some Home Office policies are widely known, others are not. It is not Home Office practice to publish their policies. These policies may be referred to in Parliament, for example, when a Home Office minister explains the government's approach or attitude to an issue, or the existence of a policy may be referred to in a court or tribunal in individual cases. Some have been set out in letters from the Home Office to certain organisations. Yet other policies have been leaked.

To understand immigration law, therefore, it is necessary also to know about the practice of the Home Office, and it is advisable to contact one of the organisations listed at the end of this chapter for advice before approaching the Home Office. It is also important to note that from 25 November 1996, the use of standard forms in making certain applications to the Home Office has been made compulsory. The Home Office have indicated that they will be strict about the completion of all sections of the form, the provision of answers to all questions and the supply of all documents in the original (or a reasonable explanation offered). An incomplete or improperly completed application will be rejected by the Home Office, with the danger of the applicant becoming an overstayer without a right of appeal. It is now more important than ever to get proper advice before making any application to the Home Office.

There are other statutes which have a bearing on immigration control: they range from nationality laws which extend or restrict rights of abode (to the Falkland Islands and Hong Kong respectively), to the Carriers' Liability Act which imposes fines on carriers who bring passengers without the required documents to the UK.

The European Union has a very significant impact on domestic immigration law. This is due to the direct effect of European Union laws on the free movement of persons, and also on a political and policy level, from increasing co-ordination and harmonisation on matters of immigration and asylum within the Union. The latter process is secretive and outside of democratic or judicial control.

STOP PRESS

The new government proposes to incorporate the European Convention on Human Rights into domestic law. The rights in the Convention are set out in Chapter 5. A Bill to incorporate the Convention is due to be published in the autumn of 1997 and this is likely to become an Act by July 1998 and to come into force not before January 1999. It is not clear at the time of writing exactly what effect this will have on our laws. It is likely that the Convention will be able to be used to challenge some of the existing procedures and judge-made law although whether the Convention will be given a higher status than statute is not so clear. Nevertheless the rights set out in this book may be enhanced by the Convention and in future the rights in the Convention will have to be considered much more seriously than they have been in the past.

Finally, the European Convention on Human Rights offers, in this context, minimum standards for the protection of the rights of migrants, their families, refugees and asylum seekers. At present, the Convention is not part of the law in the UK and is only considered by the courts as being relevant where domestic law is unclear. It is however worth noting that the Convention is probably the strongest regional human rights protection system in the world. Its principles are acknowledged by the European Union to be part of the common legal and democratic traditions of all the member states. The United Kingdom government must have regard to the principles in the Convention when formulating policies and many senior judges support the idea of making the rights under the Convention part of the law in this country. It is therefore important to view the Convention as a basis to inform the debate on rights and to be referred to in both political and legal arguments.

Persons not subject to control

British citizens are not subject to immigration control. This may seem obvious, but there are several categories of people entitled to hold British passports: only those who are described as British Citizens have a right of abode. Others such as British Overseas Citizens, British Dependant Territories Citizens, British Protected Persons, are subject to immigration control and have to fit within the immigration rules on entry and residence; as such, they are, in this respect, only British outside the country of their nationality!

Commonwealth citizens with the right of abode and Irish citizens travelling from Ireland are not subject to immigration control. As someone not subject to immigration control, you do not require permission from an immigration officer to enter and your passport will not be stamped when you travel in and out.

Commonwealth citizens have the right of abode if either:

- One of their parents was born in the UK.
- They are women who were married before 1983 to a man who was a British citizen or a Commonwealth citizen with the right of abode.

Persons subject to limited control

Citizens of countries having membership of any of three separate European entities are subject to only limited immigration control.

The European Union (EU) came into existence as a result of the Treaty of Maastricht, which came into force on 1 November 1993. The European Economic Area (EEA) took effect from the 1 January 1994, comprising the EU and five countries from the European Free Trade

Association (EFTA). On 1 January 1995, three of these EFTA countries joined the EU.

In relation to immigration control, leaving aside British citizens, nationals of the countries within the EEA are only subject to limited immigration control in the UK. That is to say, citizens of the European Union – Austria, Belgium, Denmark, Finland, France, Germany, Greece, Ireland, Italy, Luxemburg, the Netherlands, Portugal, Spain, Sweden – and those European Free Trade Association countries which are also members of the European Economic Area – Iceland and Norway – benefit from the rights of free movement within the EEA. In addition, under certain special circumstances, the families of British citizens, who are not themselves nationals of a country within the EEA, may benefit from this protection, as would the families of other EEA nationals.

It is difficult, if not impossible, to be exhaustive about what exactly is meant by 'limited control' as much depends on the circumstances of the case. In theory, those whose nationality allows for the rights of free movement are not subject to border control, and are only subject to limited controls on rights of residence in any country within the EEA.

In practice however, the exercise of the rights of free movement and residence are underpinned by economic activity, or economic self-reliance if a person is not so active. Historically, the European Court of Justice has adopted a liberal interpretation of the nature and extent of what amounts to economic activity. Thus, part-time workers or those whose earnings are so low as to require social security top-ups have been found to be within the scope and protection of the laws governing free movement. There nevertheless remain several areas of uncertainty about the extent of these rights.

The United Kingdom practice continues to be for an Immigration Officer at the port to examine the passport or other identity document of an EU/EEA national in order to establish identity and to confirm nationality. An exception is Irish citizens travelling from Ireland, who as mentioned above are not subject to control.

As a citizen of the EU or of a country within the EEA, you can come here to take up a job or to look for work, to do business or to become self-employed. There are also provisions for those who are economically inactive, but financially self-reliant. If you establish yourself in one of these activities you can get a residence permit, usually valid for five years. Although this is not compulsory by law, there are practical advantages in having one.

You can be joined by your spouse, children up to the age of twenty-one, other dependant children, grandchildren, parents, grandparents and great-grandparents. Once you have been established here for four years, you and your dependants will be considered 'settled'. Citizens of the EU have the right to vote in local and European Parliament elections.

As a citizen of the EU or of a country within the EEA, you are protected from discrimination on the grounds of sex or nationality. The extent of these rights for the purpose of this chapter, remains unclear. In the context of immigration and social security, the British government has put forward arguments which if correct, would mean that in order to enjoy any of the rights under European Union law, you must first have worked, or engaged in economic activity and obtained a residence permit. It has also been suggested that even if you have worked, you can be denied the protection of these laws, if you become unemployed and remain so for a period which the authorities say is too long. The legality of this position remains to be seen, particularly where the European Court of Justice has said that the holding of a residence permit is not necessary nor made compulsory.

Full control

Everybody else is subject to full immigration control and will be allowed to enter only with permission of an immigration officer if you qualify under the Immigration Rules to enter for a specific purpose. If you are coming to stay permanently or to work, you have to get permission from a British Embassy or High Commission abroad before travelling; this is called 'entry clearance' and could be either a visa or an entry certificate.

Citizens of many countries are 'visa nationals'. A list of these countries appears in the Immigration Rules. Being a 'visa national' means that you must always get permission before travelling, whatever you are coming for.

It is increasingly more difficult to discern any deep underlying reason for the inclusion of a country on the visa national list, or more unusually for a country to be taken off the list. It could, in the past, be said that visas were required of nationals from the poorer countries of the South, the former communist countries in Europe, the former Soviet Union and the former Yugoslavia. More recently however, the pressure for a harmonised visa list within the European Union, seems to be the determining factor. This has led to a curious situation where many Commonwealth countries with strong ties with this country are on the visa national list but countries without such ties are not. An example is Guyana, a Commonwealth country and the only visa national country in South America.

Visa nationals have to apply for permission to come here for a specific purpose and are in the main not allowed to obtain an extension for a different purpose. Thus a visa national who is here as a visitor and applies to remain here longer as a student will be refused without any right of appeal, however meritorious the case.

10.2 Coming to settle

Normally only the close relatives of people already settled here (that is, people allowed to stay permanently) will be allowed to settle with them. You must get entry clearance and satisfy other conditions before travelling. There are still long delays in processing these applications, particularly in the Indian subcontinent. Most people will only be allowed to come if their relatives can show that the person joining them can be supported and accommodated 'without recourse to public funds'.

Public funds for immigration purposes, since the changes brought about by the 1996 Asylum and Immigration Act, the Rules and Social Security regulations, now include virtually all benefits. It is a measure of the extent of the change in the law, that Child Benefit, a benefit that was paid universally regardless of means, is included within the definition of public funds.

Husbands and wives
You have to prove to an entry clearance officer (a visa issuing officer at a British diplomatic post) that:

- You are the husband or wife of the person you are coming to join and he or she is present and settled in the UK.
- You did not get married mainly in order to come to live in Britain.
- You intend to live together permanently as husband and wife.
- You have met each other.
- You have adequate accommodation for yourselves and any dependants in the UK without claiming public funds.
- You will be able to support yourselves without relying on public funds.

There are particular difficulties for people from the Indian subcontinent. The officers who issue entry certificates expect an applicant to prove that he or she qualifies under the complex and unfamiliar immigration rules. There is little regard for social and cultural differences in the way questions are asked or the way answers are interpreted. Sometimes an Entry Clearance Officer may question the credibility of an applicant who appears not to conform to a perceived social or cultural norm, and this may lead to refusal. An applicant is rarely given the benefit of the doubt. Details of family and social relationships are gone into in order to bring out 'discrepancies' which could lead to refusal. The questioning by officers is often hostile and this too leads to unjustified refusals.

If the application is successful, you will be allowed in for a year when you arrive. Before the end of that year, you must apply to the Home Office for permission to stay permanently. The Home Office must be satisfied that you and your spouse still intend to stay together and can support and accommodate yourselves without relying on public funds before this is granted.

Fiancés and fiancées

To come here to get married you have to prove similar things as husbands and wives and show in addition that you intend to get married soon after your arrival in Britain. If you are granted entry clearance, you will be allowed in for six months during which time you are expected to get married. You will not be allowed to work until you get permission from the Home Office to stay. If successful you will be granted permission to stay for an initial year, after which you will be granted settlement if you continue to satisfy the requirements.

Children

Children under eighteen may be allowed to join parents here (or to join one parent if the other parent is dead) if:

- You get entry clearance.
- Both your parents are settled here.
- Your parents have adequate accommodation for you here.
- Your parents can support you here without having to claim public funds.

If children are coming to join one parent and the other parent is still alive but not coming to live here, or coming to join a relative other than a parent, you also have to prove either:

- The parent living here has had the sole responsibility for your upbringing.
- There are serious and compelling family or other considerations making your exclusion from the UK undesirable.

These rules are very difficult to satisfy. In practice, they are not interpreted so strictly for children under twelve coming to join their mothers but this has never been written into the rules.

Adopted children under eighteen will only be allowed to come if it can be shown that the child was adopted in accordance with the proper legal procedures in the child's country, that there has been a genuine transfer of parental responsibility and adoption took place because the natural parents were unable to care for the child, the child has lost or broken ties with the natural family, and that the reason for the adoption was not to bring a child here. In common with most other applications for settlement, the ability for the sponsors to provide adequate maintenance and accommodation without recourse to public funds, must also be shown. Legal adoptions abroad are recognised if the adoption has taken place in a country on a designated list, but the other requirements will still have to be met.

Parents and grandparents

You may be able to join your children or grandchildren settled here if:

- You get entry clearance.
- You are a widow or widower over sixty-five or, if a couple, that one of you is over sixty-five.
- You can be supported and accommodated by your children here without reliance on public funds.
- You were wholly or mainly financially dependent on your children here while living in your country of origin.
- You have no other close relatives in your country of origin to whom you can turn to look after you.

In practice it is very difficult to prove all this.

Other relatives

Other relatives wanting to join family in the UK have to get entry clearance, and have to show that they are related as claimed to someone here, have been financially dependent on this relative, that they can be supported and accommodated here without recourse to public funds, and that they were living alone in the most exceptional compassionate circumstances without other close relatives to turn to. This applies only to sons, daughters, sisters, brothers, uncles and aunts of people settled here, normally only when they are over sixty-five, though it would be possible for a parent under sixty-five to apply under this rule. It is very rare for anyone to qualify to come here under this rule.

In general, the United Kingdom has a narrow definition of family for the purposes of immigration control. But for families of European Economic Area nationals, a broader definition based on extended families and shared households would apply.

10.3 Coming to work

Citizens of the European Union, and nationals of the countries within the European Economic Area, are allowed to work without requiring permission. Others wanting to come to work here need to get a work permit before travel. The employer here needs to apply to the Department of Employment for permission to employ a foreign worker, and has to satisfy restrictive conditions about your skills and experience and show there is nobody already allowed to work here who could do the job instead.

If you get a work permit you will be allowed in for four years or less if the job is for a shorter period. You will only be allowed to do the particular job with a specified employer, and do not enter the labour market here. If you change jobs, the new employer must first get a new permit for you and all the original conditions must be satisfied again. In law, work permit holders have the same rights as other workers. However, the fact that your immigration status here is dependent on a particular job with a specific employer may effectively act as a deterrent and stop you from enforcing your rights. After four years, you can qualify to settle.

The spouse and the children under eighteen of a work permit holder may be allowed to come here to join him or her as long as both parents are living or coming to live in the United Kingdom and they can be supported and accommodated without recourse to public funds. They must get entry clearance before coming and will be allowed to stay for the same length of time as the work permit holder.

Some work can be possible without a work permit. If you are coming to do one of a specific list of jobs (which includes ministers of religion, missionaries, journalists working for overseas newspapers, servants of diplomats, people working for overseas governments and international organisations), you do not need a work permit but still have to get permission before you come.

You may be allowed to come here as a writer or artist if you can show that you can support and accommodate yourself from the proceeds of your art or writing and any savings without having to take any other work or to claim benefits.

Employees of diplomatic missions are not subject to immigration control. They can remain here for as long as their employment continues, but however long they remain they never acquire any right to settle here.

If you have capital of at least £200,000 and satisfy other requirements, you may be allowed to come here to set up in business or be self-employed.

You can make your home here as a retired person if you can show a guaranteed annual income of £25,000, without having to work.

Nationals of certain countries with which the European Union has an 'Association Agreement' can come here for the purpose of setting up in business or self-employment. These countries are named in the Immigration Rules of November 1996 as Bulgaria, the Czech Republic,

Poland, Romania and Slovakia. The Association Agreement with Turkey does not allow for a similar right for Turkish nationals to become self-employed, but gives more limited rights to continue in a particular job for three years after being so allowed for an initial year. The European Union also has Cooperation Agreements with Algeria, Morocco and Tunisia, but the rights conferred by these agreements have been interpreted by the courts as being confined to non-discrimination in pay, tax and conditions at work for those nationals who already have permission to work here.

Once you have been allowed to settle there are no further immigration restrictions on what you can do here. You are able to work or set up in business without needing any extra permission. If you leave Britain, you will be allowed in again for settlement provided you have not been away for more than two years and that you confirm you are returning to stay. People who were settled and have been away for more than two years may still be allowed to settle again in certain circumstances, for example, if you have lived here for the majority of your life.

10.4 Coming for temporary purposes

If you want to visit Britain you need to satisfy an immigration officer that you are seeking to be here for a limited period of less than six months, intend to leave at the end of it and that you have enough money to support and accommodate yourself for the length of your visit without needing to work or to claim benefits. You can be supported and accommodated by someone who lives here, but you may be asked detailed questions about your relationship with them, what they do here and how they can support and accommodate you. Immigration officers may also look at your personal circumstances, such as your education, employment and family ties, and form a view about your 'incentive to return' to your country at the end of your stay. If you are a visa national, you need to get a visa in advance; if not, you can arrive at a port or airport and seek admission there. Six months is the longest time allowed to a visitor. Applications for extensions as a visitor will be refused, except in special circumstances such as illness, and may jeopardise future visits.

Study
If you want to study, you may be allowed to come here if you can show that you have been accepted for a full-time course of study at a recognised college or independent (fee-paying) school, that you have the money to pay the fees and to live here without needing to work or to claim benefits, and that you intend to leave Britain at the end of

your studies. 'Full-time' normally means at least fifteen hours of daytime classes per week, studying one subject or related subjects. Overseas students have to pay fees which cover the full cost of their courses and are not usually eligible for local authority grants.

A student will normally be allowed in for a year or the duration of the course, whichever is shorter, and can apply to the Home Office to extend this time to continue a course. If you have not yet been accepted by a college you may be allowed in for a short time in order to enrol and can then apply to the Home Office for an extension.

A student wanting a short period of post-qualification training or on-the-job experience may be allowed to stay on as a trainee on the understanding that this is temporary and that a transfer to ordinary employment will not be allowed. If a student has spent more than four years on short courses of under two years, or appears to be chopping and changing courses with no end in sight, or has not been attending studies regularly, an extension will be refused.

The spouse of a student and children under eighteen may be permitted to live here for the period of study, as long as they can be supported and accommodated without recourse to public funds. The family of a student does not have a right to stay, independently of the student. Where the student is to be here for more than a year, permission may be obtained for the spouse to take up employment.

Students may be permitted to take part-time or holiday jobs provided the college does not object and provided permission is first obtained from the Department of Employment.

Registration with the police
If you are over sixteen, not a Commonwealth or EEA national and not allowed to stay permanently but are permitted to stay in Britain for more than six months, you have to register with the local police. The police have to be informed of your name, date of birth, nationality, marital status, address, occupation and immigration status. They must be informed of any future changes in these. This requirement will only be lifted if you are later allowed to stay permanently.

10.5 Enforcement of immigration controls

There are three stages to immigration control: before entry, at the port of entry and after entry.

Before entry
All visa nationals have to obtain entry clearances from British diplomatic posts designated by the Foreign Secretary. The rules were changed so that applicants requiring visas must apply to the designated

post in the country of their nationality or where they are resident if different. Not all posts grant a full range of visas. If you are refused an entry clearance, you do not have the right of appeal if your application was to come here as a visitor, to study for not more than six months or with an intention to study without a definite place.

At the port of entry

If you had obtained entry clearance before travelling, but are refused entry here you have a right of appeal from within the country and can remain here while the appeal is pending. Immigration officers have the right to detain you while this is going on; after seven days you can apply to the immigration authorities for bail.

If you are refused entry and did not have entry clearance, you can be sent straight back. There is no longer a right of appeal against this. You can be detained at the port until there is a flight back, or while any representations made on your behalf are under consideration, and you have no right to apply for bail. However, in some circumstances, you may be allowed temporary admission requiring you to reside at a particular address and to report back at a given date and time.

After entry

If you have been allowed in for a temporary period and you are refused permission to stay longer, you can appeal against this only if your application was made to the Home Office before your permission to stay here ran out. If the application was made late there is no right of appeal and as an overstayer you are in Britain illegally.

All immigration appeals are heard in Britain, even when the appellant is abroad. An appeal is made first to a single adjudicator and then, if leave is granted, usually on a point of law only, to a three-person tribunal. Adjudicators used to be appointed by the Home Office but now both they and tribunal members are appointed by the Lord Chancellor's department. You may be represented, but legal aid is not available; few appeals succeed.

Police constables and immigration officers have the power to arrest, without warrant, anyone who has or who they suspect has committed an immigration offence. The Asylum and Immigration Act 1996 increases the number of immigration offences, increases powers of search and arrest in relation to these and provides for increased penalties for immigration offences.

It is a criminal offence not to give information to an immigration officer, or to give false information or documents. There is effectively no right of silence as the responsibility is on you to show that you qualify for the status you claim under the law. The very wide power under the immigration laws allows for the investigation and detention of suspects under these administrative provisions who do not benefit from the same level of rights as others. This leads to frequent questioning of black people about their immigration status when they come into contact with the police for any other reason, often when there is no rational cause for suspicion.

The Police and Criminal Evidence Act provides for Codes of Practice for the police in connection with the detention and questioning of people and searches of premises, but in law these do not apply to immigration officers, though they have agreed to follow them voluntarily. Breaches of these Codes of Practice have little consequence to the outcome of a case.

If you knowingly remain longer than you have been allowed by the immigration officers or the Home Office without asking permission you have become an overstayer and are committing a criminal offence. It makes no difference whether you have overstayed for many years or for a few days. You can be arrested and appear before a magistrates' court charged with this. You can be fined, imprisoned and recommended for deportation.

If you are not a British citizen, or a Commonwealth citizen with the right of abode, or a Commonwealth or Irish citizen who settled here before 1 January 1973 and who has lived here ever since, you can be recommended for deportation by a court if you are convicted of any crime for which the penalty could be imprisonment, even if you have been allowed to stay in Britain permanently. You can appeal against this as part of the sentence and it is then up to the Home Office whether to carry out the recommendation. Unless the court specifically directs your release, you will be detained while the Home Office decides what to do.

The Home Office can also make its own decision to deport people for overstaying or for breaking other conditions of stay, for example, working without permission. If it makes a decision to deport you, there is a right of appeal to the immigration appeal authorities. If you have lived here for more than seven years, compassionate aspects, as well as the law, can then be considered. If you have been here less than seven years, the appeal is only based on the facts, that is whether or not you are an overstayer. If you are married to a British citizen or someone settled here, and/or have children here who are British or are settled here, those are factors which must be taken into account by the Home Office in coming to a decision as to whether or not deportation is appropriate. The Home Office has the power to detain people it has decided to deport, even while an appeal is pending.

If a man is being deported, a decision to deport his wife and his children under eighteen (assuming that they do not have a right of abode of their own) can also be made solely on the grounds of their relationship. This will not apply if the family live in separate independent households. The children may be deported when their mother is deported, but a husband is not subject to the same risk.

The Home Office can also decide to deport you on the grounds that your presence is 'not conducive to the public good', a very vague term which can include people who have been convicted of a criminal offence but whom the court did not recommend for deportation, or people who are alleged to have made a marriage of convenience. You do have a right to an immigration appeal, but, at present, if the Home Secretary decides that your presence is non-conducive on the grounds of national security there is no appeal, nor do you have the right to representation or even to know the grounds of the Home Office's decision. You can only put your case to three 'advisers', chosen by the Home Office, who may make a secret recommendation to the Home Secretary, but this recommendation does not have to be followed. It should be noted however that the European Court of Human Rights recently held the UK to be in breach of the Convention in respect of the lack of legal safeguards and it would seem likely that this practice will be reviewed. As a result, the government has published a Bill which will create new rights of appeal. These new rights are likely to be available by the end of 1997.

Once all appeals have been exhausted, the Home Secretary can sign a deportation order against you and you can be sent out of the country. While the order is in force, you cannot return here. You can apply for the order to be revoked, either to the British post in your own country or to the Home Office, but the order is not normally revoked until it has been in force for at least three years. If the order is revoked that does not entitle you to return, but only to apply to return if you can satisfy the immigration rules.

If the Home Office claims that you entered the country illegally, you have no right of appeal until after you have been sent out of the country. You can be treated as an illegal entrant either because you entered the country without being questioned by immigration officers at all or because it is alleged that you, or even another person, misled immigration officers or did not tell them information that was relevant and, therefore, should not have been allowed in.

People alleged to be illegal entrants have no rights; they can be arrested and detained solely on the decision of an immigration official and can be held for an indefinite length of time. The Bail Act does not apply to them and they have no right of appeal until after they have been removed from the country. They may also be removed very quickly, without being given the chance to seek advice. Judicial review of the decision may be sought but it is rare for the court to reverse the Home Office's decision.

There are also provisions in the law for fares to be paid for people settled here who want to return to their countries of origin if it is 'in that person's interest to leave the UK'. People receiving in-patient treatment in mental hospitals may be sent back, under the provisions of section 90 of the Mental Health Act, to receive treatment in their country of origin, again if it is 'in the interests of the patient to remove him'; no definition of this is given and there are no legal safeguards against these powers.

10.6 Refugees

A refugee is defined by the 1951 Convention Relating to the Status of Refugees as someone who being outside their own country, has a 'well-founded fear of being persecuted for reasons of race, religion, nationality, membership of a particular social group or political opinion'.

The Convention is not part of domestic law but the Asylum and Immigration Appeals Act 1993 states that nothing in the immigration rules and practice should contravene the Convention. However, the United Nations High Commission for Refugees, human rights organisations and other leading commentators have expressed concern about the way in which the rights of refugees, guaranteed under international law, are not adequately protected and the Convention is not applied in the spirit intended.

Asylum seekers can be fingerprinted, a practice which is otherwise confined to those suspected of a criminal offence. Two successive Acts relating to asylum (in 1993 and 1996) have restricted the rights of appeal of asylum seekers: for example, where an asylum seeker is said to have an unfounded claim, or where the asylum seeker has not come directly to the United Kingdom, and most recently where an asylum seeker claims a fear of persecution in a country which the Home Secretary says there is in general 'no serious risk of persecution'. Once a person has claimed asylum, the Home Office has the power to take away any previous permission granted to remain in some other capacity.

In most cases, asylum seekers have the right of appeal against being required to leave the United Kingdom, although the time limits for appeal in certain cases are so short that it may be practically impossible to get legal advice and to prepare a case thoroughly. In cases where an asylum seeker has not arrived in this country directly from the country of persecution, the Secretary of State can issue a certificate which has the effect of removing a right of appeal against removal from within the country.

The rules and the processes relating to asylum seekers place additional hurdles. If they manage to arrive in this country without being stopped or having to transit in another country considered to be safe, asylum seekers are required to apply for asylum on arrival (not least to be able to claim benefits), to tell their story in a consistent way, not to damage or destroy any relevant document and not to undertake activities which are inconsistent with previous beliefs or said to be calculated to enhance his or her claim. The asylum seeker can also be penalised for the actions of anyone acting on his or her behalf.

Most refugees never have the opportunity of claiming asylum here or elsewhere in Europe. The visa requirement of nationals of countries which are considered to be 'refugee producing' effectively prevents most asylum seekers from ever coming here. The burden of caring for refugees invariably falls on countries closest to the country of persecution which are, more often than not, least able to provide.

The Carriers' Liability Act, which imposes sanctions against the carrier bringing improperly documented passengers (currently a fine of £2,000), is another measure that effectively denies asylum. The introduction of new laws governing asylum seekers is set against a background of increasing hostility towards refugees. Popularly held misconceptions are reinforced by politicians and others who demand tough action against 'bogus refugees and economic migrants'. In practice, this means that the Home Office is less likely to accept as refugees people fleeing from poorer countries or people who are fleeing from civil war or other circumstances. There is also an increasing trend of the UK government, in concert with other countries, mainly in Europe, to limit the scope of the Convention by giving it a narrow literal meaning.

If you are recognised as a refugee, you (and your family) will normally be allowed to stay for an initial four years and can then apply for settlement, that is, permanent residence. If the Home Office does not believe that you are a 'refugee' within the narrowest meaning of the Convention, but thinks that in the circumstances you should not have to return at present, 'exceptional leave to remain' may be granted. After seven years' exceptional leave to remain you may apply for settlement. However, you have no right under international law to continue to reside here and this will be entirely up to the Home Office.

Refugees are allowed to be joined by their families once they are recognised, but those who are granted exceptional leave to remain must wait four years before they can apply for their families to join them and must satisfy the other requirements of the Immigration Rules.

Asylum seekers are discriminated against in another vital way: access to benefits and housing. Unless you apply for asylum at the port when you first arrive, you will not be entitled to benefits, until and unless you are subsequently granted permission to stay.

Similarly, unless you apply for asylum at the port of entry, local authorities do not owe you even the minimum duty owed to other homeless people.

Several aspects of the most recent laws are still being challenged at the time of writing and it is not possible to predict the eventual outcome.

The Home Office has stated that they will continue the practice of giving permission to work if no decision has been made on your asylum application within six months. This permission would continue even if you are refused if you are awaiting an appeal.

If you are recognised as a refugee, you are protected by the Convention against discrimination. You are then free to work, change jobs or engaged in economic activity without needing any further permission from the Home Office. You will be treated as a home student for the purposes of fees and eligibility for grants.

Those with exceptional leave to remain can work but must fulfil other criteria to be entitled to educational grants.

Refugees are entitled to a Convention Travel Document, but those with exceptional leave are generally required to travel on their national passports unless they can show that this facility has been denied them.

10.7 Rights to British nationality

The British Nationality Act 1981 came into force on 1 January 1983. It defines who is British by birth and how people may become British through naturalisation or registration.

Other people who are settled here may be eligible to apply for British citizenship by naturalisation. If you are married to a British citizen it is easier to be granted citizenship. In this case, you must show that:

- You are settled here.
- You have lived here legally for at least three years and have not been out of the UK for more than 270 days in that period, nor more than ninety days in the year before the application.
- You are of good character.

There is a fee of £135 and acceptance of the application is at the discretion of the Home Office.

If you are not married to a British citizen you have to show that:

- You have been settled here for at least a year.
- You have lived here legally for at least five years and not been out of the UK for more than 450 days in those years, nor more than ninety days in the year before you apply.

- You are of good character.
- You have a sufficient knowledge of the English, Welsh or Scottish Gaelic language.
- You intend to continue to live in Britain.

There is a fee of £170 and acceptance is at the discretion of the Home Office, which also decides the standard of your knowledge of language and what being 'of good character' means; these have not been publicly defined.

In all cases of naturalisation, the Home Office had claimed that it does not have to give any reasons for refusing an application. The courts have however recently held that where the Home Office is intending to refuse you British nationality for particular reasons, it is right to afford you a chance to comment first before a final decision is made. If the reason for refusal is technical, such as your being abroad longer than allowed, the Home Office generally tell you. There is no right of appeal against refusal although you can apply again.

People who were born in the UK before 1983 were automatically British citizens by birth. The only exception to this was children whose parents were working here as diplomats at the time they were born. If you were born here after 1 January 1983 you are only automatically British if at the time of your birth:

- either of your parents was a British citizen, or
- either of your parents was allowed to stay here permanently.

If your parents were not married, only your mother's status counts. There are no plans to remove this discrimination against non-marital children.

If your parent later becomes settled, he or she can then apply for you to become British. If you are not able to inherit a nationality from either of your parents and are born stateless, and if you live here for the first ten years of your life without gaining any nationality, your parents can apply for you to become British.

10.8 Further information

Useful Organisations

Refugee Council
Bondway House
3–9 Bondway
London SW8 1SJ
Tel: 0171 582 6922

Immigration Advisory Service
County House
190 Great Dover Street
London SE1 4YB
Tel: 0171 357 6917 (advice line); 0181 814 1559 (out of hours emergencies)

Joint Council for the Welfare of Immigrants
115 Old Street
London EC1V 9JR
Tel: 0171 251 8706

Law Centres Federation
Duchess House
18–19 Warrent Street
London W1P 5DB
Tel: 0171 387 8570
For information about your nearest Law Centre

Refugee Legal Centre
Sussex House
39–45 Bermondsey Street
London SE1 3XF
Tel: 0171 827 9090
(advice line: 0171 378 6242; emergencies: 0831 598057)

UKCOSA (UK Council for Overseas Students' Affairs)
9/17 St Albans Place
London N1 0NX
Tel: 0171 226 3762

United Nations High Commission for Refugees (UNHCR)
Millbank Tower
21/24 Millbank
London SW1P 4QP
Tel: 0171 828 9191

For Citizens' Advice Bureaux, you may call these numbers for information about your nearest CAB:

0171 251 2000 in London
0171 833 2181 out of London

For other independent advice centres, you may contact FIAC (Federation of Independent Advice Centres) on 0171 274 1839.

The Immigration Law Practitioners Association at Lindsey House, 40/42 Charterhouse Street, London EC1M 6JH can provide a directory of practitioners. Please send a self-addressed envelope.

Bibliography

A. Dummett and A. Nichol, *Subjects, Citizens, Aliens and Others*, Weidenfeld and Nicholson, 1990.

D. Jackson, *Immigration and Asylum Law and Practice*, Sweet & Maxwell, 1996.

Joint Council for the Welfare of Immigrants, *Immigration and Nationality Law Handbook*, 1995

I. Macdonald and N. Blake, *Immigration Law and Practice*, Butterworths, 1995.

M. Supperstone and D. O'Dempsey, *Immigration and Asylum Law*, FT Law and Tax, 1996.

See also publications and mailings from the Immigration Law Practitioners Association, Joint Council for the Welfare of Immigrants, Greater Manchester Immigration Aid Unit, and individual Law Centres.

11

The rights of mental patients

This chapter covers:

- Applications for compulsory detention.
- Supervised discharge from hospital.
- Detention of offenders.
- Mental health review tribunals.
- Rights in mental hospitals.
- Further information.

Nearly half of all hospital patients are there because of some mental disorder. Anyone can apply voluntarily for treatment and may be admitted to hospital informally. Most patients are admitted to hospital in this way and they are entitled to leave at any time although, as an informal patient, they may be faced with the possibility of being compulsorily detained by one of the methods set out below if they do try to leave. Some patients, however, are compulsorily detained. This chapter is mainly concerned with the position of compulsorily detained patients and the rights of their relatives, as covered by the Mental Health Act 1983.

There are four categories of mental disorder which may result in detention in hospital or under special care. These are legal and not medical categories.

- Mental illness: this means any mental disorder not included in the three categories below. It includes illnesses such as schizophrenia or paranoia which may last a relatively short time, or permanent brain damage resulting from an accident.
- Severe mental impairment: this means arrested or incomplete development of mind, which includes severe impairment of intelligence and social functioning and is associated with abnormally aggressive or seriously irresponsible conduct on the part of the person concerned.
- Mental impairment: this means arrested or incomplete development of mind, which includes significant impairment of intelligence and social functioning and is associated with

> abnormally aggressive or seriously irresponsible conduct, but which does not amount to severe mental impairment.
- Psychopathic disorder: this means a persistent disorder or disability of mind, which may or may not include significant impairment of intelligence, and which results in abnormally aggressive or seriously irresponsible conduct.

Before the 1959 Mental Health Act, it was quite common for people to be detained in mental institutions because of promiscuity or other 'immoral' conduct. Such behaviour by itself may not now be considered a form of mental disorder; nor may sexual deviancy or dependence on alcohol or drugs. Such people should be detained in hospital only if they appear to be suffering from a disorder so severe that it warrants assessment or treatment and it would be necessary for their health or safety or for the protection of others that they should receive assessment or treatment and that it cannot be provided unless they are detained.

11.1 Applications for compulsory detention

An application for someone to be compulsorily detained in hospital may be made by that person's nearest relative or by an approved social worker. Except in an emergency (see below), the application must be supported by the recommendation of two doctors one of whom must be acquainted with the patient. The two doctors must not have family or business connections with the patient or with each other and one of them must be approved by the Secretary of State as having experience in dealing with mental disorder. If the application is successful, the applicant may authorise anyone to take the patient to hospital, by force if necessary.

There are three kinds of applications: assessment, treatment and emergency.

Admission for assessment
An admission for assessment may be made in cases where the disorder justifies detention to enable the doctor to decide the nature of the disorder, what treatment is needed, if any, and that detention is in the interests of the patient's health or safety or for the protection of others.

The patient may not be detained for assessment for more than twenty-eight days and the application cannot be immediately repeated. A patient may appeal within fourteen days of the admission to a mental health review tribunal (see below).

An application may be made for admission for treatment of a person outside hospital or of someone who is already an in-patient in a hospital. An approved social worker may not apply for admission for treatment until the nearest relative has been consulted, if that relative is readily available. The approved social worker cannot make the application if the nearest relative objects. Although it is not essential, it is advisable for the nearest relative to make any objection in writing to the local health authority or the approved social worker. In an extreme case, the approved social worker can challenge the decision of the nearest relative in court. The grounds for such admissions are that the person is suffering from a disorder so severe that it warrants treatment and it is necessary for that person's health or safety or for the protection of others that such treatment should be given and that it cannot be provided unless they are detained. If they are suffering from psychopathic disorder or mental impairment it is also necessary for the disorder to be susceptible to treatment.

An admission for treatment is valid for a maximum of six months. The responsible medical officer (i.e. the psychiatrist in charge of the patient) may then renew it for another six months and after that for periods of a year at a time.

Emergency admission
In an emergency, the nearest relative or an approved social worker may apply for admission for assessment with only one medical recommendation. A patient cannot be detained in this way for more than seventy-two hours unless within that time a second doctor recommends it, in which case the admission becomes an admission for assessment.

Anyone who is voluntarily in hospital can be detained for seventy-two hours on a recommendation by the doctor in charge of the patient. A nurse can also detain such a patient for a period not exceeding six hours if a doctor is not immediately available and the patient is suffering from mental disorder to such a degree that it is necessary for his or her health or safety or for the protection of others for him or her to be stopped immediately from leaving the hospital.

A police officer who finds a person in a public place who appears to be suffering from mental disorder and to be in need of care or control can take him or her to a safe place such as a police station or hospital. Such detention must not be for more than seventy-two hours and during that time an application may be made for admission for assessment or treatment.

A magistrate may issue a warrant authorising a police officer to enter any premises, by force where necessary, in which it is believed someone suffering from mental disorder is living alone and is unable to care for him- or herself or who is being neglected or ill-treated. The police officer may then remove such a person to a safe place for not more than seventy-two hours.

Discharge from hospital

The responsible medical officer or the nearest relative may discharge a patient at any time, unless the patient is subject to a restriction order (see below); but the medical officer may forbid discharge by the relative on the grounds that the patient is detained for treatment and is potentially dangerous to him- or herself or others. If that happens, the relative can appeal, within twenty-eight days, to a mental health review tribunal.

Leave of absence from a mental hospital may be granted for a specific period or up to the end of the then current period of detention.

Patients who are absent without leave may be detained and forcibly returned to hospital. If the patient is returned within twenty-eight days and the section has expired in that time, or has less than seven days to run, it is extended by up to a week to allow a renewal to be considered. If they return after more than twenty-eight days, special rules apply which the responsible medical officer must follow when considering a renewal of the section. If the section is renewed, the patient can apply to a mental health review tribunal.

11.2 Supervised discharge from hospital

A patient who is liable to be detained for treatment (but not one who is subject to a treatment order: see below), can be placed on aftercare under supervision on discharge from hospital. A supervision application can be made only by the patient's responsible medical officer, supported by written recommendations from another doctor (preferably the one who will supervise the patient in the community) and an approved social worker.

The responsible medical officer must consult and take into account the views of the patient, professional and informal carers and the nearest relative (see below).

The grounds for an application are that:

- The patient is suffering from one of the four forms of mental disorder mentioned above. Unlike admissions to hospital, the disorder does not have to be of any particular severity for this purpose.
- There would be a substantial risk of serious harm to the health or safety of the patient or the safety of other persons, or of the patient being seriously exploited, if he or she were not to receive the aftercare services to be provided after leaving hospital; and
- The patient's being subject to aftercare under supervision is likely to help to secure that he or she receives the aftercare services to be so provided.

When an application has been made, the responsible aftercare bodies may impose conditions to ensure that the patient resides at a specified place, attends at a specified place at set times for medical treatment, occupation, education and training, and allows access to his or her place of residence to the supervisor, a doctor, approved social worker or anyone authorised by the supervisor. The supervisor, or anyone authorised by him or her, has power to 'take and convey' the patient to the place where he or she is required to reside or attend for medical treatment, occupation, education or training.

An application lasts for six months and can then be renewed by the community responsible medical officer in the same way as an admission for treatment (see above). The medical officer can also end supervision at any time and the patient has a right of appeal to a mental health review tribunal (see below).

The nearest relative

The nearest relative is the first of the following who is over eighteen and resident in the UK, the Channel Islands or the Isle of Man: a legally appointed guardian, a relative the patient ordinarily resides with, husband or wife, child, father or mother, brother or sister, grandparent, grandchild, uncle or aunt, nephew or niece, anyone other than the relative with whom the patient has been ordinarily residing for five years if the patient is separated from his or her spouse. Note that:

- A husband, wife or parent need not be over eighteen.
- A person who has been living with the patient for six months as a spouse will be regarded as such if the patient's real spouse is permanently living apart from him or her.
- If the rights and powers of a parent have been taken away under the Children Act 1989, the local authority or guardian will act as the nearest relative, unless the patient is married in which case the spouse will be the nearest relative.
- An adopted child is treated as the child of the adopters.
- An illegitimate child is treated as the legitimate child of its mother.

Anyone who is a relative or spouse of the patient, or an approved social worker, may apply to a County Court for an order depriving the nearest relative of all rights concerning the patient and appointing someone else. This can be done on a number of grounds, the most important of which is that the nearest relative objects unreasonably to the patient being admitted to hospital or misuses the power to discharge.

If an order has been made displacing the nearest relative and somebody else wishes to take over the responsibilities of nearest relative, he or she may apply to the court to vary the order. This might happen if, for instance, a relative reached the age of eighteen or returned from abroad and therefore became eligible to act as the nearest relative.

Appeals

A patient can appeal to a mental health review tribunal:

- Within fourteen days of admission, if admitted for assessment.
- If admitted for treatment:

  (a) at any time within six months of admission for treatment;
  (b) within twenty-eight days when reclassified from one form of mental disorder to another;
  (c) at any time when the order for detention has been officially renewed;
  (d) within twenty-eight days if not released at the age of twenty-five and the patient is classified as suffering from psychopathic disorder or mental impairment.

- When a supervision application is accepted or renewed or the patient is reclassified from one form of mental disorder to another.
- If detained by a court order, see below.

A patient's nearest relative can appeal:

- Within twenty-eight days when the doctor has overruled the relative's order for discharge.
- Within twenty-eight days if the patient's disorder is reclassified.
- Within twenty-eight days when a patient suffering from psychopathic disorder or mental impairment is not released at the age of twenty-five.

The managers of a hospital must refer a patient's case to a tribunal if:

- The patient does not apply within six months of admission for treatment.
- The patient does not apply within six months of being transferred from guardianship to hospital.
- A tribunal has not considered the case during the previous three years.

Guardianship

A person over sixteen who is suffering from mental disorder may be put into the care of a guardian instead of being detained in hospital. The guardian may be the local health authority or anyone else. An application for guardianship should be made to the local health authority or anybody accepted by them. Patients can be transferred from hospital to guardianship and vice versa. But a transfer from guardianship to hospital needs two medical recommendations and the patient can appeal to a tribunal within six months of the transfer. The nearest relative has an absolute right of discharge from guardianship unless the patient has been transferred to hospital.

A patient suffering from psychopathic disorder or mental impairment must always be discharged from guardianship at the age of twenty-five.

11.3 Detention of offenders

Detention by court order
When a person is convicted of an offence punishable by imprisonment, the court may make a hospital order on the evidence of two doctors that the person suffers from mental disorder needing treatment. In that event, the court may not impose any sentence of imprisonment or fine nor make a probation order.

A patient may appeal to a tribunal within six months of the hospital order and then has the same rights of appeal as someone detained without a court order. The nearest relative can appeal after six months and then every twelve months.

Restriction orders
When a Crown Court makes a hospital order, it may also make a restriction order if it considers it is necessary to do so to protect the public from serious harm. In this case, the person is still sent to hospital but is subject to greater restrictions. A magistrates' court may not make a restriction order but may refer a case to the Crown Court for that purpose.

If a restriction order is made, the Home Secretary can release the patient at any time either absolutely or subject to conditions. The patient has the right to apply to a tribunal once in each year while detained, or once in each two-year period while conditionally discharged. If a person is conditionally discharged and then recalled to hospital, the Home Secretary must refer the case to a tribunal within one month of the recall.

Detention by direction of the Home Secretary
A person serving a prison sentence may, on the recommendation of two doctors, be transferred to a hospital by direction of the Home Secretary. When making a transfer direction, with or without a time limit, the Home Secretary may also make a restriction direction. This

has the same effect as a restriction order made by a court, with one exception: it lapses at the end of the prison sentence. After that occurs, the patient is in the same position as if he or she had been admitted for treatment (see above).

11.4 Mental health review tribunals

Mental health review tribunals hear appeals by mental patients or their nearest relative for the discharge of patients from hospitals and institutions, from guardianship and from a supervised discharge order. Application forms can be obtained from the patient's hospital, from the tribunal's office or from the local health authority if the patient is in the care of a guardian (see above).

The tribunal consists of three members chosen from three panels consisting of lawyers, doctors and lay members with administrative or social work experience. All three must be independent of the hospital and the local health authority concerned in the case.

Powers of the tribunal

Detentions for assessment
The tribunal must discharge a patient detained for assessment (see above) unless it is satisfied that he or she is suffering from a mental disorder severe enough to justify detention for assessment, or that detention is necessary for the patient's health or safety or the protection of other persons.

Other detentions
In all other cases (except restricted patients) the tribunal must discharge a patient if satisfied he or she is not suffering from mental illness severe enough to justify detention for treatment, or that it is not necessary for the health or safety of the patient or the protection of other persons that such treatment should be given.

In a restricted case, if the tribunal agrees that the person should be released using the provisions referred to above, but believes that the person would benefit by remaining liable to be recalled to the hospital for further treatment in future, it should order a conditional discharge.

The only appeal against a decision of a tribunal is on a point of law.

Removal of a supervised discharge order.
A tribunal can remove a supervised discharge order if it is satisfied that the conditions on which it was based are not complied with.

Procedure of the tribunal

The hearings are normally held in private at the patient's hospital. The applicant may ask for a public hearing but this may be refused if it would be harmful to the patient's interests. The applicant and the hospital representative (usually the consultant responsible for the patient) are both present and give evidence. They are entitled to hear each other's evidence and to call witnesses. They can also question each other and any other witnesses. The applicant can also address the tribunal but otherwise the tribunal conducts the proceedings as it thinks best.

The tribunal has power to take evidence on oath, to order witnesses to appear and to produce any documents. The medical member of the tribunal examines the patient before the hearing date and enquires into all relevant aspects of his or her health and treatment.

Advice and representation

It is most important that a patient should receive advice and representation when appealing to a tribunal. This can be given by a solicitor under the Legal Aid Act and is available without any form of means testing.

Expenses may be paid to the applicant, witnesses and their representatives unless the representatives are lawyers. Expenses consist of rail fares, subsistence and any loss of earnings agreed by the tribunal. It is often very useful to obtain the expert evidence of another doctor. The costs of doing so can be paid using the legal aid system.

11.5 Rights in mental hospitals

Consent to treatment

A patient in any hospital cannot be treated without specific consent, except in cases of necessity. There are exceptions for mental patients, as follows:

- Psychosurgery or the implantation of hormones to reduce male sexual drive may be given only with the consent of the patient *and* opinions from two doctors.
- The administration of medicine for three months or longer or electro-convulsive therapy may be given only either with the consent of the patient *or* opinions from two doctors.
- Any other treatment can be given if the doctor thinks fit.

It should also be noted that the above exceptions apply to treatment for the patient's mental disorder, not to any physical illness he or she may have. The restrictions on treatment do not apply to treatment which is immediately necessary to save the patient's life, to prevent a serious deterioration of his or her condition, to alleviate serious suffering by the patient or to prevent a danger to self or others. However, treatment which is irreversible or hazardous cannot be given in any of these cases except the first (i.e. if it is necessary to save the patient's life). In 1996, a number of cases were reported concerning women detained under the Mental Health Act who were forced to undergo caesarian sections without their consent. Such cases suggest that the courts are giving a wide interpretation to their compulsory treatment powers under the Mental Health Act 1983.

These exceptions do not apply to mental patients detained under the various short-term powers in the 1983 Act. Only the first exception can be applied to voluntary patients.

The right to visits

Patients have no legal right to visits, except to give them assistance in connection with a decision to release them, when they make a complaint, or to see their lawyer.

Letters

A postal packet sent by a detained patient may be withheld if a request to do so has been made by the addressee. If the patient is detained in a special hospital (Broadmoor, Ashworth or Rampton), it may also be withheld if it is likely to cause distress or danger to anyone.

Post sent to a patient in a special hospital may be withheld if it is necessary for the patient's safety or the protection of others. No letters to or from the following people can be withheld under any circumstances: an MP, an officer of the Court of Protection, the various ombudsmen, a mental health review tribunal, the managers of the hospital, a lawyer instructed by the patient or the European Commission or European Court.

Independent medical examination

A patient can be examined by an independent psychiatrist. The patient's medical notes must be shown if the psychiatrist wishes to see them. Any fee charged may be covered by the Green Form scheme.

Property

A patient's property cannot be interfered with unless he or she consents or someone is authorised to do so by the Court of Protection. The Court of Protection manages the property of people who, through mental disorder, are incapable of managing their own affairs whether or not they are in hospital.

Voting

A detained patient cannot be entered on the electoral register at the place where he or she is detained. It is a question of fact whether or not a detained patient has an established residence at some other address to which they intend to return. In 1996 the Home Office revised its guidelines relating to patients detained under the 1983 Act. These guidelines recommend that a person who is detained in hospital for six months or more is unlikely to be resident at his or her former address. A voluntary patient in hospital can register to vote at his or her former address.

Suing the staff or the hospital

No one is liable in any civil or criminal proceedings in respect of anything done under the Mental Health Act unless it was done in bad faith or without reasonable care. Civil proceedings need the permission of the High Court and criminal proceedings must be by or with the consent of the Director of Public Prosecutions.

This protection does not apply to the Secretary of State for Health or a health authority.

Jury service

Mentally disordered people resident in a psychiatric hospital or who regularly receive treatment cannot serve on juries.

STOP PRESS

The new government proposes to incorporate the European Convention on Human Rights into domestic law. The rights in the Convention are set out in Chapter 5. A Bill to incorporate the Convention is due to be published in the autumn of 1997 and this is likely to become an Act by July 1998 and to come into force not before January 1999. It is not clear at the time of writing exactly what effect this will have on our laws. It is likely that the Convention will be able to be used to challenge some of the existing procedures and judge-made law although whether the Convention will be given a higher status than statute is not so clear. Nevertheless the rights set out in this book may be enhanced by the Convention and in future the rights in the Convention will have to be considered much more seriously than they have been in the past.

11.6 Further information

Useful organisations

Law Centres – consult your telephone directory for local addresses and telephone numbers.

Mencap
123 Golden Lane
London EC1Y ORT
Tel: 0171 454 0454

MIND
Granta House,
Broadway,
London E15.
Tel: 0181 519 2122

Bibliography

Alternative Report to the United Nations Human Rights Committee, Rivers Oram Press, 1995.

Code of Practice to the Mental Health Act 1993, HMSO, August 1993

Conor Foley, with Liberty, *Human Rights, Human Wrongs – The Alternative Report to the United Nations Human Rights Committee*, Rivers Oram Press, 1995

Larry Gostin and Phil Fennell, *Mental Health: Tribunal Procedure*, Longman, 1992.

Brenda Hoggett, *Mental Health Law*, Sweet & Maxwell, 4th ed., 1996

Richard Jones, *Mental Health Act Manual*, Sweet & Maxwell, 5th ed., 1996.

MIND. Rights Guides: *Civil Admission and Discharge; Patients Involved in Criminal Proceedings; Your Rights in Hospital; Mental Health Review Tribunals*.

12

The rights of children and young people

This chapter deals with:

- Parental responsibility.
- Decision making.
- Money and financial support.
- Citizenship and nationality.
- Education and schooling.
- Children and social services.
- Children, young people and the courts.
- Further information.

Because of both their inherent vulnerability and society's attitudes towards their independence, children and young people have considerably fewer rights than adults. Children do not acquire full legal independence until they are eighteen. However, before then, the law states that children can do certain things or can be treated in particular ways at specific ages – for example, the right to drink alcohol in private at five, to buy a pet at twelve, to work part-time at thirteen and a number of different things at sixteen. For more information about this, see the bibliography on p. 318.

Over the past decade there have been a number of important changes for children's rights. There is now a far greater recognition that children and young people should be seen as people in their own right and not as possessions of their parents nor objects of investigation. The Gillick judgment (see below) recognised the rights of older mature children to make decisions concerning their lives in certain circumstances. The discrimination against non-marital children has all but disappeared. The 1989 Children Act has given children and young people greater rights to participate in decision making where social services or the family courts are involved. And the United Nations Convention on the Rights of the Child sets out a broad range of basic standards and principles relating to children's civil, political, economic, social and cultural rights. The Convention has been ratified by the government and some of its principles have been incorporated into domestic law.

But there are backward steps too, such as the introduction of the 1991 Child Support Act and recent changes to the youth justice system. The law is complex and the following inevitably simplifies to a great degree. Where in doubt, legal advice should always be obtained.

12.1 Parental responsibility

Parental responsibility is the term for parental rights and duties in relation to children and young people. The law does not actually say what this means but it has been understood to mean the rights and responsibilities to make decisions involved in all aspects of the child's upbringing, including the duty to look after the child and pay for his or her keep. Unlike the law in Scotland, there is no express requirement to promote the child's welfare. Parental responsibility lasts until the child is eighteen although the way in which it is exercised should reflect the age and maturity of the child (see below).

Parents and others

Mothers and married fathers automatically have parental responsibility for their children. This lasts even if they divorce. Unmarried fathers can obtain parental responsibility by going to court for a parental responsibility order or by entering into a special written agreement with the mother. Other people may gain parental responsibility in certain circumstances, for example, where a residence order (see below) is made by the court or on the appointment of a guardian where a parent has died. Social services get parental responsibility when a care order is made by a court but not when they are looking after a child with the agreement of the parents.

Sharing parental responsibility

Each person with parental responsibility can do what he or she thinks is best for the child. They do not have to consult with the other parent to do this but they must not do anything which infringes the law or what a court order says. If there are disagreements about how parental responsibility is being carried out the court can make a prohibited steps order (stopping a parent from doing something) or a specific issues order (telling the parent(s) to do something in a certain way).

Delegating parental responsibility

Unless there is a court order to say so, other people in charge of children, such as childminders, teachers, or foster carers do not have parental responsibility. However, they do have a duty of care to behave as a reasonable parent would do to ensure the child's safety and in emergency circumstances may take reasonable steps to promote the child's welfare.

12.2 Decision making

Unlike the law in Scotland, the Children Act does not require parents to consult with their children or take their views into account in making decisions about their upbringing. However, in an important court case decided in 1985, the court looked at this issue. It said that parental powers to control their children dwindle as the child matures. The rights of parents should give way to the child's right to make decisions when 'he or she is of sufficient understanding and intelligence' to be able to make up his or her own mind. This is known as the Gillick principle.

Names

Mothers, married fathers and others with parental responsibility have the right to choose the name of their child. They also have a duty to register the child's name with the Registrar General of Births, Marriages and Deaths within forty-two days of the child's birth.

Either parent may change the child's name unless there is a residence order which automatically stops this or a prohibited steps order which prevents the parent from doing so. With parental consent, young people may use a different name from that on their birth certificate. Applying the Gillick principle, parents should allow children of sufficient understanding to change their name even if they do not agree with this. Where there is a dispute, parents or the young person him- or herself (with the court's permission) can apply to the court for a prohibited steps or specific issues order.

Religion

Following on from the Gillick decision, young people can choose their own religion if they have the maturity to understand the implications of that decision. Again, if there is a dispute the court can be involved. If the parents thought that the religion was harmful they could ask the court to intervene by making the child a ward of court. Only parents have the right to withdraw children from religious assembly and instruction at school or to send the young person for religious instruction elsewhere provided it does not interfere with attendance.

Medical treatment

At sixteen, young people have the right to give consent to medical, dental and surgical treatment as if they were adults. This includes contraceptive advice and treatment.

Young people under the age of sixteen can give consent provided that the doctor or health worker thinks the young person is mature enough to understand what is involved in the treatment and the consequences of this. Although the law says that doctors should encourage young people to inform their parents, they may give treatment without parental knowledge or consent if the young person does not wish to involve them. These principles also apply to termination of pregnancy but in practice doctors very rarely perform abortions for under-sixteens without parental consent because of the possible risks associated with general anaesthesia.

The rights of young people under the age of eighteen to refuse consent to medical treatment are more limited and may be overridden in certain circumstances if their parents (or if they are in care, social services) disagree. This usually arises in relation to serious mental health matters, and the courts have said that the young person's refusal to give consent should be an important matter for parents, doctors and the courts in deciding whether to override the young person's views.

Leaving home

In law, under-sixteens cannot leave home unless their parents agree. Alternatively a court may make a residence order to another person such as a relative or an adult friend. This can be done on the application of the adult concerned, or by the child provided that the court has first decided that the child has sufficient understanding to make the application.

The law relating to sixteen- to seventeen-year-olds is not clear but they can probably leave home without parental consent.

The police will return young runaways under sixteen to the parents unless they have reasonable cause to believe that the child is at risk. In these circumstances the police may hold the child in police protection (not at the police station but with foster carers or in a children's home) for up to seventy-two hours pending inquiries into his or her welfare. The police will liaise with social services which may take further action for the child's protection. The police are unlikely to return over-sixteens to their parents.

Parents may take legal action for the return of a child under the age of eighteen by making the child a ward of court. However, the court is most unlikely to order that the child should go home where he or she does not want to go home, where there is evidence that the child is safe and there is a clear breakdown of the family relationship.

12.3 Money and financial support

Parents should support their children financially until they are eighteen and the 1991 Child Support Act reinforces this principle. On separation or divorce, the absent parent is responsible for paying maintenance in support of the child. This is administered, collected and enforced through the Child Support Agency (CSA), a branch of the Department of Social Security (DSS). The amount of maintenance is worked out by reference to a standard formula. In certain circumstances, the CSA should take into account the welfare of the child but the rules are very complex and the outcome may not always appear to do so. Young people have no right to make their own applications for maintenance assessment against their parents. However, over-eighteens may apply to court for maintenance where they are at school, in full- or part-time further or higher education or training.

Sixteen- and seventeen-year-olds can claim income support only in certain limited circumstances, such as the inability to work or the care of dependants. They may be able to claim a discretionary payment of income support to avoid 'severe hardship'. Matters such as the health and vulnerability of the young person and whether there are friends or relatives to support them should be taken into account by the DSS in making this decision, but many young people estranged from their parents do not receive any income support.

12.4 Citizenship and nationality

Children born in the United Kingdom before 1 January 1983 are automatically British citizens irrespective of the nationality or immigration status of their parents. Children born in the UK after that date are only British citizens if one parent (or the mother only of a non-marital child) is a British citizen or is settled in the UK at the time of the birth (see p. 288). Children and young people may apply for British citizenship by application to the Home Office for registration.

Travel and passports
Children may travel on their parents' passports until the age of sixteen. The child must be with the parent at the time of travel and his or her name must be on the parent's passport. Children of any age may have their own passport but the application must always be made by the

parent even for young people of sixteen and over, unless the applicant is married or enlisted in the armed forces.

Parents must not take their children out of the UK without the consent of the other parent, or with the permission of the court. However, a child can leave the country for up to four weeks with a parent (or anyone else) who has a residence order. Removal of a child without the consent of the parent(s) is known as child abduction. This is a very complex area about which legal advice should always be obtained. Children of sufficient understanding (see p. 316) may be able to seek a prohibited steps order stopping their parents from taking them or sending them abroad where the court considers that this is contrary to their best interests.

12.5 Education and schooling

The law relating to education is very complex and there are now a number of different kinds of state school with different forms of school government and funding. The following is a very brief summary of essential rights relating to state schools only. Independent schools fall outside the remit of the law unless they are boarding schools, in which case social services must inspect them to check the welfare, but not the education, of the children.

Compulsory education
The law makes education compulsory for all children from the age of five to sixteen. Parents must ensure that their children go to school or otherwise receive 'efficient full-time education suitable to his or her age, ability, aptitude and any special educational needs'. This means that children may be educated at home but the local education authority (LEA) must be satisfied that the education is suitable. Criminal proceedings may be brought against parents where their child is not attending school or being suitably educated. The LEA may also start court proceedings for an education supervision order. This places the child under the supervision of the LEA which has the power to make arrangements (where possible in consultation with the child and parents) to ensure that the child is properly educated.

Admissions
Schools and LEAs must allow parents their choice of state school unless that school is oversubscribed and it can be shown that admitting the child would prejudice the provision of efficient education or the use of resources in that school. Children have no independent right of choice. Parents may appeal to an LEA appeals committee against a refusal. LEAs must ensure that a child has a school place.

Curriculum

Schools must ensure that there is a broadly balanced curriculum which 'promotes the spiritual, moral, cultural, mental and physical development of pupils at the school and of society and prepares pupils for the opportunities, responsibilities and experiences of adult life'. Within this, schools must teach the National Curriculum (NC), religious education (RE) and sex education (in secondary schools only). The NC consists of the three core subjects of English, maths and science plus the foundation subjects of history, geography, technology, physical education, art, music and a foreign language (at secondary level). These subjects are evaluated by means of teacher assessment and Standard Assessment Tasks (SATs) for seven-, eleven- and fourteen-year-olds.

Parents may withdraw their children from RE at school and arrange for alternative RE during school hours. The biological facts of sex education are part of the science National Curriculum for eleven- to fourteen-year-olds. The social and emotional aspects of sex education form part of the broader curriculum from which parents may withdraw their children. Primary schools may decide whether to offer sex education and parents must be informed of the school's policy about this. Children of 'sufficient understanding' may be able to ask the court's permission to attend RE and sex education classes.

Parents, but not children, have a right to complain about the curriculum.

Special educational needs

It is estimated that about eighteen per cent of children have special educational needs (SEN). These are children with learning difficulties requiring special provision for their education. The law requires both schools and LEAs to identify and provide for children with special educational needs.

Schools are under a duty to ensure that special educational provision is made, and that the child's special needs are known to all who are going to teach the child. All schools should have a SEN Co-ordinator responsible for these tasks. Schools make provision within the normal classroom setting or by means of an individual education plan identifying specific help, possibly with further advice from other professionals. The responsibility for educational provision lies with the school and there is no formal means for parents to challenge this decision other than by making representations to the governing body.

The law requires LEAs to identify those children with more serious SEN for whom it considers it should make SEN provision. This is done by carrying out a formal multi-disciplinary assessment to decide whether to issue a statement of SEN. A statement specifies the educational provision for the child which the LEA is bound to provide and to pay for. Parents also have the right to ask the LEA for a formal assessment. The law provides parents with detailed rights to consultation at each stage of the process and there are strict time limits. If parents are not satisfied with the eventual provision contained in the statement they may appeal to a Special Educational Needs Tribunal.

Children with statements of SEN may be withdrawn from the National Curriculum. Other pupils may be excluded from part or all of the NC for up to six months. Parents can ask the headteacher to exclude their child from all or part of the NC. If they disagree with the headteacher's decision they have a right of appeal to the governing body.

Behaviour and discipline

All state schools have the right to make rules about what pupils can do both inside and outside school. There are no procedures for parents or pupils to make complaints about these issues. Some schools have behaviour policies which have been drawn up in consultation with the pupils. Corporal punishment (which includes things like throwing missiles and hair pulling as well as smacking and caning) is banned in all state schools and for children on assisted places in independent schools.

Pupils may be excluded from school permanently (expelled) or for a fixed period (suspended). Although a decision to exclude should only be made as a last resort, it is entirely up to the headteacher. Parents must be informed about the exclusion and the reasons for it and they have the right to make representations to the governing body for their child to be reinstated. Parents, but not children, may appeal against a permanent exclusion to an LEA appeals committee but the vast majority of appeals are unsuccessful. While similar procedures apply to grant-maintained schools, appeal against permanent exclusions are heard by the governing body and not the LEA. New legislation proposes to tighten up on school discipline by requiring parents to enter into contracts with schools, imposing after-school detentions without parental consent and extending the number of days per year for fixed-term exclusions.

12.6 Children and social services

Social services have a duty to promote the welfare of children in need by providing a range of services to the child and his or her family such as advice, counselling, daycare provision, and in exceptional circumstances, cash. They also have a duty to provide accommodation for children where the parents are unable to care for them for whatever reason. This is intended to be voluntary by agreement with the parents who by law are at liberty to remove the child at any time. Social services do not acquire parental responsibility for accommodated children.

Children over the age of sixteen may ask to be accommodated by social services and this request must be complied with where social services think that the child's welfare otherwise would be seriously prejudiced. In practice there is great variation between authorities about how this is interpreted. The law is unclear whether social services have a duty to accommodate under-sixteens at their own request. However, since their parents can remove them at any time its helpfulness is limited unless there are sufficient grounds for social services to take care proceedings.

Social services have a duty to make enquiries where they consider that a child may be at risk. This often includes a multi-disciplinary child protection conference which decides whether to place the child on the child protection register and, if so, draws up a child protection plan. Most children on the child protection register remain at home with their parents but the conference may recommend that social services should take legal action to protect the child.

This may involve care proceedings (see below). In an emergency, social services may apply to the court for an emergency protection order (EPO) for up to eight days. This will be granted where the court is satisfied that there is reasonable cause to believe that the child is likely to suffer significant harm if he or she is not removed to social services accommodation (or kept in an existing placement, for example, in hospital). An application for an EPO may be made without notice to the parents and in these circumstances they have the right to apply for the order to be discharged. A guardian *ad litem* is appointed at such hearings and the child is also legally represented.

Where a care order is made, social services acquire parental responsibility for the child. They share this with the parents but they can cut back the extent of the parents' responsibility in the interests of the child.

Social services have a duty to promote the child's welfare and to make plans for the child which must be reviewed every six months following more frequent initial reviews. In doing so, they must consult with the child, the parents and others concerned for the child and take these views into account (subject to the child's age and understanding) together with the child's religion, race, language and culture. They must encourage contact with parents, extended family and friends where this is in the interests of the child. Social services are also under a duty to work towards the restoration of children to their parents, extended family and friends where this is in the interests of the child;

there is a presumption in law that children should have contact with their parents unless otherwise ordered by the court.

A care order lasts until the child is eighteen unless it is discharged, or a residence order or adoption order are made. A number of different placements may take place under a care order. Social services are obliged to work towards the restoration of children to their parents' care or to the extended family or other significant adults where this is in the child's best interests. Consequently, children may live at home under a care order or be placed with relatives. Younger children who cannot be placed within their family are usually placed for adoption. Some children are placed in long-term foster care and adolescents may be placed in a children's home. Children of thirteen or over may be locked up in a children's home if they have absconded from care on a number of occasions and are thought to be at risk of significant harm. This can only happen if a court has made a secure accommodation order (unless it is less than three days). In these proceedings, children are legally represented and a guardian *ad litem* is involved.

12.7 Children, young people and the courts

Criminal cases

Young offenders
Children under the age of ten are below the age of criminal responsibility and cannot be arrested by the police or charged with any criminal offence. Younger children who persistently offend may be dealt with by social services which can offer help to the family or may start court proceedings for a care order (see below).

The rules for police questioning, search and detention of juveniles (children and young people under eighteen) are the same as for adults but juveniles have additional rights. Parents must be informed of the juvenile's arrest and detention. Except in certain circumstances, interviews should take place only in the presence of an 'appropriate adult'. This is usually the parent but may be another adult such as a social worker or youth worker if the young person is estranged from the parent(s).

The police may decide not to prosecute and instead may issue a caution. This can only be done where the crime is not a serious one, if the juvenile admits the offence and if he or she has been in relatively little trouble before. A caution is a severe reprimand by a senior police officer. It does not form part of the young person's criminal record although it may be brought up if there are court proceedings in the future (see Chapter 3.2 on criminal records).

The majority of cases are heard in the youth court which is part of the magistrates' court. Murder, manslaughter and other 'grave' offences (punishable with a maximum of fourteen years imprisonment if an adult) such as rape, arson, grievous bodily harm, robbery, aggravated burglary are heard by the Crown Court. Both courts are required to have regard to the welfare of the child but this is a weaker requirement than in the family proceedings.

The courts may impose a range of punishments such as a fine, an attendance centre order or a supervision order. Supervision orders may contain different conditions such as participation in certain activities (intermediate treatment), night restriction or a requirement that the young person lives in social services' accommodation for up to six months.

Young people cannot be sent to prison. However, fifteen- to twenty-one-year-olds can be sentenced to detention in a young offender institution. The length of detention is limited to a maximum of one year (youth court) or two years (Crown Court) for fifteen- to seventeen-year-olds but otherwise is the same length as an adult term of imprisonment. Ten- to fourteen-year-olds who have been convicted of murder or manslaughter are sentenced to detention at Her Majesty's pleasure which is indefinite detention in social services' secure accommodation and it is not subject to the usual provisions about parole available to adults. This provision has been successfully challenged in the European Court of Human Rights and new procedures are expected. Fourteen-year-olds can also be detained in secure accommodation if they have been found guilty of a grave offence. The Criminal Justice and Public Order Act 1994 introduced a new sentence for persistent young offenders. Twelve- to fourteen-year-olds may be sentenced to a secure training order (detention followed by a period of supervision for a maximum period of two years) where they have been convicted of an imprisonable offence and have been previously convicted of three or more imprisonable offences. Secure training centres are being purpose-built and pending completion those sentenced to a secure training order may be detained for not more than twenty-eight days in a place authorised by the Secretary of State.

STOP PRESS

At the time of writing the government was considering a radical review of the system of juvenile justice. It is likely that there will be detailed proposals announced during 1997 and a Bill to implement these proposals in 1998. It is unlikely that any changes will become law before 1999.

Child witnesses

A child of any age can give evidence as a witness in a criminal trial unless the court thinks that he or she is unable to understand what is involved. There are special rules about how young people can give evidence in relation to sexual or violent offences. The evidence of young people under the age of seventeen (in relation to sexual offences) or fourteen (in relation to violent offences) may be given before the trial by means of a video-recording. This evidence is transmitted by live television link at the trial so that the child does not have to appear in court. He or she may, however, have to attend court personally to answer questions put by the defendant or lawyer.

Family proceedings

Separation and divorce

The law tries to encourage parents to agree about their children's future when they separate or divorce by providing continuing parental responsibility to divorced parents and requiring the courts not to make court orders unless it is better to do so for the child. This approach has been bolstered by the introduction of mediation, a process designed to help parents reach agreement about their children. Mediation is provided by some courts and by voluntary organisations.

It is not necessary for either parent to attend court in divorce proceedings. The court merely looks at the written statement of arrangements for the children and grants the divorce unless it is concerned about the children's welfare. In these circumstances it will usually order a welfare report (see below).

New divorce law is due to be implemented in 1999. This states that couples have to wait twelve months before their divorce is granted during which time they must sort out all arrangements for their children. All couples will be required to attend a divorce information session before proceeding with their divorce and, where children are involved, they will be encouraged to consider the child's welfare and wishes and feelings and the impact on the child of divorce. Parents receiving legal aid will in most circumstances be required to attend mediation to sort things out.

Section 8 proceedings under the Children Act

Divorcing or unmarried parents may apply for a residence order, contact order, prohibited steps order or specific issues order (see above). Other people, such as relatives, can ask for the court's permission to do so and this is likely to be granted where the court considers that the application has a reasonable chance of success. Children and young people may also ask the court for permission to take a case to court but this will only be granted if the court thinks that he or she has sufficient understanding to make that application. The courts are wary of parental influence in such circumstances and seek to balance the rights of children against their welfare. Where children have been granted permission to bring a case, they are represented by their own lawyer.

In making its decision the court must put the child's welfare as its paramount consideration. This is assessed by reference to a welfare checklist of matters such as the child's physical, emotional and educational needs, the capacity of the parents (or anyone else) to care for the child and any harm he or she is suffering. It must also listen to and take into account the wishes and feelings of the child in light of his or her age and understanding. The court will usually be helped by a report prepared by a court official called a court welfare officer.

Care proceedings

Social services may apply to the court for a care order (an order for the removal of the child from home) where they consider that a child or young person is at risk. The court can only make a care order where it is satisfied that the child is suffering, or is at risk of suffering, significant harm as a result of the way the parents are caring for the child, or because the child is beyond parental control. Once these criteria have been established the court must place the child's welfare as its paramount consideration in light of the welfare checklist and must also take into account the child's wishes and feelings (see above). In particular, it must consider alternative orders such as supervision orders or residence orders to relatives or friends and whether or not it is better for the child to make no order at all. Where, for instance, there is evidence that the family is willing to cooperate with social services on a voluntary basis, there may be no need for an order. Before making a care order, the court must look at the arrangements for the child's contact with his or her parents and other significant others.

Children are parties to care proceedings and are represented by a solicitor and a guardian *ad litem*. A guardian is a social worker appointed by the court who is required to investigate the circumstances of the case and to make recommendations to the court about the child's best interests. Guardians work in partnership with the child's solicitor and frequently instruct experts such as psychiatrists or paediatricians to assist the court. Where a child of sufficient understanding disagrees with the guardian's recommendation, the solicitor must represent the child as if he or she were an adult.

Applications for supervision orders (see above) are made in the same way as for a care order and the comments made above apply to these proceedings. A supervision order means that the child will continue to live at home with the parents but with formal visits from social services. It lasts for a year but can be extended for up to three years. If the parents don't let social services see the child, the police can come to check his or her safety.

Adoption proceedings

An adoption order means that parental responsibility for the child is transferred from the birth parents to the adoptive parents and the child is regarded as having been part of the adoptive family since birth. A child can be adopted only with the consent of the birth parent(s) but this may be set aside in certain circumstances, most usually if the court is satisfied that the parents are withholding their consent unreasonably. The court is also required to put the child's welfare as its first consideration in deciding whether to make an adoption order.

Guardians *ad litem* are appointed in contested adoption proceedings to investigate and advise the court about whether adoption is in the best interests of the child. Unlike care proceedings, children are not usually represented in adoption proceedings but the court must take into account their wishes and feelings which are conveyed in the guardian's report.

Children usually have no direct contact with their birth family following adoption although it is generally considered to be good practice to provide some form of indirect contact by way of the provision of information about birth family members and/or the exchange of letters and cards. The courts have the power to make orders for contact but will not do so unless the adoptive parents are in agreement with this. At eighteen and over, young people can apply to the Registrar General for a copy of their original birth certificate and information about their birth family from the adoption agency that arranged the adoption. Adult adoptees and birth family members may also apply to the Registrar General for entry of their names on the Adoption Contact Register. Details of birth family members will be given to adoptees so that contact can be established if the adopted person wishes to pursue this.

Civil (non-criminal) cases

Where children are injured or where the authorities have failed to carry out their statutory duties, children can start their own legal proceedings. Proceedings must be brought through an adult called a 'next friend', usually the parent but may be another adult where there is a conflict of interest between the child and the parents. The next friend usually acts through a lawyer and is responsible for acting in the child's best interests. Subject to the reasonableness of the case, legal aid is available which is assessed on the means of the child and not of the next friend.

In certain limited circumstances, children may be sued and again they are represented through an adult called a guardian *ad litem*. The duties of a guardian in these circumstances are similar to those of a next friend and should not be confused with the role of the guardian *ad litem* in care proceedings.

STOP PRESS

The new government proposes to incorporate the European Convention on Human Rights into domestic law. The rights in the Convention are set out in Chapter 5. A Bill to incorporate the Convention is due to be published in the autumn of 1997 and this is likely to become an Act by July 1998 and to come into force not before January 1999. It is not clear at the time of writing exactly what effect this will have on our laws. It is likely that the Convention will be able to be used to challenge some of the existing procedures and judge-made law although whether the Convention will be given a higher status than statute is not so clear. Nevertheless the rights set out in this book may be enhanced by the Convention and in future the rights in the Convention will have to be considered much more seriously than they have been in the past.

12.8 Further information

Useful organisations

ChildLine Freepost 1111
London N1 0BR
Tel: freephone helpline 0800 1111

Children's Legal Centre
University of Essex
Wivenhoe Park
Colchester
Essex CO4 3SQ
Tel: 01206 873820 advice service Monday to Friday 2–5 p.m.

Children's Rights Office
235 Shaftesbury Avenue
London WC2H 8EL

Citizens' Advice Bureaux – consult your Yellow Pages telephone directories, or your local library to find your local office.

NSPCC Child Protection Line
67 Saffron Hill
London EC1N 8RS
Tel: freephone 0800 800500

Bibliography

At What Age Can I? Children's Legal Centre, 1996.
Children Law and Practice, Family Law, loose leaf encyclopedia.
The Law of Education, Butterworths, loose leaf encyclopedia.
Working with Young People, Children's Legal Centre, 1996.

13

The rights of workers

This chapter deals with:

- Unions.
- Contracts of employment.
- Workers' rights to privacy.
- Drug taking, drinking and workers' rights.
- Equal pay
- Maternity rights
- Health, safety, sickness and disability.
- Dismissal.
- Redundancy.
- Industrial action.
- Claims.
- Further information.

Central to any system of civil liberties is a recognition of the importance of workers' rights. In the UK, there was grudging acceptance of workers' rights in the form of the Trade Union Act 1871, which allowed trade unions to exist when hitherto they had been illegal. The expression of trade union rights in the form of calls for industrial action was made lawful by the Trade Disputes Act 1906. The foundation of modern workers' rights lies in those two statutes, now repealed, and it was not until the 1960s that attention was given to the rights of workers as individuals with the passing of legislation on minimum periods of notice and redundancy pay.

Since 1979 the government has passed a series of measures limiting the powers of trade unions and restricting the ambit of employment protection legislation. The new legislation was consolidated in the Trade Union and Labour Relations (Consolidation) Act 1992, to be followed by the Trade Union Reform and Employment Rights Act 1993 (TURER). This latter act introduced yet more stringent requirements as to union ballots, control over union finances, and maintenance of the check-off system whereby union contributions are collected by the employer. Employers were permitted to benefit employees who withdrew from union membership or negotiated terms and conditions. Members of the public could sue unions if adversely affected by unlawful industrial action. Rights were also enhanced as required by European Community Law in respect of maternity, victimisation in connection with health and safety, statutory statement of terms and conditions, transfer of undertakings and collective redundancies. The Employment Rights Act 1996 (ERA) consolidated employment protection rights while the Disability Act 1995, the enforcement provisions of which came into effect on 2 December 1996, introduced the right to make a claim to the industrial tribunal for discrimination on grounds of disability.

European Community law has had a noticeable impact in the fight for women to achieve equal pay for doing work which is the same as, or of equal value to, a man's, and in challenging other forms of discrimination on the grounds of sex. It is also the source of the protection of workers' rights on business transfers, collective redundancies, health and safety, and, as from 1996, working hours.

European Community law applies throughout the UK. Employment legislation applies in England, Wales and Scotland, and most of it applies (in the form of parallel Orders) in Northern Ireland. The Scottish and English laws of contract have different terminology but similar substance.

This chapter deals principally with the rights contained in the Acts, codes and cases arising since 1974. From the outset it is important to recall that the courts have been hostile to the concept and practice of workers' rights, particularly when these rights are advanced by way of industrial action by trade union members. Because union membership is the key to enforcing workers' rights at workplace level through collective bargaining and industrial action, union rights are dealt with first.

13.1 Unions

Why join?

Employment law has traditionally viewed workers' problems as definable in individual contracts of employment. In reality, your rights as an individual worker are largely determined by the negotiating position you have with your employer and individuals have little opportunity to influence the specific terms and conditions of employment, whereas collectively workers can and do. Furthermore, although just over one in three of the twenty-one million or so people in employment are members of trade unions, two-thirds have their terms and conditions affected by collective bargaining between their employer, or a group of employers, and trade unions.

Rights against employers

You are protected by TURER against refusal of employment, dismissal including selection for redundancy and victimisation short of dismissal on the grounds that you are or are not a trade union member. This includes seeking to become a member and taking part, at an appropriate time outside working hours but on your employer's premises, in the activities of the union. You are also protected if the grounds of your dismissal or victimisation are your trade union activities in the past, for example, when you were working for another employer, when the basis of the employer's action is fear that you will repeat those actions in your current employment.

The rights entitle you to recruit members, hand out literature, collect subscriptions and hold meetings during the times when you are not working. If management allows you to talk while you are at work, you are also allowed to talk about trade union membership and to encourage people to join.

Anything which prevents or deters you from being a member, or from taking part in the union's activities, or which penalises you for so doing, is unlawful. This includes the refusal to allow representation by a union official in accordance with agreed procedures. Generally any form of disadvantage is unlawful so long as the target of the management action is genuinely 'trade union activity'. That includes the presentation of, for example, a complaint or grievance relating to health and safety, and does not include simply the activities of a group of individuals who happen to be union members. The union content of the issue must be clear, and the management action must be taken against you as an individual and not as a form of retaliation against the union which may be seeking to organise. However, it is not unlawful for an employer who wants to change terms and conditions of employment, for example, by introducing personal contracts and when this is opposed by the trade union to give bigger pay increases to those employees who accept the change, even when the aim is to deter or penalise trade union membership.

You can make a claim to an industrial tribunal (see p. 347). Compensation is available for dismissal and victimisation of up to £45,100 with unlimited further compensation available if management refuses to comply in full with an order for reinstatement or re-engagement made by the tribunal.

The most important remedy for dismissal is an order for reinstatement. In order to make a claim, you should use the 'interim relief' procedure available while you are under notice or during the first seven days afterwards, which requires a certificate from a union official confirming that in their opinion you were dismissed because of your trade union activities and are likely to win a claim for unfair dismissal on those grounds. A very quick hearing will then be arranged by the tribunal which has power to order management to continue your contract until the full hearing of the case.

With the exception of the requirement of a union official's certificate, all of the above rights and procedures apply to someone who has been victimised or dismissed on the grounds that they refused to join or take part in the activities of a trade union.

Union recognition

Recognition means that management is prepared to negotiate with an independent trade union or unions over terms and conditions of employment. Negotiation is stronger than consultation, which is essentially a one-way process, and the mere right to represent individuals in, say, grievance or disciplinary hearings. Recognition has the advantage that the union has negotiated a procedure for the settlement of disputes and also some legal advantages flow from it. These are:

- The duty to deal with and give facilities to safety representatives appointed by the union under the Health and Safety at Work, etc. Act (see p. 339).
- Consultation on occupational pensions.
- Consultation on redundancies, on takeovers and mergers and the automatic transfer of collective agreements. Since amendments inserted in 1995 to comply with European Community law, there is an obligation on the employer to consult with appropriate representatives if no union is recognised.
- Disclosure of information, for instance, financial information, for the purposes of collective bargaining, with a legally enforceable right to obtain better terms and conditions if information is denied.
- Time off with pay for union representatives carrying out duties or training connected with collective bargaining, or without pay for union members attending internal union activities.

The right to time off can be enforced by a claim to a tribunal (see p. 347). It is available to shop stewards, staff representatives and other labour representatives. It enables them to prepare for negotiations, draw up plans, consult other members and officers, and negotiate. The amount of time off is that which is 'reasonable' for carrying out duties and training in connection with their industrial relations functions.

Quite separately, union members have the right to take time off for union activities, such as voting, attending union conferences and other matters of internal organisation. This right does not attract pay.

Union membership agreements, or closed shops, can be negotiated with management but since the Employment Acts 1988 and 1990, refusal of employment on the ground of unwillingness to join the union or victimisation on such grounds is unlawful.

All companies with 250 employees must include in their annual report a statement of the measures taken to provide information to, and to consult with, employees on matters of concern to them (Companies Act 1985).

Rights within the union

There is a right not to be unjustifiably excluded or expelled from a trade union. Exclusion or expulsion may be justified if you do not satisfy the union's rules, for example, by not being employed in a specified trade or profession, or it is due to your conduct other than having been a member of another trade union or a member of a political party. You can complain to a tribunal if your rights are infringed.

The relationship between you and your union is governed both by the union rule book and by statute. The rule book, together with custom and practice, sets up contractual rights entitling you to the benefits and the procedures contained in it. In addition, the rules of natural justice will generally apply to any disciplinary hearing within the union. These are the right to be given notice of the allegation made against you, the opportunity to state your case and to be heard by an impartial body within the union.

You have the right under the TURER not to have unjustifiable disciplinary action taken against you. You can complain to a tribunal which can set aside the decisions of the union and award compensation.

Discipline is unjustifiable if it is on the grounds of failing to participate in or support industrial action, even if a majority of the members involved voted in favour. Similarly, disciplinary action for refusing to break your contract of employment, or for following calls for action in breach of the union's rules, is unjustifiable. Disciplinary action means expulsion, fines, deprivation of benefits or any other detriment. You also have a right to terminate your union membership and not to have your union subscriptions deducted from your salary without your agreement, which must be obtained every three years. You may complain to an industrial tribunal if your employer makes an unauthorised deduction of subscriptions.

Political activities

A union may resolve to have a political fund and to require its members to pay contributions, part of which go into the fund. Activities of a party political nature must be paid for out of the political fund and not out of the general fund of the union. You have an absolute right to refuse to contribute to the political fund and must not be disadvantaged for so doing (Trade Union Act 1913). Ballots were held in all unions which had political funds, pursuant to the Trade Union Act 1984 (now the TURER), and all passed resolutions favouring the continuance of such funds. Such ballots must be conducted every ten years.

In Northern Ireland the system is reversed, in that all members are contracted out of the political fund and it requires a positive statement by an individual to join in the fund.

Election of officers

TURER provides that all officials (except certain senior officials nearing retirement) who have voting rights, or who attend and speak at the governing bodies of trade unions, must be elected by secret postal ballot every five years.

13.2 Contracts of employment

Not everyone who works has a contract of employment. Some are self-employed. Employment law generally protects only employees. In discrimination cases, people applying to become employees and people under a personal contract to do work are also covered. The distinction between employees and the self-employed is easier to see than to define. The label used is not decisive as to what the parties to the contract intended. All the relevant circumstances have to be examined to see if the person is in business on his or her own account. You may be employed even though you work through an employment agency.

Employed or self-employed?

You will generally be an employee, and not self-employed, if the economic reality of the relationship is that you are not in business on your own account, or in ordinary language, 'Are you your own boss?' You and your employer owe each other obligations which include, on your part, the requirement to obey instructions and to do the work yourself; and on your employer's part to provide work and to pay you for the work done. Since there are tax advantages to the worker and tax and other advantages to the employer in establishing self-employed status, these are superficial temptations. Self-employed workers are denied access to employment protection legislation and are unprotected by the employer's compulsory insurance against industrial injuries. Unless you genuinely want to go into business on your own account, taking the risks inherent in such a practice, you should resist offers to become self-employed. Remember that even if your employer calls you self-employed and you are self-employed for tax and national insurance purposes, you may be found to be an employee for the purposes of employment protection if you claim unfair dismissal or other statutory rights.

Certain categories of worker are given employment protection rights although strictly they are not employees. For example:

- Apprentices enter into fixed-term contracts which impose particular obligations upon the apprentice and the employer. There is a strict obligation to give and accept instruction in the trade and termination generally requires the apprentice's parents' consent.
- Civil servants work under terms of service with the Crown and do not have contracts of employment. This includes some National Health Service workers. Nevertheless, they have access to most of the employment legislation, and where they are excluded they have their own arrangements, for example, in relation to redundancy pay.
- People who hold office may or may not be employees, depending on the nature of the relationship with their 'employer'. Directors of companies, for example, may be office holders under company law and also be employees of their companies. Trade union officers hold office by virtue of their election in some cases, and are also employees of their union. Police officers hold office and are not employees.
- Homeworkers may or may not be employees, depending on the nature of the relationship and upon whether they are engaged in business on their own account, applying the 'economic reality' and 'mutual obligation' tests.
- Casual workers may be self-employed or employees only for the time when they are engaged, even though they continue to work day after day for the same employer and take on all the appearances of a regular employee. If you can establish that all your contracts as a casual worker are linked under an 'umbrella' contract, you will be able to take advantage of your rights.
- Trainees on government training schemes may or may not be employees, depending on the type of scheme and the arrangements for pay, but are covered by health and safety and discrimination legislation.

What's in a contract?

Every employee has a contract of employment which may or may not be in writing. For most people, this means a written statement of the main terms given to you shortly after you started work. Nevertheless, you are still an employee working under a contract of employment even if nothing is written down. The fact that you have agreed to work and your employer has agreed to pay you constitutes a contract of employment. True, if a dispute arises as to the rate of pay or entitlement to bonus, it will be more difficult for you to prove your version is correct, but that does not detract from the fact that you have contractual rights. A contract will generally consist of terms and conditions which may be identified in any of the following forms.

Written statement

Within two months of your starting work, your employer must provide you with a statement, in writing, of the particulars of your terms of employment (ERA) if you work eight hours or more per week. These must include:

- The name of your employer;
- The date your employment started and whether any previous employment is regarded as continuous with it;
- The rate of pay or the method of calculating it and how often it is paid;
- Hours of work;
- Entitlement to holidays, holiday pay, sick pay, and whether or not a pension scheme exists;
- The length of notice required to be given by each side;
- Job title;
- If your employment is not intended to be continuous the period for which it is expected to continue, if it is for a fixed term the date on which it is to end;
- Your place or places of work, whether you are required to work outside the UK;
- Whether any collective agreements directly affect your terms and conditions of work.

These particulars must be given in a single document unless they refer to another accessible document for particulars of incapacity, sick pay or pensions, or notice requirements. Any disciplinary rules which apply to you must be specified as well as the name of any person to whom you can apply if you have a grievance or are dissatisfied with any disciplinary action, and the procedure which you must follow. Details of disciplinary rules need only be given if your employer employs at least twenty people. Another accessible document such as a Company Handbook which contains this information may be referred to.

If you are not given a written statement you can make a claim to a tribunal and if successful you would get compensation (see p. 347).

The written statement provides strong evidence of what the agreed terms are, but does not in itself constitute the contract of employment. As the written statement is just your employer's account of what are the terms of your contract, you can challenge the terms in it if they are not those to which you agreed. Even if you have signed to acknowledge receipt of the statement, it is not itself a contract. It is best only to agree to sign that you have received the document and not that you accept its contents being true so that if you later want to challenge any of the contents you are free to do so. You must be notified of any changes to your terms and conditions not later than one month from such changes taking effect. Again you may be referred to an accessible document which contains the information as to such changes. Only changes which you or your union on your behalf have agreed to are binding upon you. If your employer unilaterally attempts to impose a change upon you, you are entitled to record that you do not agree to the change and hold your employer to the original agreement. Your employer may counterattack by dismissing you and offering you a new contract with the new terms. If you claim unfair dismissal, the industrial tribunal would have to decide whether the employer had good business reasons for the changes and whether in all the circumstances the dismissal was fair.

Collective agreements

Frequently many of these terms and conditions will be determined by agreements negotiated by trade unions on your behalf. The fruits of the negotiations between unions and employers are usually incorporated into your contract of employment, since either your written statement or the custom and practice at your workplace will generally say so. Collective agreements generally set terms and conditions such as wages, hours, holidays and sick pay and will also provide the machinery for the resolution of disputes, discipline and grievances.

Itemised pay statement

Every time you are paid you are entitled (ERA) to a written statement setting out the gross pay, any variable or fixed deductions, net pay and, if not all the pay is paid in the same way, the method of payment for each part, for example, where a bonus is paid less frequently than basic pay. If you have fixed deductions for each pay period, it is sufficient for management to give you a statement in advance of what the fixed deductions are, and they must reissue it at least annually. If you are not given an itemised pay slip then you can make a claim to a tribunal (see p. 347).

Works rules

Management may publish on notice boards or in employee handbooks a set of works rules. These do not necessarily form part of your contract, so that if you break any of them you may not automatically be breaking your contract of employment. At most, they are management's instructions about how the job is to be done and are not to be treated as rules cast in stone – they can be challenged if you make a claim to a tribunal arising out of, for example, your dismissal for breaking one.

Wages council orders and Agricultural Wages Boards

In 1909, protection was given to workers in industries where there is low trade union organisation and where workers are notoriously prone to exploitation. The Wages Act 1986 cut down the rights of workers engaged in a range of industries including catering, garment manufacture and retailing. On 30 August 1993, all wages councils were abolished.

The Agricultural Wages Board remains in place and sets minimum rates and rest days for agricultural workers. If agricultural workers are not paid the minimum rate wages, inspectors employed by the Department of Employment can prosecute the employer. A court can order the employer to pay a fine and to make payments of arrears of wages or repayment of deductions unlawfully made (for example, for accommodation). In addition, proceedings can be brought either by you or the wages inspector in the county courts.

Breach of contract

Since it takes two to make a contract, changes to it must be agreed by both. Otherwise there is a breach of contract which, if it is sufficiently serious, entitles you to say the contract is at an end and to walk out. Alternatively, as explained above, you can refuse to accept that the serious action or omission by your employers has brought the contract to an end and you can continue to work, while reserving your rights to make a claim in the courts for breach of contract. A breach occurs when either party fails to carry out the agreed terms, or terms which have been implied by the courts or by custom and practice, or when you are dismissed with no or insufficient notice, unless you have committed 'gross misconduct' (see p. 342). A sufficiently serious breach of contract will also entitle you to bring a claim of unfair dismissal (see p. 342).

Contractual obligations

This section contains the main contractual obligations between you and your employer.

Payment of wages

The method and frequency of wages or salary are as set out in your written statement. If deductions are made unlawfully from your pay you can make a claim to a tribunal (ERA) (see p. 347). Deductions are lawful only if you have given your consent in writing or if this is provided for in your contract. However, there are exceptions allowing management to make deductions in respect of: overpayment of wages and expenses; payments by law to public authorities; payments to third parties, for example to trade unions, or deductions following a strike or other industrial action. The law as to unlawful deductions applies not just to employees but to all workers provided they have undertaken to do the work personally.

Hours of work

Hours of work are determined by agreement either with you or with trade unions. There have been no restrictions on the maximum or minimum number of hours to be worked by men or women, or the times of the day and days of the week when work may take place. The European Communities Working Time Directive which came into force on 23 November 1996 provides for:

* a maximum working week of forty-eight hours a week measured over a four-month reference period, (or six or twelve months by agreement with the unions);
* a minimum of three weeks' annual leave, (four from 1999);
* stipulated rest periods;
* a maximum average of eight hours' work in any twenty-four hour period for night workers and free health assessments.

There are, however, numerous exemptions to the new regulations, both for certain industries and for certain types of workers. There are some restrictions on the hours of young people below the age of eighteen. Until 1995, you had to have worked for at least sixteen hours a week, or alternatively for eight hours a week for more than five years to be entitled to most employment protection rights. These rules have now been abolished so the numbers of hours you work is no longer relevant to your employment rights. There is no statutory obligation to offer holidays, or to pay for them, or even to offer or pay for bank holidays.

Obligation to provide work

As long as management pay you they have no obligation to provide work. The right to work may be enforced only by:

*   Employees who are offered the opportunity to earn commission or a bonus (and therefore cannot achieve this if they are denied the right).
*   Artists, actors, singers and performers whose careers are advanced by exposure.
*   Highly skilled craft workers who need to keep their hand in.

Claims for lost belongings

Although management is under an obligation to provide adequate storage accommodation for your clothing if you work in a factory, they are not generally liable to recompense you for losses unless they are aware of a history of thefts and have done nothing, or they know you are required to bring tools or clothing to work in order to carry out your job. In that case, it is more likely that you can claim.

Right to search

There is no right to search you, for example, on leaving the work premises, unless you have agreed this in your contract or accepted it by long-standing custom and practice. Security officers have no general powers to search or detain you.

Injuries at work

If you are injured at work you can claim compensation on the basis that your employer has not provided a safe system of work.

Suspensions and layoffs

Management have no right to impose a suspension or lay-off without pay and without your agreement. Suspension with pay pending the investigation of an allegation of misconduct against you is often provided for in agreements, but unilateral suspension without pay for economic or disciplinary reasons is unlawful. If you are dismissed because management's needs for your work have diminished, you can claim redundancy pay (see p. 344) if you are suspended or reduced to less than half-pay for more than four weeks. If there is no work at all, you can also claim a guarantee payment of £14.50 per day (1996) for up to five days a quarter (ERA).

Personal data

You are entitled to see personal data held by your employer on computer or in a form other than manual records (Data Protection Act 1984). If the data is inaccurate, you can apply to a County Court or the High Court for its rectification or removal, and you can claim damages for loss you have suffered and for distress caused to you. Your employer must comply with a request for the data within forty days (see also p. 112).

Duties of fidelity and confidentiality
You owe a duty of fidelity to your employer while you work and some aspects of that survive your leaving. While you are employed, you must not disclose confidential information, but you can use information which you remember (you must not remove and use your ex-employer's documents after you leave) unless there are clear written restrictions in your contract – known as restrictive covenants – forbidding this. Then, such restrictions will be upheld provided they do not stop you earning a living and they are reasonable for the protection of your ex-employer's interests. A covenant is unreasonable if it restricts you for too long or to too narrow a geographical area, or if it excludes you from your main types of work. Information relating to your employer's specific trade secrets must be kept confidential even after you leave.

While employed, you must work only for the one employer during your working hours, but in the absence of some implied restriction on your working for others, you can work in your own time as you wish. Any money you make arising out of your employment belongs to your employer and you must account for it. If you produce written material for publication, your employer has the copyright over it. If you make inventions or create patents, management gets the benefit provided your normal duties include the likelihood of your making inventions. If you invent something of outstanding benefit to management, you can claim a fair share of the profits (Patents Act 1977).

Duty to obey instructions
You are under a duty to obey instructions, provided these are lawful, reasonable and within the scope of the contract you have agreed. Other instructions will constitute breaches of the contract, for example, if you are instructed to do something which is against the criminal law, or which is unsafe, unreasonable or outside the scope of the duties you have agreed to perform. If your contract is in any way illegal (for example, because of your intention to avoid tax by being paid cash in hand), you can claim no rights under it or benefit from the employment legislation except in respect of sex and race discrimination.

Previous convictions
You are under no obligation to disclose previous convictions, unless you are applying for a job in certain professions or occupations where

disclosure is obligatory. You are entitled to answer 'no' to questions aimed at probing convictions which have become 'spent' after periods of time, for example, five years for a fine (Rehabilitation of Offenders Act 1974, see Chapter 3, 'The right of privacy'). Answering negatively is neither a lie nor grounds for dismissal.

For information on discrimination at work see Chapter 9, 'The right not to be discriminated against'.

References
On leaving, management is not obliged to give you a reference. However, if your employer provides a reference there is a duty to take reasonable care to see that any reference is fair and accurate. There is an implied term in a contract of employment requiring the exercise of due care and skill in the preparation of a reference. If, as a result of a bad reference which is the result of a failure to take care, the employee suffers loss, for example a job, then he or she may claim damages in the county court. Legal aid is available.

Time off
You have a right to time off without pay to be a member of a local council, health authority, school or college governing body, water authority, police authority, board of prison visitors or magistrates' bench, or for jury service. If this right is denied you can claim to a tribunal (see p. 347)(ERA). The amount of time off is that which is 'reasonable' taking into account the effect of your absence on your employer's business.

Whistleblowers
Workers who bring attention publicly to unsafe or unsound industrial or working practices may well find themselves in danger of victimisation by their employers. There are very few specific provisions in the law aimed at protecting such workers and their freedom of speech. A worker can rely on the unfair dismissal legislation, although it may often be possible for an employer to show that as a result of the whistleblowing activities there has been misconduct. The claim by the employer will be that the worker has broken the obligation to be faithful to his employer (a duty that has been much developed by the courts in recent years). It is often the case, however, that employers alive to the political embarrassment of declaring that the whistleblowing activity was the real reason for the dismissal will be caught out by presenting a patently sham reason for their action. The worker may be able to show, for instance, that there has been no real damage to the employer or that the employer had not warned the worker it would lead to dismissal.

In addition, an employer may sue workers who have disclosed confidential information. In no circumstances can a worker reveal the trade secrets of the employer (which are widely defined sometimes to include simple processes). Ex-employees may also be prevented by their contract of employment from revealing other information confidential to the employer – to stick, the clause must not prevent the worker from being able to work in the future and the information must be defined. Injunctions may be obtained where such contracts are broken leading to lengthy 'gagging' of ex-employees in some cases.

Whistleblowing cases have often concerned Health Service employees, for example, Graham Pink and Wendy Savage. As cuts are made in funding and conditions in hospitals deteriorate, there is more and more pressure on those inside the system to prevent them from speaking out. Indeed, guidance notes for staff on relations with the media have been published by the NHS which stress patient confidentiality and internal grievance procedures. A further problem in this area is the tension between often highly restrictive contractual clauses against speaking out and the rules of professional conduct which allow and indeed require nurses to act whenever they see falling standards of care. Where professional codes are incorporated into the contract of employment, it is arguable that the final decision remains with the worker according to his or her professional rules. Professional codes often require individual responsibility for decisions which can remove much managerial prerogative in the assessment of whether the 'whistleblowing' is in breach of contract.

There is a right not to be unfairly dismissed or victimised if a worker (who is a health and safety representative) takes action when he or she believes workers to be in serious and imminent danger (ERA). Whether this extends to whistleblowing activities has yet to be tested – the wording is clearly open to restrictive interpretation by the courts. At the time of writing there were proposals to give statutory rights to whistleblowers. Any changes would be unlikely to take effect before 1999.

13.3 Workers' rights to privacy

Whilst at present there is no general law on privacy in this country, there is recourse to the European Convention on Human Rights. Article 8 provides that everybody has the right to respect of his/her private life, and correspondence (except where restrictions are necessary, for example in the interests of public safety or for the prevention of crime and/or disorder). This right is important in the employment context.

There is an implied term in the contract of employment that employers will not without reasonable and proper cause conduct themselves in a manner calculated or likely to destroy, or seriously damage, the relationship of confidence and trust between themselves and their employees. If an employer opens your personal mail or tapes your telephone calls, their conduct may be interpreted as breaching this term, entitling you to resign and claim unfair constructive dismissal (see p. 342). Furthermore, it is an offence under the Interception of Communications Act 1985 to 'intercept' communications by post or by a telecommunications system in the UK. Lawful interception of communications requires a warrant, which will be granted only in certain circumstances, including the detection or prevention of serious crime, and in the interests of national security (see Chapter 3, 'The right of privacy'). If you suspect that your employer is intercepting your mail or telephone calls, etc., then you may complain to the Interception of Communications Tribunal who will investigate your complaint. The Act does not cover eavesdropping on an employer's own telephone system. The European Court of Human Rights recently decided that it is a violation of article 8 of the Convention for an employer to do so without a warrant. The Court decided that the police surveillance of Alison Halford's telephone calls while she was an employee is a breach of Article 8. The government will now need to change the law to regulate such surveillance. It is hoped that new legislation will protect the privacy of employees not just when making personal calls but in other situations when there is a reasonable expectation of privacy. Any legislation is unlikely to take effect until 1999.

A large number of employers now employ video surveillance on their premises, and require workers to wear name badges, particularly in the retail and banking industries. The former may be related to reasons of security and would, in most cases, be viewed by a tribunal as reasonable in the circumstances. Excessive surveillance, for example, in changing rooms, may be viewed as unreasonable. The wearing of name badges has become to be perceived as a useful tool in customer relations, and, again, will usually be justified on these grounds, as well as security.

Some employers have introduced alcohol and drug screening of workers, but as a matter of law an employer is unable to do so without your consent. The same requirement applies to searches for drugs and alcohol. If such searches are to be contracted out to a third party such as a security firm, then this should be the subject of a specific provision within the contract of employment.

If you refuse to consent to a search, whether or not there is a specific provision within the employment contract, it would be an assault to proceed with the search, and you may be entitled to resign in protest, claiming constructive dismissal. For this reason, your contract of employment may provide that refusal to cooperate with a search is a disciplinary offence.

13.4 Drug taking, drinking and workers' rights

Drug addiction, like alcoholism, should be treated like an illness. The Advisory Conciliation and Arbitration Service (ACAS) in its advice booklet 'Discipline at Work' urges employers to have a policy covering both problems. However, employers usually treat drug taking as misconduct. Reasons given are that drug taking, unlike alcohol, can be a criminal offence and employers themselves can commit an offence under the Misuse of Drugs Act 1971 if they know that illegal drugs are being used or distributed on their premises. Tribunals usually find that dismissal is a reasonable response to drug taking or being under the influence of drink or drugs at work. Factors that a tribunal are likely to take into account include: whether the conduct was on or off duty; safety at work; contact with children or young people; the effect on the employer's reputation and business, and the illegality of the employee's actions. So off-duty conduct will not usually merit dismissal in itself, though it may if it affects the employee's ability to do the job or the employer's reputation. Even if the employee has been convicted of a drug offence, the employer must conduct a proper investigation before dismissing, otherwise it will be unfair as there may be mitigating circumstances. In one case, for instance, the employee did not smoke the cannabis found in his garden.

Personal problems causing temporary drug taking or drinking have sometimes been seen as a factor that employers should take into account and restrict themselves to a warning rather than dismissal. Tribunals often accept that an employer is entitled to assume that there is a safety risk in drug taking or drinking without there being any evidence. So a worker up on disciplinary charges connected with drugs or alcohol would do well to provide evidence that there was no safety risk.

The Transport and Works Act 1992 has introduced new measures which include a new criminal offence relating to people controlling vehicles (trains, trams, etc.) whilst being unfit through drink or drugs.

13.5 Equal pay

You are guaranteed equal pay if you are doing work which is the same as, or broadly similar to, that of a man in the same employment as you or employed in the same service, or if you are covered by a job evaluation scheme which gives you similar scores to a man doing different work, or if you are doing work which you consider to be of equal value to a man's. Pay is widely defined and includes all aspects of remuneration including pension contributions. In addition, Article 119 of the Treaty of Rome enables you to claim in an industrial tribunal for discrimination in pay matters which is overt and direct even if you cannot point to a male worker. For example, entitlement to redundancy payment or pension benefit which differs between men and women is unlawful even though there may be no man with whom you can compare yourself. The Equal Pay Act excludes claims for pensions and retirement benefits, but you are still entitled to claim under it as a result of the rulings of the European Court on the effect of Article 119 which where necessary replaces UK law.

In a job evaluation scheme, if your job scores less than that of the man under you, you will have to prove that the scheme discriminates by, for example, giving undue weight to characteristics and abilities commonly possessed by men, or undervalues those of women. You can also compare yourself with a man who is doing work which is of 'equal value' to yours whether or not his job has been evaluated under a job evaluation scheme. You make your claim to a tribunal (see p. 347) which will decide whether to refer your claim for analysis to an independent expert appointed under the Equal Pay Act or decide the issue themselves. Unless your employer can convince the tribunal that there are no 'reasonable' grounds for making the comparison, or that the difference in pay is due to some non-sex-based reason referred to as 'a material factor', your claim is then assessed. If an expert is appointed to carry out the assessment, the tribunal may accept or reject the expert's report.

As explained above, management may defend the inequality in a claim under any part of the Equal Pay Act by saying that the difference is genuinely due not to sex but to a 'material factor'. If women generally are paid less than men for work of equal value, the material factor has to be objectively justified by the employer. The measures chosen by the employer must correspond to a real need on the part of the employer and be appropriate to achieving the objects pursued and be necessary to that end. Reasons for the inequality of pay put forward as material factors may include additional responsibility, the pressure of market forces, seniority.

If you win, the tribunal can award arrears of pay for up to two years prior to the making of the claim and can change the terms of your contract to give you equality. In 1996 the European Court was being asked to rule as to whether the two-year limit on compensation was in breach of Article 119 as it prevented women being fully compensated.

13.6 Maternity rights

A pregnant worker who has two years' service with the same employer has four rights: to be paid time off for antenatal leave, to maternity leave, to statutory maternity pay and not to be dismissed on account of her pregnancy (ERA). As a result of the Pregnancy Directive, since 1995 all workers irrespective of service are protected from dismissal related to pregnancy or maternity and entitled to fourteen weeks' leave. An employee with at least two years' service with her employer has a right to return from maternity leave up to twenty-nine weeks from the week in which the baby is born. If your employer suspends you from your work during your pregnancy on health and safety grounds you must be paid. If your employer infringes these rights you can claim unfair dismissal in an industrial tribunal, (see p. 342).

In order to be entitled to maternity leave, you must notify management in writing at least twenty-one days before the start of your leave of your pregnancy, the expected week of childbirth and when you intend to go on maternity leave. If you have the right to return after the twenty-nine weeks referred to above, at the same time you should confirm that you intend to return. In these circumstances:

* You can also be asked in writing after your confinement to confirm your intention to return;
* You must give twenty-one days' written notice of the date on which you intend to return;
* Your employer can seek medical confirmation;
* You yourself can postpone the date of return by up to four weeks on medical grounds.

You may be entitled by your contract or collective agreement to be paid while you are on leave, and to be paid above the minimum statutory maternity pay (SMP) levels. You can take advantage of whichever is better. SMP is available if you have been employed for twenty-six weeks including the fifteenth week before the expected week of confinement, and you have average weekly earnings above the lower earnings limit for the purposes of social security contributions (£61 in 1996) (Social Security Contributions and Benefits Act 1993). You need not be working at the fifteenth week, providing your contract continues into it (for example, you could take some holiday entitlement). SMP is available from the eleventh week before confinement and lasts for eighteen weeks.

You do not get SMP if your pay is below the lower earnings level (£61 in 1996). You are entitled to SMP at 90 per cent of your average earnings for the first six weeks of absence provided you have been employed for two years at sixteen hours per week (or for five years at eight hours per week) by the fifteenth week before confinement. You then receive twelve weeks' pay at the lower rate (£54.55 in 1996).

No dismissal

It is automatically unfair to dismiss you for a pregnancy-related reason or to fail to offer you a suitable available vacancy. If a redundancy has occurred during your maternity leave and it is not reasonably practicable to give you your old job back, you must be offered suitable alternative employment on no less favourable terms.

13.7 Health, safety, sickness and disability

Health and Safety at Work Act 1974

This Act imposes duties on all employers to ensure so far as is reasonably practicable the health, safety and welfare of their employees. This means providing safe plant and systems of work, and making arrangements for the safe handling, storage and transport of all articles used at work. Information, instruction, training and supervision should be provided so as to ensure employees' health and safety.

If management break these obligations, the Health and Safety Executive inspectors can issue prohibition or improvement notices requiring the work to be stopped or the machinery to be improved and they also have power to prosecute.

If your trade union is recognised for collective bargaining (see p. 321), you have the right to appoint union safety representatives who are given rights under the Act to time off with pay and to carry out inspection of the workplace and of relevant documents. Employers must consult safety representatives on health and safety arrangements. Claims for time off can be made to a tribunal or complaints about safety can be made to the Health and Safety Executive.

Regulations and a Code of Practice set out employers' obligations to provide first-aid facilities, including first-aid boxes and trained first-aiders, the number depending on the nature of the risk and the number of employees. In hazardous workplaces, there should be one qualified first-aider where more than fifty persons are employed and two where more than 150 are employed.

Accidents and industrial diseases causing the loss of more than three days' working time must be notified to the Health and Safety Executive.

The Fire Precautions Act 1971 requires a fire authority to give a certificate to the occupiers of any workplace other than low-risk premises where an exemption has been granted or when there are fewer than twenty employees. This imposes duties on employers to ensure that fire precautions and means of escape are provided and maintained.

Employers must keep workplaces clean, at a reasonable temperature (a minimum of 16°C or 13°C when the work requires severe physical effort), free from humidity, well ventilated, well lit, well provided with toilets and clean floors. Dangerous machinery must be guarded or, when this is not practicable, other suitable steps taken. Cranes must be kept in good mechanical order and be regularly inspected. If you are working on processes involving danger to your eyes, you must be provided with and wear eye protection. Adequate drinking water and washing facilities must be provided. The atmosphere must be kept free of harmful dust and fumes.

Some of these obligations apply in all circumstances – they are 'absolute' duties and any breach of them will be a breach of the law. On the other hand, some depend on what is practicable, in which case a lesser standard will suffice. Many of these obligations arise from regulations implementing European Community directives which came into force on 1 January 1993. They replace many of the previous Factories Act 1961 provisions.

Mines and quarries
Extensive protection is given to workers in these industries. Inspectors may be appointed by a union under the Mines and Quarries Act 1954; they are given specific powers and duties to enforce the legislation.

Construction sites
These must be kept safe, excavations and demolitions must be fenced or secured and machinery must also be fenced.

Agriculture
Agriculture, forestry and nurseries are covered by the Agriculture Act (Safety, Health and Welfare Provisions) 1956 and regulations made under it.

Other industries
Specific regulations cover, for example, working with asbestos, wood, civil engineering, lead, nuclear radiation and in foundries.

Sanctions
For breach of any of the above, the Health and Safety Executive may bring proceedings in the criminal courts and may issue prohibition and improvement notices.

Compensation

In addition to possible prosecution, many breaches of the above laws give rise to claims by injured workers for breach of statutory duty or negligence. Every employer is under an obligation to provide:

- A safe system of work.
- Competent staff, i.e. if another worker is careless you can sue the employer for failing to supervise him or her.
- A safe place of work.
- Safe and adequate plant, machinery and materials, and adequate supervision.

A civil claim is made in either the County Court or the High Court depending on the seriousness of the injury or the disease you have contracted. Legal aid is available. You must claim within three years of the injury or disease, although you can sometimes claim later if you did not know that you were suffering from an injury or disease which is attributable to your employer's negligence. If successful, you will be awarded damages to compensate you for your injury and for financial losses such as loss of wages and expenses.

Sick pay

Many contracts and collective agreements contain arrangements for payment during times of sickness. If these are better than the minimum statutory sick pay (SSP) you are entitled to them by your contract. If you have made sufficient social security contributions, you will be entitled to SSP, payable by your employer. Provided you earn more than the lower earnings' level, (£61 in 1996) you qualify for SSP for the first twenty-eight weeks of absence, excluding the first three days. You get SSP at one flat rate which was £54.55 in 1996. You are entitled to no more than twenty-eight weeks' SSP in any three-year period.

13.8 Dismissal

The termination of a contract of employment by the unilateral act of your employer is a dismissal. It can take many practical forms. You may be dismissed with or without or with less than your contractual notice. You may be made redundant or offered early retirement. You may resign in protest at your employer's words or behaviour – this is called constructive dismissal if your employer's action is serious enough. You may be given an ultimatum in which you can either resign or be dismissed. You may be the victim of a process of 'squeezing out' over a period of time. If you are on a fixed-term contract, management may refuse to renew it on its expiry. Or they may refuse to take you back after a strike, or to re-engage you after your dismissal during a strike. Or they may refuse to offer you a job after you have been on maternity leave.

In reality, there are only two kinds of dismissal in law upon which you can take action. You can either claim wrongful dismissal, which is when you are given less than your contractual period of notice or denied access to agreed procedures prior to dismissal (that is all it means); or you may claim unfair dismissal because the reason given by your employer, or found by a tribunal on your claim, is insufficient, and management acted unreasonably in dismissing you for that reason in all the circumstances (ERA).

Notice

You are entitled to periods of notice depending on your length of service and the written statement (see p. 327) must include a note of your contractual entitlement. After one month's service you are entitled to one week's notice and thereafter at the rate of one week for each year of service, up to a maximum of twelve weeks. Of course, your contract may provide for longer periods than this, but if nothing is said, you are entitled to a 'reasonable' amount of notice which may exceed the statutory minimum.

If you do not get your contractual or statutory notice, you can claim in the industrial tribunal or sue for breach of contract in the County Court. If you have been denied access to a contractual procedure for challenging dismissal, your notice period is extended by the notional period during which you would have pursued your rights internally.

You lose your right to notice if you are dismissed for gross misconduct, a term not defined in any statute but taken to mean conduct by you which shows that you no longer intend to be bound by the contract and which, if proved, deprives you of your rights.

Reasons for dismissal

Provided you have been employed for two years at the date of dismissal, you are entitled to particulars, in writing, of the reasons for your dismissal. Following a written request, management must provide them within fourteen days. If this is not forthcoming, you can make a claim to a tribunal (see p. 347) which has the power to declare the reason for dismissal and to award two weeks' pay. If you are claiming unfair dismissal, you should seek written particulars in any event and add this to your claim if management does not comply.

Unfair dismissal

In order to claim unfair dismissal, you must have been continuously employed for at least two years unless you are claiming on the basis of race, sex, trade union discrimination, or dismissal related to pregnancy. You can claim at any stage up to the age of sixty-five, unless there is a lower normal retirement age at your workplace.

If you bring a claim to a tribunal (see p. 347), management must show what the reason was for your dismissal. Some dismissals are automatically unfair, for example, a dismissal for a pregnancy-related reason, or because the employee was an employee representative, or the reason for the dismissal was because the employee had made a complaint against the employer that his or her statutory rights had been infringed (ERA). If the dismissal does not fall into one of these categories, the reason for the dismissal must fit into one of the following categories: conduct, capacity, redundancy, a legal restriction (for example, not having proper working papers), or some 'other substantial reason' which could justify the dismissal. Few employers have difficulty putting forward a reason, so the main dispute focuses on the reasonableness of the employer in deciding to dismiss for that reason. Since the circumstances in which dismissal arises are numerous and varied, there is not space here to deal with this complex area of the law. Clear rules have emerged for dealing with sickness, reorgan-isations, criminal acts committed within the employment context, poor performance and refusal to obey instructions. Nevertheless, each case is to be treated on its own merits and tribunals on the same facts could reach quite different conclusions.

Remedies for unfair dismissal
If you win your case, the tribunal must first consider whether you wish to be reinstated and, if so, must decide whether it is just and equitable to order that. If not, compensation should be awarded to take account of the losses you have suffered up to the date of the hearing and the amount of time you are likely to be unemployed, or if you have a job, to compensate you for any loss in pay in the new job. If you have claimed unemployment benefit, the amount of benefit you have received is deducted from the award of compensation. In addition, you should also get a payment equivalent to a redundancy payment (see below) which is called a basic award.

After dismissal, you must take steps to try and find alternative work and if you do not, your compensation may be reduced by a percentage. Also, it may be reduced and the tribunal may refuse to order reinstatement if you have contributed to your dismissal by your own actions.

In 1994–95, only 39 per cent of applicants who reached a tribunal hearing succeeded. The median award of compensation was £3,289. Reinstatement was awarded in 1.6 per cent of successful cases.

Breach of procedure

The existence of a disciplinary procedure in your contract of employment or collective agreement is important for both unfair and wrongful dismissal. If you are denied your rights, you may claim an injunction in the High Court to prevent management acting upon your dismissal or taking other disciplinary action until the procedure has been exhausted. This means you are to be treated as still employed, although perhaps not being required to work, until the full trial of your case for wrongful dismissal. You can get legal aid for this. Also, in unfair dismissal proceedings, a failure to go through either the agreed procedure or to adopt the rules of natural justice (giving notice of an allegation, an opportunity for you to say what you think, and an open-minded management) may result in the dismissal being unfair. In other words, a potentially fair dismissal can be made unfair if proper and reasonable procedures are not followed.

13.9 Redundancy

Redundancy occurs when management's requirements for work of the particular kind you are employed to do have ceased or diminished, either temporarily or permanently. If you are dismissed for this reason, or put on short-term working (receiving less than half pay) or are laid off for four weeks or more, you can claim a redundancy payment (ERA).

The payment is based on your age, length of continuous service and weekly pay. You are entitled to one and a half weeks' pay for each year of continuous employment when you are aged between forty-one and sixty-three inclusive, one week's pay between the ages of twenty-one and forty inclusive, and half a week's pay for each other year.

Weekly pay does not include all your earnings and so, for example, voluntary overtime is excluded but regular commission and bonuses are included. The maximum weekly pay allowable for redundancy purposes is £210 as of 1996.

You lose your right to a redundancy payment if you turn down an offer made by your employer to re-engage you on a new contract if the offer is of suitable alternative employment – the kind of work which would be regarded as suitable for you – and you have unreasonably refused to take it. The unreasonableness is judged by what your own circumstances are.

Before you are made redundant, you have a right to claim a reasonable amount of time off with pay in order to look for work or to retrain. And, if you accept an offer of new employment with the same employer or one of its associates, you have the right to a four-week trial period during which time you can quit the job and be regarded as redundant. In other words, you do not prejudice your rights by taking the job for a trial period.

As with unfair dismissal, you need two years' continuous employment to qualify for these redundancy terms. Your entitlement to redundancy pay is reduced if you have reached the age of sixty-four.

If management dispute that there is a redundancy situation, for example, by claiming that there has simply been a reorganisation of the business without any lessening of the requirements for employees, or if you dispute the amount of money paid to you, you can make a claim to a tribunal (see p. 347), though you will lose your right to redundancy pay in the circumstances described above. If your employer has gone bust, you can make a claim for redundancy pay and other outstanding debts including notice and holiday pay to be made by the Secretary of State for Employment (ERA and Insolvency Act 1986).

Consultation

If an employer is proposing to make at least twenty employees redundant within a period of ninety days or less there is an obligation to consult employee representatives about a proposal to make any dismissal (TURER). There is a minimum consultation period: thirty days if twenty or more employees are to be dismissed, ninety days for a hundred or more. Employee representatives are either trade union representatives or representatives elected by the employees. The employer may choose which if there is a choice. If the union or any employee representative claims that there has been no or inadequate consultation, it can make a claim to a tribunal which can then make a 'protective award' of compensation in favour of the employees who have been dismissed without the necessary consultation having taken place.

Takeovers, mergers and transfers

If the business in which you work is transferred as a going concern to another employer, the Transfer of Undertakings Regulations 1981 protect your terms and conditions with the new employer. Recognition of your union and all your contractual terms go over to the new employer. If you are dismissed as a result of the transfer, you can claim unfair dismissal which will be automatically unfair unless management proves that the dismissal was on account of an organisational or technical reason associated with the transfer.

Payment

The total amount of any redundancy payment is to be paid by your employer, without reimbursement from the state. You are entitled to a written statement of the calculation.

13.10 Industrial action

There is no right to strike in the UK. What is regarded as a fundamental or constitutional right in other countries becomes an immunity from some forms of civil action in the courts in the UK. Persuading people not to work and to break their contracts has always been unlawful in common law. If it is done in contemplation or furtherance of a trade dispute, as narrowly defined by the Trade Union and Labour Relations Act 1974, and if a ballot in favour of the action has been held, union leaders are 'immune' from normal civil liability.

Restrictions on the freedom to strike are placed on police and prison officers, apprentices (who must make up the time) and merchant seafarers; limited action by postal workers is also restricted by law.

A trade dispute is a dispute between workers and their own employer about terms, conditions, suspension, duties, engagement of workers, allocation of work, discipline, union membership, negotiating procedures and union facilities. In the course of such a dispute you can persuade people not to work. But if you do it on behalf of the union because you are a lay or full-time officer, or if the union adopts your actions, the union must conduct a ballot, and such calls for action will only be lawful if taken within four weeks of the result of a successful ballot. The ballot must ask all those likely to be asked to breach their contracts whether they are in favour.

It does not matter what form the industrial action takes – it can be a strike, work to rule, ban on overtime (whether it is voluntary or compulsory), withdrawal of cooperation, boycotts – they are all forms of industrial action and involve breaches of contract. As such, all those engaged in action are liable to their employers for breach of contract. In practice, employers do not sue their workers for the losses suffered by them as a result of each worker's breach of contract. What is more likely is an action against the union. Unions can be sued in their own name for damages if industrial action is taken which is unlawful. Much 'secondary action', that is, action taken against an employer who is not a party to the main trade dispute, is unlawful. If the union has organised this, an injunction can be granted to prevent it, and claims for damages of up to £250,000, depending on the size of the union, can be awarded.

It is equally likely that employers may dismiss all of those engaged in industrial action. If all of you who take industrial action at the same workplace are dismissed and none is re-engaged within three months, none of you has any claim. After the three-month period, selective re-engagement is permissible. This means that you are always at risk whatever form of action you take. You have no claim if at the time of dismissal you are taking part in unofficial industrial action.

Employers sometimes withhold pay for all or part of the time that you have been engaged in limited industrial action. They are entitled only to deduct a proportion of pay representing the proportion of your time lost by your action.

Since the Employment Act 1988, ballots in favour of industrial action must be taken at each workplace where workers are to be called upon. Action in pursuit of union membership agreements (see p. 323) is always unlawful.

Picketing of your own workplace (but nowhere else) during the course of a dispute is lawful provided that your purpose is peacefully to persuade people not to work or to communicate information. A Code of Practice (and one court decision) recommends that there be a limit of six pickets on each entrance, but different numbers may be appropriate in different circumstances. Offences under public order legislation (see p. 11) are the most likely criminal charges to arise out of picketing.

13.11 Claims

Most claims in this chapter are brought before industrial tribunals. Legal aid is not available, but an extension to the Green Form for preparation and/or counsel's advice can be granted. Appeals from industrial tribunals go to the Employment Appeal Tribunal for which legal aid is available. Legal aid is also available if you are taking a case such as an injunction to the High Court. Help can be obtained from the Equal Opportunities Commission, the Commission for Racial Equality or, in certain cases, from the Commissioner for the Rights of Trade Union Members.

Claims in time
The first point to check is whether you are in time to bring a claim. Deadlines are strict, usually three months from the action complained of. Make sure you fill in, or have filled in on your behalf, the 'Originating Application to an Industrial Tribunal' form (IT1) and that it reaches the Central Office of Industrial Tribunals for England and Wales, or for Scotland or for Northern Ireland, within the appropriate time.

Documents
The organisation against which you are claiming – usually an employer but sometimes a trade union – will reply in a set form. You may ask for further particulars of any matter they raise, and you can also be asked to give particulars. Before commencing proceedings in a race relations or sex discrimination claim, you may issue a questionnaire

seeking to obtain information from your employer about the actions and policies you are challenging. If you have been dismissed, write a letter seeking particulars, in writing and within fourteen days, of the reasons for your dismissal.

An important step in the proceedings is the 'discovery of documents'. You are entitled to see all documents relevant to your claim, including internal notes and minutes, which are particularly important in respect of claims for discrimination. If the employers do not provide documents, you can seek an order from the tribunal to this effect.

Representation

You can be represented at a tribunal by anyone you like. If you are claiming unfair dismissal, the employers start the case and bring their witnesses. Otherwise you start.

If you think the hearing is likely to last more than one day you should tell the tribunal so that they can fix a block of time for it. Otherwise the case will be adjourned with an interval in between.

The case is generally conducted by the Chairman (the statutory term) who is a lawyer, but the tribunal also consists of a person nominated by employers' organisations and one by employees' organisations. They have an equal say in the decision.

Awards

Tribunals can award compensation, make recommendations of reinstatement or re-engagement, and order employers to rectify discriminatory acts and policies.

STOP PRESS

The new government proposes to incorporate the European Convention on Human Rights into domestic law. The rights in the Convention are set out in Chapter 5. A Bill to incorporate the Convention is due to be published in the autumn of 1997 and this is likely to become an Act by July 1998 and to come into force not before January 1999. It is not clear at the time of writing exactly what effect this will have on our laws. It is likely that the Convention will be able to be used to challenge some of the existing procedures and judge-made law although whether the Convention will be given a higher status than statute is not so clear. Nevertheless the rights set out in this book may be enhanced by the Convention and in future the rights in the Convention will have to be considered much more seriously than they have been in the past.

Appeals

Appeals on points of law go to the Employment Appeal Tribunal (EAT) in London or Edinburgh or to the Northern Ireland Court of Appeal. The EAT consists of a High Court Judge and a person nominated by employers and one by employees. Legal aid is available. You may be represented by anyone you like at the EAT, and appeal from its decisions lies to the Court of Appeal, the Court of Session in Scotland or the House of Lords. This can only be on a point of law, and you must have the permission either of the EAT or the Court of Appeal or Court of Session in order to take the case further.

13.12 Further information

Useful organisations

The best source of advice is your trade union. The TUC will direct you to an appropriate union. Their address is:

Congress House
Great Russell Street
London WC1B 3LS
Tel: 0171 636 4030.

Advisory Conciliation and Arbitration Service (ACAS)
Regional offices in Newcastle, Leeds, London, Bristol, Birmingham, Nottingham, Manchester, Liverpool, Glasgow, Cardiff and the Labour Relations Agency in Belfast.

Commission for Racial Equality
Elliott House
10–12 Allington Street
London SW1E 5EH
Tel: 0171 828 7022

Equal Opportunities Commission
Overseas House
Quay Street
Manchester M3 3HN
Tel: 0161 833 9244

Equal Opportunities Commission for Northern Ireland
Chamber of Commerce House
22 Great Victoria Street
Belfast BT2 2BA
Tel: 0232 242752

Fair Employment Agency
Andras House
60 Great Victoria Street
Belfast BT2 7BB
Tel: 01232 240020

Health and Safety Executive
2 Southwark Bridge Road
London SE1
Tel: 0171 717 6000

Labour Relations Agency
Windsor House
9–15 Bedford Street
Belfast BT2 7NU
Tel: 01232 321442

Bibliography

J. McIlroy, *Industrial Tribunals*, Pluto Press, 1982.
R. W. Painter and K. Puttick, *Employment Rights*, Pluto Press, 1993 (new edition forthcoming 1998).
C. Palmer, *Discrimination at Work*, Legal Action Group, 1992.
D. Pannick, *Sex Discrimination Law*, Oxford University Press, 1986.
M. Rowland, C. Kennedy and I. McMullen (eds), *The Rights Guide to Non-means-tested Benefits*, Child Poverty Action Group (annually).
E. Slade, *Tolley's Employment Handbook* (10th edn), Tolley, 1991.
Lord Wedderburn, *The Worker and the Law*, Penguin, 1986.

14

The rights of travellers

This chapter deals with:

- The right to travel.
- The right to stop.
- The right to a site.
- The right to housing.
- The right to education.
- The right to healthcare.
- The right to welfare benefits.
- The right not to be discriminated against.
- Further information.

14.1 The right to travel

As with most other rights under English law, you can do what you like, unless it breaches criminal law or someone else's rights under civil law. As a traveller, you are subject to broadly the same laws as anyone else. So you have the right to pass and repass on the highway, but no special right to stop and park your caravan or other vehicles. Although there is planning guidance from central government which encourages local planning authorities to consider the needs of 'gypsies' (persons of nomadic habit of life who travel around for economic reasons), civil and criminal powers to evict people, or direct them to leave land, can be used against anyone, whether they are a 'gypsy' (as defined above), other traveller, or anyone else. In particular, new powers under the Criminal Justice and Public Order Act 1994 apply to what people are doing (trespassing) and not specifically to those who are doing it. A local authority has to consider the welfare needs of anyone it is considering whether to evict or direct to leave the land. If that person is a 'gypsy', then the authority must consider leaving that person on its land, if no great nuisance is being caused. The police 'may' consider welfare needs of people they are considering whether or not to direct to leave the land.

14.2 The right to stop
Where can you stop, legally, and park and live in a caravan? The answer to this is: a legal site. A legal site is:

- A piece of land you own, which has any necessary planning permission. You are the owner and occupier.
- A piece of land owned by someone else, including a local council, which is laid out as a site with any necessary planning permission, with a site licence and where the site operator and yourself have agreed you can stay. You are a licensee, with very limited rights if it is a local authority gypsy caravan site.
- A piece of land, not necessarily laid out as a site, where no planning permission or site licence for the parking of an inhabited caravan is required because you are doing seasonal agricultural or forestry work for the landowner (usually a farmer), or in a limited number of other cases where you are staying for short periods on open fields.
- A piece of land where one or more caravans have remained continuously for over ten years and where no valid planning enforcement notice has been served nor planning application turned down during that time. In these cases, if you own the land or the landowner allows you to stay, you can apply for a Certificate of Lawful Established Use and Development (CLEUD) and that Certificate is the same as a full planning permission. If you can prove that caravans have been on the land since at least 1963 or even 1948, then the local planning authority will not be able to take planning enforcement action against that number of caravans or fewer.

Other than the four cases above, you may be liable to have planning (enforcement) action taken against you or be moved on, except in certain cases where the owner of the land you are on is unknown.

What follows is a checklist to help you identify not only how much the right to stop has been reduced, but also which powers may be used against caravans or other vehicles on any particular type of land.

Someone else's land
Local authorities no longer have any duty to provide caravan sites for 'gypsies'. So it is no longer possible for gypsies or travellers to argue that councils have to provide a site for them, under English law, and therefore cannot move them on.

Any private or company landowner who finds people with vehicles stopping on their land can ask those people to leave. If the occupiers do not leave, then, as long as there are more than two people and more than six vehicles occupying, the landowner can ask the police or a local authority covering that area to use their powers under the Criminal Justice and Public Order Act 1994 to order them to leave. If there are at least two occupiers but fewer than six vehicles, then the landowner will need to show damage to the land or abusive, threatening or insulting behaviour by the occupiers, for local authority or police powers to be useable. The occupiers commit an offence if they fail to leave as soon as possible after being so directed.

Further provisions give the police extra powers to seize vehicles (and to charge for their removal, retention and destruction); create new criminal offences of trespassing with the intent of intimidating others or obstructing or disrupting their activities, and give local authorities the power to ban assemblies of over twenty people.

Local authorities, before using their powers against any occupier, have to consider the occupiers' welfare needs. Where the occupiers are 'gypsies', a local authority has to consider whether such people have to be moved.

Land owned by a local authority; highway land

Additional powers exist for local authorities, including those who are highway authorities. So the authority does not need to use the 1994 Act powers. However, the same rules on welfare needs and considering whether or not people have to be moved apply as detailed earlier. A local authority, under the 1994 Act, has extensive powers to direct people to leave its land, ask a local magistrates' court for an order to itself move caravans (if the people do not move first) and/or prosecute the occupiers of the caravans which have not moved when directed.

Own land

Whether or not the area is designated, if you live on land where you have freehold or leasehold title, you may still fall foul of the law. If it is not a legal site, you must get planning permission and a site licence. If you do not seek planning permission from your local district, borough or unitary council, it may decide to take out a planning enforcement notice (and even a stop notice) on you. A planning enforcement notice will require you to cease using the land as a site, after a specified date. A stop notice will require you to cease to do so immediately. However, if you later get planning permission to run a site, the local planning authority may have to pay you compensation if they have served a stop notice on you earlier. If you do not appeal against any enforcement notice, or you do not win your appeal, you can subsequently be fined, face High Court injunctions to prevent the occupation of your land, and even, finally, be imprisoned for contempt of court and have your land sold to pay unpaid fines. It is, however, rare for all these to happen.

If you are able to show that your planning application has been turned down due to your race or ethnic group, there would have been a breach of the Race Relations Act 1976. If this has happened to you (or you suspect it has), contact the Commission for Racial Equality at the address at the end of this chapter.

The Department of the Environment issued advice in early 1994 on planning provision for gypsy sites. That circular should be followed by local authorities when they produce their development plans (which show what should be allowed where in the area they cover), and deal with planning applications by 'gypsies'.

Planning authorities considering planning applications should always consider both the proposed use of the land and the personal circumstances of the applicant and their immediate family. If the Council turns down the application (or issues an enforcement notice, because no application has been made), the applicant or person enforced against may appeal to the Secretary of State for the Environment. That often results in an appeal hearing, and at least exchanges of correspondence before an appeal decision is made.

In 1996 the European Court of Human Rights gave judgment in a case brought by June Buckley, a gypsy. She had applied retrospectively to her district council for planning permission for her three caravans. Permission was refused and enforcement proceedings were taken against her. June Buckley argued that she had been prevented from living with her family on her own land and following a traditional gypsy lifestyle, in breach of the right to respect for her private and family life under Article 8 of the European Convention. The Court found that Article 8 did apply to her case but on the particular facts the Court found by six votes to three that the Convention had not been breached because adequate account had been taken of her position in the planning proceedings.

Type of land

If you have no title to the land, the type of land may decide if and how anyone can be moved from it. Outside cities, highway verges are both wider and more plentiful in rural areas, as is common land. There are many powers to prosecute and/or move on travellers (or anyone else) under the Highways Acts, but some councils and some police do not wish to make matters worse by using these powers, unless it is really necessary. In the case of common land, there may be legal complications about moving you on, unless that bit of common is already covered by an express ban on caravan parking. If it is, there should be a sign up saying so.

Some of the powers enable prosecution, some enable eviction and some do both. It is always important to check paperwork to see what the effect of the legal action will be, if it is successful.

Who owns the land?
If the land is neither highway verge nor common land and has a definite owner, the length of time you can stop on it will depend on a number of factors, including the number of caravans and the way that you and other travellers behave, as well as the level of complaint from others round about. Councils with too few sites may feel that it is unwise to evict you too quickly. Others may not feel limited by this. Action depends on the decision of the particular landowner. If the landowner wishes to take action, this will usually be done through the High Court in London or Cardiff or the County Court nearest to where the land is.

If the landowner wants to let you stay
In this case, unless you are a seasonal worker or staying only days on open land, the landowner may be pressed by planning officers to move you and, if you have gathered in numbers for a festival or other event, you could be prosecuted for unlawful assembly.

14.3 The right to a site

There has never been a 'right to a site', even though local housing authorities have duties to provide 'accommodation' for certain people, and those people may wish to live on a caravan site. Local authorities used to have a duty to provide enough sites for 'gypsies' in their area. Now they just have powers to provide them. Caravan sites originally established for 'gypsies', however, remain so.

If you are seeking a site place, you should keep in touch (preferably in writing) with the local council you have most connection with, hold on to evidence of your continuing stay in the area, and keep pressing for the building of a necessary site.

14.4 The right to housing

It can obviously be very difficult for any nomadic person to secure rights to housing. It is hard enough if you are not nomadic and settle in an area with some legal accommodation. Some areas have large numbers of families in hotels or bed and breakfast accommodation. If you are single or childless and neither elderly nor disabled, it will be difficult for you to get council housing, whether or not you are a traveller. All housing authorities have their own distinct rules for acceptance onto their housing lists and for deciding who gets priority once they are on the list. If you are a traveller, you face daily difficulties if you have no legal accommodation to stop on or in, and these are dealt with elsewhere in this section. But it is important for you to remember that you have the right to seek council housing and to be considered for it, just as much as anyone else. You may also have rights to be provided with (or helped to get) accommodation by a local council housing department if you are judged to be 'homeless' (for example, you are being evicted from a piece of land or a highway verge, and you have nowhere legal to go and live in your caravan), and have a 'priority need' for accommodation (if you have children living with you, or elderly or disabled people). If it is decided that you are homeless and have such a priority need, then the council can avoid its duty to provide you with accommodation only by showing either that you have a 'local connection' with another council's area that is stronger than your connection with theirs, or that you made yourself intentionally homeless (for example, you were in housing or on a legal site, perhaps even some time ago, but left this legal accommodation for no good reason, or for a reason which was the fault of you or a member of your family living with you). It is important to note that there is no duty on any council housing authority to provide you with a site for your caravan.

If you are looking for settled accommodation, or even if you want to put your name on a waiting list for a possible caravan site, you should visit the local council housing offices, preferably in the area that you have most connection with, unless there is a good reason for selecting another area (risk of violence from another member of the family, or someone else, for example). When you visit the housing offices, ask them what sort of provision is available. Do they have a site for travelling people? Does it have spare places on it? Where is it and how do they decide who goes on to it? If you have no interest in such a site, instead give the housing officer all the details about your living arrangements in your caravan. Remember that there are two separate ways of getting council accommodation and that you can apply to be put on a council house waiting list without being homeless. Before you leave the council office, ask them for a record of your applications, and ask them to let you know their decisions in writing. Keep all the paper they give you in a safe place. If you apply to be dealt with as homeless, the council housing department should give you a quick answer. If necessary, visit them regularly. Find out the name of the housing officer or other person that you need to speak to and try to speak to the same person each time. If you are applying for a council house (or 'social housing' provided by a housing association, as is now more common), make sure you keep in contact with the housing department by telephone or letter as the council house waiting lists are revised every six months or year in many areas and you have to make sure that you stay on the list each time until they make you an offer. It is possible to be on more than one council house waiting list at once.

Finally, you have the right to see all information on the housing department files. You may have to pay a charge if you want copies. If you do not read, or feel more confident with someone assisting you, then ask a sympathetic councillor, council travellers' officer, teacher, health visitor or some other person that you trust to go with on those visits, who could not only give you assistance, but also act as an independent witness.

Duties to house the homeless have been changed by recent law. There is only a duty to provide temporary accommodation for anyone immediately, although councils can keep reviewing the matter and extending the temporary accommodation, where there is a good case for it.

14.5 The right to education

Traveller children aged between five and sixteen have the same legal right to education as anyone else. Parents of traveller children aged four will have the rights to nursery vouchers when these are introduced.

It is obviously difficult to claim or seek these rights if you do not have a legal place to stop. If your child is of school age, then simply take the child to the state school nearest to where you are and ask them to provide education. It will be very helpful, both for the child and the local education authority, if you present children at school at age five or even shortly before. However, do not hesitate to take them at any age, even if there have been difficulties in getting your children to school at an earlier age. You have a legal duty to present them at school, and the local education authority has a legal duty to provide them with appropriate full-time education. Once you have met the school secretary, headteacher or another teacher, they may say that there will or could be difficulties which stop them admitting your child. It is important for you to stand your ground. Those practical difficulties are for the school or the local education authority to work out. If they ask you to go away for a few days, ask them exactly why you are being asked to do so. It is a good plan to be firm but polite. If one or more of your children is refused education at a school, or there are many obstacles put in front of her or him, then you should approach the Chief Education Officer for that council by going to the local town or county hall.

Many traveller children start school later than five and attend only from time to time. If you keep moving because of work or other reasons, then you only have to make sure that your children are in school for two hundred half days (one hundred full days) during the September to July school year. If your children have started late or attended irregularly, they may be judged to have special needs, which may include remedial help with reading or even the necessity for them to go to a special school. There are rules about the way in which this decision on special needs is made, and if you cannot read well you will need the assistance of someone who can help you through this process.

In conclusion, remember that your school-age children have a right to be educated and a right to have their needs considered in the same way as any other child. If the school or education department is planning to make (or making) decisions that you do not understand or disagree with, keep asking them questions at every stage, so that they tell you exactly what they are doing, why they are doing it, and what the likely result will be. What is most important is that you do not give up and withdraw your child or children from school if you do not understand what is happening. Taking a child away from school is more likely to damage the child's education than to get a council to change a decision it has made.

The Children Act 1989 puts responsibilities on courts and local authorities to make decisions about children in the best interests of those children. A number of court decisions have indicated that local authorities have to protect the interests of children, when they are in that authority's area, including when the authority is considering whether or not to evict families which include those children.

14.6 The right to healthcare

Everyone has a right to healthcare from the National Health Service. What this means in practice is that no hospital should ever turn away someone who is the victim of accident or illness, whoever that person is and whether or not they have paid any national insurance contributions. When you go to a dentist or take a prescription to the chemist, however, you will only get certain benefits free or at a reduced price if you are a child, someone who suffers from a long-term illness or disability (for example, diabetes) or if you receive income support, a pension or family credit.

Although many travellers go to casualty departments when they have an accident or illness, it is much more sensible to register with a local doctor if you are in an area, or expect to be, for more than a few weeks. Lists of doctors should be available at main Post Offices, and the best way is to visit the doctor you pick from the list and give her or him the exact details of those members of your family who wish to register with them (dates of birth and so on). Some doctors are prevented from taking extra people onto their list if it is already too long, and so you may have to go to several doctors before you find one that will allow you to register with her or him. If you are turned down by all the doctors, whether or not it is because you are a traveller, find the address and phone number of the Family Health Services Authority in the local phone book. Contact them (if possible in writing, after a telephone call) telling them that you have been turned down by the doctors concerned, the reasons you have been given by the doctors, and any other reasons you believe may have affected the decision.

If there is an accident or illness within your family and you believe it may be unsafe to move the person concerned, you can telephone any local doctor and ask for emergency help. Try to make sure that there is somebody else with you when you make that call, if that is possible, so there is no doubt that you made it and when you made it.

In practice, health visitors may have more contact with your family and friends, especially around the time that any children are born. Ask a health visitor for advice about registering with a doctor and for help with getting your rights to healthcare, even if you are regularly being moved from place to place.

The major changes to the National Health Service within the last few years are deterring some doctors from accepting traveller and other mobile families onto their lists. It is becoming increasingly important for all Health Service consumers to assert their rights to healthcare.

14.7 The right to welfare benefits

It is commonly believed that if you do not have a settled address then you are not entitled to welfare benefits. This is untrue. You are as entitled to welfare benefits if you move around as if you stay in the same place. But it is obviously more difficult to claim them; you may get long delays while the papers relating to you go from office to office of the Benefits Agency. Agency officers may also presume fraud, or the intention to defraud, more easily in those who are more mobile.

If you and any members of your family that you live with do not have any income, or only a very small one, then you can apply for income support on form SP1 (pensioners) or A1 (everyone else) available from a social security office. You can also apply on form IS1 which you can get from a Post Office or social security office. If you are on a site or in a house, you may be able to claim housing benefit and for this you approach the local council housing benefit department. If you have children under sixteen living with you, you are entitled to child benefit, whatever income you have. If you do not have a settled house or site to stop on, your child benefits may be paid at the end of each three months, unless you can make an arrangement for it to be paid through a close friend, relative or council officer, or it can be added to any income support that you are receiving each week.

You may also be entitled to other benefits, such as those for the disabled and people who look after them. You can get leaflets about all these from main Post Offices or discuss them with the local social security office. At the end of this chapter, there are details of a guide to many of these benefits and how to claim them. Particular difficulties often arise with lost birth certificates or with people proving their identity. These two issues may well be linked. If you are having difficulty with either of them, approach your local advice centre, Citizens' Advice Bureau or local social services department to help you get your money, especially if it is an emergency.

Unless you are not required to be 'available for work', due to your age, pregnancy, lone parent status, etc., you claim Job Seekers Allowance from a Job Centre. In order to receive this, you are not only required to be 'available for work' but also 'actively seeking work' and have a current 'Jobseekers' Agreement' with the Job Centre. The rules for receiving Jobseekers Allowance do not allow those seeking work to place too many restrictions on the type of work they are prepared to accept and may result in having to take a job that is not linked to particular skills or that they would not normally choose.

14.8 The right not to be discriminated against

This subject is dealt with elsewhere within this book in general terms (see Chapter 9), but the following relates particularly to discrimination against 'gypsies' (falling within one or more racial or ethnic groups of such).

The National Union of Teachers has described the prejudice against travellers as being similar to that suffered by many other ethnic minorities, and sometimes as fierce. For many years, it was said that the Race Relations Acts covered gypsies as much as any one else, but no one was ever prosecuted for incitement to racial hatred against gypsies (and in very few other cases, either, it must be said) and there are only two notable cases that the Commission for Racial Equality dealt with concerning travelling people (see below).

Recent changes in the law and practice now mean that a gypsy applicant (and far from all travellers will come within the racial or ethnic definition 'gypsy') for a planning permission or a council house is covered by the Race Relations Act 1976. If someone produces material, including a leaflet, book, play, film, television or radio programme which is likely to stir up racial hatred against gypsies, then they can be criminally prosecuted, providing the Attorney General consents to the prosecution. The Court of Appeal decided in the summer of 1988 that gypsies were one or more ethnic groups and were protected by the Race Relations Act. A 'No Travellers' sign on a public house could indirectly discriminate against gypsies, as they would be a large proportion of the group 'travelling' (that is, caravan-dwelling) who would be refused service. Unless, therefore, there is justification for the sign, it is in breach of the law.

If you have been refused service in a shop or a pub, or been prevented from entering premises normally open to any member of the public by an objectionable sign, or you know of planning policies which ban all gypsy caravan sites being approved in an area, or in some other way you suffer discrimination in treatment by virtue of your origins as a traveller, then it is extremely important that you complain rather than expecting that it is something that you have to put up with. Complain to the local Community Relations Council for your area, if you know where it is, or complain directly to the Commission for Racial Equality in London, whose address is below.

STOP PRESS

The new government proposes to incorporate the European Convention on Human Rights into domestic law. The rights in the Convention are set out in Chapter 5. A Bill to incorporate the Convention is due to be published in the autumn of 1997 and this is likely to become an Act by July 1998 and to come into force not before January 1999. It is not clear at the time of writing exactly what effect this will have on our laws. It is likely that the Convention will be able to be used to challenge some of the existing procedures and judge-made law although whether the Convention will be given a higher status than statute is not so clear. Nevertheless the rights set out in this book may be enhanced by the Convention and in future the rights in the Convention will have to be considered much more seriously than they have been in the past.

14.9 Further information

Useful organisations

The Advisory Committee for the Education of Romany and Other
Travellers (ACERT)
Moot House
The Stow
Harlow
Essex CM20 3AG
Tel: 01279 418666

Commission for Racial Equality
Elliott House
10–12 Allington Street
London SW1E 5EH
Tel: 0171 828 7022

Friends and Families of Travellers Support Group
33 High Street
Glastonbury
Somerset
BA6 9HT
Tel: 01458 823371

The Gypsy Council for Education, Welfare and Civil Rights
8 Hall Road
Aveley
Essex
RM15 4HD
Tel: 01708 868986

National Gypsy Council
Greenhills Caravan Site
Hapsford
Helsby
Warrington
Cheshire
WA6 0SS
Tel: 01928 723130

The Romany Guild
c/o 61 Blenheim Crescent
London
W11 2EG
Tel: 0171 727 2916

The Romany Rights Association
c/o Eli Frankham
The Bungalow
Romon Bank
Walpole Street
St Andrews
Wisbech
Cambridgeshire
PE14 7HP
Tel: 01945 780326 or 475698

Telephone Legal Advice Service for Travellers (TLAST)
Cardiff Law School
University of Wales, College of Cardiff
PO Box 427
Cardiff
CF1 1XD
Tel: 01222 874580

Bibliography

C. Brand, *Mobile Homes and the Law*, Sweet and Maxwell, 1986.
Brief guides to part of the Act by TLAST (see above).
Criminal Justice and Public Order Act 1994, Stationery Office.
Department of the Environment Circulars 1/94 and 18/94, Stationery Office.
B. Forrester, *The Travellers' Handbook*, Interchange Books, 1985.
Mobile Homes – an Occupiers Guide, Shelter, 1988.
National Welfare Benefits Handbook, Child Poverty Action Group, annual.

Index

PLUTO PRESS ✦ ESSENTIAL READING

THE PRISONS HANDBOOK
Mark Leech
'A useful sourcebook ... Prisoners, their families and friends will find [it] very useful ... it should be in every prison and public library'
Prison Service Journal
The only comprehensive guide to the penal system in England and Wales. Now in a new edition, it is on the Home Office list of books required to be in every prison library. Each prison has a detailed entry; listing key officials, visiting, education and facilities. An advice section spans reception to release, and legal rights in prison. With an extensive legal section, lists of helpful organizations, Internet sites and other key resources, this is an indispensable reference book.
Aug 97 • 448pp • 230x150mm • Pb • £45.00 • 0 7453 1225 X

THE VIDEO ACTIVIST HANDBOOK
Thomas Harding
'You must read this book if you are in any way involved with campaigning' **Robby Kelman, Greenpeace**
This excellent book is both a practical guide to video activism and a political briefing for the burgeoning protest movement worldwide. Arguing that the powers that control the media and the practices that govern it have stifled political debate and marginalised the concerns of ordinary people, it charts the recent rise in non-violent direct action and shows how activists are challenging the mainstream media's view of the world by producing and distributing their own programming.
Aug 97 • 192pp • Photos • 215x135mm • Pb • £11.99 • 0 7453 1169 5 • Hb • £35.00 • 0 7453 1174 1

CIVIL RIGHTS AND THE INTERNET
Edited by Jonathan Cooper
The Internet offers new opportunities and threats to all our basic liberties: civil rights, privacy and freedoms of expression. Published in association with Liberty, this important book looks at how the freedom of use and accessibility of this world-wide phenomenon is being eroded, both by governments (reacting as politically 'undesirable' information becomes freely available) and by private concerns and pressure groups raising moral panics.
Mar 98 • 240pp • 215x135mm • Pb • £13.99 • 0 7453 1294 2 • Hb • £40.00 • 0 7453 1299 3

ENVIRONMENTAL ACTION
Edited by Martyn Day
This invaluable guide examines all aspects of the legal process available to campaigners (including several Eurodirectives). From claiming damages for injury from pollution, to nuisance claims and criminal law, the contributors explain what the law is, how it can work, and where to find help and advice. Essential information is given on legal aid and the Criminal Justice Act, and case studies are used to explain the law in a way that is both clear and empowering.
Dec 97 • 416pp • 215x135mm • Pb • £14.99 • 0 7453 1190 3 • Hb • £50.00 • 0 7453 1191 1

PLUTO PRESS ◀▶ ESSENTIAL READING

ABORTION: *The Arguments for Choice*
Ann Furedi

In this highly controversial book, Furedi reveals that through a sophisticated battery of arguments intended to undermine public confidence in abortion law and practice, the anti-choice movement is now pressing claims that concern even those who are disposed to support reproductive rights. Furedi exposes and refutes the inaccuracies in their claims, and clarifies the facts of the arguments. Covering the clinical, legal, ethical, and social issues, this is essential reading for all concerned with the arguments for and against abortion.
Mar 98 • 144pp • 215x135mm • Pb • £9.99 • 0 7453 1153 9 • Hb • £30.00 • 0 7453 1154 7

PREGNANCY AT WORK: *A Guide to Health and Safety*
Regina Kenen

Compiled in association with the Maternity Alliance, this invaluable guide is specifically written for working women, trade unionists, health and safety officers and employers. Using case studies, Kenen illustrates particular occupational hazards and possible solutions, pointing out where to get help and advice and providing practical strategies for negotiating healthier solutions to the dangers. Kenen presents a wealth of related material, covering relevant legislation, rights and benefit, and a thorough listing of helpful organisations.
Feb 98 • 256pp • 215x135mm • Pb • £10.99 • 0 7453 1286 1 • Hb • £35.00 • 0 7453 1291 8

Visit the Pluto Web-site at http://www.leevalley.co.uk/plutopress

Please complete this **order form** (prices subject to change) and send to:
(UK only) Pluto Press, **FREEPOST**, ND 6781, London N6 5BR. Outside UK please send orders to: Pluto Press, 345 Archway Road, London N6 5AA. Or fax on +44 (0) 181 348 9133. **Payment must include P&P as follows: UK 10% of order value, min £2; Europe 15% of order value, min £3.50; outside of Europe 20% of order value, min £5.**

Title	Author	ISBN	Pb/Hb	Price	Qty

☐ I enclose a cheque for £_____ (inc P&P) (made payable to Marston Book Services)

☐ Please debit my credit card (specify type) _____ for £ _____
(inc P&P)

☐ Please send me a copy of the 1997 Complete Catalogue

Card No: ☐☐☐☐☐☐☐☐☐☐☐☐☐☐☐☐ Expiry Date: /

Name .... Signature

Card Address ....

Delivery (if different) YR97